# HOW 8

# A HANDBOOK FOR OFFICE WORKERS 8E

## James L. Clark
Professor, Business Department
Pasadena City College

## Lyn R. Clark
Professor, Office Administration Department
Los Angeles Pierce College

SOUTH-WESTERN College Publishing

*An International Thomson Publishing Company*

| Publishing Team Director: | John Szilagyi |
|---|---|
| Developmental Editor: | Susan Freeman Carson |
| Production Editor: | Kelly Keeler |
| Production House: | Julia Chitwood |
| Designer: | Michael Stratton |
| Marketing Manager: | Steve Scoble |

**Library of Congress Cataloging-in-Publication Data**

Clark, James Leland, 1929–
    HOW 8 : a handbook for office workers / James L. Clark, Lyn R.
Clark.—8th ed.
        p.    cm.
    Rev. ed. of: HOW 7. 7th ed. c1995
    Includes bibliographical references and index.
    ISBN 0-538-86319-6
    1. Commercial correspondence—Handbooks, manuals, etc.   I. Clark,
Lyn.   II. Clark, James Leland, 1929–      HOW 7.
HF5726.C55   1997
808'.06665—dc21                                                      97-17711
                                                                          CIP

        3  4  5  6 **D1** 2  1  0  9  8  7
Printed in the United States of America

I(T)P®
International Thomson Publishing
South-Western College Publishing is an ITP Company. The ITP trademark is used under license.

# Contents

# Preface

*HOW 8: A Handbook for Office Workers*, Eighth Edition, is designed to assist office professionals and business writers in preparing successful written business communications. *HOW 8* maintains the style, format, and content that have made it a success through seven editions. But today's business professionals must be ready to meet the challenges of technology in a competitive global economy. With this in mind, *HOW 8* has been completely updated to reflect the most current use of technology in the office, including E-mail and the Internet.

*HOW 8* serves as a reference book—to answer specific questions regarding punctuation, grammar, capitalization, number usage, word usage, forms of address, abbreviations, format, and document transmission as they relate to the preparation of business letters, memorandums, reports, manuscripts, résumés, faxes, E-mail, agendas, itineraries, meeting minutes, and press releases. *HOW 8* presents detailed and precise information for writing, formatting, and transmitting business documents. It focuses specifically on the needs of business and office technology students, office personnel, prospective office managers, business writers, and other business professionals.

## A Comprehensive Reference Manual for Business

*HOW 8* is succinct, yet comprehensive. It covers thoroughly the principles of grammar, punctuation, capitalization, number usage, word hyphenation and division, and abbreviation format in simple, easy-to-understand language. Each rule is illustrated with examples or example sentences related to business circumstances or conditions. In addition, nearly 200 word confusions—ones such as *affect/ effect, ensure/insure*, and *principal/principle*—are differentiated by simple definitions and discriminating examples.

Content and formats for various business documents are covered thoroughly in *HOW 8*. All the major parts of a business letter, forms of address for domestic and foreign correspondence, and commonly used letter styles are discussed and illustrated, along with the basic formats for writing memorandums. To assist readers with the entire document processing cycle, *HOW 8* provides detailed procedures for preparing business documents on computer-based equipment.

## A Current Manual for Today's Workplace

The following information is new to *HOW 8*:

- Specific instructions and examples for preparing résumés that will be scanned and assessed by electronic applicant tracking systems (see Chapter 12).
- Chapter on information sources—printed materials, electronic resources, and on-line resources. This chapter also covers Internet access and available resources on the Web (see Chapter 15).
- Comprehensive instructions for initiating an E-mail setup, sending messages, receiving messages, and attaching files (see Chapters 10 and 13).
- Business math applications, which add to *HOW 8*'s position as a comprehensive resource for business professionals (see Chapter 4).

- Expanded guidelines for preparing visuals, citing sources, setting up listings, using main and text headings, compiling preliminary pages and bibliographies, and formatting a report provide added value for report writers (see Chapter 11).
- Instructions and examples for preparing itineraries, agendas, press releases, and meeting minutes further enhance the usability of this book as a business writer's resource (see Chapter 11).

## Features to Help You Find Instant Solutions

Several features, besides the table of contents and the extensive index, increase the functional use of *HOW 8* as a reference book:

1. **Solution Finders**—comprehensive topic indexes at the beginning of each chapter enable readers to locate easily solutions to their problems.
2. **Two-color format**—rules are printed in red and examples are printed in black so that principles may be located, read, and understood quickly.
3. **Example headings**—boldfaced headings differentiate aspects of each rule so that specific examples and applications may be located immediately.
4. **Spiral binding**—the lie-flat feature of spiral binding permits readers to compare readily their questions with the examples.
5. **Glossary of grammatical terms**—a listing with definitions and examples of all the grammatical terms used in this book may be accessed for further clarification of any language principle.

Information you need may be located easily and quickly in *HOW 8* by using a four-step process.

1. Find the chapter you need by turning to the list of contents shown on the outside back cover.
2. Turn to the Solution Finder at the beginning of that chapter by using the page-edge chapter divider tab.
3. Locate the information you need in the Solution Finder. Each main topic is listed alphabetically followed by subsections of that topic and their corresponding section numbers.
4. Turn to the appropriate section within the chapter by referring to the page guide references (the section numbers shown at the top right corner of the odd-numbered pages).

If information cannot be located through surveying the contents listed on the back cover, use the comprehensive index at the end of the book to find the appropriate section.

## Supplementary Materials for Instructors and Students

*HOW 8* may be employed as a classroom text or supplement for instructing potential office employees, administrative assistants, business writers, and managers—anyone who deals with the preparation of written business documents.

The following supplementary materials are available for instructors and students:

***Workbook for HOW 8.*** (ISBN 0-538-87042-7) This 300-page supplement reinforces the major principles presented in the reference manual. It contains exercises that are coordinated specifically with sections in *HOW 8* and are designed to provide students with realistic learning applications, not just isolated sentence exercises. Workbook exercises enable students to apply the rules governing punctuation, capitalization, number usage and applications, grammar, word confusions, abbreviations, spelling, proofreading, and editing. In addition, students receive practice in using correct address formats, formatting business letters and memorandums, indexing names for filing, and locating reference sources on the Internet.

*Instructor's Manual and Key.* (ISBN 0-538-86321-8) This supplement includes over 120 instructional transparency masters that contain the major punctuation, grammar, capitalization, and number-usage principles in *HOW 8* and correspond directly with the exercise applications in the workbook. All transparency masters in the instructor's manual have been revised and reproduced in a print format. Other teaching materials in the instructor's manual include a familiarization exercise and a series of business letter and memorandum problems.

*NEW! The Professional Writer's Electronic Resource (PoWER).* (ISBN 0-538-87895-9) This on-line reference and interactive study guide reviews and reinforces grammar, spelling, and punctuation rules. It also covers mechanics and usage in writing letters, memos, reports, and proposals. It draws references and exercises from *HOW 8* as well as from Mary Ellen Guffey's *Business English, Essentials of Business Communication*, and *Business Communication: Process and Product*. The software includes pretests, posttests, examples, lessons, and exercises. The software is also available in a Network Version (ISBN 0-538-87897-5).

The principles of grammar and usage incorporated in *HOW 8* coordinate with and reinforce those presented in Mary Ellen Guffey's books. This coordination means that students can move from one book to another without experiencing contradictory usage or style guidelines.

## User Profile

*HOW 8* may be used by students in word processing, keyboarding, business English, business communication, transcription, legal office, medical office, or office procedures courses—all courses that require the processing of written words. It functions as a resource for class assignments—answering questions on language applications, punctuation, document framework, and document format. Use of the handbook enables students to produce more nearly correct business documents. This reference book continues to be a valuable resource as students enter the business environment and encounter actual assignments in business writing and document preparation.

Leaders of seminars designed to improve communication proficiency will find *HOW 8* a useful tool for assisting participants in improving their language competence, mechanics of expression, and knowledge of document framework and formats.

*HOW 8* serves as a reference for all persons in business who are responsible for communicating through the written word. Similar to the indispensable dictionary, this handbook compresses other essential reference information into a single source for producing effective business documents. It is targeted for use in businesses by managers, administrative assistants, secretaries, word processors, and all others who have responsibility for producing effective written communications. However, persons in all fields of business, education, government, medicine, and law will benefit from using *HOW 8* as a reference in preparing written documents for their professional position and their personal business circumstances.

## Acknowledgments

We thank the following reviewers for their assistance in the preparation of this reference book:

Beverly Amoroso, Kirkwood Community College
Janet Hempstead, Hudson Valley Community College
Shirley Kutevac, Kent State University, Trumbull Campus
Marianna P. Larsen, Utah State University
Marsha Lewis, Itawamba Community College
Kay Mackey, Richland Community College
Paul J. Martello, Bryant and Stratton Business Institute
Myrtie Bain Peterson, Casper College
Betty Stiles, Des Moines Area Community College

James and Lyn Clark
E-mail: ClarksHOW@aol.com

# Chapter 1

# Punctuation

# Punctuation Solution Finder

## Punctuation Solution Finder (*continued*)

## Punctuation Solution Finder (*continued*)

# Comma

## 1–1.   Series

a.   In a sentence containing a series of three or more equally ranked parts (words, phrases, or short clauses), place a comma after each part except the last one. Be sure to use a comma before the conjunction (*and, or, nor*).[1]

**words**

Our $4.99 luncheon special includes a salad, sandwich, beverage, and dessert.

Next year's budget will permit us to hire in this branch office an accountant, an administrative assistant, and a word processing specialist.

**phrases**

A new manager was hired to supervise office services, improve our records management system, and implement more cost-effective procedures.

**short clauses**

Karen Jones made the sale, Chris Lopez approved the contract, and Ralph Harris directed me to ship the computers immediately.

b.   Commas are not used when the parts of a series are all joined by conjunctions.

**words**

Only checks **or** bankcards **or** purchase orders are acceptable.

**phrases**

For the last year we have contracted with A-Z Building Services to clean the offices nightly **and** maintain the grounds weekly **and** provide general repairs as needed.

c.   Although generally avoided, *etc.* is sometimes used to indicate "and so forth" at the end of a series. If used, *etc.* is set off by commas; it is never preceded by the word *and*.

**within a sentence**

Checking accounts, savings accounts, money market accounts, certificates of deposit, **etc.**, are described fully in this brochure.

**end of a sentence**

We plan to visit all our branch offices this year—New York, Los Angeles, San Francisco, Chicago, **etc.**

---

[1]Some periodicals and literary writers prefer to omit the comma before the conjunction in a series. For business writing, however, always use the comma before the conjunction to promote ease of reading and clarity.

**d.** A comma is not used before an ampersand (&) in an organizational name unless the organization officially uses the comma in its name.

**no comma**

Her first interview is with Gates, Hamilton & Gates.

**comma**

Augner, Haight, Liggett, & Phelan is a long-established accounting firm in the Chicago area.

## 1–2. Parenthetical Expressions

**a.** Transitional words and expressions that are considered unnecessary for the grammatical completeness of a sentence and that *interrupt its natural flow* are set off with commas. A partial list of such parenthetical expressions follows:

| | | |
|---|---|---|
| according to our records | however | obviously |
| accordingly | in addition | of course |
| after all | incidentally | on the contrary |
| all in all | in conclusion | on the other hand |
| all things considered | indeed | on the whole |
| also | in effect | otherwise |
| as a matter of fact | in essence | perhaps |
| as a result | in fact | periodically |
| as a rule | in general | secondly |
| at any rate | in my opinion | so |
| at the same time | in other words | that is |
| besides | instead | then |
| between you and me | in summary | therefore |
| by the way | in the first place | thus |
| consequently | in the meantime | too |
| even so | likewise | under the circumstances |
| finally | moreover | unfortunately |
| for example | namely | what is more |
| fortunately | needless to say | without a doubt |
| furthermore | nevertheless | yes |
| hence | no | |
| | no doubt | |

**beginning of a sentence**

**Needless to say,** he is planning to attend the meeting.

**end of a sentence**

The store will be closed over the Labor Day weekend, **without a doubt.**

**within a sentence**

A large crowd, **nevertheless,** attended the exhibit.

**b.** Sometimes words and phrases used as parenthetical expressions *do not interrupt* the flow of a sentence. In such cases no commas are used with the expression.

**beginning of a sentence**

**Perhaps** the package will arrive in Dallas by Monday.

**end of a sentence**

Our manager is planning to visit New York City **too**.

**within a sentence**

She was **indeed** concerned about the omissions in the financial analysis.

**c.** Exclamations at the beginning of a sentence are parenthetical expressions that require a comma.

**Oh,** what a surprise to see Ms. Hilton in court again!

**Ah,** we will have difficulty transferring these holdings into liquid assets!

**d.** Enumerations or explanations used as parenthetical expressions *within a sentence* are set off by commas, dashes, or parentheses. Use commas when the enumerated or explanatory information has no internal commas, dashes when the information contains commas within it, or parentheses when the information is considered to be only incidental to the rest of the sentence.

**commas**

Only one company**, namely, Consolidated Enterprises,** bid on the contract.

**dashes**

He reported income from several sources**—namely, salary, interest, dividends, and rentals—**on his last income tax return.

**parentheses**

Our vice president toured several Ohio cities **(Cleveland, Columbus, and Toledo)** to find a suitable plant site.

**e.** A parenthetical expression introducing an enumeration or explanation *after a complete thought* may be set off with either (1) commas or (2) a semicolon and a comma. If the enumeration or explanation itself is a complete thought or contains internal commas, use a semicolon and a comma. Otherwise, use commas.

**commas**

We are expecting two exceptionally large orders next week**, namely,** from Reed's Department Store and Payco.

There are several ways we can cut our expenses during the next quarter**, for example,** by reducing our advertising budget.

**semicolon and comma**

This customer ordered new furniture for her living room; **namely, a sofa, two chairs, two lamp tables, and an occasional table.**

**f. Short introductory prepositional phrases essential to the meaning of a sentence should not be mistaken for parenthetical expressions. These phrases answer specifically questions such as *when, where, why,* or *how*. Introductory prepositional phrases containing fewer than five words (but not containing a verb form) generally flow smoothly into the sentence and are *not* followed by a comma.**

**when?**

**In the future** please place your orders with our Eastern Washington office.

**At your convenience** please fill out and return the enclosed form.

**where?**

**At this conference** we met agents from all parts of the United States.

**In this case** we are able to grant only a partial refund of the purchase price.

**why?**

**For that reason** we have turned over your account to our attorney for collection.

**On this basis** we have decided to expand our operations in the South.

**how?**

**In this way** you will be able to cut your travel costs significantly.

**With this program** you can speed up the operation of any desktop computer by at least 20 percent.

**g. Adverbs used as parenthetical expressions do not require commas.**

**However** brilliant his work may be, Mr. Rogers will not be promoted until his disposition improves.

**Obviously** concerned about the drop in sales, our manager called a meeting of all sales personnel.

**Too** many agents have not yet submitted their monthly sales summary.

## 1–3. Direct Address

**When calling a person by name, title, or affiliation, use commas to set off the reference. Speaking directly to individuals or groups requires their names be set off by commas because these names are used in direct address. For words used in direct address within a sentence, capitalize only (1) proper nouns and (2) personal and professional titles.**

**beginning of a sentence**

**Ladies and gentlemen,** congratulations on your achievements!

**Mrs. Phelps,** you have been promoted to assistant vice president.

**within a sentence**

Will you please, **Dr. Jones,** send us your check for $50 by March 30.

The book you have ordered, **Professor,** is presently out of stock.

Please examine for yourselves, **ladies and gentlemen,** how this proposal will affect you.

You, **fellow golfer,** will now be able to cut strokes from your game with this new Leading Edge driver.

**end of a sentence**

You are certainly a competent assistant, **Ms. Boyer.**

You also should be concerned about this issue, **fellow American.**

## 1–4. Appositives

**a.** Appositives are word groups that rename or explain the nouns or pronouns they follow. These descriptive words usually add extra information and are set off by commas. (See 1-4b and 1-4c for exceptions.)

**within a sentence**

All the reports were submitted to Ms. Hartford, **our sales manager,** for approval.

Our vice president, **Mr. Voddon,** will be in Denver all next week.

**end of a sentence**

At your suggestion we contacted a representative in your nearest branch office, **the Hillsdale office.**

She had reservations on the 5:30 p.m. flight, **the last flight to San Francisco that day.**

**b.** Restrictive appositives—descriptive word groups that are *needed to identify* the person or thing further described—are not set off by commas. These restrictive appositives tell *which one* or *which ones* and are essential to the meaning of the sentence.

**necessary for identification—tells which one or which ones**

The book *Terminology for the Automated Office* will be released next week.

Your student **Larry Green** has an appointment to see you tomorrow.

We **board members** are responsible for ensuring that each child in our community receives a quality education.

**unnecessary for identification**

His latest book, *College English*, was released last December.

Your best student, **Ann Freeman,** has an appointment to see you next week.

c. **Closely related one-word appositives or those forming parts of proper names do not require commas.**

**closely related one-word appositives**

My sister **Ellen** has received two promotions within the last year.

I **myself** plan to attend the organizational meeting in Memphis.

In this area the state legislation sets forth only general guidelines for us **teachers**.

**proper name**

His last two novels dealt with the lives of Alexander **the Great** and Richard **the Lionhearted**.

d. **College degrees and abbreviations written after individuals' names are set off by commas; the abbreviations *Jr.* and *Sr.* and Roman numerals, however, are not set off by commas unless an individual chooses to include them.**

**Abbreviations such as *Inc.* and *Ltd.* after company names are also set off by commas if a particular company elects to include them.**

**commas with college degree or abbreviation after name of individual**

Marilyn Drengson, **Doctor of Divinity,** will deliver the main graduation address.

Caroline R. Ryan, **Ph.D.,** is the author of *Executive Decision Making*.

Our firm will be represented by Alan Moskley, **Esq.**[2]

**no commas with *Jr., Sr.,* or Roman numeral after name of individual**

Mr. Lowell T. Harrison **Jr.** has just been promoted to executive vice president.

Please send copies of the contract to David Warburton **Sr.** and the other names listed in the attached letter.

Only Robert T. Link **II** has access to the safety deposit box.

Donald J. Ellington **III** has just been appointed secretary of state.

**commas with abbreviations after company names**

A. G. Edwards & Sons, **Inc.,** has moved its offices to Wilshire Boulevard.

Clothiers, **Ltd.,** is one of the largest jobbers on the West Coast.

---

[2]Courtesy or professional titles are not used with the abbreviation *Esq. Esq.* may be used after the name of a lawyer. It replaces the courtesy title (*Mr., Mrs.,* or *Ms.*) and the professional title *Attorney-at-Law*.

### no commas with abbreviations after company names

We have contracted with Ricon MED **Inc.** to install the wheelchair lifts in our hospital vans.

Most of the stocks in this estate are held by DEAN WITTER REYNOLDS **INC.**

Your crystal order from Cash & Co. **Ltd.** will be shipped from Ireland within the next week.

**e.** Words or expressions referred to simply as words or expressions should be written in italics rather than set off by commas. If an italic font is not available, underscore or place in quotation marks the words or expressions.

### italics

Too many writers use *insure* when they should use *ensure*.

### underscored

The word **convenience** is often misspelled in business letters.

### quotation marks

The phrase **"Thanking you in advance"** is an outdated expression that should be avoided in business letters.

## 1–5.   Dates and Time Zones

**a.** Dates containing combinations of weekday, calendar date, and year require commas. Place a comma *after each element* used unless, of course, the element concludes a sentence. Remember *always* to place a comma *after* the year when a calendar date and year appear within the sentence.

Commas are not used with a calendar date expressed alone.

### calendar date expressed alone

On **February 28** our books were audited by the Internal Revenue Service.

### calendar date and year

On **February 28, 1998,** our books were audited by the Internal Revenue Service.

### weekday and calendar date

On **Tuesday, February 28,** our books were audited by the Internal Revenue Service.

### weekday, calendar date, and year

On **Tuesday, February 28, 1998,** our books were audited by the Internal Revenue Service.

**b.** Expressions of month and year are written without commas.

The Internal Revenue Service audited our books in **February 1998**.

In **March 2000** we will release our new line of products.

**c.** Set off by commas any time zones used with clock times.

Our flight will leave Denver at 9:35 a.m., **MST,** and arrive in New York at 3:18 p.m., **EST.**

We received your fax from Japan at 10:40 a.m., **PDT.**

## 1–6. Addresses

**a.** The parts of an address written in sentence form are separated by commas.

**name and complete address**

Please send the check to **Ms. Harriet Buckley, Manager, Accounting Department, American Paper Company, 2996 Grandview Avenue, N.E., Suite 312, Atlanta, Georgia 30305-3245,** by May 1.

**complete address only**

Mr. Livingston may be reached at **740 Gayley Avenue, Los Angeles, California 90025.**

**b.** Use commas to set off a state following the name of a city. Likewise, use commas to set off a country following the name of a city. Remember to use the second comma after the state or country name when it appears in the middle of a sentence.

**within a sentence**

The letter was sent to Kansas City, **Missouri,** in error.

Please confirm this order from Frankfurt, **Germany,** at the company's E-mail address.

**end of a sentence**

On our tour we will visit Boston, **Massachusetts.**

Next month we will be opening new offices in Brisbane, **Australia.**

## 1–7. Coordinating Conjunctions

**a.** The words *and, but, or,* and *nor* are coordinating conjunctions. Place a comma before any of these words that separate two independent clauses (complete thought units) in a compound sentence. No comma is used if both clauses are not totally independent and could not stand alone as separate sentences. (See Section 1-18 for use of a semicolon instead of a comma.)

### two independent clauses

Several of our staff members should reach their sales goals by the end of this month, **and** they will then be eligible to win a bonus vacation to Hawaii.

There are still 43 orders to fill, **but** we will close for vacation as scheduled.

You may have the interest added to your account, **or** we can send you a monthly check for the interest earned.

We have not purchased any appliances from this distributor within the past three months, **nor** have we requested an extension of our credit line.

You may, Mr. Villano, obtain up-to-date flight schedules from our Web site on the Internet, **and** you can make your reservations at the same time.

Over one hundred of our clients indicated an interest in attending our free seminars, **but** we can, unfortunately, only accommodate half of them in this series.

### no second independent clause

I plan to complete this project by Wednesday but cannot promise that it will reach your desk before Monday.

We are aware that sales have increased in your district and that another salesperson should be assigned to your territory.

**b.**  **In imperative sentences (command statements), the subject *you* is understood. Separate with a comma two independent clauses, whether one or both are in the imperative form.**

Ship the books to me at Grant Occupational Center, **but** send the invoice to the bookstore manager at Eastern College.

Please call Dr. Greenberg's office tomorrow morning, **and** his nurse will let you know what time the doctor is expected to finish surgery.

**c.**  **When a simple adverb, an introductory phrase, or a dependent clause precedes and applies equally to two clauses, the second clause is not a totally separate thought unit. Consequently, no comma is placed before the conjunction.**

### simple adverb

**Please** call the doctor's office tomorrow morning and arrange to have your appointment changed to next week.  (The adverb *please* refers to both call and arrange. Therefore, the second clause is not an independent thought unit and a comma is not required.)

### introductory phrase

**During the next month** our board members will visit several sites in Memphis and they will select one for our new branch office.  (*During the* *next month* applies equally to both clauses. Consequently, the second clause is not an independent thought unit and a comma is not required.)

### dependent clauses

**When Mr. Howard calls**, ask him for his new address and send him 100 copies of our revised price list. (Subject *you* is understood in both clauses. *When Mr. Howard calls* applies to both clauses. Therefore, the second clause is not an independent thought unit and no punctuation mark is required.)

**As soon as we receive your response,** we will notify our distributor and he will ship your order the next day. (In this case *As soon as we receive your response* applies to both clauses; therefore, no punctuation mark is needed before the conjunction *and*.)

**d.** **Omit the comma in short compound sentences connected by *and*. For simplicity, "short" in these cases *may be* interpreted as those compound sentences containing up to 12 or 13 words.**

Format five additional disks and use them to back up this subdirectory.

John wrote the letter and his supervisor signed it.

I received the inquiry yesterday and my assistant contacted the client immediately.

## 1–8.   Independent Adjectives

**Use commas to separate two or more independent adjectives that modify a noun. No commas are needed, though, when the first adjective modifies the second adjective and the noun as a unit. To identify independent adjectives, (1) reverse the adjectives, (2) read the adjectives independently, and (3) read the sentence with the word *and* between the adjectives. If the sentence makes sense and means the same thing with the adjectives read in these ways, then commas should be placed between them.**

### independent adjectives

Be sure to enclose a **stamped, addressed** envelope with your inquiry.

The president had surrounded herself with **efficient, intelligent** assistants.

We received a **demanding, discourteous, unprecedented** letter from your company.

### first adjective modifies second adjective and noun

The posters were lettered in **large bold print**.

He received several **attractive business offers**.

The room was filled with **old local newspapers** dating back to the 1960s.

Does the press release describe Liza's **dazzling blue evening gown**?

## 1–9. Introductory Clauses

**a.** An introductory dependent clause is separated from the rest of the sentence by a comma. Introductory dependent clauses contain a subject and a verb and usually begin with one of the words listed below:

| as ⎫ | | after | provided | until |
|------|--------------------|----------|----------|----------|
| if ⎬ are most common | although | since | whenever |
| when ⎭ | | because | so | while |
| | | before | unless | |

**When Mr. Jones received his $10,000 inheritance,** he invested the money in mutual funds.

**So that we may reach a decision by March 14,** please submit the papers within the next two days.

**b.** A shortened form of an introductory clause is separated from the rest of the sentence by a comma.

**If so,** the delivery of these materials may be delayed. (If that is so, . . . .)

**As agreed,** we will offer the contract to the lowest qualified bidder. (As we agreed, . . . .)

**Whatever the reason,** without a sales receipt we cannot accept returned merchandise at a higher price than the current selling price. (Whatever the reason may be, . . . .)

**c.** Occasionally an introductory clause may follow another introductory word group. In such cases place a comma only after the introductory clause.

Mrs. Jones said that **when these accounts are paid,** we will reinstate their credit privileges.

I hope that **before you file your income tax return,** you will check with our tax attorneys on this issue.

**d.** When an introductory clause is followed by two main clauses, place a comma only after the introductory clause.

**When Gerald addresses prospective clients,** he speaks clearly and he answers all questions courteously.

**If you wish employment with our company,** fill out the enclosed application form and mail it in the enclosed envelope.

**e.** When a sentence contains two introductory clauses, place a comma only after the second clause.

**If you decide to purchase this system and after you have received the president's authorization,** please submit all the specifications on our standard purchase order form.

## 1–10. Introductory Phrases

**a.** An introductory infinitive phrase (a verb preceded by *to*) is followed by a comma.

**To arrive at an immediate decision,** the Board of Directors called an emergency stockholders' meeting.

**To carry out the original plans,** Ms. Morii hired two additional employees.

**b.** An introductory participial phrase (a verb form used as an adjective) is followed by a comma.

**Hoping to obtain several large orders,** Mr. Irwin embarked upon a selective advertising campaign.

**Concerned about the sudden decrease in sales,** Ms. Alexander flew to the West Coast office.

**c.** An introductory prepositional phrase (a group of words that include a preposition and an object) is separated from the rest of the sentence by a comma if it contains a verb form *or* five or more words.[3] After an introductory prepositional phrase that contains no verb form and fewer than five words, use a comma only if the comma is necessary for clarity.

A partial list of prepositions used to begin introductory prepositional phrases follows:

| about | among | behind | during | on | until |
|-------|-------|--------|--------|----|-------|
| above | around | below | for | over | up |
| after | at | between | from | through | upon |
| along | before | by | in | under | with |

**verb form**

**Upon receiving the papers,** Swift & Company filed suit against its former parent company.

**After reviewing the case,** the judge decided in favor of the defendant.

**By enrolling today,** you are assured of receiving a place in the class that begins on March 1.

**After calling you,** I notified our insurance company of the theft.

**five or more words**

**During the past few days of litigation,** both sides have made significant concessions.

**Between July 1 and August 31,** all our stores will be closed on Mondays.

**Within the next few days,** you should receive a written confirmation from the Hawaiian Village Hotel.

---

[3]Some authorities suggest four words.

### no verb form and fewer than five words

**About three months ago** our laboratories released several new medical breakthroughs to the press.

**Through your efforts** we have been able to locate new customers for our towels and linens.

**For over two weeks** our offices have been without air-conditioning.

**On September 30** we will open our new branch office in London.

### comma necessary for clarity

**After the class,** discussion on this issue will continue until 3 p.m. in Conference Room 14.

**In my office,** files dating back to 1989 are stored in three of the cabinets.

**Until next Monday,** morning deliveries will be accepted only between 8:30 and 10 a.m.; afternoon deliveries, between 3 and 5 p.m.

**d.** An introductory phrase that follows another introductory word group is treated as if the opening introductory word group were not included. In other words, mentally omit the opening expression, and punctuate the introductory phrase according to the rules in Section 1-10a–c.

### infinitive phrase

Mr. Wilson explained that **to meet our production deadline,** we would have to work overtime the remainder of the week.

### participial phrase

Ms. Winston expressed concern over the poor handling of complaints by our customer service representatives; and **speaking calmly and empathetically,** she demonstrated how they should handle irate customers.

### prepositional phrase, fewer than five words

We were notified that **on Monday** we will resume our regular schedule.

May we assure you that **within the next week** your order will be shipped from our warehouse.

### prepositional phrase, five or more words

I hope that **in view of the urgency of the situation,** we will obtain the full cooperation of our staff.

We expect that **during this rapid growth period,** many investors will attempt to acquire our company.

**e.** Any phrase that acts as the subject or is part of the predicate is not followed by a comma.

**phrase that acts as a subject**

**To answer your question** would require several days' research on the part of our staff.

**Helping his employees prepare for advancement** does not rank high among Mr. Green's management attributes.

**phrase that is part of the predicate**

**From the intensive police investigation** came some new evidence that led to the apprehension of the suspected arsonists.

## 1–11. Restrictive and Nonrestrictive Phrases and Clauses

Restrictive phrases and clauses modify and contribute substantially to the main idea of a sentence and are essential to its meaning. They tell *who, what*, or *which one* and are not set off with commas.

Nonrestrictive phrases and clauses add an additional idea and do not significantly change or contribute to the main idea of a sentence. They are unessential word groups; that is, they are not needed by the main clause to tell *who, what*, or *which one*. Set off nonrestrictive phrases and clauses from the rest of the sentence with commas. Notice that phrases and clauses directly following proper nouns are nonrestrictive.

a. Relative clauses (those beginning with *who, whose, whom, which*, or *that*) are either restrictive (no comma) or nonrestrictive (comma required).

**restrictive and essential to meaning**

Office employees **who are able to use a spreadsheet program such as Excel or Lotus** can obtain well-paying jobs. (Tells *which kind* of office employee.)

**nonrestrictive and not essential to meaning**

Ms. Kennedy, **who readily uses Excel and Lotus,** can obtain a well-paying job. (Additional idea. Clause following a proper noun.)

In the first example the clause "who are able to use a spreadsheet program such as Excel or Lotus" limits the type of office employees who "can easily obtain well-paying jobs." In the second example "who readily uses Excel and Lotus" is of no assistance in *identifying* Ms. Kennedy but is merely an additional idea. Therefore, this example is a nonrestrictive clause that is set off by commas.

**restrictive and essential to meaning**

All students **who are enrolled in history classes** will take part in organizing World Affairs Day. (Tells *which* students.)

**nonrestrictive and not essential to meaning**

Joseph, **who is enrolled in a history class,** will take part in organizing World Affairs Day. (Additional idea. Clause following a proper noun.)

**b.** Careful writers will use *that* for restrictive clauses (no comma) and *which* for nonrestrictive clauses (comma required).

### restrictive

The stores **that are located in the Flintridge Mall** are sponsoring a free parking lot carnival this weekend.

All our insurance programs **that appeal to young adults** should be featured in this new brochure.

### nonrestrictive

Her new book, **which was scheduled for spring publication,** will be released next December.

We have canceled our winter sales meeting, **which was scheduled from December 11–13 in Miami.**

**c.** Dependent adverbial clauses (ones that begin with words such as *if, as, when, since, because*, etc.) that follow the main clause may be restrictive (no comma) or nonrestrictive (comma required). Restrictive clauses (1) answer such questions as *when, why, how*, or *whether* or (2) limit the main idea of the sentence. Nonrestrictive clauses, however, add an additional idea that does not alter the meaning of the main clause.

### restrictive and essential to meaning

We will ship your order **as soon as your account is approved.** (Tells *when*.)

National Food Products has doubled its monthly sales **since the advertising campaign began.** (Tells *when*.)

Please send us this information by March 1 **so that we may update our records.** (Tells *why*.)

Our company president retired last month **because his doctor recommended a six-month leave of absence.** (Tells *why*.)

You can receive this handsome carrying case free of charge **if you will fill out and return the enclosed questionnaire.** (Tells *how*.)

We can still promise you the discount price **if we receive your order on or before July 15.** (Tells *whether*.)

We cannot install the additional equipment you requested **unless we receive an authorization from your main office.** (Limits main idea.)

You may order additional items at the advertised sale prices **as long as our current supply of merchandise lasts.** (Limits main idea.)

### nonrestrictive and not essential to meaning

He has written his letter of resignation, **although I do not believe he will submit it.** (Additional idea.)

She will continue with her plans for introducing a new product, **whatever the competition might be.** (Additional idea.)

Next week our Board of Directors will tour our new South Haven plant, **where we will be hiring several hundred new employees.** (Additional idea.)

**d.** A dependent clause or a short independent clause used to provide an extra idea within a sentence is nonrestrictive and is set off with commas (or dashes for emphasis).

### interrupting dependent clause

Sales figures for last year, **as you can see from the financial reports,** were nearly 10 percent higher than we had projected.

On Tuesday morning, **when you arrive for the meeting,** please give the manuscript to my secretary.

We can, **as I see the situation,** complete this project at least a month before its deadline date.

This year's line of holiday greeting cards—**although the cards are larger and more exquisite**—is less expensive than last year's.

### interrupting short independent clause

Ms. Moore is, **I believe,** the only applicant who presently resides out of the state.

We will, **I hope,** be able to supply you with this information by July 1.

**e.** Participial, infinitive, or prepositional phrases appearing within a sentence may be restrictive (no comma) or nonrestrictive (comma required), depending on whether or not they tell *who, what, what kind,* or *which one.* Phrases that answer these questions are restrictive (no comma).

### participial restrictive

All employees **planning to participate in the stock option program** must sign up by July 1. (Tells *which ones.*)

### participial nonrestrictive

Mr. Daly, **planning to participate in the stock option program,** has agreed to conduct seminars on this employee benefit. (Additional idea. Phrase following a proper noun.)

### infinitive restrictive

We are planning **to sign up for the program** by July 1. (Tells *what.*)

### infinitive nonrestrictive

The stock option plan offers employees an excellent investment opportunity, **to mention only one company fringe benefit.** (Additional idea.)

### prepositional restrictive

The advertising brochures **for our August sale** will be ready June 30. (Tells *which ones.*)

Manufacturers **like us** find themselves in financial difficulty today. (Tells *what kind*.)

Clients **like the Atkinsons** make the real estate business a pleasure. (Tells *what kind*.)

### prepositional nonrestrictive

We are planning, **in response to numerous requests,** to open our city ticketing agencies on Sundays as well. (Additional idea.)

Small appliance manufacturers, **like us,** are in financial difficulty today. (Additional idea.)

## 1–12. Contrasting, Limiting, and Contingent Expressions

Contrasting, limiting, or contingent expressions are set off with commas. Words often used to introduce contrasting and limiting expressions include *not, never, but, seldom*, and *yet*.

### contrasting expression

She had considered selling her stocks, **not her rental property,** to increase her liquid assets.

### limiting expression

The association will give us four tickets, **but only for members of our sales staff.**

### contingent expression

**The sooner** we are able to contact our investors in Chicago, **the sooner** we will be able to finance this new project.

**The more money** you can invest, **the greater the return** you can expect.

## 1–13. Omitted Words

Commas are often used to indicate the omission of words when the context of the sentence makes the omitted words clearly understood.

Four new secretaries were hired in the Accounting Department; three, in the Policy Issue Department. (Three *new secretaries were hired* in the Policy Issue Department.)

Last week Mr. Higgins dictated three complete reports; this week, two complete reports. (This week *Mr. Higgins dictated* two complete reports.)

Our B-124 contract expired on June 14; the B-127 contract, June 16; and the B-132, June 21. (The B-127 contract *expired on* June 16, and the B-132 *contract expired on* June 21.)

21

## 1–14. Punctuation for Clarity

**a.** Two identical verbs that appear together in a sentence are separated by a comma.

Whoever **wins, wins** a trip to Hawaii.

Whoever **travels, travels** at his own risk.

Whatever irregularities **occurred, occurred** without the knowledge of the president.

**b.** Words repeated for emphasis are separated by a comma.

**Many, many** years ago this company was founded by Bernard Harris.

It has been a **long, long** time since one of our vice presidents has visited the East Coast offices.

**c.** A word or phrase at the beginning of a sentence that could be read incorrectly with the words that follow is set off by a comma.

**Ever since,** she has been employed by the Hirschell Corporation of Boston.

**The month before,** the corporation expanded its operations to Brazil.

**From the beginning,** students are expected to proofread their own work carefully.

**In our business,** letters are written primarily to sell goods and services and to collect money.

**d.** A name written in inverted form is separated by a comma between the last name and the first name.

Irwin, Carl      Luers, Barbara R.

## 1–15. Short Quotations

**a.** A short quoted sentence is set off from the rest of the sentence by a comma. When the quoted sentence is broken into two parts, commas are required before and after the interjected thought.

**beginning quotation**

"All employees will receive two days' paid vacation after the contract is completed," said Mr. Adams.

**interrupted quotation**

"All employees will receive two days' paid vacation," said Mr. Adams, "after the contract is completed."

**ending quotation**

Mr. Adams said, "All employees will receive two days' paid vacation after the contract is completed."

**b.** Unless a beginning quotation is interrupted, omit any separating commas when the quoted sentence is a question or an exclamation.

**question**

"When will the bids for this contract be opened?" asked Ms. Snow.

**interrupted question**

"When," asked Ms. Snow, "will the bids for this contract be opened?"

**exclamation**

"What a wonderful opportunity you have given our staff!" exclaimed Mr. Stevens.

**interrupted exclamation**

"What a wonderful opportunity," exclaimed Mr. Stevens, "you have given our staff!"

**c.** No comma is needed to set off a quotation or part of a quotation that is woven into a complete sentence or one that is not a complete thought.

**woven into sentence**

The chairperson operated on the premise that "A stitch in time saves nine."

John is reported to have said that " . . . no vacancies will be filled until June 1."

**incomplete sentence**

Please mark the top of this package "This Side Up."

The personnel manager advised me "to submit my application as soon as possible."

He merely answered "yes" to all the questions.

**d.** When a comma and a quotation mark fall at the same point in a sentence, *always* place the comma inside the closing quotation mark. Periods, too, are *always* placed inside the closing quotation mark.

"Please arrive at the airport by 9 p.m.," requested Mrs. Chambers.

Her last magazine article, "Western Travel," appeared in *Automotive Digest*.

John said, "Be sure to mail your report by June 11."

**e.** For placement of question marks and exclamation marks with closing quotation marks, see Sections 1-44a and 1-46c.

## 1–16. Numerals

**a.** Expressed in United States format, numerals of more than three digits require commas.

1,320     63,481     963,481     1,293,070     23,092,946     450,500,000

**b.** Two independent figures appearing consecutively in a sentence are separated by a comma.

Two consecutive numbers that act as adjectives modifying the same noun are *not* separated by a comma. Instead, write the first number in words and the second one in figures. If the first number cannot be expressed in *one or two words*, place it in figures also.

**independent figures**

Of this **$23,000, $12,000** is secured by real property.

During **1997, $876,000** worth of sales were financed through this plan.

By October **1, 43** people had submitted applications.

**two numbers modifying a noun, word-figure form**

I will need **thirty 12-inch** rulers for my accounting class.

Each package contains **twelve 2-inch** nails.

Be sure to order **twenty-four 100-watt** bulbs for the lamps in the doctors' waiting rooms.

**two numbers modifying a noun, figure-figure form**

While you are at the post office, please purchase **125 32-cent** stamps.

The prescription was for **250 10-milligram** tablets.

When the carton fell, **127 40-watt** bulbs were broken.

**c.** Commas are omitted in years, house numbers, zip codes, telephone numbers, decimal fractions, metric measurements, and any label-numeral combinations. In metric measurements use a space to separate all numerals containing more than four digits.

**year**

1998          1780          2007

**house number**

9732 Porter Street          19573 Bestor Boulevard

**zip code**

Northridge, CA 91324          Bothell, WA 98041-3011

**telephone number**

(212) 482-9768, Ext. 4412      *or*      212-482-9768, Ext. 4412

**decimal fraction**

0.2873

**metric measurement**

1200 kilometers          10 200 kilometers

### label-numeral combination

Serial No. 83621      page 1276      Room 1890      Invoice 43798

**d.** Volume numbers and page references are separated by commas.

Please refer to Volume XI, page 9.

The article appeared in Volume X, July 1995, page 23.

**e.** Measurements (such as weights, capacities, dimensions, etc.) are treated as single units and are not interrupted by commas.

### weight

Their new baby weighed **8 pounds 7 ounces.**

### dimension

He is **5 feet 10 inches** tall.

The room measurements are **20 feet 6 inches** by **18 feet 4 inches.**

### time period

Our flight time was estimated to be **2 hours 40 minutes.**

## Semicolon

### 1–17. Independent Clauses Without Coordinating Conjunctions

**a.** A semicolon is used between two or more closely related independent clauses (complete thoughts that could stand alone as separate sentences) that are not connected with a coordinating conjunction (and, but, or, nor).

### two independent clauses

Several orders were delayed in the Milwaukee office last month; Ms. Williams will check into our shipping procedures there.

Plan to attend the next American Management Association meeting; you will certainly find this association to be well worth your time.

### three independent clauses

Mr. Horowitz drafted the contract specifications last week; Ms. Ames consulted the firm's attorneys on Monday; Mr. Dotson signed and mailed the company's offer on Wednesday.

**b.** Short and closely related independent clauses may be separated by commas.

### two short independent clauses

Pittsburgh Bank issued the checks, TSI mailed them to clients.

**three short independent clauses**

The monitor flashed, it emitted sparks, it went blank.

He came, he looked around, he left.

## 1–18. Independent Clauses With Coordinating Conjunctions

Two independent clauses linked by a coordinating conjunction *(and, but, or, nor)* are generally separated with a comma. Lengthy, complicated sentences containing internal commas in either or both clauses, however, may be punctuated with a semicolon between the two clauses.

**clauses separated with a comma**

She planned to attend the Chicago meeting, **but** several important matters interfered with her plans.

Yes, Mr. Dale, we have on hand your current order, **but** we can ship it only after your account is up-to-date.

We were pleased with the results of the survey, **and** you will, of course, receive a copy of the summary.

Yes, you may mail in your monthly payment, **or** you may take it to one of our fast, convenient pay stations.

**clauses separated with a semicolon**

Several large orders were recently placed through the Dayton office; **and** Ms. Baca, our national sales manager, has commended the sales staff for its diligent efforts in making such rapid progress in a new office.

You, of course, need not attend the committee meeting scheduled for June 4; **but** I believe, Mr. Plotkin, you will find reading the minutes of this meeting helpful before you address the Board of Directors next week.

## 1–19. Independent Clauses With Transitional Expressions

Two independent clauses (complete thoughts) separated by a transitional expression require a semicolon. A partial list of common transitional expressions follows. In addition, those words and phrases listed in Section 1-2a may be considered transitional expressions when they separate two closely related complete thoughts.

| | | | |
|---|---|---|---|
| accordingly | indeed | notwithstanding | then |
| besides | in fact | on the contrary | therefore |
| consequently | in other words | on the other hand | thus |
| furthermore | likewise | otherwise | yet |
| hence | moreover | so | |
| however | nevertheless | still | |

A comma is used after a transitional expression of more than one syllable or where a strong pause is needed after a one-syllable expression.

**transitional expression with one syllable**

The library will have difficulty obtaining a budget increase this year; **thus** members of your staff should not plan to receive all the books specified on this requisition.

**transitional expression containing more than one syllable**

New catalogs will be shipped to our customers the first week in February; **therefore,** we anticipate a 20 percent sales increase for the months of February, March, and April.

## 1–20. Series Containing Internal Commas or Complete Thoughts

**a.** Items in a series are usually separated by commas. When, however, one or more of the parts contain internal commas, use semicolons to separate the items.

Representatives from Boston, Massachusetts; Los Angeles, California; and Denver, Colorado, were not present at the conference.

Among those present at the convention were Mr. Harmon Fieldcrest, president of Fieldcrest Steel Industries; Dr. Joyce Morton, research director for the University of Wisconsin; Mr. Garland Hansen, vice president of Wisconsin State Bank; and Ms. Georgia Fillmore, secretary-treasurer of CRA Consultants, Inc.

**b.** Three or more independent clauses (complete thoughts) comprising a series are separated by semicolons. Only very short clauses are separated by commas.

**series of independent clauses**

Nearly 7,000 circulars were mailed to prospective clients in 1991; over 15,000 circulars were mailed in 1996; and next year we plan to mail over 10,000 new brochures as well as 20,000 circulars.

**series of independent clauses with internal commas**

Mr. John Harris, our company president, will arrive on Saturday; Mrs. Olga Williams, one of our vice presidents, will arrive on Monday; and Ms. Carol Watson, our company treasurer, will arrive on Tuesday.

**series of short independent clauses**

The tenant called yesterday, we investigated his complaint immediately, and the roof will be repaired tomorrow.

## 1–21. Enumerations and Explanations

**a.** Certain words and phrases are used to introduce enumerations or explanations that follow an independent clause (complete thought). Some common introductory expressions follow:

| | | |
|---|---|---|
| for example (e.g.) | for instance | that is (i.e.) |
| namely (viz.) | that is to say | |

If the enumeration or explanation following the introductory expression *contains commas* or *forms another complete thought*, use a semicolon after the opening independent clause and a comma after the introductory expression.

### enumeration containing commas

Many factors have contributed to the sharp increase in production costs during the last three months; **namely,** price increases in raw materials, wage increases for electrical workers, and overtime salaries for the entire production staff.

### explanation forming another complete thought

To open its Syracuse office, Caldwell Industries advertised for a number of new employees; **that is to say,** not all its employees were willing to transfer to the new location.

**b.** Some independent clauses followed by expressions that introduce enumerations and explanations require a comma, not a semicolon, after the independent clause. If the enumeration or explanation that follows the introductory expression does *not* contain commas or form another complete thought, use commas after the independent clause and the introductory expression.

### enumeration without internal commas

As a member of our user group, you are eligible to purchase additional computer peripherals through our discount program, **for instance,** an automatic control panel or a modem.

### explanation forming an incomplete thought

You may wish to call Ms. Hendrix for further advice, **for example,** to inquire which filing system would be more efficient for your office.

**c.** Enumerations or explanations used as parenthetical expressions within a sentence are not set off by semicolons. Use commas when the enumerated or explanatory information has no internal commas; use dashes or parentheses when the information contains internal commas.

### commas

Your accounting procedures, **for example, posting customer deposits,** can be streamlined with our new computer system.

### dashes

Because of current economic conditions, we must find new vendors for some of our multimedia equipment—**e.g., video cameras, video playback units, and LCD panels**—to stay within our budget allocations.

### parentheses

Your recommendations (**namely, increasing our staff, improving our hiring procedures, and revamping our testing program**) were approved unanimously by the board.

**d.** Complete thoughts that introduce enumerations or explanations without an introductory expression are followed by a colon, not a semicolon.

Several new items were introduced in this popular line: gloves, scarves, and hosiery.

The following people were present at the sales managers' meeting: Roberta Adams, Horace Brubaker, Phillip Haledon, and Susan McCloskey.

Only 82 teachers attended the ARTA state conference: apparently many of our members did not receive their brochures in time to plan for this event.

## 1–22. Semicolon Placement

Always place the semicolon outside closing quotation marks and parentheses.

### quotation marks

Last month Mr. Harrison promised, "I will mail you a check the 1st of next month"; but we have received no money or explanation from him.

### parentheses

Several members of the Accounting Department were ill last week (with the flu); consequently, our end-of-month reports will be a week late in reaching the home office.

# Colon

## 1–23. Formally Enumerated or Listed Items

**a.** Use a colon after an independent clause (complete thought) that introduces a formal listing or an enumeration of items. Words commonly used in introductory independent clauses include *the following, as follows, these,* and *thus.* Sometimes, however, the introduction is implied rather than stated directly. Use a colon following both direct and implied introductions.

### direct introduction

Mrs. Robinson ordered the following new furniture and equipment for her offices: three desks, six chairs, two sofas, two microcomputers, and one laser printer.

These rules should be observed for a successful job interview:
1. Dress appropriately.
2. Appear interested in the company and the job.
3. Answer questions courteously.
4. Thank the interviewers for their time.

**implied introduction**

Several kinds of microcomputers were on display: IBM, Compaq, DEC, Apple, Tandy, Dell, and Xerox.

In determining whether to use a colon or a semicolon for introducing enumerated items, use the colon when the enumeration is not preceded by a transitional introductory expression such as *namely, for example, e.g., that is*, or *i.e.* If an introductory expression immediately precedes the listing, use a semicolon before the expression and a comma after it. (See Section 1-21a for examples.)

**b.** The colon is *not* used to introduce listings of items in the following situations: (1) when an intervening sentence separates the introductory sentence and the enumerated items, (2) when the enumerated items follow a "being" verb or are the object of a verb, (3) when the enumerated items are the object of a preposition, and (4) when the listing is immediately preceded by an enumerating expression.

**no colon: intervening sentence**

The following new silverware patterns will be available January 1. They will be introduced to our dealers next month.
1. Fantasia
2. Sunburst
3. Apollo
4. Moonglow

**no colon: following a "being" verb or acting as the object of a verb**

The words most commonly misspelled **were** *convenience, occasionally, commodity, consequently*, and *accommodate*. (Not: " . . . were: *convenience, . . . .* ")

Examples of Web browsers **include** Netscape Navigator, Mosaic, and Internet Explorer. (Not: " . . . include: Netscape . . . .")

**no colon: object of a preposition**

The first lesson introduces the user **to** the menu bar, the tool bar, and the power bar. (Not: " . . . to: the menu . . . .")

Sales meetings are scheduled **for** January 3, February 4, March 7, and April 9. (Not: " . . . for: January 3, . . . .")

**no colon: listing after enumerating expression**

Please order some additional supplies; **namely,** 8 1/2- by 11-inch plain bond paper, legal-size envelopes, and letter-size manila file folders.

## 1–24. Explanatory Sentences

Separate two sentences with a colon when the second sentence explains, illustrates, or supplements the first.

### explanation

During the next three months, we will gross approximately 50 percent of our annual sales: major toy purchases occur during September, October, and November.

### illustration

Our new advertising campaign will be directed toward buyers of economy cars: we will stress efficient gas mileage, low maintenance costs, and reliability.

### supplement

Several new customers complained about the delay in receiving their charge account plates: they wished to have them in time to complete their holiday shopping.

## 1–25. Long Quotations

**Long one-sentence quotations and quotations of two or more sentences are introduced by a colon.**

**Long quotations of two or more sentences (and usually more than three lines) omit the quotation marks and appear as separate paragraphs. They are indented from the left and right margins and separated from the main text by single blank lines at the beginning and the end of the quotation.**

### long one-sentence quotation

Ms. Judy Dolan, personnel manager of Hartnell Corporation, reported in her annual summary: "Graduates from the University of Southern California's School of Business have been placed in a number of our divisions, and they have risen to middle-management positions within a three-year period."

### long quotation of two or more sentences

One item of importance was noted from the board minutes of March 16:

> Two new products, which will revolutionize word processing, will be introduced on July 1. Trade journal publicity and direct mail advertising will be the major vehicles for distributing information about these products. Efforts by the sales staff for July and August will be directed specifically at marketing the Model AB 1781 and the Model AB 2782 communication networks.

As you can see from the board minutes, we will soon be involved . . . .

## 1–26. Special-Purpose Uses for the Colon

a. **In business letters a colon is placed after the salutation when the mixed punctuation format is used (see Section 10-22).**

Dear Bill:     Dear Ms. Corrigan:     Gentlemen:

**b.** **Use the colon to separate hours and minutes in expressions of time.**

We will arrive at **8:30 a.m.** on Tuesday, March 24.

At **12:15 p.m.** Ms. Hardesty is scheduled to address the Compton Chamber of Commerce.

**c.** **In expressing ratios, use the colon to represent the word *to*.**

The label instructions recommend proportions of **4:1**.

The union members voted **2:1** against accepting the new contract.

**d.** **The colon is often used to separate items in literary references.**

**between title and subtitle**

Dr. Mary Ellen Guffey's latest book, *Business Communication: Process & Product*, 2nd Ed., is now in stock in our college bookstore.

**between place of publication and publisher in footnotes and bibliographies**

Clark, James L., and Lyn R. Clark. *HOW 8: A Handbook for Office Workers*, 8th Ed. Cincinnati: South-Western College Publishing, 1998.

**between volume and page number in footnotes and bibliographies**

[10]Virginia C. Beauchamp and Robert M. Dougherty, "Organizational Communications: Frameworks for Making Yours 'People Oriented,'" *The Bulletin for the Association of Business Communication* 60 (March 1997): 36–38.

**biblical citation**

As an introduction to his sermon, the minister quoted Isaiah **24:1** (Chapter 24, verse 1).

## 1–27. Colon Format and Use With Other Punctuation Marks

**a.** **In computer-generated (or typewritten) copy, space twice after a colon.[4]**

May I please have the following documents by next week: copies of the rental agreement, the returned check, and the 30-day notice to move.

**b.** **Place the colon outside closing quotation marks and parentheses.**

**closing quotation mark**

Please distribute to the following staff members copies of Lynn Haile's latest article, "Closing the Sale Effectively": Mina Balejian, Charles Ballesteros, Paul Kellogg, and Kyung Kim.

---

[4]Some authorities recommend a single space after a colon for desktop publishing formats. To promote ease of reading for business documents, though, space twice after a colon in all computer-generated documents.

**closing parenthesis**

Several contractors are being considered for the new project (Mountain Hills):  Wyeth & Sons, Burnside Developers, and Hartman and Associates.

c. In vertical listings introduced by a colon, conclude each item in the listing with a period only if the items are complete sentences.

Single-space the items in a vertical listing. If any item in the listing contains more than one line, double-space between the items. If all the items in the listing consist of a single line, you *may either* leave one blank line between each item *or* just single-space the listing. Always place one blank line before and after a listing.

In business letters and memorandums, vertical listings may be indented from the left and right margins *or* may assume the margins of the main text.[5] Items in a listing may or may not be numbered.

**complete sentences, numbered items, standard margins**

We have discontinued manufacturing our Model 1040A microwave oven for the following reasons:

1. The popularity of our smaller ovens has decreased continually during the past eighteen months.
2. Manufacturing costs and prices differ only slightly from those for our standard-size ovens.
3. Two other models smaller than our standard-size ones have been more popular.

**incomplete sentences, unnumbered items, indented margins**

Effective July 1 new rates will be in force for the following types of policies:

> Jewelry riders on home owners' policies
> Liability coverage for drivers under 25 years of age
> Earthquake riders on all casualty policies
> Term life insurance for males 65 and older

## 1–28. Capitalization With Colons

a. When a colon is used to introduce a horizontal listing of items, the first letter after the colon is not capitalized unless it begins a proper noun. Capitalize the first letter of each item in a vertical listing.

**lowercase letter in horizontal listing**

Place the following items in the tray:  the original invoice, the duplicate invoice, and the shipping copy.

---

[5]See Section 11-9 for guidelines governing the format and preparation of horizontal and vertical listings in reports and manuscripts as well as in business letters and memorandums.

### proper noun capitalized

Four employees were promoted last week: Teresa Caruana, Sue Rigby, Lloyd Bartholome, and Arthur Rubin.

### capitalized letters in vertical listing

You may pay for your Empress Vacation Time-Share package in a number of ways:

Personal check
Credit card—Visa, MasterCard, or American Express
Eighteen monthly installments of $637.50

Do not miss the opportunity to get in on the ground floor of this . . . .

**b.** Do not capitalize the first letter after a colon when the second sentence explains or supplements the first unless the letter begins a proper noun.

### lowercase letter begins second sentence

Your account has been temporarily frozen:  outstanding bills for $327 still remain unpaid.

### proper noun capitalized

The $1,000 award was given to Warren Weber:  Dr. Weber's paper was judged to be the best by a panel of three judges.

**c.** Capitalize the first word after a colon when the colon introduces a formal rule or principle stated as a complete sentence.

Apply the following rule in preparing all your business correspondence: Always place commas and periods inside closing quotation marks.

Mr. Wilson emphasized the importance of strict adherence to the following policy:  In case of absence all employees must notify their immediate supervisor by 8:30 a.m. that day.

**d.** When two or more sentences follow a colon, capitalize the first letter of each sentence.

Several suggestions emerged from the discussion:  To begin with, an engineering firm should be consulted to determine the extent of damage to the property.  Then a building contractor should be contacted for estimates to repair the damage.  Finally, financial institutions should be surveyed to obtain the best terms for reconstructing the property.

**e.** Capitalize the first letter of sentences or phrases introduced by words such as *Note, Attention, Warning, Caution, For Rent,* or *For Sale.*

**Warning:** All cars parked illegally will be towed away at vehicle owner's expense.

**Caution:** Please hold children by hand.

**For Rent:** Large three-bedroom home with family room, fireplace, air-conditioning, and pool.  Phone (617) 555-3542.

**f.** Capitalize the first word of quoted material that follows a colon.

Mr. Rosen informed the board about expansion plans for this year: "Since property on the corner of Tampa and Nordhoff has already been purchased, construction of our new branch office will begin early this spring so that we can open this office in September or October."

# Dash

## 1–29. Parenthetical Elements, Appositives, and Summaries

**a.** Parenthetical elements and appositives are usually set off from the rest of the sentence by commas. When the parenthetical element or appositive contains internal commas, however, substitute dashes (or parentheses) for the separating commas.

In printed, desktop publishing, or word processing material, use an em dash—a character that appears as a solid line and is twice the length of a hyphen. In typewritten material form the dash by typing two hyphens with no space before, between, or after.

**parenthetical element with internal commas**

Last month Ms. Arntson—with the hope of increasing sales, recruiting new employees, and establishing sources of supply—made several trips to the East Coast.

**appositive with internal commas**

Three state dignitaries—Governor Charles Inacker, Attorney General Mary Sanchez, and Secretary Gregory Pappas—attended the opening session of the convention.

**b.** Use a dash to set off a brief summary from the rest of the sentence.

Thanksgiving, Christmas, and New Year's Day—these are the only holidays the store will be closed.

White, black, navy, red, and tan—you have your choice of these five colors.

**c.** To achieve greater separation, use dashes instead of commas to set off abrupt parenthetical elements or those requiring emphasis. Appositives requiring emphasis may also be separated from the rest of the sentence with dashes instead of commas.

**abrupt parenthetical element**

Her only concern—notwithstanding her interest in job security—was finding employment in an organization where opportunities for advancement were numerous.

### emphatic parenthetical element

Several orders were rerouted to the Milwaukee office—not to the Salt Lake City branch.

### emphatic appositive

Additional heavy-duty equipment—bulldozers and graders—was needed to complete the project.

**d.** **For emphasis use a dash in place of a comma or a semicolon to introduce an example or explanation.**

### example requiring emphasis

Insurance coverage adequate five years ago may no longer fulfill the purpose for which it was designed—for example, if current inflationary trends continue, fire and theft insurance may not cover the replacement costs of the insured properties.

### explanation requiring emphasis

Our sales of greeting cards have increased 25 percent since 1996— namely, from $1 million to $1.25 million.

**e.** **Afterthoughts or side thoughts generated from the text, but not necessarily part of it, may be separated from the rest of the sentence by dashes.**

### side thought

All members of our staff were invited to the conference on simplifying communication procedures—only Ms. Harris was unable to attend the session.

### afterthought

Mrs. Wilson had planned to finish installing the new software this afternoon—at least John thought she had planned to do it then.

## 1–30. Hesitations in Verbal Reports

**Use dashes to indicate hesitations, faltering, or stammering in reports of conversations, testimonies, or speeches.**

Ms. Morrow: Yes, Mr. President—we expect perhaps oh—a— 35 percent increase in sales during the next year.

Mr. Schatz: Well—perhaps a new inventory-control system will solve some of the current problems.

## 1–31. Source of Quotations

**A dash is placed before the source of a quotation when the source is listed after the quotation.**

"We can expect a great decrease in our unemployment rate during the next ten months."

—H. J. Scott

"The difference between the right word and the almost right word is the difference between lightning and the lightning bug."

—Mark Twain

## 1–32. Format and Placement of Dash

**a.** In printing, in desktop publishing, or with word processing programs, use an em dash (not a hyphen or an en dash) to form the dash; leave no space before or after the em dash. Form the dash on a typewriter by typing two hyphens consecutively; leave no space before, between, or after the hyphens.

A dash never begins a new line, but it may appear at the end of a line.

**em dash**

Several influential community organizations—the Kiwanis Club, the Chamber of Commerce, and the Rotary Club—sponsored Marian C. Crawford for the vacant seat on the board of education.

**typewritten dash**

Three cities--Atlanta, New Orleans, and Fort Worth--are still under consideration for our new plant site.

**end of line**

Our contract negotiations—after reaching an impasse on December 20— were resumed on January 5.

**b.** The only punctuation mark that may precede an opening dash is a period in an abbreviation. Closing dashes may be preceded by a period in an abbreviation, a question mark, or an exclamation mark.

**opening dash after abbreviation**

Prices quoted on all Eastern furniture were f.o.b.—freight charges from Pennsylvania to Los Angeles amounted to $834.

**closing dash after question mark**

A new kind of after-dinner mint—do you know which one I mean?— was introduced by the Sweitzer Candy Company last month.

# Period

## 1–33. End of Sentence

Place a period at the end of a declarative sentence, an imperative statement or command, an indirect question, and a polite request.

Polite requests end with a period even though they may appear to have the format of a question. A polite request (1) asks the reader to perform a specific action and (2) is answered by the reader's compliance or noncompliance with the request. (See Section 1-41e for additional information and examples.)

### declarative sentence

We have received free introductory offers from America Online, CompuServe, and Prodigy.

Several new products were introduced to the stockholders at the April 5 meeting.

### imperative statement

Fill in and mail your application for admittance by April 30.

Please check to ensure you have locked all entrances and engaged the security system before leaving the store.

### indirect question

She asked who was responsible for planning and coordinating the sales meeting.

Most of the telephone calls have been inquiries asking where we have moved our store.

### polite request

Will you please send us your check for $174.55 by May 1.

May I have your E-mail address so that I can send you this information.

## 1–34. End of Independent Phrase

Independent phrases, those phrases representing implied complete thoughts not directly connected with the following thought, are concluded with a period.

**Now, to get to the point.** Will you be able to accept responsibility for conducting a sales campaign during June?

**Yes, for the most part.** Our salespeople have increased their sales since the new incentive program was established.

## 1–35. Abbreviations and Initials

a. Abbreviations are usually concluded with periods. However, after abbreviations for business and governmental organizations, associations, radio and television stations, federal agencies, and certain professional designations (*CLU, CPA, CPS, PLS*), the periods are omitted. (See Section 1-39a for spacing following the period.)

**period after abbreviation**

Fletcher, Hagan, Ross, and Company **Inc.** released several new stock issues.

**periods after abbreviations**

Mr. Haynes requested that all orders be sent on a **c.o.d.** basis.

Most of these products were manufactured in the **U.S.A.**

**no periods with certain abbreviations**

I hope the educational project director for **NASA** will be able to address our convention.

Did you purchase additional **IBM** stock?

**b.** Place a period after an initial. Leave one space between the period and the next word.

Ms. Roberta **D.** Holt accepted the invitation to address the convention participants.

We have tried for several days to contact **A. F.** Elliot.

## 1–36. Outlines

**a.** Use periods after letters and numbers in alphanumeric outlines, except those enclosed in parentheses. Leave two blank spaces before beginning the contents of the item.

Use periods after whole numbers in decimal outlines. Leave two blank spaces after the last typed character before beginning the contents of the item.

**alphanumeric outline**

```
I.  . . . . . .
    A.  . . . . . .
    B.  . . . . . .
        1.  . . . . . .
        2.  . . . . . .
            a.  . . . . . .
            b.  . . . . . .
                (1)  . . . . . .
                (2)  . . . . . .
                    (a)  . . . . . .
                    (b)  . . . . . .
                        1)  . . . . . .
                        2)  . . . . . .
                            a)  . . . . . .
                            b)  . . . . . .
II.  . . . . . .
```

**decimal outline**

```
1.  ......
    1.1  ......
    1.2  ......
         1.21  ......
         1.22  ......
               1.221  ......
               1.222  ......
                      1.2221  ......
                      1.2222  ......
                              1.22221  ......
                              1.22222  ......
                                       1.222221  ......
                                       1.222222  ......
2.  ......
```

**b.** Use periods after complete sentences in outlines and listings. No punctuation mark is placed after an incomplete thought.

**periods—complete sentences**

A.  Two new processes were developed as a result of the experiments.
   1.  Lamination of fiberglass to wooden surfaces contributes to vessel buoyancy.
   2.  Sealing of surfaces prevents excessive moisture absorption.

**no periods—incomplete sentences**

A.  New Processes
   1.  Lamination of fiberglass to wooden surfaces
   2.  Sealing of surfaces

## 1–37.  Decimals

Periods are used to signify decimals.

Of the customers responding to our survey, only **34.7** percent rated our service as "Excellent."

Last year Mr. Phoenix paid $120 for the 2,000 sales announcements; this year he paid **$145.50** for the same kind and number.

## 1–38.  Ellipses

An ellipsis (a series of three periods with a space before, between, and after the series) is used for emphasis in advertising material or for showing omissions in quoted material. In showing omissions, indicate the completion of a thought with an additional period. (See Section 1-52 for further information on the use of ellipses.)

**emphasis**

Place your order today . . . for relief from tension headaches . . . for ending miserable aches and pains . . . for a happier, tension-free you.

**omission**

The president read from the consulting company's report: "Basically, operations for the next year should be conducted according to the attached plan .... Several of your current operations personnel should ... implement the recommended procedures."

## 1–39. Period Format

**a.** No space is placed between a decimal point and a number or after a period within an abbreviation. However, within a sentence one space follows an initial or the concluding period in an abbreviation. In copy prepared on a word processor or typewriter, allow two spaces after a period at the end of a sentence.[6]

**decimal—no space**

Since 1996 costs of manufacturing materials have risen **18.5** percent.

**period within abbreviation—no space**

All prices quoted are **f.o.b.**

**initial—one space**

John **R.** Gardner was elected chair of the committee.

**abbreviation within sentence—one space**

**Dr.** Sussman has scheduled **Mrs.** Johnson for surgery at 9 **a.m.** on June 23 in Encino Hospital.

**end of sentence—two spaces**

Please submit proof that the property taxes have been **paid.** As soon as we receive copies of your canceled check, we can close escrow.

**b.** Use only one period to end a sentence, even though the sentence may end with an abbreviation.

She is scheduled to arrive between 9 and 10 a.m.

Mr. Kirk's mail is to be forwarded to him in Washington, D.C.

**c.** A period is always placed inside the closing quotation mark.

Ms. Allison promptly replied, "No funding requests will be honored after July 1."

Our editor was pleased with your magazine article, "New Ideas for Home Builders."

**d.** A period is placed inside the closing parenthesis when the words in parentheses are a complete sentence. When words in parentheses

---

[6]For desktop publishing some authorities recommend one space after a period that concludes a sentence. To promote ease of reading in documents written for business, use two spaces after a period that concludes a sentence.

are not a complete thought and are part of another sentence, place the period outside the closing parenthesis.

**complete sentence in parentheses**

Several executives left the company after the merger. (They were disappointed with the new leadership.)

**incomplete sentence in parentheses**

Only three items were discontinued after the consulting analysts completed their investigation (last March).

# Question Mark

## 1–40. Direct Questions

Conclude a direct question that requires an answer with a question mark.

How many times have you tried to contact Ms. Cates?

Of all the people at the board meeting, how many would you estimate were disappointed with the salary proposal?

## 1–41. Statements With Questions

**a.** When a sentence contains a statement followed by a direct question, conclude the sentence with a question mark. Separate the statement from the question with a comma, dash, or colon, depending upon the nature of the statement.

**question mark with comma**

I would recommend that we contact at least three other vendors before selecting a permanent source of supply, wouldn't you agree?

**question mark with dash**

They were satisfied with the report—weren't they?

**question mark with colon**

Each of us should consider the following question:  what can we do to improve the profit picture for next year?

**b.** Conclude a statement that contains a short, direct question with a question mark.

You have filed your income tax return, have you not, for the last taxable year?

Our rental payments are current—aren't they—for the leased offices in the Bradley building?

**c.** A statement that is meant as a question is concluded with a question mark.

You still expect to leave for Cleveland tomorrow morning?

The conference has been delayed until April?

**d.** **A period, rather than a question mark, is placed after an indirect question.**

Mr. Joyner asked when we expected our Albany office to release the information.

Ms. Schmidt inquired about the possibility of her placing several students in our Accounting Department as trainees in a cooperative work-experience program.

**e.** **Polite requests phrased as questions are followed by periods rather than question marks because they are considered to be commands or "please do" statements. A polite request (1) asks the reader to perform a specific action and (2) is answered by having the reader either take or ignore the action requested instead of responding with a "yes" or "no." Both components *must* be present for a period to be used; otherwise, a question mark is correct.**

### polite request requiring period

Will you please send us three copies of your latest financial report.

May I please have this information by the end of the month.

Won't you take a few minutes now to fill in the questionnaire and return it in the enclosed envelope.

May we count on your support with a "yes" vote on Proposition 11.

### direct question requiring question mark

Would you be willing to address envelopes for the senator's reelection campaign? (Requires "yes" or "no" response.)

May we call on you next week for a demonstration? (Requires "yes" or "no" response.)

Wouldn't you like to be the proud owner of a new Supra 28 personal computer? (Does not require reader to return a "yes" or "no" response, but no *specific* action is requested.)

May we have your support in the future? (Does not require reader to return a "yes" or "no" response, but no *specific* action is requested.)

May I compliment you on your outstanding performance in meeting this year's sales quota? (No "yes" or "no" response is required; however, no *specific* action is requested.)

## 1–42. Expressions of Doubt

**Doubt in expressing statements of fact may be signified by enclosing a question mark in parentheses.**

His last visit to the South was in 1995 (?).

She earns $2,400 (?) a month.

## 1–43. Series of Questions

When a sentence contains a series of questions, place a question mark at the end of each question. Only the first letter of the sentence is capitalized unless a question in the series begins with a proper noun or is a complete thought. Leave one space after a question mark that appears within a sentence; leave two spaces after the concluding question mark.[7]

**series of incomplete questions**

What are the primary responsibilities of the president? the executive vice president? the treasurer?

Who requested copies of the report—the judge? the insurance company? the plaintiff's attorney?

**series of proper noun questions**

Will the new flight route have a stop in San Diego? Los Angeles? San Francisco?

**series of independent questions**

Several important issues were discussed at the conference last week: What style trends will be popular during the next decade? What comfort demands will the public make on furniture manufacturers? How much will price influence consumer furniture purchases?

## 1–44. Question Mark Placement and Format

a. Question marks may be placed either inside or outside the closing quotation mark or parenthesis.

When a complete question is contained within the quotation or parenthetical remark, place the question mark inside the closing quotation mark or parenthesis. If the entire sentence, not just the quotation or parenthetical remark, comprises the question, place the question mark outside the closing quotation mark or parenthesis.

Use only one concluding punctuation mark at the end of a sentence.

**complete question contained in parentheses**

We received official notification last week **(did your notice arrive yet?)** that we must vacate our offices by the 1st of the month.

The committee informed me that J. Wilson Edwards has been appointed manager of the Phoenix office. **(Did you approve this appointment?)**

---

[7]Although some desktop publishing authorities recommend only one space after the concluding punctuation mark, use two spaces to promote ease of reading in business documents.

**complete question contained in quotation marks**

"Will the entire original cast be present for the opening night in Philadelphia?" asked a local reporter.

The Governor then inquired, "Who is in charge of this committee?"

**question encompasses entire sentence**

Will you be able to ship this order by May 15 (earlier if possible)?

Have you finished reading the article "Investment Opportunities Abroad"?

**b.** If an entire sentence and a quotation within the sentence are both questions, use only the first question mark—the one appearing inside the closing quotation mark.

Did the president ask, "When will the directors hold their next meeting?"

**c.** In word processing-generated and typewritten copy, leave one space after a question mark that appears within a sentence and two spaces after a question mark that appears at the end of a sentence.[8]

**one space**

Should I place these supplies on the desk? in the cabinet? in the storeroom?

**two spaces**

What time should we leave for the airport?   When is your flight scheduled to depart?   What time do you expect to arrive in Atlanta? May I please have answers to these questions by this afternoon.

## Exclamation Mark

### 1–45.  Use of Exclamation Mark

To express a high degree of emotion, use an exclamation mark after a word, phrase, clause, or sentence.

**word**

What!  You mean the materials will not arrive until next week?

**phrase**

How beautiful!  The designer certainly used a great deal of color and imagination in creating this pattern.

---

[8]Some desktop publishing authorities suggest using only one space after a concluding punctuation mark, but use two spaces in business documents to promote ease of reading.

**clause**

**If he attends!** He'd better attend, or Mr. Ramirez will get a new assistant.

**sentence**

Yes, she finally got an interview!

## 1–46. Exclamation Mark Placement and Format

**a.** In word processing-generated and typewritten copy, leave two spaces after the exclamation mark before beginning the next word.[9]

**b.** The exclamation mark should be used sparingly in business documents, and placing exclamation marks in two consecutive sentences or thought units should be avoided. Instead, use commas, periods, or question marks to complete an exclamatory thought.

**exclamation with comma**

**Oh,** I don't see how we can possibly meet the contract deadline without working overtime!

**exclamation with period**

**No!** Mr. Jones has not resigned.

**exclamation with question mark**

**What!** You expected the completed analysis last week?

**c.** Exclamation marks may be placed before or after the closing quotation mark or parenthesis.

When a complete exclamatory remark is a quotation or is enclosed in parentheses, place the exclamation mark inside the closing quotation mark or parenthesis. If the entire sentence, not just the quotation or parenthetical element, comprises the exclamatory expression, place the exclamation mark outside the closing quotation mark or parenthesis.

Use only one concluding punctuation mark at the end of a sentence.

**complete exclamatory expression in quotation marks**

At the time of the emergency, one of the employees shouted, **"Break down the door!"**

**complete exclamatory expression in parentheses**

He obtained the help of several advisors **(what a mistake that was!)** to assist him in selecting the project subcontractors.

---

[9]Some desktop publishing authorities recommend only one space, but for business documents use two spaces to foster reading ease.

Management was shocked at the employees' reactions to the new process. **(Only 4 percent of the staff welcomed the new procedures!)**

**exclamatory expression encompasses entire sentence**

**If you wish to take advantage of these bargains, you will have to act now (today)!**

**I cannot believe Marie Huffinger's statement, "Only 3 percent of the merchandise was returned"!**

# Quotation Marks

## 1–47. Direct Quotations

Direct quotations contain the exact wording used by a writer or speaker. Place one-sentence quotations and short two-sentence quotations within quotation marks.

Use commas to introduce most one-sentence quotations. Long one-sentence quotations and quotations of two or more sentences are introduced by a colon.

Quotation marks are not used for indirect quotations that do not use the exact wording of the reference.

**direct quotation**

**"The economy cannot help slowing down by next year,"** said Dr. Roger Watson, a renowned economist.

**"Although this stock has split three times since 1981,"** explained Ms. Mooneyhan, **"you cannot anticipate that it will continue to do so."**

One of the reporters shouted, **"Look out! The building is collapsing."**

Mr. Goldman explained in his February 8 memo: **"Because my wife became ill Monday morning and was hospitalized that afternoon, I was unable to attend the meeting. Please send me a copy of the minutes."**

**indirect quotation**

Kriss Powell, our production manager, said that our manufacturing costs per unit will increase at least 30 percent within the next year.

## 1–48. Long Quotations

Long quotations of two or more sentences (and usually more than three lines) are written without the quotation marks and appear as separate paragraphs. They are indented from the left and right margins and separated from the main text by single blank lines at the beginning and the end of the quotation.

The speaker brought out the importance of management communication when she made the following statement:

> To exercise the function of leadership, there must be effective communication.  If a leader cannot communicate, there is no leader because information cannot pass between the two groups. For instance, in management one cannot delegate duties and authority without effective communication.

Effective communication is paramount to effective leadership in . . . .

## 1–49.  Short Expressions

a. When short expressions—such as words used in humor, technical words used in a nontechnical way, coined expressions, or slang words—need to be emphasized or clarified for the reader, they are placed in quotation marks. These same words are often shown in italics instead.

### slang words

Mr. Rhodes has difficulty working with others on the production team because he always wants to be **"in the driver's seat."** (or *in the driver's seat*)

### technical words used in a nontechnical way

Mr. Rollins announced that **"all systems are go"** for the new golf course and condominium project in Scottsdale. (or *all systems are go*)

b. Place in quotation marks the definitions of words or expressions. Italicize (or underscore if italics are not available) the word or expression defined.

### defined word

According to some economists, a *recession* is actually a **"little depression."**

### defined expression

The French term *faux pas* means **"a social blunder."**

c. References to the words *marked*, *labeled*, *stamped*, or *signed* are placed in quotation marks.

Be sure to mark all packages **"Glass—Handle With Care."**

The envelope was stamped **"Addressee Unknown, Return to Sender."**

The letter was signed **"Philip Armstrong"** but contained no return address on either the letter or the envelope.

## 1–50.  Literary Titles

Titles of various kinds of literary or artistic works such as magazine or newspaper articles, chapters of books or pamphlets, unpublished manuscripts, episodes in television series, acts in plays or musicals, short poems, lectures, songs, and themes are placed within quotation marks.

Names of books, magazines, pamphlets, newspapers, and other complete published or artistic works that contain subdivisions, however, are placed in italics (or underscored if italics are not accessible). (See Section 3-6 for further information and examples of titles placed in italics or underscored.)

**book and chapter title**

The chapter **"Principles of Office Organization"** contained in *Office Management and Automation* was helpful in implementing our office reorganization.

**musical and song title**

Of all the songs from the musical production *Man of La Mancha*, **"The Impossible Dream"** is probably the most well recognized.

**episode in television series**

For the past four years, **"To Serve Man"** has been aired on our network's Thanksgiving Day marathon of episodes from the *Twilight Zone*.

**lecture title**

Her last lecture, **"Combating Inflationary Trends,"** was very well attended.

## 1–51.  Quotations Within Quotations

Use single quotation marks to signify a quotation within a quotation. If your software does not support single quotation marks, use the apostrophe key.

For quoted material within single quotation marks, return to using quotation marks.

**quotation within a quotation**

The report stated, "According to the U.S. Chamber of Commerce, **'The problem of air and water pollution must be solved within the next decade if our cities are to survive.'"**

**quotation within single quotation marks**

The newspaper quoted the attorney as saying, "When I asked the defendant, 'Did you endorse the check **"Robert S. Parry"**?' he replied, 'No, I did not.'"

## 1–52.  Ellipses

An ellipsis (a series of three periods with a space before, between, and after the series) is used to show an intentional omission of quoted material:

(1) If the omission begins the quoted sentence, use an ellipsis to begin the quotation.

(2) If the omission occurs within a sentence, use an ellipsis to substitute for the omitted words.

(3) If the omission occurs at the end of a sentence, use an ellipsis and then add the closing punctuation mark for the sentence.

(4) If one or more sentences have been omitted after the quoted sentence or sentences, first conclude the last sentence with the appropriate punctuation mark and then follow with an ellipsis to show the omission.

**omission at beginning of quotation**

The instructions stated, " . . . and turn knob in clockwise direction." (Remember to leave one space between the opening quotation mark and the first period in the ellipsis, one space between the periods, and one space after the closing period in the ellipsis.)

**omission within sentence**

The new sign was worded to discourage nonresidents from parking in the private lot: "Violators will be towed . . . cars will be released only upon payment of a $200 fine."

**end-of-sentence omission**

The guarantee reads: "All repairs that are not covered under the warranty will be made at a 25 percent discount . . . . "

One of the directors inquired, "How many miles is the home office from our various branch offices; i.e., Houston, Dallas, Oklahoma City, Atlanta, . . . ?"

**one or more sentences omitted**

The directive stated specifically: "Please ship our international orders by September 1 . . . .   Our European distributors must have their merchandise by October 1." (Close the sentence with a period. Place one space before each period in the ellipsis; place two spaces after the final period in the ellipsis before beginning the next sentence.)

The marketing manager wrote in her August 1 memo, "Will you be able to attend the conference in Baltimore? . . .   We will need to set up our display booths on September 9." (Use a closing punctuation mark followed by an ellipsis with a space before, between, and after each period. Place two spaces after the final period in the ellipsis before beginning the next sentence.)

## 1–53. Capitalization With Quotation Marks

**a.** Capitalize the first word of a complete sentence enclosed in quotation marks.

"Please call me before 10 a.m. tomorrow," requested Mrs. Edwards.

Andrew replied, "Yes, I will be able to attend the conference on July 28."

**b.** **Capitalize incomplete thoughts enclosed in quotation marks only if the quoted words themselves are capitalized. First, last, and main words[10] in quoted expressions preceded by "stamped" or "marked" are usually capitalized.**

### capitalized

His check was returned from the bank marked **"Insufficient Funds."**

**"Handle With Care"** was stamped on the package.

Did you mark the invoice **"Paid in Full"**?

### not capitalized

Mrs. Atkins asked us to spend **"as little time as possible"** on this project.

## 1–54. Quotation Mark Placement

**a.** **Periods and commas are always placed inside the closing quotation mark; semicolons and colons, outside the closing quotation mark.**

### period

The purchase requisition stipulates, "Cancel this order if the merchandise cannot be delivered by the 1st of July."

### comma

"Our operating costs must be lowered," said Mr. Collins.

### semicolon

The consultant's report stated emphatically, "A thorough analysis of the company's data and information processing system should be undertaken"; however, no steps have been taken to initiate such an analysis.

### colon

Mrs. Cox recommended that the following vacation policy be adopted "unless a better one can be formulated": (1) Employees should select their vacation time on the basis of seniority and (2) conflicts should be resolved by the employees themselves, whenever possible.

**b.** **When a complete question or exclamation is contained within the quotation, place the question mark or exclamation mark inside the closing quotation mark. If the entire sentence comprises the question or exclamation, then place the appropriate mark outside the closing quotation mark. If both the quotation and the entire sentence are questions, use only the first question mark.**

---

[10]*Main words* are all words EXCEPT (1) the articles *a*, *an*, and *the*; (2) the coordinating conjunctions *and*, *but*, *or*, and *nor*; (3) the word *to* in an infinitive (*to* sing); and (4) prepositions with three or fewer letters (e.g., *of*, *for*, *in*, *on*, *by*).

**complete question within quotation**

He asked, "Where are the annual reports filed?"

**entire sentence comprises question**

Do you have a copy of her latest article, "Air Pollution Control"?

**complete exclamation within quotation**

"Do not," exclaimed Mr. Rey, "leave the lights burning all night again!"

**entire sentence comprises exclamation**

Our new sales manager is a real "go-getter"!

**question within a question**

Did Mr. Heinze inquire, "What time will our flight depart?"

## Apostrophe

### 1–55. Possessives

a. When a noun, singular or plural, does not end with a pronounced *s*, add an apostrophe and *s* (*'s*) to form the possessive case.

**singular noun**

Yes, I found the request on my **assistant's** desk.

**Lisa's** father owns these three restaurants.

Most of the **company's** profits were earned during the first quarter of this year.

**plural noun**

**Women's** fashions are much more colorful this year.

Most of our discounted **children's** toys have already been sold.

This garment is made from 100 percent **sheep's** wool.

b. When a noun, singular or plural, ends with a pronounced *s*, generally add an apostrophe (*'*) to form the possessive case. However, an apostrophe and *s* (*'s*) may be added to singular nouns ending in a pronounced *s* if an additional *s* sound is also pronounced.

**singular noun—add ' only**

**Mrs. Simons'** attendance record during the past five years has been perfect.

Most of these museum pieces were found among **Athens'** ruins.

**plural noun—add ' only**

Our staff reviews **customers'** accounts every 60 days.

Yesterday one of our agents sold the **Simonses'** home.

**singular noun with additional *s* sound—add *'s***

We have been invited to our **boss's** home for dinner on April 27.

The **class's** scores on this examination were exceptionally high.

Ask **Mr. Jones's** assistant for a copy of the report.

Were you present in court during the **witness's** testimony?

c. **Possessives are generally formed on nouns that represent people, animals, and other living entities (animate objects) or nouns related to time, distance, value, or celestial bodies. For other types of nouns (inanimate objects), show possession with an *of* phrase.**

**animate possessive**

The **employees'** representatives will meet with us on July 15.

Were the **horse's** hooves lacerated during the race?

Preserve your **hair's** color and luster with Richman's Protein+ conditioning shampoo.

How can we be assured that the **tree's** roots will not crack the walls of the swimming pool?

Our **company's** steadily declining profits eventually led to the replacement of all its executive officers. (The word *company* is animate because it is composed of animate objects—people.)

**time possessive**

This **year's** profit and loss statement showed a gain of nearly 12 percent.

Enclosed is a check for three **months'** rent.

**Yesterday's** mail was still lying on her desk unopened when this **morning's** mail arrived.

**distance possessive**

Our office is just a **stone's** throw from the airport.

The thief rushed by within **arm's** length.

**value possessive**

She ordered several thousand **dollars'** worth of laser printer paper.

You owe me 50 **cents'** change.

**celestial possessive**

During the summer months the **sun's** rays can be extremely harmful if one is not careful.

Is **Mars'** atmosphere suitable for human survival?

**inanimate possessive**

The **terms of the loan** were extended another six months. (Not *loan's terms*)

Who broke the **base of the pot**? (Not *pot's base*)

d. **Form the possessive of compound nouns by having the last word show possession.**

She was designated her **father-in-law's** beneficiary.

Our next Christmas party will be held at the **chairman of the board's** home.

My two **sisters-in-law's** business is doing well.

e. **When two or more nouns have joint ownership, only the last noun shows possession. When the nouns represent individual ownership, however, each noun must show possession.**

**joint possession**

**Bill and Sheryl's** new assistant has worked at ABCO Corporation for three years. (Bill and Sheryl share the same assistant—joint possession.)

**The Harrises and the Bradys'** new boat was damaged in the storm. (The Harrises and the Bradys own the same boat—joint possession.)

**individual possession**

**Mary's and Henry's** offices have been relocated to the new wing of our building. (Mary and Henry have different offices—individual possession.)

**The Schaeffers' and the Gonzalezes'** houses are on the same street. (The Schaeffers and the Gonzalezes live in different houses— individual possession.)

f. **The possessive of indefinite pronouns such as *anyone, everyone, someone, anybody, everybody, somebody,* and *nobody* is formed by using the same rules that apply to possessive nouns.**

It is **anyone's** guess when we will be able to resume production.

**Somebody's** car is blocking the entrance to the parking lot.

g. **The possessive forms of personal or relative pronouns (such as *its, yours, theirs,* or *whose*) do not include apostrophes. These pronouns are often confused with verb contractions, all of which contain apostrophes.**

**possessive pronoun**

Although the company had **its** greatest sales volume last year, it still failed to show a profit.

I met Ralph, **whose** father is a major stockholder in our company.

### contraction

It's (It is) one of our most profitable lines.

I met with Pamela, **who's (who is)** the production editor on this project.

h. **Possessives of abbreviations are formed by using the same rules that apply to possessive nouns.**

### abbreviation not ending with *s*

The **CPA's** report was comprehensive.

**NASA's** new space project is scheduled for a 2001 launching.

### abbreviation ending with *s*

**Barker Bros.'** annual sale will be held next week.

All **R.N.s'** badges are to be turned in at the end of each shift.

You may wish to follow the **IRS's** advice in this instance. (Use *'s* instead of just an apostrophe because of the extra pronounced syllable.)

i. **Use the possessive case of a noun or a pronoun before a gerund (an *-ing* verb used as a noun).**

### noun

**Don's** accounting of the convention expenses was incomplete.

### pronoun

We would appreciate **your** returning the enclosed form by March 31.

j. **When a possessive noun is followed by an explanatory expression (an appositive), use an apostrophe only in the explanatory expression. When this form of writing sounds awkward, as it does in most cases, show possession by using an *of* phrase.**

### apostrophe

Ms. Madden, **our production manager's**, office is being remodeled.

### *of* phrase

The office **of our production manager**, Ms. Madden, is being remodeled.

k. **Many organizations with plural possessives in their names have omitted the apostrophe; organizations with singular possessives have tended to retain the apostrophe. The precise format used by the organization itself should be followed.**

### plural possessive

We have just been approved for a loan from the **Farmers** Bank and Trust Company.

**singular possessive**

The contract was issued to **Linton's** Manufacturing Company.

l.   Sometimes the possessed item is not explicitly stated in a sentence, but it is understood or clearly implied. In such cases the ownership word still uses an apostrophe to show possession.

This year the holiday party will be held at **Steve's**.

Be sure to meet me at the **doctor's** by 2 p.m.

The wallet found in the corridor was **Mr. Lopez's**.

Deliver this floral arrangement to the **Briggses'**.

This month's sales are considerably higher than last **month's**.

## 1–56.   Additional Uses of the Apostrophe

a.   Use the apostrophe to form contractions.

**single-word contraction**

acknowledged  **ack'd**        national  **nat'l**        cannot  **can't**

**two-word contraction**

you would  **you'd**        is not  **isn't**        I have  **I've**

b.   The apostrophe is used for clarity to form the plural of all isolated lowercase letters and the single capital letters *A*, *I*, *M*, and *U*.

**plural of lowercase letter**

Be sure to dot your **i's** and cross your **t's**.

How many times have I reminded you to watch your **p's** and **q's**?

**plural of capital letters *A*, *I*, *M*, and *U***

Mr. Craig's daughter received three *A's* on her report card.

Avoid using too many *I's* in the business letters you write.

c.   The apostrophe may be used for the single quotation mark to signify a quotation within a quotation.

Terry reported, "The president opened the forum with **'We're going to drive QuickWrite's sales back up to and beyond its former high!'**"

d.   The apostrophe may be used to signify the omission of figures in expressing a year.

Job prospects for the class of **'99** look favorable—especially in the computer industry.

e.   In technical material the apostrophe may be used as a symbol for *feet*.

12' × 15' (room)            5' 3" (height)            80' × 110' (area)

# Parentheses

## 1–57. Nonessential Expressions

Parentheses are used to set off and subordinate nonessential expressions that would otherwise confuse the reader because (1) they give supplementary information that has no direct bearing on the main idea or (2) they call for an abrupt change in thought. References and directions are examples of expressions that are often enclosed in parentheses.

### abrupt change in thought

I wrote to Mr. Furstman **(I tried to call him, but there was no answer)** and asked him to contact us before October 4.

### reference

All major repairs over $3,000 must first be cleared through proper channels. **(See Bulletin 8 dated March 2.)**

### directions

Please send 500 copies of our annual report to each of our European offices. **(Send them by air M-Bag mail.)**

## 1–58. Numerals

Numerals in legal, business, and professional documents are often shown in parentheses to confirm a spelled-out figure.

All work is guaranteed for ninety **(90)** days.

Compensation for services rendered will not exceed three thousand dollars **($3,000)**.

The committee may not consider any bid over nine thousand nine hundred ninety-nine dollars **($9,999)**.

On March 4 our client received a check for two thousand eight hundred forty-three dollars and seventy-five cents **($2,843.75)**.

## 1–59. Enumerated Items

Enclose in parentheses numbers or letters used to enumerate lists of items within a sentence.

See Section 1-36a for the use of parentheses with alphanumeric outlines.

### numbers

Please supply me with the following information for the current year: **(1)** the number of new employees, **(2)** the number of people who retired, **(3)** the number of people who resigned, and **(4)** the number of people terminated by the company.

**letters**

This report supplies the following current information for Marengo County:  **(a)** salary trends, **(b)** unemployment statistics, and **(c)** placement requests.

## 1–60.   Parentheses With Other Punctuation Marks

a.   **Words, phrases, and clauses enclosed in parentheses in the middle of a sentence function as part of the sentence in applying rules of punctuation and capitalization.**

**word**

We will fly to Fort Lauderdale **(Florida)** for our annual convention.

**phrase**

Ms. Haven will gross nearly $800,000 **(as compared to a $500,000 average)** in sales this year.

**clause**

Our new manager **(several members of our staff met him last week)** will conduct a communications seminar in the spring.

b.   **When an incomplete thought enclosed in parentheses ends a sentence that requires a period, place the period outside the closing parenthesis.**

According to our legal counsel, this procedure violates laws in only two states **(Minnesota and Wyoming).**

Several members of the committee will meet in Kansas City this weekend **(if possible).**

c.   **When a complete thought enclosed in parentheses ends a sentence that requires a period, the two parts are treated separately. Place a period at the end of both sentences, with the final period appearing inside the closing parenthesis.**

Yes, your order was shipped on April 17.  **(You should receive it within seven to ten days from the shipment date.)**

Several members of our staff attended the ATLW conference this year. **(This year's conference was held in Honolulu.)**

d.   **If an interrupting word, phrase, or clause shown in parentheses requires a question mark or exclamation mark, use such a mark of punctuation only if the sentence ends with a different mark.**

**parenthetical question**

Our new manager **(do you know Colleen Merrell?)** will arrive in Los Angeles tomorrow.

Were you informed that our new price list **(has your copy arrived yet)** will go into effect on October 1?

### parenthetical exclamation

Have you heard about the recent enormous price increases **(I can't believe them!)** in single-family dwellings?

Living conditions **(you can scarcely call them that)** are absolutely deplorable in this section of the city!

e. **Place commas, semicolons, and colons outside the closing parenthesis.**

### comma

If you plan to attend the president's retirement banquet (on May 16**),** please send your reservations to Terry Thomsen by Monday, May 12.

### semicolon

His report deals primarily with the importance of our country's major transportation systems (railroads, inland waterways, motor trucks, pipe lines, and air transportation)**;** therefore, little emphasis was given to rising transportation costs.

### colon

On February 15 Ms. Haddad will introduce two new product lines (for women's fashion departments)**:** the Sportswoman Series and the Sun and Surf Coordinates.

## Brackets

### 1–61. Use of Brackets

a. **Use brackets to insert an explanation, a correction, or a comment in quoted material.**

**To show that an error in quoted material appeared in the original document, enclose the term *sic* (meaning "so" or "this is the way it was") in brackets.**

Mr. Gilmer stated in his report: "With new equipment to speed up the production process **[he did not specify what new equipment was needed]**, substantial savings can be mad **[sic]** in both material and labor costs."

b. **Brackets may be used within parentheses to indicate even another subordinate idea.**

The auction of Rita Rothchild's possessions (including jewelry, furs, furniture, movie costumes **[from 1945 through 1975]**, china, silverware, and other memorabilia) is scheduled for July 17 and 18.

### 1–62. Brackets With Other Punctuation Marks

**The placement of other punctuation marks with brackets follows the same principles outlined for parentheses in Section 1-60.**

# Asterisk

### 1–63. Use of Asterisk

**Asterisks may be used to call the reader's attention to footnotes in a document when they appear infrequently and occur at widely spaced intervals. The asterisk follows other punctuation marks, except the dash, closing parenthesis, or closing bracket.**

#### after most punctuation marks

A recent government report states, "Air traffic is expected to double within the next decade."*

#### before dash, closing parenthesis, or closing bracket

We are studying the works of Ray Bradbury*—one of our leading contemporary science fiction writers.

Companies that have hired outside consultants to develop cost-cutting procedures have reported good results. (Several articles supporting the effectiveness of outside consultants have recently appeared in leading professional journals.*)

Many national magazines (such as *Time*, *Newsweek*, and *Business Week* [May and June issues*]) have published informative, interesting articles on using the Internet.

# Diagonal

### 1–64. Use of Diagonal

**Use a diagonal (also called a "solidus," "slash," or "virgule") between (1) letters in some abbreviations, (2) numerals in fractions, and (3) the expression *and/or* to show that the terms are interchangeable. No space appears before or after the diagonal.**

#### abbreviation

Please address the envelope as follows:  Mrs. Maureen Smith, **c/o** Mr. George Martin, Display Manager, Wilson Disc Company, 1141 Western Avenue, Los Angeles, California 90024.

#### fraction

Costs have increased **1/2** percent since last week.

To reupholster the reception room sofa will require **12 3/4** yards of fabric.

#### and/or

Authorizations for future purchases may be obtained from Ms. Jorgensen **and/or** Mr. Kline.

# Underscore

### 1–65.  Use of the Underscore

The underscore is generally not used in computer-generated or printed copy. Other font attributes—italics, bolding, bolded italics, and varying font sizes—have been substituted for the underscore.

In typewritten copy the underscore is used to emphasize such items as headings; words that would normally be italicized; and titles of books, magazines, newspapers, pamphlets, and various other published or artistic works (See Section 3-6). Continuous lines, with no spacing between words, are used for underscoring. Except for periods with abbreviations, punctuation marks immediately following underscored material are not underscored.

**italicized word**

He always misspells the word <u>convenience</u>.

**magazine title**

According to an article in <u>Business Week</u>, most movies are currently being filmed outside the United States.

**artistic work with subdivision**

"Jack the Ripper" was the first episode on this season's television series <u>Unsolved Mysteries</u>.

**abbreviation**

Be sure to place <u>a.m.</u> in lowercase letters.

**punctuation mark following standard underscored material**

Did the bookstore order sufficient copies of <u>Merriam-Webster's Collegiate Dictionary, Tenth Edition</u>?

# Ampersand

### 1–66.  Use of the Ampersand

a.  The ampersand (&), a symbol that represents the word *and*, is used primarily to express the official name of some business organizations.

**ampersand in company name**

Johnson & Johnson was the subcontractor for the project.

A. G. Edwards & Sons, Inc., is handling the sale of this new stock issue.

### use of *and* in company name

All merger talks with Merritt **and** Sons have been delayed until the end of our fiscal period.

b. **When the ampersand represents *and* in a series, use a comma before the ampersand only if the organization does so in its official name.**

### no comma before the ampersand

The law offices of Levitt, Myers & Cohen represented the plaintiff in this case.

### comma before the ampersand

Fall fashions from Liz, Lee, & Co. should arrive in our store by the middle of July.

# Chapter 2

# Hyphenating and Dividing Words

pre/

## Hyphenating and Dividing Words Solution Finder

# Hyphenating Words

## 2–1.    Compound Nouns and Verbs

Often two or more words act as one idea. Nouns and verbs in this class may be written as separate words, written as single words, or hyphenated. Consult an up-to-date dictionary to determine the exact form of compound nouns and verbs.[1]

**separate words, nouns**

| | | | |
|---|---|---|---|
| sales tax | editor in chief | life insurance | charge account |
| data processing | air conditioner | port of entry | voice mail |

**single words, nouns**

| | | | |
|---|---|---|---|
| checkbook | workforce | salesperson | paycheck |
| spreadsheet | database | stepfather | moneymaker |

**hyphenated words, nouns**

| | | | |
|---|---|---|---|
| brother-in-law | attorney-at-law | by-product | self-interest |
| double-talk | face-lift | go-around | air-conditioning |

**separate words, verbs**

| | | | |
|---|---|---|---|
| to set up | to mark down | to step down | to call in |
| to stand out | to trade in | to slip up | to double up |

**single words, verbs**

| | | | |
|---|---|---|---|
| to upgrade | to keyboard | to downsize | to landscape |
| to videotape | to download | to handpick | to mastermind |

**hyphenated words, verbs**

| | | | |
|---|---|---|---|
| to tape-record | to air-condition | to triple-space | to cross-examine |
| to ill-treat | to jury-rig | to double-check | to piece-dye |

## 2–2.    Compound Adjectives

When two or more words appearing together act as a single idea to describe a noun or pronoun, these words function as a compound adjective. In many cases compound adjectives are hyphenated; in other cases they are not. Use the following guidelines to determine whether or not a compound adjective should be hyphenated.

a.    A number of compound adjectives are listed and shown hyphenated in the dictionary. These adjectives may be considered *permanent* compounds. They are hyphenated whenever they are used as adjectives in a sentence, no matter where they appear in the sentence — before or after the nouns or pronouns they modify.

---

[1]All spellings and hyphenations used in this manual are based upon *Merriam-Webster's Collegiate Dictionary,* 10th Ed. (Springfield, Mass.: Merriam-Webster, Incorporated, 1996).

**permanent compound adjective before a noun or pronoun**

| | |
|---|---|
| up-to-date | **up-to-date** equipment |
| well-known | **well-known** brands |
| part-time | **part-time** employment |
| snow-white | **snow-white** hair |
| smooth-tongued | **smooth-tongued** salesperson |
| small-scale | **small-scale** operation |
| hands-off | **hands-off** policy |
| machine-readable | **machine-readable** text |
| no-fault | **no-fault** insurance |
| public-spirited | **public-spirited** citizens |

**permanent adjective compound following noun or pronoun**

None of these files are **up-to-date**.

If your job is **part-time**, please check the appropriate box on the enclosed form.

These clothing manufacturers are **well-known** throughout the country.

Mailing addresses on envelopes from major corporations are usually **machine-readable**.

You cannot deny that this community is **public-spirited**.

**b.** Sometimes compound nouns are used as single-thought adjectives to describe other nouns or pronouns. When these combinations are shown as *open compounds* (not hyphenated) in the dictionary, they are not hyphenated when they are used as compound adjectives.

| compound noun | compound noun used as compound adjective |
|---|---|
| data processing | **data processing** center |
| life insurance | **life insurance** policy |
| money market | **money market** account |
| human resources | **human resources** management |
| finance company | **finance company** records |
| charge account | **charge account** customer |
| high school | **high school** teacher |
| word processing | **word processing** software |
| income tax | **income tax** return |
| department store | **department store** personnel |
| mobile home | **mobile home** sales |
| real estate | **real estate** commission |

**c.** Many single-thought word groups that function as compound adjectives are not shown in the dictionary. Such word groups are known as *temporary compounds.* These temporary compounds are hyphenated and written in singular form (where applicable) when they appear *before* the nouns or pronouns they describe. They are not hyphenated, however, when they appear after the words they modify.

### temporary compound before noun or pronoun—hyphenated

We have already installed **voice-activated** software in several of our computers.

All **city-owned** property is exempt from these county taxes.

A **well-established** legal firm has been retained to represent our interests.

Capture that **never-to-be-forgotten** moment with pictures by Mardell!

The mayor's **not-too-cordial** attitude toward the press was evident.

### temporary compound in singular form before noun or pronoun—hyphenated

This property has a **123-foot** driveway leading up to the house.

The Holtzes are interested in purchasing a **four-bedroom** home.

The Walters' **7-pound-12-ounce** son was born yesterday at 5 a.m.

All vehicles are expected to abide by the **65-mile-an-hour** speed limit on this highway.

### temporary compound following noun or pronoun

We have investigated using software that is **voice activated**.

None of the properties on this block are **city owned**.

This firm has been **well established** in the Chicago area for nearly thirty years.

Your wedding should be a day that is **never to be forgotten**.

Mr. Simms' greetings this morning were certainly **not too cordial**.

The driveway leading up to the house is **123 feet** long.

The Holtzes' new home has **four bedrooms**.

At birth the Walters' baby weighed **7 pounds 12 ounces**.

The speed limit on this highway is **65 miles an hour**.

**d.** When *two separate* proper nouns or *two separate* common nouns are combined to form single-thought adjectives before other nouns or pronouns, these compounds are hyphenated.

### separate proper nouns used as an adjective

This morning's issue of the newspaper carried several articles on **Chinese-American** relations.

Your **Chicago-London** flight has been delayed until tomorrow.

### separate common nouns used as an adjective

Today's training session will deal with **union-management** relations.

Most of the classes offered by our institute maintain a 15 to 1 **student-teacher** ratio.

**e.** The components of a *single* proper noun are not hyphenated when they are used as an adjective.

We have been negotiating with a **Far Eastern** firm for the last three months.

How many **University of Nebraska** alumni have you been able to locate in Salt Lake City?

**f.** Adverbs ending in *ly* that are combined with adjectives to form a single modifier are not hyphenated.

I understand that your session sparked the most **hotly debated** issues at the conference.

Dr. Stevens is an **exceptionally gifted** nuclear physicist.

**g.** Two separate colors stated in a compound modifier are hyphenated. Other adjectives, however, used in conjunction with colors are not hyphenated unless the combination is a permanent compound shown in the dictionary.

**two separate colors**

This **blue-green** fabric was selected for upholstering the sofas in the hotel lobby.

The artist used **red-orange** hues effectively in portraying the Hawaiian sunset.

**adjective combined with color**

The **bluish green** water magnified the size of the iridescent, colorful fish.

Place these artists' prints against a **snow-white** background to accentuate their deep color contrasts. (The adjective *snow-white* is shown hyphenated in the dictionary.[2])

The **bright red** flag can easily be seen from a distance.

Ask all our sales representatives to wear **dark gray** suits to the exhibition.

The **emerald green** cover of your new book stands out quite visibly.

**h.** When a series of hyphenated adjectives has a common ending, use suspending hyphens.

Have these announcements printed on **8 1/2- by 11-inch** bond paper.

Please order a supply of **1/16- and 1/8-inch** drill bits.

Most of the awards were given to **tenth- and eleventh-grade** students.

---

[2]*Merriam-Webster's Collegiate Dictionary*, 10th Ed. (Springfield, Mass.: Merriam-Webster, Incorporated, 1996), 1113.

All construction bids for this hillside are based on **one-, two-, and three-level** family dwellings.

i. **Amounts in the millions and billions, percentages, and nouns used with numerals or letters are *not* hyphenated when they function as compound adjectives.**

**dollar amounts in the millions and billions**

How will the president deal with the projected **$1 billion** decline in the Gross Domestic Product?

Nearly **2.5 million** people in the United States use our soap.

**percentages**

You will receive a **10 percent** discount on all orders placed before October 1.

There will be a **1/2 percent** increase in our state sales tax effective July 1.

**nouns used with numerals or letters**

Will our new employee be rated in as a **Grade 1** administrative assistant?

How many **Vitamin C** tablets are in each container?

Please ship these **Model 85A** wall units by October 1.

j. **Simple fractions are hyphenated *only* when they are used as compound adjectives.[3]**

**compound adjective**

John sold his **one-fourth** ownership in the company for $575,000.

Amendments to our bylaws require a **two-thirds** majority approval by our voting membership.

**simple fraction as noun**

Only **one third** of the stockholders responded to the questionnaire.

The Board of Directors voted to reinvest **one half** of this year's profits in additional research and development projects.

## 2–3. Prefixes

a. **Words beginning with *ex* (meaning "former") and *self* are hyphenated; those beginning with *pre*, *re*,[4] and *non* are generally not hyphenated. Words beginning with *co* and *vice* may or may not be**

---

[3]"Table of Numbers," Footnote 5, *Merriam-Webster's Collegiate Dictionary,* 10th Ed. (Springfield, Mass.: Merriam-Webster, Incorporated, 1996), 798.

[4]The words *re-collect* meaning "to collect again," *re-cover* meaning "to cover anew," *re-create* meaning "to create again," *re-lease* meaning "to lease again," *re-present* meaning "to present again," *re-press* meaning "to press again," *re-sign* meaning "to sign again," *re-sort* meaning "to sort again," and *re-tread* meaning "to tread again" are exceptions to this rule. Note that without the hyphens these words would have completely different meanings.

hyphenated. **Use your dictionary to check the hyphenation of words with these two beginnings.**

### ex and self

Bob Hubbard, the **ex-baseball** star, is now in the real estate business.

Our **ex-chairman** still has all the committee records in his files.

To be successful in sales, a person should have an outgoing personality and project **self-confidence**.

Employee **self-satisfaction** contributes to raising both morale and productivity.

### pre, re, and non

All the floppy disks we use have been **preformatted**.

Where will the **preemployment** interviews be held?

Please **recheck** all the total columns carefully.

We should have the wheels on this truck **realigned**.

Tuition **reimbursements** will not be made to **nonaccredited** educational institutions.

You may wish to initiate legal proceedings against Phillips Bros. for **nonpayment** of its account.

### co

| | | |
|---|---|---|
| co-edition | co-occurrence | codefendant |
| co-owner | coauthor | coinsurance |

### vice

| | | | |
|---|---|---|---|
| vice-chancellor | vice-consul | vice admiral | vice president |

**b.** **When a prefix is added to a proper noun, place a hyphen between the prefix and the proper noun.**

We found that many firms operating in the South today date back to **pre-Civil War** times.

If you cannot promise a **mid-September** delivery date, cancel the order.

To some people a 4th of July without fireworks would be **un-American**.

## 2–4. Numbers

**a.** **Compound numbers from 21 to 99 are hyphenated when they appear in word form.**

**Ninety-six** of our agents responded to the questionnaire, but we are still awaiting replies from **twenty-four** more.

**b.** **In numbers over 99, components other than compound numbers are not hyphenated.**

The lessee shall pay a sum of **Two Thousand Eight Hundred Seventy-five Dollars and Twenty-four Cents** ($2,875.24) to the lessor.

c.   Simple fractions not used with units of measure are expressed in word form. These fractions are hyphenated *only* when they function as compound adjectives.

**simple fraction used as noun**

Nearly **two thirds** of our employees voted to ratify the new contract.

Can you believe that over **three fourths** of the microcomputers purchased in our industry last year were for management personnel?

**simple fraction used as compound adjective**

Our company wishes to purchase a **one-fourth** interest in the new shopping mall planned for the Pinehurst area.

A **two-thirds** majority vote is needed to pass this proposition, which will appear on the November ballot.

d.   When a number-noun combination functions as a *single unit* (a compound adjective) to describe another noun, (1) express the noun part of the compound adjective in singular form and (2) separate the words in the compound adjective with a hyphen. Only in percentages, amounts in the millions and billions, and capitalized noun-number combinations are the hyphens omitted.

**hyphen—number-noun compound adjective**

We have a **three-year** lease on this building.

Our highways have a **65-mile-an-hour** speed limit.

Drivers are charged **50-cent** tolls along this turnpike.

He just started a **$2,500-a-month** job.

The Joneses' **7-pound-8-ounce** baby girl was born on December 25.

**no hyphen—percentage**

We experienced a **25 percent** sales increase this year.

**no hyphen—amount in the millions**

Ridgewood Inc. announced a **$3 million** profit for the year.

**no hyphen—capitalized noun-number combination**

Your Evansdale **Model 380** curio cabinet should arrive in our store within the next three weeks.

e.   In word processing-generated copy, use an en dash (if possible) to represent the terms *to* or *through* between two numerals. In typewritten copy, though, the hyphen may be used to replace these terms.

As you requested, your vacation has been scheduled from July **3–18**.

Refer to pages **70–75** for further instructions.

# End-of-Line Word and Word-Group Divisions

Where possible, avoid dividing words at the end of a computer-generated or typewritten line because complete words are easier to read, easier to understand, and neater in appearance. Sometimes, however, word divisions at the end of a line are necessary to avoid overly uneven line lengths or, in justified copy, awkward-appearing lines with large spaces between words.

Particular rules need to be observed in dividing words and certain word groups correctly at the end of a line. Some of these rules should be adhered to strictly; others are flexible in their application, especially in desktop published copy. The following sections address (1) words and word groups *never* to be divided, (2) word divisions to be avoided, if possible, and (3) rules and guidelines for proper end-of-line word and word-group divisions.

**2–5.  Words and Word Groups Never to Be Divided**

Some words and certain word groups may not be divided under any circumstances:

**a.**  Do not divide one-syllable words, including those that end in *ed*.

**one-syllable words**

| | | | | | |
|---|---|---|---|---|---|
| freight | straight | threats | thought | through | bread |

**one-syllable *ed* words**

| | | | | | |
|---|---|---|---|---|---|
| called | changed | weighed | planned | striped | shipped |

**b.**  Do not set off a single-letter syllable at either the beginning or the end of a word.

**beginning of a word**

| | | |
|---|---|---|
| i tinerary | a warded | e nough |
| i dentify | o mitted | u niform |

**end of a word**

| | | | | | |
|---|---|---|---|---|---|
| radi o | bacteri a | health y | photocop y | criteri a | rati o |

**c.**  Do not set off a two-letter syllable at the end of a word. At least three characters of a divided word must appear on the next line.

| | | |
|---|---|---|
| present ed | compa ny | month ly |
| build er | week ly | debt or |

**d.**  Do not divide abbreviations unless a hyphen already appears within the abbreviation. Hyphenated abbreviations may be divided after the hyphen.

**not divided**

| | | | |
|---|---|---|---|
| UNESCO | AMSLAN | U.S.A. | Sept. |
| Ph.D. | B.Eng.S. | B.A. | UCLA |
| equiv. | c.o.d. | A.S.S.R. | bdrm. |

**may be divided**

AFL-CIO KMET-TV NBEA-WBEA

e. Do not divide month and day; *a.m.*, *p.m.*, *noon*, or *midnight* from clock time; percentages from the word *percent*; page numbers from page references; or other such closely related word-and-number combinations.

If you are using a word processor, place a hard space between the components of the combination to keep all parts on the same line.

**month and day**

November 25 January 5 May 1

**a.m., p.m., noon, or *midnight* with clock time**

| | | |
|---|---|---|
| 10 a.m. | 6:30 a.m. | 2 p.m. |
| 4:05 p.m | 12 midnight | 12 noon |

**percentage with the word *percent***

| | | |
|---|---|---|
| 0.5 percent | 1 percent | 8.25 percent |
| 42.5 percent | 100 percent | |

**page number with page reference**

page iv page 23 page 241 page 1073

**other word-and-number combinations**

| | | | |
|---|---|---|---|
| 7 ounces | Room 341 | Model 4A | No. 437892 |
| Check 873 | 6 inches | 210 miles | 43 yards |
| 32 cents | Suite 310 | Chapter 3 | size 12 |

f. Do not divide contractions or numerals.

**contractions**

| | | |
|---|---|---|
| wouldn't | doesn't | haven't |
| should've | you're | o'clock |

**numerals**

| | | | | |
|---|---|---|---|---|
| $15,487 | 1,240,500 | 3 billion | 4,500 | $2.5 million |

g. Do not divide the last word in more than two consecutive lines.

h. Do not divide *the last word in a paragraph* or *the last word on a page*.

## 2–6. Words to Avoid Dividing, If Possible

Although adherence to the following rules is desirable, situations may occur where end-of-line word divisions are unavoidable. Observe these rules—unless doing so would result in an extremely ragged right margin.

**a.** Avoid dividing words containing six or fewer letters.

forget     person     better     number     listen     filter

Avoid dividing a word after a two-letter prefix.

| | | |
|---|---|---|
| en large | re warding | im portant |
| de pendent | un necessary | |

**b.** Avoid dividing a word at the end of the first line of a paragraph in typewritten copy. Desktop published copy and copy generated by word processing software do not generally follow this guideline.

**c.** Avoid dividing a word at the end of the last full line of a paragraph in typewritten copy. Desktop published copy and copy generated by word processing software do not generally follow this guideline.

## 2–7.   Rules and Guidelines for Dividing Words

Divide words *only* between syllables. Use an up-to-date dictionary or a word division manual to locate the correct syllabication of words to be divided. All word divisions shown in this reference manual are based on the syllabication shown in *Merriam-Webster's Collegiate Dictionary,* Tenth Edition, the 1996 printing, published by Merriam-Webster, Incorporated.

Words containing several syllables often require forethought to determine the appropriate place to separate the word. Use the following guidelines to determine where to divide a word:

**a.** Divide hyphenated and single-word compounds at their natural breaks.

**hyphenated compound**

vice-/chancellor[5]     self-/esteem     Governor-/elect
brother-/in-/law

**single-word compound**

common/place     hand/made     break/down     sales/person

**b.** Where possible, divide words after a prefix or before a suffix.

**prefix**

anti/body     super/intendent     mis/fortune     sub/stantiate

**suffix**

evasive/ness     corpora/tion     unemploy/ment
conscien/tious

**c.** Divide words between double letters *except* when the root word itself ends with the double letters and is followed by a suffix.

---

[5]The slash (/) as used here and in the following sections of this chapter signifies appropriate places for dividing words at the end of a line.

**divided between double letters**

bul/letin          accom/modate          neces/sarily
vacil/late         mil/len/nium

**divided after double letters**

business/like      fulfill/ment      helpless/ness      install/ing

**d.** Divide words between two vowels pronounced separately.

continu/ation      experi/ence      gradu/ation      influ/ential

**e.** Divide words *after*, not before, a single vowel pronounced as a syllable except when the vowel is part of a suffix.

**single vowel**

clari/fication     apolo/gize      congratu/lations      bene/ficial

**suffix vowel**

accept/able        collaps/ible      forc/ible
collect/ible       allow/able

## 2–8. Guidelines for Dividing Word Groups

Certain word groups are preferably divided in specific places. Use the following guidelines to separate dates, names of individuals, addresses, numbered items, copy containing dashes, and copy containing ellipses. If you are using a word processor, place a hard space between any parts in the word group that should appear on the same line.

**a.** Divide dates between the day and the year, but *not* between the month and the day.

January 7,/1999     *not* January/7, 1999
April 15,/2000      *not* April/15, 2000

**b.** Full names of individuals are ideally divided directly before the last name, but they may be divided before a middle name. Do not, however, divide a name after a courtesy title, before a middle initial, or before an abbreviation.

Names preceded by long professional titles *may also be* divided between the title and the first name or between words in the title.

**divided before last name**

Ms. Marilyn/Farrar        *not*  Ms./Marilyn Farrar
Dr. Roberta P./Rosenberg  *not*  Dr./Roberta P. Rosenberg
                                 Dr. Roberta/P. Rosenberg

Mr. William/Harrison Jr.  *not*  Mr./William Harrison Jr.
                                 Mr. William Harrison/Jr.

**divided before middle name or last name**

Lorraine/Hoover/Clark    Khristopher/William/Savage

**divided also after long title or between words in a long title**

Lieutenant/Harvey/Petrowski

Assistant/Professor/Alice H./Duffy

c.   Avoid, where possible, dividing a street address directly after the house number. Street addresses are preferably divided between the street name and the street designation (*Street, Avenue, Boulevard, Lane,* etc.). If the street name contains more than one word, the address may also be broken between words in the street name.

**division of single-word street name**

1138 Monogram/Avenue         One Park/Street

20 Wilshire/Boulevard          3624 59th/Place

**division possibilities of street name containing more than one word**

6800 Coldwater/Canyon/Avenue        218 East/Hawes/Street

17325 San/Fernando/Mission/Boulevard     849 North/73rd/Street

d.   Geographical locations in addresses may be divided between the city and state and the state and zip code. They may also be divided between words in cities and states containing more than one word.

Dubuque,/Iowa/52001

Poughkeepsie,/New/York/12601-1032

San/Diego,/California/92109-2134

e.   Divide a numbered or lettered horizontal listing directly before the number or letter, but not directly after.

An affirmative action officer gave these reasons:  (1) fewer job openings, (2) enrollment declines in the student population, and (3) an increase in the mandatory retirement age for teachers.

f.   A sentence with a dash may be broken after the dash, but not directly before it.

The Board of Directors will agree that your policies are excellent— a step in the right direction.

When our peak sales subside at the end of this year—in January— we plan to move our offices to San Francisco.

g.   A sentence may be divided directly after an ellipsis, not directly before. At least one word of the sentence must appear on the same line before the ellipsis.

If you are using a word processor, place a hard space before and between the periods in an ellipsis to prevent the periods from word wrapping incorrectly to the next line.

As the article stated, "The mayor's campaign issues focus on . . . crime prevention in our city."

According to the *Newsweek* article, "As the number of network access providers continues to grow, prices for services will drop. . . . Such factors will result in substantially fewer providers."

pre/

# Chapter 3

# Capitalization

U.S.

## Capitalization Solution Finder

## Capitalization Solution Finder (*continued*)

Capitalization

3

U.S.

## 3–1. Beginning Words

**a.** Capitalize the beginning words of sentences, quoted sentences, independent phrases, lines of poetry, and items in an outline.

**sentence**

**All** employees are requested to work overtime until the inventory has been completed.

**quoted sentence**

The guarantee states, "**Defective** parts will be replaced free of charge."

**independent phrase**

**Now,** to the important point.

**poetry**

**By** the rude bridge that arched the flood,
**Their** flag to the April's breeze unfurled,
**Here** once the embattled farmers stood,
**And** fired the shot heard round the world.
— Emerson

**outline**

1. **Specific** instructions
   a. **Type** of product
   b. **Tools** needed for assembly
   c. **Diagrams** illustrating assembly

**b.** The initial letter of an incomplete quoted thought that is woven in with the rest of the sentence is not capitalized unless the first word is (1) a proper noun, (2) preceded by identification words such as *marked* or *stamped*, or (3) capitalized because of another rule of capitalization.

**lowercase**

Mr. Reyes was directed to "**take** care of this situation immediately."

**proper noun**

Mr. Stone's response was simply "**General** Motors common stock."

**preceded by identification words *marked* or *stamped***

This package should be stamped "**Priority Mail.**"

Your check was returned by the bank marked "**Insufficient Funds.**"

**another rule of capitalization**

Be sure to read "**The** 700 Club" in this week's issue of *Time*.

**c.** In standard salutations used for correspondence, capitalize the first word and any nouns contained in the salutation. For salutations directed to undetermined individuals, capitalize the first word and all *main*[1] words that follow.

Capitalize only the first word of a complimentary close.

### standard salutation—first word and all nouns

Dear Mr. Jones:          Gentlemen:          My dear Friend:

Dear fellow American:     Ladies and Gentlemen:

### salutation to undetermined individual—first word and all main words

To Whom It May Concern:

To Stockholders of Record on May 1, 1999:

### complimentary close

Sincerely yours,          Cordially yours,          Yours very truly,

**d.** The first word following a colon is generally not capitalized. Capitalize the first word, however, when the material following the colon (1) begins with a proper noun, (2) consists of two or more sentences, (3) begins a vertical listing, (4) presents a formal rule, or (5) requires emphasis.

### first word not capitalized

Our maintenance crew has requested us to order the following garden supplies: **lawn** seed, liquid fertilizer, and insect spray.

We are experiencing a two months' delay in our production schedule: **the** warehouse fire set us back considerably.

### proper noun following colon

Three colleges are involved in the project: **DeKalb** Community College, MiraCosta College, and the City College of New York.

### two or more sentences following colon

Here are two important questions to consider: **Will** enlarging our facilities at this time be economically feasible? **Is** the current market able to assimilate any increased production?

### vertical listing following colon

Please send us copies of the following items:
1. **Lease** agreement with Property Management Associates
2. **Statement** of income and expenses for 1998
3. **Budget** of projected income and expenses for 1999

### item of special emphasis following colon

Wanted: **Student** to work weekends and holidays.

---

[1]*Main* words are all words except the articles *a, an, the*; the conjunctions *and, but, or, nor*; the word *to* used with an infinitive; and prepositions containing two or three letters (*of, for, on*, etc.)

Note: **Several** of our employees were listening to the World Series during working hours.

### formal rule following colon

Please use the following procedure in preparing all our correspondence: **Format** all letters in the modified-block letter style with blocked paragraphs and mixed punctuation.

**e.** Unless the word is a proper noun, the first word of a complete thought contained in parentheses *within a sentence* is not capitalized. A complete thought contained in parentheses that appears immediately after a sentence is treated as a separate unit, and the first word is capitalized.

### parentheses within sentence—first word not capitalized

Several minor changes (**these** were recommended by Mr. Lloyd) will be made in the final draft.

### parentheses within sentence—proper noun capitalized

Your recommendations (**Ms.** Williams approved all of them) will be incorporated into the marketing survey.

### parentheses at end of sentence—first word capitalized

A group of marketing students wishes to tour our main plant in Atlanta. (**The** students will arrange for their own transportation.)

## 3–2.   Proper Nouns and Adjectives[2]

**a.** Proper nouns (words that name a particular person, place, or thing) and adjectives derived from proper nouns are capitalized. Capitalize the names of persons, cities, states, countries, rivers, mountains, streets, parks, colleges, buildings, shopping centers, malls, developments, organizations, ships, airplanes, specific events, etc.

### proper noun

We have opened a new branch office in **Austin, Texas**.

Our offices are in the **Atlantic Richfield Building** on **Fifth Street**.

The **Orange County Fair** will be held in **Petit Park** this year.

When will the **Brownsville Shopping Mall** be ready for occupancy?

We flew to **Florida** on a **Boeing 747** to meet our cruise ship, the **Song of Norway**.

Next month **John** and **Lisa** will take a raft down the **Colorado River**.

How much is the toll for the **Golden Gate Bridge**, which crosses **San Francisco Bay**?

---

[2]The capitalization principles that follow are based primarily on those suggested by *The Chicago Manual of Style,* 14th Ed. (Chicago: The University of Chicago Press, 1993).

### adjective derived from proper noun[3]

Football and baseball are typical **American** sports.

Be sure to order **Roquefort** dressing and grated **Swiss** cheese for the salad bar.

The **Socratic** method is often used in debates.

Your decorator selected **Vandyke** brown carpeting for the executive offices.

How much **Canadian** money do you have in your wallet?

The use of the **Heimlich** maneuver has saved many people from choking to death.

Our store, the Furniture Guild, always carries an extensive inventory of **Victorian** furniture.

**b.** **When well-known descriptive terms, such as nicknames, are used in place of proper nouns, they are capitalized.**

My territory includes all sales districts west of the **Rockies.** (Rocky Mountains)

Most of his business trips have been to the **Windy City.** (Chicago)

**Old Hickory** was particularly popular with the frontiersmen. (Andrew Jackson)

Several of our colleagues from the **Big Apple** will attend the convention. (New York City)

**c.** **Sometimes proper nouns, such as widely used commercial products, acquire common noun meanings through popular usage.[4] As a result, they are not capitalized. Always capitalize, however, specific brand or trade names of products. Any words that describe the type or kind of product (such as *refrigerator, vacuum cleaner, television, computer,* or *printer*) are not capitalized unless they represent a coined derivative that is considered part of the trade name.**

### common noun meaning

Be sure that each address on this mailing list has a **zip code.**

Before computer-aided design these drawings were all done in **india** ink.

Our restaurant serves **french** fries with all sandwiches.

Copies of the **braille** alphabet may be obtained from the Foundation for the Junior Blind.

---

[3]The capitalization of all adjectives derived from proper nouns is based on entries shown in *Merriam-Webster Collegiate Dictionary,* 10th Ed. (Springfield, Mass.: Merriam-Webster, Incorporated, 1996).

[4]Check an up-to-date dictionary to determine which proper nouns have acquired common noun meanings and are no longer capitalized. The examples shown here are based on entries from *Merriam-Webster's Collegiate Dictionary,* 10th Ed. (Springfield, Mass.: Merriam-Webster, Incorporated, 1996).

Reproductions of this statue can easily be made from plaster of **paris**.

How many **china** patterns does Regency carry in its line?

The old-fashioned **venetian** blinds in our reception area should be replaced with attractive vertical blinds.

Did the **thermos** break when it fell off the shelf?

You will find dining at Adagio's Ristorante an **epicurean** delight.

The demand for cars with **diesel** engines is declining steadily.

**brand or trade name with common noun product**

Did you order a **Sony portable television**?

Our new **Frigidaire freezer** was delivered today.

Please deliver this **Macintosh computer** to Dr. Mitchell's home.

The **Xerox copier** in our office enables us to copy images from colored paper.

Does your pharmacy chain carry **Kleenex tissues** exclusively?

**product name part of trade name**

Your **Amana Radarange** will give you many years of service.

Contact your nearest **Griffin Press-Tiles** dealer for pricing information.

All **IBM Personal Computers** in our office have long been replaced with IBM Personal System 2 computers.

Almost every day for lunch Mr. Rosen orders either a **Filet-O-Fish** or **Chicken McNuggets** from McDonald's.

## 3–3.  Abbreviations

Most abbreviations are capitalized only if the words they represent are capitalized. Exceptions to this rule are the abbreviations of academic degrees and certain coined business expressions. Refer to Section 5-11 for the proper format of abbreviations commonly used in business.

**lowercase words represented by lowercase abbreviations**

Please send 5 **doz.** hammers **c.o.d.**  (*dozen* and *collect on delivery*)

You may contact me anytime after 5:30 **p.m.**  (*post meridiem*)

**capitalized words represented by capitalized abbreviations**

She sat for the **CPS** examination last May.  (*Certified Professional Secretary*)

Mrs. Johnson was awarded a bachelor of arts degree from **UCLA** in 1993.  (*University of California, Los Angeles*)

**exceptions**

Our university offers **B.S.** and **M.S.** degrees in psychology through the College of Letters, Arts, and Sciences. (*bachelor of science* and *master of science*)

On this application form please include any other names by which you may be known and precede them with the initials **AKA**. (*also known as*)

## 3–4. Numbered or Lettered Items

Nouns followed by numerals or letters are capitalized except in the case of page, paragraph, line, size, and verse references.

The word *number* is abbreviated except when it appears at the beginning of a sentence.

**capitalized nouns**

A reservation is being held for you on **Flight** 487 to Chattanooga.

Please check **Invoice** B3721 to verify that all items have been shipped.

Did you receive our order for your **Model** 23D china case?

The meeting is scheduled to be held in **Room** 132 of the Barnard Business Building.

**lowercase nouns**

Refer to **page** 3, **paragraph** 2, of the contract for the schedule of project completion.

We are sold out of **size** 10 in our Style 483 blazer.

**the word *number* abbreviated within a sentence**

Have you had an opportunity to restock our supply of **No.** 10 white envelopes?

I believe that my policy, **No.** 68341, covers this kind of injury.

This invoice was paid with our Check **No.** 1253 dated January 25.

**the word *number* written out at the beginning of a sentence**

**Number** 145-MD has been out of stock for over three months.

## 3–5. Personal and Professional Titles[5]

a. Capitalize the courtesy titles *Mr., Ms., Mrs., Miss, Master,* and *Dr.* when they precede and are used in conjunction with persons' names.

Capitalize also a title representing a person's profession, company position, military rank, service rank, religious station, or political office when it precedes and is used directly with a person's name in place of a courtesy title.

---

[5]The principles presented here are based upon those contained in *The Chicago Manual of Style*, 14th Ed. (Chicago: The University of Chicago Press, 1993), 240–244.

**A title representing family relationship or nobility is capitalized when it appears before the name of an individual and is used directly with the name.**

### courtesy title

Please send copies of this report to **Mr.** Donald Curry and **Dr.** Scot Ober.

Both **Ms.** Bielich and **Mrs.** Scher-Padilla have agreed to serve on the selection committee for this position.

Please inform **Master** Todd Jaffarian that he has been selected as one of the finalists in the "eight-year-old" category of our children's contest.

### professional title

The meeting will be chaired by **Professor** Wanda Stitt.

### title indicating company position

Although **President** Newton attended the stockholders' meeting, he asked **Vice President** Eleanor Chu from our Minneapolis branch to present the earnings report for this year.

### military or service rank title

All medical problems should be referred to **Major** Michael Zimmerman.

These kinds of police matters are under **Captain** Murillo's jurisdiction.

### religious title

Please ensure that **Archbishop** Lucatorto receives copies of these financial reports.

The **Reverend** William Trump will be the guest minister for next Sunday's services.

The family has requested that **Rabbi** Cogan conduct the service.

### political title

We are looking forward to meeting with **Mayor** Charles Bowshier next Friday.

Please ask **Senator** Rhodes to authorize payment of this invoice.

What time will the networks air **President** Clinton's address?

### title showing family relationship

As soon as **Aunt** Elizabeth's house is sold, her attorney will set up the trust fund.

These U.S. Savings Bonds were given to the children by **Grandpa** Fairbanks.

### title of nobility

Several of the recent articles in this magazine have dealt with the life of **Prince** Charles.

This style of furniture dates back to the era of **Queen** Victoria.

**b.** A person's title—professional, business, military, service, religious, political, family, or one pertaining to nobility—is not capitalized when it is followed by an appositive.

She consulted with her **doctor, Linda Montgomery,** about the accident.

I went to see the **executive vice president, F. Ross Byrd.**

Please consult with the **captain, John Blakely,** before making any changes in the boundaries of this precinct.

Such decisions are made solely by the **president, Bill Clinton.**

Rebecca Dentino inherited the property in Denton, Texas, from her **uncle, Mitchell Marcus.**

**c.** In running text do not capitalize a title following a person's name.

**political title**

Tonight at 8 p.m., EST, Bill Clinton, **president** of the United States, will appear on national television.

Next month Al Gore, **vice president** of the United States, will arrive in Memphis for a tour of the city.

Robert Haller, **senator** from Georgia, received an award for outstanding service.

This new bill is awaiting only the signature of Pete Wilson, **governor** of California.

**military title**

Marie Stewart's manuscript deals with the life of Ulysses S. Grant, **commander in chief** of the Union army.

Captain Hogan, the **company commander,** has received new orders from headquarters.

**business title**

You may wish to subpoena Janet Horne, **president** of AMCO Products, to appear in court on May 11.

Carl Irwin, **director of marketing,** wrote the report.

**professional title**

You will need to address this inquiry to Dr. Phil Stein, **dean of academic affairs.**

If you wish additional information, please contact Laura Jeffreys, **professor of business,** at Simpson Community College.

**religious title**

Pastor Ellis Jones, **minister** of Ascension Lutheran Church, will deliver the graduation address at Concordia College.

We have invited Dr. David Schultz, **rabbi** of Temple Beth Torah, to give the invocation at the opening banquet of the conference.

**d.** When a person's title is used in place of his or her name, the title is generally not capitalized. In cases of direct address, however, capitalize the title if it replaces the name.

Do not capitalize common nouns such as *sir, madam, ladies,* or *gentlemen* used in direct address.

### title used in place of name

I was pleased to be able to meet with the **secretary of state** last week.

Please invite the **governor** to attend the conference.

The **auditor** indicated that our books were in order.

After the meeting the **president** directed her **executive assistant** to inform all the department managers that the **director of marketing** had resigned.

### title capitalized in direct address

Did I pass the test, **Professor**?

If you wish to change your schedule, **Captain,** please notify me by Friday, May 5.

Yes, **Doctor,** we have your reservation for May 8.

### common noun not capitalized in direct address

I believe, **ladies and gentlemen,** that all our sales personnel will meet their quotas this year.

**e.** A person's title is always capitalized in business correspondence when it appears in the inside address, signature line, or envelope address.

Mrs. Delieu Scopesi, **Director of Human Resources**

Dr. Donald Phelps, **Chancellor**

**f.** When the title of an executive officer is used in that organization's formal minutes, bylaws, or rules, it is capitalized. Also capitalize the title of a high-ranking government official when it is used in a formal context (an introduction or acknowledgment).

The **Treasurer's** report was read and approved.

The **President** will be responsible for the negotiation of all labor contracts.

We gratefully acknowledge the contribution of George L. Bach, **Governor** of Alaska, to promoting research in the conservation of our natural resources.

**g.** Descriptive terms such as *ex, elect, late,* and *former* are not capitalized when they are combined with a title.

**ex**

Since **ex**-President D. J. Morgan was appointed chairman of the board, our company has prospered.

**elect**

Councilman-**elect** Norman Rittgers will be sworn in on January 2.

**late**

The **late** President Eisenhower was an avid golfer.

**former**

A copy of the report was sent to **former** President Bush.

**3–6. Published and Artistic Works Containing Subdivisions**

Capitalize the first letter of the principal words in the title of a published or artistic work. Articles (*a*, *an*, *the*), conjunctions (*and*, *but*, *or*, *nor*), and prepositions with three or fewer letters (*of*, *in*, *on*, *to*, *for*, etc.) are not capitalized unless they appear as the first or last words of the title or as the first word of a subtitle following a colon. The *to* in infinitives (*to write*, *to exercise*, *to study*) is also not capitalized unless it appears as the first word in the title or subtitle.

Italicize (or underline, if an italics font is not available) the titles of complete published and artistic works that contain subdivisions. Use italics for the titles of books, magazines, newspapers, booklets, pamphlets, compact disks, plays, musicals, operas, television series, musical albums, and other similar works that contain subdivisions such as chapters, articles, columns, acts, episodes, or songs. Italicize or underline also the titles of movies.

**book**

A copy of *The Random House Dictionary of the English Language* arrived yesterday.

*DuPont, the Autobiography of American Enterprise* may be purchased at your local bookstore.

Copies of Computers and the Electronic Age will be available next month.

**book with subtitle**

This question is answered on page 26 of *HOW 8: A Handbook for Office Workers,* Eighth Edition.

**magazine**

Use the enclosed coupon to renew your subscription to the *Journal of Higher Education.*

Have you read the latest issue of Better Homes and Gardens?

**newspaper**

An article in *The Wall Street Journal* yesterday discussed sales trends in our industry.

We will place an advertisement in the <u>Los Angeles Times</u> for nurses and nurses' assistants.

**pamphlet or booklet**

Distribute copies of *How to Write Effective E-mail Messages* to all members of our administrative staff.

*Your Attitude Is Showing* is a publication that should be given to all new employees.

Be sure to print at least 500 copies of our new booklet, <u>Employee Programs and Benefits</u>, for distribution to all our employees.

**compact disk**

For this report I obtained a significant amount of information from Microsoft's *Encarta '97*, an interactive multimedia encyclopedia.

**play or musical**

Neil Simon's new play, *Jake's Women*, was originally performed at the Stevens Center of the North Carolina School of the Arts.

Yesterday we saw the last performance of *Les Miserables*; next month *Phantom of the Opera* will open.

Richard Chamberlain played the leading role in the Los Angeles production of <u>My Fair Lady</u>.

**television series**

Weekly episodes of *Frasier* may currently be viewed on NBC television.

**movie title**

The latest remake of *Father of the Bride* stars Steve Martin.

Next month local theaters will schedule children's matinees for showings of Disney's *Snow White and the Seven Dwarfs*.

The movie <u>Twelve Angry Men</u> is still considered to be a classic among American films.

## 3–7.  Subdivisions of Published and Artistic Works

**a.** Capitalize the main words and place in quotation marks the titles of individual chapters, sections, articles, columns, acts, episodes, or songs contained in complete published and artistic works such as books, magazines, booklets, pamphlets, newspapers, compact disks, plays, musicals, operas, television series, and musical albums.

**chapter in a book**

The final chapter, "Application of Information Processing Procedures," contributed greatly to the success of *Office Systems and Management*.

**section in a pamphlet**

Please review the section "Filling Out the Application" before you apply for a job.

**article in a magazine**

Did you read "Successful Ideas for the Indoor Gardener" in last month's issue of *Ladies' Home Journal*?

**column in a newspaper**

Potter's "Financial Outlook" predicted a rising stock market during the next quarter.

**section in a compact disk**

More detailed information about the big bang theory may be found in "Cosmology" in Microsoft's *Encarta '97*.

**act in a play or musical**

During the second act, "Homecoming," many people in the audience were tearful.

**episode in a television series**

Next week's scheduled broadcast, "Holiday in London," of *Worldwide Travels* has been postponed.

Rerun marathons of *The Twilight Zone* usually include the popular episode "To Serve Man."

**b.** **In a published work capitalize the first letter of subdivisions such as *preface*, *contents*, *appendix*, and *index* when they refer to a specific work.**

**specific work**

The rule for punctuating words in a series may be found in the Appendix.

Consult the Index to see on which page the explanation of molecular theory begins.

**general reference**

The index generally follows any appendixes that may be included in a book.

## 3–8. Published and Artistic Works Without Subdivisions

**Capitalize the first letter of the principal words in any title. (See Section 3-6 for an explanation of *principal words*.)**

**Place in quotation marks the titles of television shows, radio programs, poems, songs, paintings, sculptures, and essays—any such published or artistic works that do not contain subdivisions with subtitles.**

**radio program**

Next month we will begin airing our new radio talk show, "Around Cincinnati With Al and Ed."

**poem**

Her poem "A Mother's Love" has been published in poster format.

**song**

For his audition Robert Harris chose to sing "Why Can't the English?"

## 3–9. Unpublished Works

**a.** Place the titles of unpublished essays, manuscripts, reports, theses, and dissertations in quotation marks. Capitalize the first letter of the principal words in the title.

**title of a report**

Copies of "Report on Progress in Areas of Public Concern" were distributed to the board members last week.

**title of a thesis or dissertation**

Casey Wong's thesis, "Differences in Accounting Practices of Three Major Accounting Firms As Compared With Accounting Theory Taught in the Three Leading Accounting Textbooks," was approved by the committee last week.

**b.** Capitalize the main words and place in quotation marks the titles of lectures and sermons.

Dr. Lipmann's dynamic presentation, "Politics and Education," concluded with a challenge the audience could not overlook.

## 3–10. Headings and Text Headings

**a.** In all published or unpublished written works, capitalize the principal words in main headings, secondary headings, centered text headings, and side (or margin) text headings. (See Section 3-6 for an explanation of *principal words*.)

| | |
|---|---|
| The Age of the Universe | Origins of Communication |
| The Steady-State Theory | Communication Through the Ages |
| The Big Bang Theory | Communicating at a Distance |
| Evolution of the Universe | Developments on the Horizon |

**b.** In published and unpublished written works, capitalize only the first word and any proper nouns in paragraph text headings.

**Investment in Europe and other foreign markets.** During the last year the company has established offices in Frankfurt, London, Paris, Mexico City, and Tokyo. With an overseas staff of 23 and a home office staff of 6 dedicated to enlarging our foreign markets, we expect to . . . .

## 3–11. Computer Software Program Titles

Capitalize the main words in computer software program titles. Note that in some cases main words are capitalized and written without an intervening space. Follow the format used by the manufacturer. (See Section 3-6 for an explanation of *principal* or *main words*.)

**software title written as separate words**

Did you use **Microsoft Word** to prepare this manuscript?

Our company has decided to use **Quattro Pro** as its spreadsheet program.

**software title written without spaces**

What version of **WordPerfect** is your law office presently using?

For high-impact business graphics, you may wish to use **CorelFLOW**.

## 3–12. Punctuation Format for Literary and Artistic Titles

**a.** Titles of literary and artistic works are often used in appositive expressions; that is, they are used to rename a previously mentioned noun. In cases where the title is not needed to identify the work, set it off from the rest of the sentence with commas. Where the title is needed for identification, no commas are used.

**title unnecessary to determine which article**

His latest article, "Marketing Changes in the Automotive Industry," recommended a startling departure from current practices.

**title necessary to determine which book**

The book *Escape to Riches* should soon make the best-seller list.

**b.** Periods and commas are *always* placed before the closing quotation mark; semicolons and colons *always* follow the closing quotation mark.

**period and comma before closing quotation mark**

Hawaii is the location of our new episode, "Mousetrap."

Your last article, "Computerized Accounting Procedures in the Banking Industry," was certainly helpful to me in planning our new procedures.

**semicolon and colon after closing quotation mark**

Several hundred readers have requested reprints of your article "Diversifying Your Investment Portfolio"; these reprints will be mailed within the next three weeks.

The following newscasters appear nightly in "Kansas City Reports": Rod Whitcomb, Erika Lovejoy, Steve Markham, and Lisa Darnell.

**c.** Question or exclamation marks appearing with and at the end of quoted titles are placed before the closing quotation mark. If the question or exclamation mark in a title appears at the end of the sentence, no other form of punctuation is required. On the other hand, if the sentence, not the title, is a question or exclamation, place the ending punctuation mark outside the closing quotation mark.

**quoted title phrased as question in middle of sentence**

The article "Are You Getting the Most for Your Investment Dollars?" will appear next month in our quarterly newsletter to all banking customers.

Have you read the article "Are You Getting the Most for Your Investment Dollars?" that appeared in our last month's newsletter?

**statement with quoted title phrased as question at end of sentence**

This week's feature article was entitled "What Is Earthquake Readiness?"

**question with quoted title phrased as question at end of sentence**

Have you read this week's feature article, "What Is Earthquake Readiness?"

**quoted title separate from question**

What percent of our subscribers read "Talk of the Town"?

### 3–13. Academic Courses and Subjects

a. The names of numbered courses and specific course titles are capitalized.

**names of numbered courses**

How many students are enrolled in **Computer Science** 43?

To fulfill your degree requirements, you must complete the following courses: **Psychology** 182, **Anthropology** 1, and **Music** 30.

**specific course title**

You are scheduled to teach two sections of **Survey of Business Law** next semester.

Last year Tina took **Speech 125, Introduction to Public Debate.**

b. Capitalize only proper nouns in the names of academic subject areas.

**subject area**

Please encourage Ms. Harris to take an **accounting** class this spring.

Our college offers over 20 different **history** classes.

**subject area containing proper noun**

I earned an "A" in my **business English** class.

Perhaps you should take a course in **conversational French** before you leave for Paris.

## 3–14. Academic Degrees

**a.** References to academic degrees are generally not capitalized unless they are used after and in conjunction with the name of an individual.

**general reference**

Bill Clark will be awarded a **bachelor of science** degree this June.

She earned her **master's** last summer.

**after person's name**

Joyce Mooneyhan, **Doctor of Divinity**, will deliver the opening address.

**b.** Capitalize abbreviations of academic degrees appearing after a person's name. Remember, though, that the *h* in *Ph.D.* appears in lowercase form.

James Bennett, **D.D.S.**, is an excellent dental surgeon.

We have asked Louise Peebles, **D.B.A.**, to be our speaker.

Make your check payable to Lawrence W. Erickson, **M.D.**

Marcia McKenzie, **Ph.D.**, will join our clinic in June as a staff psychologist.

## 3–15. Organizations

**a.** Principal words in the names of all organizations—business, civic, educational, governmental, labor, military, philanthropic, political, professional, religious, and social—are capitalized. Articles (*a, an, the*), conjunctions (*and, but, or, nor*), and prepositions with three or fewer letters (*of, in, on, to, for*, etc.) are not capitalized.

Boston Chamber of Commerce
Los Angeles Board of Education
Arizona Department of Motor
   Vehicles
Stanford Research Institute
United States Department of
   Defense
Foundation for the Junior Blind
DreamWorks

Young Republican Club
National Council of Churches
Porter Valley Country Club
Tactical Air Command
Illinois Bar Association
American Cancer Society
Metro-Goldwyn-Mayer

**b.** When the word *the* precedes the organizational name and is officially part of the name, it must be capitalized.

We received two letters from **The** Prudential Insurance Company.

**c.** When the common noun element of an organization's name is used in place of the full name, it is generally not capitalized. In formal documents and in specific references to national government bodies, however, capitalize the shortened form.

**general communication**

All employees of the **company** are allowed ten days' sick leave each year.

The **board of education** convened for a special meeting yesterday to consider the budget crisis.

Two members from our local **chamber** received presidential appointments.

So far only two members of the **city council** have agreed to support our rapid transit proposal.

**formal communication**

As agent for the **Association,** I am authorized to sign the convention contracts.

On July 15, 1998, the **Company** acquired several additional holdings.

**national government bodies**

This important bill is now before the **House.** (United States House of Representatives)

Three **Cabinet** members were interviewed by the press. (President's Cabinet)

When will **Congress** reconvene? (United States Congress)

Who is presently majority leader of the **Senate?** (United States Senate)

This issue is now before the **Supreme Court.** (United States Supreme Court)

d.  Government terms such as *federal, government,* and *nation* are often used in place of their respective full names. Because they are used so often and are considered terms of general classification, they are not capitalized.

*federal*

Veterans Day is a holiday for all **federal** employees.

*government*

The **government** is concerned about inflation and its effect on the economy.

Loans such as these are fully guaranteed by the **federal government**.

*nation*

The **nation** has been able to overcome a number of crises.

e.  Principal words in the official name of a division or department within a business organization are capitalized. When a division or department is referred to by its function because the official or specific name is unknown, do not capitalize this reference.

Always capitalize main words in a division or department name used in a return address, an inside address, a signature block, or an envelope address.

**official or specific name**

Please notify the **Department of Human Resources** if you are going to be absent from work.

This contract must be signed by two members of the **Board of Directors**.

A check for this amount must first be approved by the manager of our **Accounting Department**.

We will send a copy of our official findings to your **Department of Research and Development**.

Will you be able to send a member from your **Information Processing Department** to the conference?

**official or specific name unknown**

The efficiency of your **accounting department** can be increased by using our new computer software.

A member of your **advertising department** may wish to contact one of our account executives to take advantage of this rare opportunity.

**return address, inside address, signature block, or envelope address**

Mr. Gary Packler, Manager, Credit Department

f. **Capitalize the principal words in the names of departments, bureaus, divisions, offices, and agencies in government organizations.**

We will forward this information to the **Department of Health and Human Services** within the next week.

Have you contacted the **Bureau of Indian Affairs** about this matter?

You may obtain copies of the proposed freeway route from the **Division of Highways**.

This case is under investigation by the **Office of Internal Affairs**.

To work for the **Federal Bureau of Investigation,** you must first receive a security clearance.

g. **Capitalize the main words in the names of specific departments, divisions, and offices within educational institutions. Main words in the names of schools or colleges within universities are also capitalized.**

**educational departments, divisions, or offices**

Each year the **Music Department** of Banning High School sponsors a spring music festival.

Does Professor Joyce Arntson teach in the **Social Science Division?**

Please send your application for admission to the **Admissions Office** by November 1.

All such budget requests must be submitted to the **Office of Educational Services** by June 30.

**university schools or colleges**

I am presently taking courses in the **School of Business and Economics** at Kentview State University.

The major in which you are interested is offered in the **College of Letters, Arts, and Sciences.**

## 3–16. Geographical Locations

**a.** The names of places—for example, specific continents, countries, islands, states, cities, streets, mountains, valleys, parks, oceans, lakes, rivers, canals, bays, and harbors—are capitalized. When a geographical term (such as *city, street, bay,* or *island*) appears directly after a place name, it is considered part of the name and is capitalized. Terms used in this way are capitalized in both singular and plural forms.

A geographical term appearing before the name of a place is generally not capitalized. Capitalize the term only if (1) it is part of the official name or (2) it is used by the governing bodies of that place as part of an official name.

**specific place**

Our products are distributed throughout **North America.**

Does any airline have a direct flight from **Kansas City** to **New York City**?

Customers in the **Hawaiian Islands** will soon be serviced by their own branch office in **Honolulu.**

The magazine article dealt mainly with camping facilities on the **Colorado River.**

We have a number of tours that take foreign visitors to **Yellowstone National Park.**

Many of our shipments are brought here through the **Panama Canal.**

Property taxes in **Ventura County** have risen steadily during the past five years.

**specific places—geographical term in plural form**

The excursion will include trips on both the **Mississippi and Missouri Rivers.**

Most of our discoveries have been in the **San Bernardino and San Gorgonio Mountains.**

The new shopping mall is located on the corner of **59th and State Streets.**

**geographical term appearing before specific place — not capitalized**

Most of our business is conducted within the **state** of Utah.

Will your tour include the **city** of London?

The **city** of Los Angeles was selected as the site for our next convention.

The estimated 2001 population for the **county** of Ventura is 653,609.

**geographical term appearing before specific place — capitalized**

Most of our suppliers are located in the **City of Industry**. (Geographical term part of city name.)

The **City of Los Angeles** has approved a new budget plan. (Geographical term used by governing body as part of official name.)

Did the **State of California** adopt a new automobile insurance plan for low-risk drivers? (Geographical term used by governing body as part of official name.)

**b.** Capitalize nicknames of geographical locations and names of regional areas that have evolved as a result of usage.

**geographical nicknames**

All our pineapples come directly from the **Aloha State**. (Hawaii)

When were the Olympics held in the **City of Angels**? (Los Angeles)

How many times each year must you go to the **Big Apple**? (New York City)

This year our convention will be held in the **Windy City**. (Chicago)

**regional names emerging from usage**

Many of our clients are from **Upstate New York**.

Police reports indicate that the **Lower East Side** has the highest crime rate in our city.

Merchants from the **Greater Los Angeles Area** have banded together to support this worthwhile project.

Many residents in the **Bay Area** are concerned about the pollution occurring in San Francisco Bay.

**c.** Points of the compass are capitalized when they are used as simple or compound nouns to designate *specific regions*. Points of the compass are not capitalized, however, when they are used to indicate *direction* or *general localities*.

**specific regions**

Firms connected with the aerospace industry are heavily concentrated in the **West** and **Southwest**.

Our company has increased its trade to the **Far East**.

The festival was held in **East Los Angeles**.

101

Sales in our **Southern Region** have increased 25 percent during the past year.

Within the next month we will expand our operations into **East Texas**.

### directions

My territory includes all states **east** of the Mississippi River.

The consultant's report recommended that our new plant be located just **northwest** of Baltimore.

To avoid the harsh winter weather, many retirees travel **south** or **west** during the snow season.

By taking the **eastbound** on-ramp, you will get to the center of Madison.

### general localities

The **southern** part of our state is suffering a severe drought.

Our delivery service is restricted to the **east** side of Miami.

Customers from the **northwest** section of the city have registered more complaints than customers from any other sector.

Did you survey most of the **western** states?

This new weather stripping is guaranteed to protect you against the severity of **northern** winters.

**d.** Words derived from simple or compound nouns representing *specific* regions are capitalized.

A number of **Midwesterners** have inquired about our franchises.

**Southern Californians** are known for their casual lifestyle.

This survey includes responses only from **Easterners**.

Atlanta is known for its **Southern** hospitality.

## 3–17. Dates, Time Periods, and Events

Capitalize days of the week, months of the year, holidays (including religious days), specific special events, and specific historical events or periods.

The names of seasons, decades, and centuries are generally not capitalized. If, however, a season is combined with a year, capitalize the season.

### day of week and month

Our committee will meet the first **Monday** in **March, June, September,** and **December.**

### holiday

Will our store be closed on **New Year's Day** this year?

Each year **Veterans Day** is observed on a different date.

**specific special event**

Our company will celebrate its **Silver Anniversary** next year.

**National Secretaries' Week** is traditionally observed during the latter part of April.

This year the **Maricopa County Fair** will be held from September 4 through September 27.

How many of your staff members will be attending the **NBEA Convention** this year?

**historical event or period**

In our **Information Age** the Internet is taking an increasingly important role.

The stock market crash of 1929 brought the **Roaring Twenties** to a dismal end and catapulted our country into the **Great Depression**.

During the **Industrial Revolution** children were often forced to work long hours under intolerable conditions.

**season**

Our biggest sales item during this **spring** season has been the Model 550 patio set.

None of the **winter** coats we ordered have arrived yet.

If you wish to enroll for the **fall** semester, please submit your application by August 15.

We have received your application for admission for the **Winter 1999** quarter.

**decade**

During the last year a number of movies portraying life in the **sixties** have been released.

This company was founded in the early **fifties** by Jonathan Hunt.

**century**

Technological developments during the **twentieth century** have advanced the human race further than all other developments during our previous history.

Many of Mr. Ryan's critics believe that he operates his business on **nineteenth-century** management principles.

## 3–18. Ethnic and Religious References

a. Ethnic-related terms (references to a particular language, race, or culture) are capitalized. Generic terms such as *black, white*, and *brown* when used in reference to race are generally not capitalized.

**language**

A knowledge of both **German** and **English** is required for the job.

**race**

The census indicated that many **Asians** are living in this area.

Courses in **African-American** history and culture are taught in many major colleges and universities throughout the United States.

Several **black** leaders have requested to address the city council on this issue.

**culture**

Cinco de Mayo is observed with many festivities in the **Mexican-American** community.

The predominant native language of **Hispanics** is Spanish, but a significant number claim Portuguese as their native tongue.

**b.** **Capitalize references to specific religious groups.**

Massive opposition from **Catholic, Protestant**, and **Jewish** clergy led to the defeat of this proposed legislation.

A **Mormon** temple will be built on this site in 2001.

## 3–19. Celestial Bodies

Capitalize the names of celestial bodies—planets, planet satellites, stars, constellations, and asteroids. Do not capitalize the terms *earth, sun*, and *moon*, however, unless they are used as the names of specific bodies in the solar system.

**capitalized**

We have been studying the orbital paths of **Mars** and **Earth**.

Can you pick out the **North Star** or the **Big Dipper** among the many stars in the sky?

When will **Earth** next pass between the **Sun** and the **Moon**?

The background of the scene embraces a darkened sky highlighted only by an array of stars and **Saturn** with its bright rings.

**lowercase**

Television broadcasts of the first **moon** landing were viewed by millions of Americans.

None of the pieces from the satellite found their way back into the **earth's** atmosphere.

Rays from the **sun** can damage your skin and subsequently cause skin cancer.

# Chapter 4

# Number Formats and Applications

# Number Formats and Applications Solution Finder

# General Format

## 4–1.   General Rules for Numbers

**a.**   A number that begins a sentence *must be* expressed in word form. When the number cannot be written in one or two words, however, change the word order of the sentence so that the number does not begin the sentence. Then write the number in figures. This number rule takes precedence over all others.

**number written in words**

Twenty-four people responded to our advertisement for an accountant.

**sentence order rearranged for figure form**

The questionnaire was answered by **260** respondents.  (Not: *Two hundred sixty* [or *260*] respondents answered the questionnaire.)

**b.**   Numbers *one* through *ten* used in a general way are written in words. Write such numbers above *ten* in figures, except those used to begin a sentence (See Section 4-1a). This rule applies only to those numbers not governed by any other number-usage rule.

**number *ten* or below**

Would you please ship us **four** additional copies of this software program.

**number above *ten***

We have received **12** letters of complaint about service in our Springfield office during the last month.

Thirty-three of our present employees will not be moving with us to our Santa Maria location.

**c.**   Approximations above *ten* that can be expressed in one or two words may be written in either figures or words. Keep in mind that figures are more emphatic and conform to the rule for the use of general numbers.

**approximation written in figures**

Nearly **300** people sent telegrams to the mayor.

**approximation written in words**

He expected over **fifty** people for the conference.

**d.**   Numbers below *100* that are written in word form are hyphenated if they are written as two words; that is, compound numbers *21* through *99* are hyphenated if they are spelled out.

Twenty-seven of the homes in this tract were sold last month.

**e.**   Round numbers in the millions or billions are expressed in a combination of figures and words. Only *one million* used as an

Numbers

4

*approximation* is usually written in all word form; otherwise, it is written *1 million*.

### round number

Captain Maez has flown nearly **2 million** miles since he earned his wings.

### round number with fraction

Our company manufactured over 3½ **billion** pens last year.

### round number with decimal

Will we exceed our production quota of **1.2 million** automobiles?

### *one million* as an approximation

Look to establish additional locations in cities with populations of more than **one million**.

### *1 million* as an exact figure

We will recover all development and marketing costs once we have sold **1 million** of these special bolts.

## 4–2. Related Numbers

**a.** Numbers used in a comparable or corresponding manner in the same document are considered related numbers and should be expressed in the same form. Therefore, write numbers *one* through *ten* in figures when they are used with related numbers above ten.

Of the **130** items inspected, only **2** were found to be defective.

Next week we will deliver the **3** reams of bond paper, the **24** boxes of envelopes, and the **2** file trays that were back ordered for you. (Note that items appearing in a series are always considered to be related.)

**b.** Round numbers in the millions or billions are expressed in figures when they are used with related numbers below a million or with related numbers that cannot be expressed in a combination of words and figures.

### combined with number below 1 million

Our production of umbrellas rose from **970,000** to **2,000,000** this year.

### combined with number over 1 million written in figures

During the past two years, our circulation has risen from nearly **3,000,000** copies to **3,875,500** copies.

**c.** Unrelated numbers used in the same sentence are considered individually to determine whether they should be expressed in words or figures.

### unrelated numbers in same sentence

Please send each of the **four** vice presidents **15** copies of our monthly report.

For this banquet each of the **14** tables should seat **eight** people.

**combination of related and unrelated numbers in same sentence**

Our warehouse inventory of **22** dishwashers, **17** refrigerators, and **8** washing machines must be distributed among our **three** stores.

These new packing boxes hold **four** cartons that contain **12** bottles each whereas the old boxes held **six** cartons that contained **6** bottles each.

## 4–3. Number Format

a. Numbers expressed as figures are separated by commas into groups of three digits. Exceptions include years, house numbers, telephone numbers, fax numbers, zip codes, serial numbers, page numbers, decimal fractions, and metric measurements. Metric measurements of five or more digits are separated into groups of three with spaces.

**commas in figures with more than three digits**

4,782       17,750       385,450       2,865,000       1,567,874,500

**no commas in certain figures**

1999              Serial No. 14896-AN              1111 Figueroa Street
page 1032       Evansville, IN 47701-1957       (805) 555-6132
0.7534           1000 kilometers

**space in metric measures with five or more digits**

Our dairy delivers over **45 000** liters of milk daily to homes in this city.

b. When two independent figures appear consecutively (one directly after the other) in a sentence, separate the figures with a comma.

By **1998, 52** homes had been built around the golf course.

Of the **325, 72** questionnaires were not returned.

c. Two consecutive numbers that act as adjectives modifying the same noun are *not* separated by a comma. Instead, write the first number in words and the second one in figures. If the first number cannot be expressed in *one or two words*, place it in figures also.

**two numbers modifying a noun, word-figure form**

We processed your order for **twelve 48-inch** glass tabletops yesterday.

Each package contains **twenty 3-inch** nails.

Did you order **seventy 50-watt** bulbs?

Each box contains **twelve 6-pack** cartons of Coke.

Our contract calls for **three 25-second** commercials during this broadcast.

The contractor plans to build **thirty-six 5-bedroom** houses on this land.

**two numbers modifying a noun, figure-figure form**

Please purchase **150 32-cent** stamps from the post office.

The bank has agreed to finance your purchase of a **1997 30-foot** mobile home.

The prescription was for **175 25-milligram** tablets.

**d.** Separate volume numbers from page references with commas. Weights, capacities, and measures that consist of several words are treated as single units and are not separated by commas.

**volume and page number**

This information may be found in **Volume IV, page 289.**

**weight as a single unit**

The Millers' newborn weighed **7 pounds 3 ounces** at birth.

**capacity as a single unit**

In conventional terms the capacity of the pitcher is **2 quarts 1 cup.**

**measure as a single unit**

Mr. Knight verified that the room length measured **28 feet 4 inches.**

The flight time has been calculated to be **4 hours 20 minutes.**

**e.** The plural of a figure is formed by adding *s*.

How many **7s** do you see in this serial number?

The **1900s** will be noted for man's first successes in space travel.

# Figure Form

## 4–4. Money

**a.** Amounts of money *$1 or more* are expressed in figures. Omit the decimal and zeros in expressing whole dollar amounts, even if they appear with mixed dollar amounts.

**money expressed in figures**

We paid **$284.95** for this new Microlite cellular telephone.

**omission of decimal and zeros**

The list of purchases included items for **$6.50, $3, $79.45, $200,** and **$265.**

**b.** Amounts of money *less than $1* are expressed in figures combined with the word *cents* unless they are used in conjunction with related amounts of *$1 or more*. Unrelated amounts of money appearing in the same sentence, however, are treated separately.

**amounts less than $1**

Last week the basic bus fare was increased from **60 cents** to **75 cents**.

**related amounts of money**

To mail the three reports, I paid **$.85, $1.40**, and **$2** in postage.

**unrelated amounts of money**

The tax on this **$8** item was **52 cents**.

c. Round amounts of money in millions or billions of dollars are expressed in combined figure and word form except when they are used with related dollar figures below a million or related amounts that can be expressed in figures only.

**round amount**

The cost of the new building was over **$12 1/2 million**.

Nearly **$3.5 billion** in assets provides the customer confidence that has made Liberty Fed the largest federal savings bank in the country.

**related to amount less than $1 million**

We estimate that **$850,000** will be needed to retool the Wilmington plant and **$2,000,000** will be needed for the Van Nuys plant.

**related to amount that can be expressed in figures only**

Our sales decreased from **$12,458,000** last year to less than **$12,000,000** this year.

d. Amounts of money in legal documents are expressed in words followed by the figure amount contained in parentheses. The word *and* is used only to introduce cents included in a money amount written in word form.

**round dollar amounts**

The amount of indebtedness incurred by the defendant during this period was **Ten Thousand Five Hundred Eighty-three Dollars ($10,583)**.

The Company shall pay up to **One Thousand Dollars ($1,000)** within 90 days upon receipt of a valid release statement.

**dollar amount with cents**

A check for **Two Thousand Four Hundred Sixty-one Dollars and Forty-eight Cents ($2,461.48)** was received from Westin Industries on May 3.

## 4–5. Decimals and Percentages

a. Numbers containing decimals are expressed in figures. To prevent misreading, place a zero before a decimal that does not contain a whole number or begin with a zero.

**decimal with whole number**

Our trucks average **12.843** miles per gallon of gasoline.

**decimal beginning with 0**

This part must be made within **.002** inch of specifications.

**decimal not containing whole number or beginning with 0**

Only **0.4** percent of all items manufactured this year were rejected because of defective workmanship.

**b.** Write percentages in figures followed by the word *percent*. The percent symbol (%) is used only for statistical or technical tables or forms.

**percent used in sentence format**

Last month we were able to decrease our energy consumption by only **1 percent**.

This year's travel expenses are up **8 percent** over last year's.

A **12 1/2 percent** pay increase was granted to all office employees.

We anticipate a **0.5 percent** increase in sales tax this year—from **6 percent** to **6.5 percent**.

**% used in statistical tables or forms**

32.5%        80%        99.9%        4.3%        6%        0.8%

## 4–6.    U.S. Standard Weights and Measures

**a.** For quick comprehension express in figures the amount something weighs or measures. Weights and measures (inches, feet, yards, miles, kilometers, ounces, pounds, tons, grams, pints, quarts, gallons, liters, each, dozen, gross, reams, pecks, bushels, degrees, acres, etc.), however, are written out fully in words. Abbreviations or symbols representing these units are limited to use in business forms or statistical materials.

**general use**

This carton is **3 pounds 6 ounces** in excess of the U.S. Postal Service limitations.

Over **2 tons** of waste material leave the plant daily.

Place the **8 reams** of copy paper in the storeroom.

Approximately **150 square yards** of carpeting will be needed for this office.

Use **3-inch** screws for this job.

**use for forms and statistical materials**

4 doz.        12 yd.        84°        9#        9 ft.        85 lb.        12 ea.

**b.** Standard measures of length may be expressed in mils, inches, feet, yards, rods, furlongs, miles, and leagues. Standard weights may be expressed in grains, drams, ounces, pounds, hundredweights, and tons. Standard capacities may be expressed in teaspoons, tablespoons, ounces, cups, pints, quarts, gallons, pecks, and bushels. The following tables provide equivalents for various standard measures of length, weight, and capacity:

### standard measures of length

| | | |
|---:|:---:|:---|
| 1 mil | = | 0.001 inch |
| 1 inch | = | 1,000 mils |
| 12 inches | = | 1 foot |
| 3 feet | = | 1 yard |
| 16.5 feet | = | 1 rod |
| 40 rods | = | 1 furlong |
| 8 furlongs or 5,280 feet | = | 1 mile |
| 3 miles | = | 1 league (land) |

### standard measures of weight

| | | |
|---:|:---:|:---|
| 1 grain | = | 0.036 drams |
| 1 dram | = | 27.34 grains |
| 16 drams or 437.5 grains | = | 1 ounce |
| 16 ounces or 7,000 grains | = | 1 pound |
| 100 pounds | = | 1 hundredweight |
| 2,000 pounds | = | 1 ton |

### standard measures of capacity

| | | |
|---:|:---:|:---|
| 3 teaspoons or 0.5 ounce | = | 1 tablespoon |
| 2 tablespoons | = | 1 ounce |
| 16 tablespoons or 8 ounces | = | 1 cup |
| 2 cups or 16 ounces | = | 1 pint |
| 2 pints, 4 cups, or 32 ounces | = | 1 quart |
| 4 quarts or 128 ounces | = | 1 gallon |
| 8 quarts | = | 1 peck |
| 4 pecks | = | 1 bushel |

## 4–7. Metric Weights and Measures

**a.** The most common metric measurements are based on meters, grams, and liters. Prefixes indicating fractions and multiples of these quantities follow:

**fractions**

deci (1/10)     centi (1/100)     milli (1/1000)

**multiples**

deka (× 10)     hecto (× 100)     kilo (× 1000)

**b.** Express metric measurements in figures. Use a space to separate numbers of five or more digits into groups of three. No space or comma is used with four-digit figures.

### regular metric measures

We will be using **1.75-liter** bottles for our large-size apple juice.

Our new package of pie crust sticks weighs 11 ounces, which equals **311 grams** or **3.11 hectograms**.

### four-digit figures

The distance from Memphis to Boston is over **2000 kilometers**.

The central office ordered **1500 kilograms** of flour and **1200 kilograms** of sugar to be delivered to our bakeries throughout the state.

### five-digit figures

His 5 acres is equal to approximately 2 hectares, that is, approximately **20 000 square meters**.

**c.** **For general correspondence spell out units of measure. Abbreviate units of measure only in technical writing, medical reports, or any kind of forms.**

### general correspondence

10 millimeters          4 liters          80 kilometers

### technical writing, medical reports, or forms

60 mm          6 mg          25 km          100 cc

**d.** **The following tables show equivalents for metric and standard measures of length, weight, and capacity:**

### equivalents for measures of length

| Metric to Standard | Standard to Metric |
|---|---|
| 1 kilometer = 0.6214 (5/8) mile | 1 mile = 1.609 kilometers |
| 1 meter = 1.0936 yards | 1 yard = 0.9144 meter (exact) |
| 1 meter = 39.37 inches | 1 foot = 0.3048 meter (exact) |
| 1 centimeter = 0.3937 (2/5) inch | 1 inch = 2.54 centimeters (exact) |

### equivalents for measures of weight

| Metric to Standard | Standard to Metric |
|---|---|
| 1 ton (or tonne) = 1.1023 tons | 1 ton = 0.90721 ton (or tonne) |
| 1 kilogram = 2.2046 pounds | 1 pound = 453.592 grams |
| 1 kilogram = 35 ounces | 1 ounce = 28.35 grams |
| 1 gram = 0.035 ounce | |

### equivalents for measures of capacity

| Metric to Standard | Standard to Metric |
|---|---|
| 1 hectoliter (hl) = 2.838 bushels | 1 bushel = 35.239 liters |
| 1 liter (L) = 0.264 liquid gallon | 1 liquid gallon = 3.785 liters |
| 1 liter (L) = 1.057 liquid quarts | 1 liquid quart = 0.946 liter |
| 1 liter (L) = 0.908 dry quart | 1 dry quart = 1.101 liters |
| 1 milliliter (ml) <br> 1 cubic centimeter (cc) } = 0.034 fluid ounce | 1 fluid ounce = 29.573 milliliters |

## 4-8.   Numbers Used With Nouns, Abbreviations, and Symbols

a.   Numbers used directly with nouns are placed in figures. Page numbers, model numbers, policy numbers, and serial numbers are just a few of the instances in which numerals are used with nouns. The words preceding the numerals are usually capitalized except for page, paragraph, line, size, and verse references. (See Section 3-4 for capitalization format.)

**model number**

We ordered your **Model 3** printer for our Information Processing Center.

Our **Model No. 87** magazine rack has been discontinued.

**policy and serial numbers**

Please return your copy of **Policy 1284691D** to the home office.

Our IBM computer, **Serial No. A32-74603552**, was reported missing from the office.

**page number**

You will find a picture of this economy unit on **page 21** of our current catalog.

b.   Direct reference to the word *number* is the most common instance in which figures are used with an abbreviation. The word *number* is abbreviated in this case except when it appears at the beginning of a sentence.

We expect to replace our camera equipment with your **No. 378** series.

The following checks were returned by your bank: **Nos. 487, 492, and 495.**

**Numbers 381, 1209, and 1628** were the winning raffle tickets.

c.   The use of symbols is generally avoided in business writing. However, for preparing forms (such as invoices and orders), charts, tables, and other documents where space is limited, symbols are used liberally. Numbers expressed with symbols are written in figures.

2/10, N/30          8%          #455

# Time

## 4-9.   Dates

a.   When the day is written after the month, use cardinal figures (*1, 2, 3*, etc.). Ordinal figures (*1st, 2nd, 3rd*, etc.) are used for expressing days that appear before the month or that stand alone.

**month followed by day**

**March 23, 2000,** is the deadline for filing your claim.

115

Your **October 15** payment is now 30 days past due.

**day appearing before month**

We expect payment in full by the **10th of April.**

Our new offices should be ready for occupancy by the **3rd of June.**

**day used alone**

Your reservations for the **9th** and the **24th** have been confirmed.

Please send us your rental payment by the **1st** of each month.

**b.** Dates used in most domestic business correspondence are expressed in terms of month, day, and year with a comma separating the day and year. In military and international correspondence, dates are generally written day, month, and year without an intervening comma.

**domestic business correspondence**

November 27, 1999

**military or international correspondence**

27 November 1999

**4–10. Clock Time**

**a.** Figures are used with *a.m., p.m., noon,* or *midnight* to express clock time. Omit the colon and zeros with even times, even if they appear in conjunction with times expressed in hours and minutes.

The terms *noon* and *midnight* may be used with or without the figure *12.* When these terms are used with other clock times containing *a.m.* and/or *p.m.,* however, include the figure *12.* Never use *a.m.* or *p.m.* following *12, noon,* or *midnight.*

**_a.m., p.m., noon, midnight_ with figures**

His plane was scheduled to arrive at **1 p.m.,** but the actual arrival time was **1:27 p.m.**

Our next plant tour will begin at **10:30 a.m.** and conclude by **12 noon.**

The afternoon shift is scheduled from **4 p.m.** until **12 midnight.**

**_noon_ and _midnight_ with the figure _12_**

She left promptly at **12 noon.**

The new shift starts at **12 midnight.**

This postal station is open Saturdays from **8 a.m.** until **12 noon.**

New hours for our coffee shop are from **8 a.m.** until **12 midnight** daily.

**_noon_ and _midnight_ without the figure _12_**

May we please have your answer before **noon** on July 30.

All envelopes containing tax payments must be postmarked before **midnight**, April 15.

**b.** **Either word or figure form may be used with** *o'clock*.

We must leave the office by **eight o'clock** [or **8 o'clock**] if we are to arrive at the airport on time.

**c.** **Phrases such as "in the morning," "in the afternoon," or "at night" may follow clock times expressed with** *o'clock* **but not with** *a.m.* **or** *p.m.*

Coffee breaks are scheduled at **10 o'clock in the morning** and at **3 o'clock in the afternoon**.

By **two o'clock in the afternoon**, our campus is almost empty; but by **seven o'clock in the evening**, it is filled with students attending night classes.

**d.** **When even clock hours of the day are expressed without** *a.m.*, *p.m.*, **or** *o'clock*, **use word form. Either word or figure form may be used, however, when both hours and minutes are expressed.**

**exact hour**

The board meeting is scheduled to begin at **eight** tonight.

**hour and minutes**

The committee meeting was not adjourned until **6:30** [or **six-thirty**].

The power shut off at **9:05** [or **five after nine**] this morning but resumed operation before **10:30** [or **ten-thirty**].

## 4–11.  Periods of Time

**a.** **Periods of time relating to** *days, weeks, months,* **or** *years* **that can be expressed in one or two words are usually written in word form when they are used in a general way. Periods of time that cannot be expressed in one or two words are written in figure form.**

**General references to clock hours, minutes, or seconds are treated as general numbers: numbers** *ten* **and below are written in word form and numbers above** *ten* **are written in figure form.**

**general time period—days, weeks, months, or years**

During the last **sixteen months**, we have shown a slight profit.

We have been in this location for **thirty-two years**.

The auto workers' strike lasted **117 days**.

**general references to clock time**

Each candidate's speech is limited to **five minutes**.

We offer **24-hour** repair service to all our subscribers.

Numbers

4

**b.** Time-period data related to specific loan lengths, discount rates, interest rates, payment terms, credit terms, or other such information dealing with definite business contracts are expressed in figures.

This loan must be paid in full within **90 days**.

We give a 2 percent discount on all invoices paid within **10 days** of the invoice date.

You have been granted a 9 percent loan for **6 months**.

## 4–12. Ages and Anniversaries

Ages and anniversaries that can be expressed in one or two words are generally written in word form; those that require more than two words are written in figures. Figures are also used when an age (1) appears directly after a person's name; (2) is used in a legal or technical sense; or (3) is expressed in terms of years, months, and sometimes days. Note that no commas are used to separate the years, months, and days in the expression of ages.

### general expression of ages and anniversaries

David will be **twenty-seven** on August 9; his son John will be **three** the same day.

The staff was surprised that Mrs. Wong retired the day after her **fifty-fifth** birthday.

Next month we will celebrate our manager's **twenty-fifth** anniversary with the company.

Our city will celebrate its **150th** anniversary in 2001.

### age after name

Ms. Soderstrom, **47**, was promoted to branch manager last week.

### age used in technical or legal sense

Employees no longer must retire at the age of **65**.

The legal voting age is **18**.

At **25** you will be eligible for these reduced insurance rates.

### age in years, months, and days

According to our records, the insured was **35** years **5** months and **28** days of age upon cancellation of the policy.

# Addresses and Telephone Numbers

## 4–13. Addresses

**a.** House numbers are expressed in figures except for the house number *One*. No commas are used to separate digits in house numbers.

**One** Alpha Street                   **One** East Broward Boulevard

**4** Headquarters Plaza North         **18817** Clearview Avenue

**b.** Street names that are numbered *ten* or below are expressed in word form with ordinal numbers (*First, Second, Third*, etc.). Street names numbered above *ten* are written in ordinal figures (*st, nd, rd, th*).

**street name *ten* or below**

All visitors to New York City must stroll down **Fifth** Avenue.

Mail your payment to our office at 200 West **Second** Street, Winston-Salem, North Carolina 27101-4036

**street name above *ten***

Please send this order to 1111 **23rd** Street, Denver, Colorado 80205-2145.

His former address is listed as 3624 West **59th** Place.

**c.** Apartment numbers, suite numbers, box numbers, and route numbers are expressed in figure form.

1883 Creek Avenue, Apt. **4**          Post Office Box **1584**

Plaza Medical Building, Suite **102**   Rural Route **2**

**d.** Zip codes are expressed in figures (without commas) and typed a single space after the state. Address lines containing zip + 4 are written in the same manner as those containing five-digit zip codes. The only difference is that the four extra digits are separated from the zip code with a hyphen.

**sentence format**

Ms. Sherman requested that the refund be sent to her at Pasadena City College, 1570 East Colorado Boulevard, Pasadena, California **91106-2003**.

Redirect this order to Palmer Enterprises, 1586 North Cicero Avenue, Chicago, Illinois **60651-1618**.

**inside address or envelope address**

Mr. Arthur M. Manuel                   Mrs. Janice Harrington
7820 ½ South Eighth Avenue             1073 23rd Street, Apt. 2
Inglewood, CA **90305-1004**           Moonachie, NJ **07074**

Ms. Eleanor Chu, Vice President
Parke-Dunn Pharmaceutical Company
74 West Michigan Mall, Suite 300
Battle Creek, Michigan **49017-3606**

## 4–14. Telephone and Facsimile (Fax) Numbers

Telephone and facsimile (fax) numbers are expressed in figures. When the area code is included, place it in parentheses before the number.

As an alternate format you may omit the parentheses and separate the area code from the telephone or fax number with a hyphen.

Extension numbers, preceded by the abbreviation *Ext.*, follow telephone numbers. If an extension number concludes a sentence, use a single comma to separate it from the telephone number. However, if an extension number appears in the middle of a sentence, use commas before and after it.

### telephone or facsimile (fax) number

You may reach our representative at **728-1694**.

Please ask the doctor to fax the prescription for this prosthesis to **363-6534**.

### area code with telephone or facsimile (fax) number

Please fax a copy of this proposal to me at **(714) 555-5235**.

Call our toll-free number, **800-885-3322**, to place your order.

### area code, telephone number, extension

You may reach me any weekday at **(617) 555-7139, Ext. 3712**.

We were requested to call **(213) 347-0551, Ext. 244**, within an hour.

## Special Forms

### 4–15.  Fractions

**a.**  Simple fractions that can be expressed in two words are written in word form. Fractions written in word form are not hyphenated unless they are used as compound adjectives.[1]

### simple fraction used as a noun

We have already met **three fourths** of our production quota for this year.

Only **one third** of our agents returned the questionnaire.

### simple fraction used as a compound adjective

A **two-thirds** majority vote is needed to ratify the contract.

Our investment syndicate wishes to purchase a **one-fourth** interest in the proposed new shopping center.

**b.**  Figures are used to express (1) long and awkward fractions, (2) fractions combined with whole numbers, or (3) fractions used for technical purposes.

### long and awkward fraction

The study indicated that $21/200$ of a second is needed for the average person to begin reacting in emergency situations.

---

[1]"Table of Numbers," Footnote 5, *Merriam-Webster's Collegiate Dictionary*, 10th Ed. (Springfield, Mass.: Merriam-Webster, Incorporated, 1996), p. 798.

**fraction combined with whole number**

Our new plant is located **3½** miles from here.

**fraction for technical use**

Our department is temporarily out of stock of ⅝-inch roundheaded metal screws.

**c.** Use the extended character set of your word processing program to key fractions that are written in figures. Those commonly found are ½, ¼, ¾, ⅓, ⅔, ⅛, ⅜, ⅝, and ⅞.

Fractions written in figures that are not found in extended character sets of word processing programs are formed by using the diagonal to separate the two parts. If possible, format the first number for superscript in a smaller font and format the second number at the normal position in that same font. When fractions available in extended character sets are used with those not available in these sets, key all fractions by using the diagonal construction.

In mixed numbers not constructed by extended character sets or other font attributes, leave one space between the fraction and any whole number used with the fraction.

**fraction keyed through an extended character set**

Our supply of ¾-inch nails is running low.

**mixed number keyed through an extended character set**

We shipped **8⅔** tons of beef last week.

Our employees averaged **31½** hours of sick leave last year as compared to **24¼** hours this year.

**fraction keyed using a diagonal**

These **15/16**-inch screws have been designed especially to assemble the Model 1585A cabinets.

All these parts must be manufactured within **1/100** inch of specifications.

**mixed number keyed using a diagonal**

Each chair to be recovered in the restaurant will require **3 5/6** yards of fabric.

These panels are exactly **23 11/16** inches wide.

## 4–16. Ordinals

**a.** Ordinal numbers (*first, second, third,* etc.) that can be written in one or two words are generally expressed in word form except those appearing in (1) dates before the month or standing alone and (2) numbered street names above *ten*.

**general use**

Mr. Cox was elected to represent the **Thirty-fourth** Congressional District.

Mrs. Lang was criticized for managing the company according to **nineteenth**-century practices.

**dates**

Our next audit is scheduled for the **1st of August**.

Your order will be shipped by the **15th** of this month.

Please submit your report by the **1st** of the year.

**numbered streets**

Our new store is located at 820 West **Third** Avenue.

I plan to meet Mr. Siegel at noon on the corner of Main and **42nd** Streets.

**b.** Ordinals expressed in figure form end in *st, nd, rd,* or *th.*

This note is due the **1st** of March.

May we have your response by the **22nd** of November.

This year marks the **123rd** anniversary of our city.

Our new offices are located at 1560 **12th** Avenue.

## 4–17. Roman Numerals

**a.** When typing Roman numerals for chapter or outline divisions, use capital letters to form the numbers. In using word processing programs with an outline feature, adjust the tab settings so that the periods align for Roman numerals as well as for other divisions in the outline.

Use capital letters for expressing years written in Roman numerals.

**table of Roman numerals**

| Arabic Numeral | Roman Numeral | Arabic Numeral | Roman Numeral |
|---|---|---|---|
| 1 | I | 16 | XVI |
| 2 | II | 17 | XVII |
| 3 | III | 18 | XVIII |
| 4 | IV | 19 | XIX |
| 5 | V | 20 | XX |
| 6 | VI | 30 | XXX |
| 7 | VII | 40 | XL |
| 8 | VIII | 50 | L |
| 9 | IX | 60 | LX |
| 10 | X | 70 | LXX |
| 11 | XI | 80 | LXXX |
| 12 | XII | 90 | XC |
| 13 | XIII | 100 | C |
| 14 | XIV | 500 | D |
| 15 | XV | 1,000 | M |

**chapter divisions**

Please submit your review of **Chapter IX** by June 1.

**divisions in an outline**

   **I.** Hardware Requirements
  **II.** Network Capabilities
 **III.** Software Requirements
 **IV.** Training Programs

**year expressed in Roman numerals**

Chiseled at the top of the archway was the year the old stone church had been built—**MDCLXXXVI.** (1686)

**b.** The preliminary sections of a report such as the letter of transmittal, the table of contents, and the list of tables are numbered with lower-case Roman numerals. Number the pages consecutively using *i, ii, iii, iv, v,* etc.

# Business Calculations

## 4–18. Rounding Numbers

When answers to arithmetic calculations contain a number of digits after the decimal, they may be rounded for ease of understanding. For example, amounts of money in business calculations are commonly rounded to the nearest cent.

Use the following three-step process to round numbers:

(1) Identify the number of digits needed to the right of the decimal.

(2) Increase the last digit by one if the number to its right is *5* or greater.

(3) Eliminate the extra digits after the decimal point.

**figure rounded to three decimal places**

$45.6667 = $45.666|7 = $45.667   5.125463% = 5.125|463% = 5.125%

**figure rounded to two decimal places**

$45.6667 = $45.66|67 = $45.67     5.125463% = 5.12|5463% = 5.13%

**figure rounded to one decimal place**

$45.6667 = $45.6|667 = $45.7      5.125463% = 5.1|25463% = 5.1%

**figure rounded to whole number**

$45.6667 = $45.|6667 = $46       5.125463% = 5.|125463% = 5%

## 4–19. Converting Fractions to Decimals

To convert fractions to decimal form, divide the numerator (top or first number) by the denominator (bottom or second number).

Numbers

4

123

$$\tfrac{1}{2} = 1 \div 2 = 0.5 \qquad \tfrac{2}{3} = 2 \div 3 = 0.667 \qquad \tfrac{5}{6} = 5 \div 6 = 0.8333$$

$$\tfrac{3}{4} = 3 \div 4 = 0.75 \qquad \tfrac{7}{8} = 7 \div 8 = 0.875 \qquad \tfrac{11}{16} = 11 \div 16 = 0.6875$$

## 4–20. Converting Decimals to Percents

To convert decimal numbers to percent form, move the decimal two places to the right and add a percent sign. If an additional digit is needed, add *0*.

| | |
|---|---|
| 0.2 = 20% | 0.65 = 65% |
| 0.7152 = 71.52% | 1.1582 = 115.82% |

## 4–21. Converting Percents to Decimals

To convert percentages to decimal form, move the decimal two places to the left. Omit any *0*s at the end. For decimal forms without whole numbers, place a *0* before the decimal to avoid misreading.

| | |
|---|---|
| 70% = 0.7 | 95% = 0.95 |
| 32.62% = 0.3262 | 185.25% = 1.8525 |

Decimal equivalents and percentages for common fractions are shown in the following table:

| Fraction | | Decimal | Percent | Fraction | | Decimal | Percent |
|---|---|---|---|---|---|---|---|
| 1/3 | | .3333 | 33.33% | 1/12 | | .0833 | 8.33% |
| 2/3 | | .6667 | 66.67% | 2/12 | (1/6) | .1667 | 16.67% |
| 1/4 | | .25 | 25% | 3/12 | (1/4) | .25 | 25% |
| 2/4 | (1/2) | .50 | 50% | 4/12 | (1/3) | .3333 | 33.33% |
| 3/4 | | .75 | 75% | 5/12 | | .4167 | 41.67% |
| 1/5 | | .20 | 20% | 6/12 | (1/2) | .50 | 50% |
| 2/5 | | .40 | 40% | 7/12 | | .5833 | 58.33% |
| 3/5 | | .60 | 60% | 8/12 | (2/3) | .6667 | 66.67% |
| 4/5 | | .80 | 80% | 9/12 | (3/4) | .75 | 75% |
| 1/6 | | .1667 | 16.67% | 10/12 | (5/6) | .8333 | 83.33% |
| 2/6 | (1/3) | .3333 | 33.33% | 11/12 | | .9167 | 91.67% |
| 3/6 | (1/2) | .50 | 50% | 1/16 | | .0625 | 6.25% |
| 4/6 | (2/3) | .6667 | 66.67% | 3/16 | | .1875 | 18.75% |
| 5/6 | | .8333 | 83.33% | 5/16 | | .3125 | 31.25% |
| 1/8 | | .125 | 12.5% | 7/16 | | .4375 | 43.75% |
| 2/8 | (1/4) | .25 | 25% | 9/16 | | .5625 | 56.25% |
| 3/8 | | .375 | 37.5% | 11/16 | | .6875 | 68.75% |
| 4/8 | (1/2) | .50 | 50% | 13/16 | | .8125 | 81.25% |
| 5/8 | | .625 | 62.5% | 15/16 | | .9375 | 93.75% |
| 6/8 | (3/4) | .75 | 75% | 1/20 | | .05 | 5% |
| 7/8 | | .875 | 87.5% | 1/25 | | .04 | 4% |

## 4-22. Determining the Percent of a Total

The percent of a total is found by dividing each part by the total.

### Percentage of Department Sales

| Dept. | Sales | Calculation | Decimal | Percent |
|-------|-------|-------------|---------|---------|
| A | $42,875 | $42.875/$122,200 | 0.351 | 35.1% |
| B | $22,900 | $22,900/$122,200 | 0.187 | 18.7% |
| C | $56,425 | $56,425/$122,200 | 0.462 | 46.2% |
| Total | $122,200 | | 1.000 | 100.0% |

## 4-23. Computing Sales Tax

Calculate sales tax by multiplying the purchase amount by the sales tax percentage. Convert the sales tax percentage to a decimal equivalent to perform the calculation.

### State and Local Sales Taxes

| Amount of Sale | Sales Tax | Calculation | Amount of Sales Tax | Total Amount |
|----------------|-----------|-------------|---------------------|--------------|
| $72.35 | 5% | $72.35 × .05 | $3.62 | $75.97 |
| $145.80 | 7½% | $145.80 × .075 | $10.94 | $156.74 |
| $890.50 | 8¼% | $890.50 × .0825 | $73.47 | $963.97 |

## 4-24. Determining Mileage Expense

Individuals using their vehicles for business purposes are usually reimbursed for the expenses they have incurred. Reimbursement often takes the form of paying the individual a set amount of money for each mile driven on the employer's behalf. This reimbursement is known as *mileage expense*.

Use the following procedures to determine mileage expense:

(1) Subtract the beginning miles from the ending miles on the odometer to obtain the total miles traveled.

(2) Multiply the total miles traveled by the amount of money (usually cents) allowed per mile.

### Mileage Expense Calculations

| Trip | Beginning Mileage | (−) Ending Mileage | (=) Total Mileage | (×) Mileage Allowance | (=) Total Expense |
|------|-------------------|--------------------|-------------------|-----------------------|-------------------|
| A | 23,481 | 23,735 | 254 | $.35 | $88.90 |
| B | 41,775 | 42,804 | 1,029 | $.28 | $288.12 |
| C | 50,099 | 53,777 | 3,678 | $.22 | $809.16 |

## 4-25. Calculating Simple Discounts

Simple discounts are often given for quantity purchases and on sale merchandise. These discounts are usually stated as a percentage decrease of a regular price.

125

Use the following procedures to calculate the dollar amount of the discount and the cost of the purchase:

(1) Convert the percent of discount to its decimal equivalent.

(2) Multiply the regular price by the decimal equivalent of the discount to obtain the discount amount.

(3) Subtract the discount amount from the regular price to find the cost of the purchase.

### Simple Discount Calculations

| Regular Price | Discount | Calculation (Decimal Equivalent) | Amount of Discount | Cost of Purchase |
|---|---|---|---|---|
| $120.40 | 30% | $120.40 × .30 | $36.12 | $84.28 |
| $885.90 | 45% | $885.90 × .45 | $398.66 | $487.25 |
| $2,570.50 | 12% | $2,570.50 × .12 | $308.46 | $2,262.04 |

## 4–26. Determining Percent of Increase or Percent of Markup

Annual sales for a year may be greater than the previous year (the base year). Owners may wish to know what percent these sales increased over the base year. Business people purchase goods at a certain price (the base price) and sell them at a higher price. These people may wish to know their percent of markup over the base price. Percent of increase and markup are the same; they are calculated identically.

Use the following procedures to calculate percent of increase and percent of markup:

(1) Subtract the base figure (sales, price, etc.) from the more recent or higher figure to obtain the difference.

(2) Divide the difference by the base figure.

(3) Convert the resulting decimal to a percentage.

### Percent of Increase

| 1998 Sales | 1997 Sales (Base Year) | Amount of Increase | Increase ÷ Base Year | Percent of Increase |
|---|---|---|---|---|
| $987,695 | $765,782 | $221,913 | 0.290 | 29.0% |
| $87,843 | $76,289 | $11,554 | 0.151 | 15.1% |
| $6,841,980 | $6,543,902 | $298,078 | 0.046 | 4.6% |

### Percent of Markup

| Selling Price | Cost (Base Price) | Amount of Markup | Markup ÷ Base Price | Percent of Markup |
|---|---|---|---|---|
| $18.98 | $12.43 | $6.55 | 0.527 | 52.7% |
| $49.99 | $25.70 | $24.29 | 0.945 | 94.5% |
| $149.50 | $62.00 | $87.50 | 1.411 | 141.1% |

## 4–27. Determining Percent of Decrease or Percent of Markdown

Annual sales for a year may be less than the previous year (the base year). Owners may wish to know what percent these sales decreased over the base year. Business people price goods at a certain price (the base price) and then later sell them at a lower price. These people may wish to know their percent of markdown over the base price. Percent of decrease and markdown are the same; they are calculated identically.

Use the following procedures to calculate percent of decrease and percent of markdown:

(1)  Subtract the base figure (sales, price, etc.) from the more recent or lower figure to obtain the difference.

(2)  Divide the difference by the base figure.

(3)  Convert the resulting decimal to a percentage.

### Percent of Decrease

| 1997 Sales (Base Year) | 1998 Sales | Amount of Decrease | Decrease ÷ Base Year | Percent of Decrease |
|---|---|---|---|---|
| $764,950 | $583,415 | $181,535 | 0.237 | 23.7% |
| $53,966 | $46,630 | $7,336 | 0.136 | 13.6% |
| $2,980,655 | $2,743,062 | $237,593 | 0.080 | 8.0% |

### Percent of Markdown

| Original Price (Base Price) | Discounted Price | Amount of Markdown | Markdown ÷ Base Price | Percent of Markdown |
|---|---|---|---|---|
| $15.98 | $10.50 | $5.48 | 0.343 | 34.3% |
| $69.99 | $49.99 | $20.00 | 0.286 | 28.6% |
| $125.00 | $109.00 | $16.00 | 0.128 | 12.8% |

## 4–28. Finding the Amount of Simple Interest

Simple interest is calculated (1) by multiplying the amount borrowed (principal) (2) by the rate of interest charged (3) by the years (time) for which the principal was borrowed. For loan periods less than a year, time is calculated on either a 365-day year (exact interest) or a 360-day year (ordinary interest).

### Simple Interest Calculations

| Amount Borrowed | Rate | Time | Calculation (Amount × Rate × Years) | Interest |
|---|---|---|---|---|
| $4,500 | 5% | 2 years | $4,500 × .05 × 2 | $450.00 |
| $12,600 | 8½% | 42 months | $12,600 × .085 × (42/12) | $3,748.50 |
| $20,200 | 12% | 90 days | $20,200 × .12 × (90/365) | $597.70 |

# Chapter 5

# Abbreviated Forms

c.o.d.

## Abbreviated Forms Solution Finder

c.o.d.

# Abbreviations

## 5–1. Use of Abbreviations

**a.** Use abbreviations only when you are confident the reader understands their meaning. Confine your primary use of abbreviations to (1) business forms; (2) suitable technical documents; and (3) tables, charts, graphs, and other such visual aids.

**b.** Limit your use of abbreviations in running copy. If used, spell out the words and place the abbreviation in parentheses the first time the words are used.

Before taking this deduction, you may wish to check with the **Internal Revenue Service (IRS)** on its legitimacy. Several recent **IRS** rulings in this area may affect your ability to use these losses as a deduction.

**c.** Use consistently throughout your document the same form for an abbreviated word or sequence of words.

Application deadlines for admittance to **California State University, Northridge (CSUN)** are due by March 1. Housing requests for **CSUN** and other state universities are due by June 1. (Not: *Cal State Northridge*)

## 5–2. Titles

**a.** The abbreviations *Mr., Ms., Mrs.,* and *Dr.* are used for courtesy titles.

| | |
|---|---|
| **Mr.** Peter Miller | **Mrs.** Carole Eustice |
| **Ms.** Frances Cates | **Dr.** James Korkosz |

**b.** Write out a civil, educational, military, or religious title used before and in conjunction with a person's full name or last name only. Lengthy titles (those containing more than one word) may be abbreviated, however, when they appear before a person's *full* name and brevity is required.

**title written out—with full name**

I believe **Professor** Sharlene Pollyea is in charge of the project.

**title written out—with last name only**

Dear **Governor** Reece:

Address the letter to the attention of **Lieutenant Governor** Miller.

**title abbreviated—with full name**

Please invite **Lt. Col.** Donald Curry to the meeting. (Lieutenant Colonel)

**c.** Abbreviate and capitalize personal titles (*Jr., Sr., Esq.,* etc.), professional designations (*CPA, CLU, R.N., R.P.T.,* etc.), or academic degrees (*M.D., Ph.D., Ed.D., LL.B., M.L.S.,* etc.) that follow a person's name. Except for *Jr.* and *Sr.,* a comma is used before and after an abbreviation appearing within a sentence and before an abbreviation appearing at the end of a sentence.

Abbreviations of academic degrees and professional designations are separated by periods except for the designations *CPA* (Certified Public Accountant), *CPS* (Certified Professional Secretary), *PLS* (Professional Legal Secretary), and *CLU* (Chartered Life Underwriter).

**personal title**

John A. Wrigley **Jr.** was elected to the Lynwood City Council.

The airline reservation is for Robert J. Brown **Sr.**

Please send a copy of the report to Robert Lucio, **Esq.,** by March 1.

**professional designation**

Cynthia Armstrong, **CPA**, was present at the meeting.

The charge nurse during that shift is Eric Blake, **R.N.**

**academic degree**

Our new college president, David Wolf, **Ph.D.,** met with the Board of Trustees yesterday.

First fill the prescriptions written by Dorothy Salazar, **M.D.**

## 5–3.   Organizations

**a.** The names of well-known business, educational, governmental, professional, military, labor, philanthropic, and other organizations or agencies may be abbreviated. No periods or spaces are used to separate the individual letters.

**business organizations**

| | |
|---|---|
| ALCOA | Aluminum Co. of America |
| ARCO | Atlantic Richfield Co. |
| BA | BankAmerica Corp. |
| GE | General Electric Co. |
| GMC | General Motors Corp. |
| IBM | International Business Machines Corp. |
| ITP | International Thomson Publishing |
| TWA | Trans World Airlines, Inc. |

**educational organizations**

| | |
|---|---|
| ERIC | Educational Resources Information Center |
| NYU | New York University |
| PCC | Pasadena City College |
| UCLA | University of California, Los Angeles |

**government organizations**

| | |
|---|---|
| CIA | Central Intelligence Agency |
| FBI | Federal Bureau of Investigation |
| FCC | Federal Communications Commission |

| | |
|---|---|
| FDA | Food and Drug Administration |
| FTC | Federal Trade Commission |
| HUD | Department of Housing and Urban Development |
| ICC | Interstate Commerce Commission |
| OSHA | Occupational Safety and Health Administration |
| SSA | Social Security Administration |
| SEC | Securities and Exchange Commission |
| UNESCO | United Nations Educational, Scientific, and Cultural Organization |
| USDA | U.S. Department of Agriculture |
| USPS | U.S. Postal Service |
| VA | Veterans Administration |

**professional organizations**

| | |
|---|---|
| ABA | American Bankers Association; American Bar Association |
| ABC | Association for Business Communication |
| AIA | American Institute of Architects |
| AIB | American Institute of Banking |
| AMA | American Medical Association |
| ARMA | Association of Record Managers and Administrators |
| NBEA | National Business Education Association |
| PSI | Professional Secretaries International |

**other organizations**

| | |
|---|---|
| AAA | American Automobile Association |
| AFL-CIO | American Federation of Labor and Congress of Industrial Organizations |
| BBB | Better Business Bureau |
| NAACP | National Association for the Advancement of Colored People |
| NOW | National Organization for Women |
| YMCA | Young Men's Christian Association |
| YWCA | Young Women's Christian Association |

b. **Television and radio station call letters are written in all capital letters without periods or spaces.**

ABC     CBS     CNN     KFI     KNXT     PBS     NBC

c. **In the names of business firms, abbreviations such as *Co., Corp., Inc., Ltd.,* and *Mfg.* are used only if they are part of the official organizational name.**

We ordered the parts from Corway **Mfg.** Co.

Johnson Products **Inc.** will receive the contract.

## 5–4.   Dates and Time

a. **Spell out days of the week and months of the year. Abbreviate them only in lists, tables, graphs, charts, illustrations, or other such visual presentations where space is limited.**

133

**days and months spelled out in text**

Our next committee meeting will be held on **Monday, January 18.**

Next **Tuesday, October 8,** will mark the company's fifth anniversary.

**days of the week abbreviated in graphics**

| Sun. | Mon. | Tues. (Tue.) | Wed. | Thurs. (Thu.) | Fri. | Sat. |
|------|------|-------------|------|---------------|------|------|
| Su | M | Tu | W | Th | F | Sa |

**months of the year abbreviated in graphics**

| Jan. | Feb. | Mar. | Apr. | May | June (Jun.) |
|------|------|------|------|-----|-------------|
| July (Jul.) | Aug. | Sept. (Sep.) | Oct. | Nov. | Dec. |

**b.** The abbreviations *a.m.* (ante meridiem) and *p.m.* (post meridiem) are used for expressing clock time. They are placed in lowercase letters followed by periods. No space follows the first period.

Would you prefer to take the flight at 8:45 **a.m.** or the one at 2 **p.m.?**

He arrived at 3:30 **p.m.**

**c.** United States time zones—*EST* (Eastern Standard Time), *CST* (Central Standard Time), *MST* (Mountain Standard Time), *PST* (Pacific Standard Time), *AST* (Alaska Standard Time), and *HST* (Hawaiian Standard Time)—are usually abbreviated. Time zones for daylight saving time are abbreviated *EDT, CDT, MDT, PDT,* and *ADT.* Hawaii does not go on daylight saving time.

Our operators are available to take your orders from 8 a.m. to 9 p.m., **EST.**

According to the latest report, his plane will arrive in Denver at 6:05 p.m., **MDT.**

**d.** The abbreviations *B.C.* (before Christ) and *A.D.* (anno Domini) are sometimes used in expressing dates. Both follow the year and are shown in capital letters with periods. In formal writing, however, *A.D.* appears before the year.

**B.C.**

Professor Farhood claims that the statue dates back to 400 **B.C.**

**after the year**

Ms. Lopez's thesis deals with the rise of Christianity from 200 to 350 **A.D.**

**before the year**

The Spanish legions, under the leadership of Galba, conquered Rome in **A.D.** 68.

**5–5. Standard Units of Measure**

Common units of measure such as distance, length, temperature, volume, and weight are usually spelled out in business documents.

Abbreviations, however, may be used on invoices, packing slips, and other business forms where space is limited. In abbreviating units of measure, place periods after one-word abbreviations and use the singular form. Omit the periods in abbreviations representing more than one word.

### general business documents

All perishable goods shipped over **100 miles** should be kept below **40 degrees** Fahrenheit.

### business forms, one-word abbreviations

**12 ft. 2 in.** (12 feet 2 inches)          **3 lb. 2 oz.** (3 pounds 2 ounces)

### business forms, multiple-word abbreviations

**80 wpm** (80 words per minute)          **65 mph** (65 miles per hour)

## 5–6.  Metric Units of Measure

**a.** In regular business documents metric units of measurement are generally written out. However, in business forms and tables and in scientific and technical writing, they are often abbreviated. These abbreviations are written without periods, and the singular and plural forms are the same. Common abbreviations for measurements related to distance, weight, and volume follow:

### prefixes

| | | | | | | |
|---|---|---|---|---|---|---|
| deka | **da** | (x 10) | | deci | **d** | (1/10) |
| hecto | **h** | (x 100) | | centi | **c** | (1/100) |
| kilo | **k** | (x 1000) | | milli | **m** | (1/1000) |
| mega | **m** | (x 1 000 000) | | | | |
| giga | **g** | (x 1 000 000 000) | | | | |

### common units of measure

| | | | | | |
|---|---|---|---|---|---|
| meter | **m** | centimeter | **cm** | kilometer | **km** |
| gram | **g** | kilogram | **kg** | milligram | **mg** |
| liter | **L** | milliliter | **ml** | | |

cubic centimeter    **cc**          square meter    **sq m**

kilobyte    **KB**          megabyte    **MB**          gigabyte    **GB**

**b.** The abbreviation for *liter* is a capital *L* because the lowercase letter "l" and the numeral "1" (one) for many fonts look the same. Therefore, to avoid confusion, the capital *L* is used instead.

**1 L** milk      *but*      **1 ml** vaccine (abbreviation is clear)

**c.** Temperatures in the metric system are expressed on the Celsius scale. This term is abbreviated *C*.

37°C          25°C

**d.** Express abbreviations relating to kilometers per hour with a diagonal.

The maximum speed permitted on this highway is **105 km/h** (65 mph).

Slow down to **40 km/h** (25 mph) in the school crossing zone.

## 5–7. Business and General Terms

**a.** When the word *number* is not followed by a numeral, spell it out. The abbreviation *No.*, however, is used when a numeral directly follows the term unless the term begins the sentence.

The stock **number** of the item you requested is **4-862**.

We plan to discontinue stocking these **No. 1370** metal plates.

Please ship us three **Model No. 17A** electric motors.

**Number 18-A** replacement shelves are no longer stocked in our warehouse.

**b.** Most commonly abbreviated business and computer terms are typed in all capital letters with no spaces or periods separating the letters. A few business terms, when used in business correspondence, however, are written in lowercase letters separated by periods. See Section 5-11 for an additional listing of business and computer terms.

**capitalized abbreviation of business term**

PERT   (program evaluation and review technique)
GDP   (gross domestic product)
LIFO   (last in, first out)
FIFO   (first in, first out)
SOP   (standard operating procedures)

**capitalized abbreviation of computer term**

RAM   (random-access memory)
CPU   (central processing unit)
CRT   (cathode-ray tube)
EDP   (electronic data processing)
OCR   (optical character recognition)

**lowercase letters for abbreviation in correspondence**

c.o.d.   (collect on delivery)
f.o.b.   (free on board)

**c.** Capitalize and abbreviate the word *extension* (*Ext.*) when it appears in conjunction with telephone numbers.

You may reach me at 987-9281, **Ext.** 1201, any weekday between 10 and 11 a.m.

Please call me collect at (714) 555-3827, **Ext.** 248.

**d.** Some commonly abbreviated terms are derived from Latin expressions. They are generally typed in lowercase letters and are followed by a period at the close of each abbreviated word.

**abbreviations from Latin expressions**

| | | | |
|---|---|---|---|
| e.g. | (for example) | viz. | (namely) |
| et al. | (and others) | ibid. | (in the same place) |
| i.e. | (that is) | loc. cit. | (in the place cited) |
| etc. | (and so forth) | op. cit. | (in the work cited) |
| cf. | (compare) | a.m. | (after midnight until noon) |
| pro tem. | (temporarily) | p.m. | (after noon until midnight |
| id. | (the same) | B.C. | (year before Christ) |
| P.S. | (postscript) | A.D. | (year after Christ) |
| N.B. | (note well) | ca. | (approximately; around) |

## 5–8. Plurals

Apostrophes are not used to form the plurals of abbreviations; most plural abbreviations are formed by adding only *s* to the singular form. Some words, however, use the same abbreviation for the singular and plural forms.

**plural formed by adding *s***

hr., **hrs.**          IOU, **IOUs**

mgr., **mgrs.**        CPA, **CPAs**

c.o.d., **c.o.d.s**    R.N., **R.N.s**

**singular and plural forms identical**

deg., **deg.**       ft., **ft.**       in., **in.**

## 5–9. Addresses and Geographical Expressions

**a.** For addresses in business correspondence, street designations such as *Boulevard, Street, Avenue, Lane, Place,* and *Road* are spelled out. *Boulevard,* however, may be abbreviated (*Blvd.*) if space is limited for expressing long street names.

**street designation spelled out**

Ms. Lila Green
462 Olive **Avenue**
Iowa City, IA 52240

Woodcutt Escrow Company
5700 Jefferson **Boulevard**
Columbus, OH 43266-0309

c.o.d.

Abbreviations

5

**Boulevard abbreviated with long street name**

Mr. James F. Campenelli
1873 San Fernando Mission **Blvd.**
San Francisco, CA 94127

b. Terms indicating direction (*North, South, East, West*) that precede a street name are spelled out. Compound directions such as *N.W. (Northwest)*, however, are abbreviated when they are used before or after the street name.

**simple direction before street name**

851 **East** Lake Street

**compound direction with street name**

7059 Capitol Avenue, **N.E.**          4411 **S.W.** 34th Street

c. The U.S. Postal Service recommends that the names of states be abbreviated on all mailings by using the official state designations. (They are typed in capital letters with no periods or spaces.) These two-letter state designations are shown in Section 5-12 and on the page opposite the inside back cover.

However, since modern optical scanning equipment no longer requires the use of the two-letter designations, either the full state name or the two-letter state designation may be used, depending on which form more nearly balances with the other lines of the address. If both forms provide balance, use the two-letter state designation.

**zip code designation**

Mrs. Marjory Clark, PLS
Los Angeles Pierce College
6201 Winnetka Avenue
Woodland Hills, **CA** 91371

**state spelled out fully**

Fielder Publishing Company
9836 West Seventh Avenue
Ridgewood, **New Jersey** 07541

d. Since 1974 the U.S. Postal Service has recommended a format for addressing envelopes that uses all capital letters, abbreviations, and no internal punctuation marks. As yet, this format has not been widely accepted for individually typed correspondence or even computer-generated form correspondence; its use has been mainly with standard bulk mailings. This format is described fully in Section 10-29.

e. A period is placed after each abbreviated word in geographical abbreviations. Only with the two-letter state designations recommended by the U.S. Postal Service are the periods omitted.

**capital letters**

| U.S.A. | (United States of America) | U.K. | (United Kingdom) |
|--------|---------------------------|------|------------------|
| U.A.R. | (United Arab Republic) | G.B. | (Great Britain) |

**capital and lowercase letters**

So. Nev.   (Southern Nevada)              Ire.   (Ireland)

**postal service designation**

MT   (Montana)                            IA   (Iowa)

## 5–10.   Abbreviation Format

**a.**   The capitalization of abbreviations is generally governed by the format of the original word or words. Proper nouns are always capitalized while common nouns generally appear in lowercase letters. Some common noun abbreviations, however, are capitalized.

**capital letters for proper noun**

His father is a member of the **AFL-CIO**.

**lowercase letters for common noun**

Please send the order **c.o.d.**

**capital letters for some common nouns**

How many **VCRs** did our sales staff sell during the holiday season?

Be sure to ask the **TV** repair service to send the bill to our home office.

**b.**   Abbreviations that appear in all capital letters are generally typed without periods or spaces. Exceptions are (1) geographical expressions, most professional designations, and academic degrees, which are typed with periods but no spaces and (2) initials in a person's name and most abbreviations containing capital and lowercase letters, which are typed with both periods and spaces.

**general rule—no periods and no spaces**

We heard the news from an **NBC** reporter.

Be sure to turn your dial to **KBIG** for beautiful music.

**geographical expressions—periods with no spaces**

Their travel agency in Bonn sponsored several tours of the **U.S.A.** last summer.

Please submit these completed forms to the **U.S.** Department of Agriculture.

Our new store location is 800 Tufts Avenue, **S.W.**

**professional designations—periods with no spaces**

Jodi Myers, **R.P.T.**, is the physical therapist who is handling this case.

Will Robert Soto, **R.N.**, be the new director of our nursing program?

**academic degrees—periods with no spaces**

Mr. Fujimoto earned an **M.A.** in music last June.

Sharon Lund O'Neil, **Ph.D.**, was offered the position.

**initials—periods and spaces**

Please deliver this report to Ms. **J. T.** Kelley.

Only Gerald **H.** Monroe applied for the position.

**abbreviations with capital and lowercase letters—periods and spaces**

So. Calif.   (Southern California)          N. Mex.   (New Mexico)

c.  In abbreviations beginning with lowercase letters, a period is generally placed after each letter or group of letters representing a word. No space appears between periods and letters in compound abbreviations. Periods are not used, however, in abbreviations of metric measurements and compound abbreviations representing "measures per time."

**general rule—periods**

| | | | |
|---|---|---|---|
| c.o.d. | (collect on delivery) | mgr. | (manager) |
| a.m. | (ante meridiem) | qt. | (quart) |
| ft. | (foot or feet) | amt. | (amount) |

**metric measurements—no periods**

| | | | |
|---|---|---|---|
| mm | millimeter | ml | milliliter |
| cm | centimeter | kg | kilogram |
| cc | cubic centimeter | | |

**time measurements—no periods**

| | | | |
|---|---|---|---|
| rpm | revolutions per minute | wam | words a minute |
| wpm | words per minute | mph | miles per hour |

d.  If an abbreviation containing a period falls at the end of a sentence that requires a period, use only a single period. In a question or an exclamation, place a closing question or exclamation mark directly after the period appearing in the abbreviation.

**period**

The hotel clerk awakened Mr. Sykiski at **8 a.m.**

**question mark**

Did you send the order **c.o.d.?**

**exclamation mark**

The plane was three hours late arriving in the **U.S.A.!**

## 5-11. Abbreviations of Terms Commonly Used in Business

| Abbreviation | Term |
|---|---|
| A.A. | associate in arts (degree) |
| acct. | account |
| A.D. | anno Domini (in the year of our Lord) |
| ad, advt. | advertisement |
| ADT | Alaska Daylight Time |
| addl., add'l | additional |
| Adm. | admiral (military title) |
| adm., admin. | administration, administrative |
| afft. | affidavit |
| agcy. | agency |
| agt. | agent |
| AI | artificial intelligence |
| a.k.a., AKA | also known as |
| a.m. | ante meridiem (before noon) |
| amt. | amount |
| ans. | answer |
| AP | accounts payable |
| approx. | approximately |
| APR | annual percentage rate (of interest) |
| Apr. | April |
| AR | accounts receivable |
| ARM | adjustable rate mortgage |
| A.S. | associate in science (degree) |
| ASAP | as soon as possible |
| ASCII | American Standard Code for Information Interchange |
| assoc., Assoc. | associate, associates |
| assn., Assn., assoc., Assoc. | association |
| asst., ass't. | assistant |
| AST | Alaska Standard Time |
| ATM | automated teller machine |
| att. | attachment |
| attn. | attention |
| atty. | attorney |
| Aug. | August |
| AV | audiovisual |
| av., avg. | average |
| ave. | avenue |
| B.A., A.B. | bachelor of arts (degree) |
| bal. | balance |
| B.B.A. | bachelor of business administration (degree) |
| bbl. | barrel, barrels |
| B.C. | before Christ |
| BIOS | basic input-output system |
| bit | binary digit |
| bl. | bale, bales |
| B/L, BL | bill of lading |

c.o.d.

Abbreviations

5

| Abbreviation | Term |
| --- | --- |
| bldg. | building |
| BO | back order |
| bps | bits per second |
| bros., Bros. | brothers |
| B.S. | bachelor of science (degree) |
| B/S, BS | bill of sale |
| bu. | bushel, bushels |
| c | copy |
| C | Celsius |
| CAD/CAM | computer-aided drafting/computer-aided manufacturing |
| CAI | computer-aided instruction |
| cap. | capital |
| Capt. | captain |
| CAT | computer-aided transcription |
| cc | cubic centimeter |
| cc, CC | carbon copy, courtesy copy |
| CD | certificate of deposit |
| CD-ROM | compact disk read-only memory |
| CDT | Central Daylight Time |
| CEO | chief executive officer |
| CFO | chief financial officer |
| cg | centigram |
| CGA | color graphics adapter |
| chg. | charge |
| c.i.f., CIF | cost, insurance, and freight |
| CLU | Certified Life Underwriter |
| cm | centimeter |
| c/o | care of |
| co., Co. | company |
| COBOL | Common Business Oriented Language |
| c.o.d., COD | collect on delivery |
| Col. | colonel (military title) |
| COLA | cost-of-living adjustment |
| COM | computer output microfilm |
| comm. | commission |
| cont. | continued |
| COO | chief operating officer |
| corp., Corp. | corporation |
| CPA | Certified Public Accountant |
| cpi | characters per inch |
| cps | characters per second |
| CPS | Certified Professional Secretary |
| CPU | central processing unit |
| cr. | credit |
| CRT | cathode-ray tube |
| CST | Central Standard Time |
| ctn. | carton |
| cu. | cubic |
| cwt. | hundredweight |

c.o.d.

| Abbreviation | Term |
|---|---|
| D.A. | doctor of arts (degree) |
| D.B.A. | doctor of business administration (degree) |
| d.b.a., DBA | doing business as |
| DBMS | data base management system |
| D.D. | doctor of divinity (degree) |
| D.D.S. | doctor of dental surgery (degree) |
| Dec. | December |
| depr. | depreciation |
| dept. | department |
| disc., dis. | discount |
| dist. | district |
| distr. | distributed, distribution, distributor |
| div. | dividend; division |
| DJIA | Dow Jones Industrial Average |
| DOS | disk operating system |
| doz., dz. | dozen |
| DP | data processing |
| dpi | dots per inch |
| dr. | debit |
| dr. | dram, drams |
| Dr., Drs. | doctor, doctors |
| DSS | decision support system |
| DST | daylight saving time |
| dstn. | destination |
| dtd. | dated |
| DTP | desktop publishing |
| dup. | duplicate |
| D.V.M. | doctor of veterinary medicine (degree) |
| ea. | each |
| ed. | editor |
| Ed.D. | doctor of education (degree) |
| EDP | electronic data processing |
| EDT | Eastern Daylight Time |
| e.g. | for example |
| EGA | enhanced graphics adapter |
| enc., encl. | enclosure |
| EOF | end of file |
| e.o.m., EOM | end of month |
| Esq. | Esquire |
| EST | Eastern Standard Time |
| ETA | estimated time of arrival |
| exp. | expense |
| ext., Ext. | extension |
| F | Fahrenheit |
| f.a.s., FAS | free alongside ship |
| FAQ, FAQs | frequently asked question(s) |
| fax | facsimile |
| f.b.o., FBO | for the benefit of |
| Feb. | February |
| FIFO | first in, first out (inventory) |

c.o.d.

Abbreviations

5

c.o.d.

| Abbreviation | Term |
| --- | --- |
| f.o.b., FOB | free on board |
| FORTRAN | FORmula TRANslator |
| Fri. | Friday |
| frt. | freight |
| ft. | foot, feet |
| ft-tn | foot-ton, foot-tons |
| fwd. | forward |
| FY | fiscal year |
| FYI | for your information |
| g | gram |
| gal. | gallon, gallons |
| GB | gigabyte (billion bytes) |
| GDP | gross domestic product |
| gen. | general |
| Gen. | general (military title) |
| GIGO | garbage in, garbage out |
| GM | general manager |
| gr. | gross |
| GUI | graphical user interface |
| hdlg. | handling |
| HMO | health maintenance organization |
| HP, hp | horsepower |
| HQ, hdqrs. | headquarters |
| hr., hrs. | hour, hours |
| HST | Hawaii Standard Time |
| ID | identification data |
| i.e. | id est (that is) |
| in. | inch, inches |
| inc., Inc. | incorporated |
| incl. | includes, including |
| info | information |
| ins. | insurance |
| int. | interest |
| intl., intnl. | international |
| inv. | invoice |
| invt. | inventory |
| I/O | input/output |
| IOU | I owe you |
| ips | inches per second |
| IQ | intelligence quotient |
| IRA | individual retirement account |
| Jan. | January |
| J.D. | doctor of jurisprudence, doctor of law (degrees) |
| K | thousand (in reference to computer disk or memory) |
| K, KB | kilobyte(s) (thousand bytes) |
| kg | kilogram, kilograms |
| km | kilometer, kilometers |
| km/h | kilometers per hour |
| L | liter |

| Abbreviation | Term |
|---|---|
| l., ll. | line, lines |
| LAN | local area network |
| laser | light amplification stimulated emission radiation |
| lb. | pound, pounds |
| L/C | Letter of Credit |
| l.c.l., LCL | less-than-carload lot |
| LIFO | last in, first out (inventory) |
| LL.B. | bachelor of laws (degree) |
| lpm | lines per minute |
| Lt. | lieutenant |
| ltd., Ltd. | limited |
| m | meter |
| M.A. | master of arts (degree) |
| Maj. | major (military rank) |
| Mar. | March |
| max. | maximum |
| MB, M | megabyte, megabytes (million bytes) |
| M.B.A. | master of business administration (degree) |
| MC (represents emcee) | master of ceremonies, mistress of ceremonies |
| M.D. | doctor of medicine (degree) |
| mdse. | merchandise |
| MDT | Mountain Daylight Time |
| memo | memorandum |
| Messrs. | Misters |
| mfg., Mfg. | manufacturing |
| mfr., mfrs. | manufacturer, manufacturers |
| mg | milligram, milligrams |
| mgmt. | management |
| mgr. | manager |
| MHz | megahertz |
| mi. | mile, miles |
| min. | minute, minutes; minumum |
| MIS | management information system |
| misc. | miscellaneous |
| ml | milliliter, milliliters |
| mm | millimeter, millimeters |
| MO | mail order |
| MO | money order |
| mo., mos. | month, months |
| modem | modulator/demodulator |
| Mon. | Monday |
| M.P.A. | master of public administration (degree) |
| mpg | miles per gallon |
| M.P.H. | master of public health (degree) |
| mph | miles per hour |
| Mr. | Mister |
| Mrs. | Mistress |
| M.S. | master of science (degree) |
| MST | Mountain Standard Time |

c.o.d.

Abbreviations

5

| Abbreviation | Term |
| --- | --- |
| M.S.W. | master of social work (degree) |
| n/30 | net in 30 days |
| NA | not applicable; not available |
| ND | no date |
| No., Nos. | number, numbers |
| Nov. | November |
| NSF | not sufficient funds |
| nt. wt. | net weight |
| OC | overcharge |
| OCR | optical character recognition |
| Oct. | October |
| o.d., OD | overdraft |
| OAG | *Official Airline Guide* |
| OK | okay |
| opt. | optional |
| org. | organization |
| orig. | original |
| O/S | out of stock |
| OS | operating system (computer) |
| OTC | over-the-counter |
| oz. | ounce, ounces |
| p., pp. | page, pages |
| PABX | private automatic branch exchange |
| PBX | private branch exchange |
| PC | personal computer |
| pd. | paid |
| PDT | Pacific Daylight Time |
| PERT | program evaluation and review technique |
| p and h, P/H | postage and handling |
| Ph.D. | doctor of philosophy (degree) |
| phone | telephone |
| photo | photograph |
| PIN | personal identification number |
| pkg. | package |
| P & L, P/L | profit and loss |
| p.m. | post meridiem  (after noon) |
| P.O. | post office |
| P.O., PO | purchase order |
| p.o.e., POE | port of entry |
| ppd. | postpaid, prepaid |
| PR | public relations |
| pr., prs. | pair, pairs |
| pres. | president |
| PROM | programmable read-only memory |
| P.S., PS | postscript |
| PST | Pacific Standard Time |
| pt. | part; pint, pints |
| pt., pts. | point, points |
| qr. | quire, quires |
| qt. | quart, quarts |

c.o.d.

| Abbreviation | Term |
|---|---|
| qtr. | quarter, quarterly |
| qty. | quantity |
| RAM | random-access memory |
| R & D | research and development |
| recd. | received |
| reg. | registered; regular |
| req. | requisition |
| ret. | retail; retired |
| retd. | returned |
| rev. | revised, revision |
| RFD | rural free delivery |
| rm. | ream, reams |
| ROM | read-only memory |
| rpm, RPM | revolutions per minute |
| R.S.V.P., RSVP | respond, if you please |
| rwy., ry. | railway |
| /S/ | signed by |
| SASE | self-addressed, stamped envelope |
| Sat. | Saturday |
| scuba | self-contained underwater breathing apparatus |
| sec. | second, seconds |
| sec., secy., sec'y | secretary |
| sect. | section |
| Sept., Sep. | September |
| Sgt. | sergeant |
| shpt. | shipment |
| shtg. | shortage |
| S.O., SO | shipping order |
| SOP | standard operating procedure |
| sq. | square |
| std. | standard |
| stge. | storage |
| stmt. | statement |
| Sun. | Sunday |
| Thurs., Thu. | Thursday |
| TQM | total quality management |
| treas. | treasurer |
| Tues., Tue. | Tuesday |
| TV | television |
| TWX | Western Union Teleprinter Exchange Service |
| UPC | Universal Product Code |
| VAT | value-added tax |
| VCR | video cassette recorder |
| VDT | video display terminal |
| VGA | video graphics array |
| VIP | very important person |
| vol. | volume |
| V.P. | vice president |
| vs., v. | versus |
| wam | words a minute |

c.o.d.

Abbreviations

5

| Abbreviation | Term |
|---|---|
| WAN | wide area network |
| WATS | Wide Area Telephone Service |
| Wed. | Wednesday |
| whsle. | wholesale |
| wk., wks. | week, weeks |
| w/o | without |
| wp | word processing |
| wpm | words per minute |
| wt. | weight |
| WWW | World Wide Web |
| WYSIWYG | What you see is what you get. |
| yd. | yard, yards |
| yr., yrs. | year, years |
| zip, ZIP | Zone Improvement Plan |

## 5–12. Abbreviations of States and Territories

| State or Territory | Two-Letter Postal Designation | Standard Abbreviation |
|---|---|---|
| Alabama | AL | Ala. |
| Alaska | AK | — |
| Arizona | AZ | Ariz. |
| Arkansas | AR | Ark. |
| California | CA | Calif., Cal. |
| Canal Zone | CZ | C.Z. |
| Colorado | CO | Colo., Col. |
| Connecticut | CT | Conn. |
| Delaware | DE | Del. |
| District of Columbia | DC | D.C. |
| Florida | FL | Fla. |
| Georgia | GA | Ga. |
| Guam | GU | — |
| Hawaii | HI | — |
| Idaho | ID | — |
| Illinois | IL | Ill. |
| Indiana | IN | Ind. |
| Iowa | IA | — |
| Kansas | KS | Kans., Kan. |
| Kentucky | KY | Ky. |
| Louisiana | LA | La. |
| Maine | ME | — |
| Maryland | MD | Md. |
| Massachusetts | MA | Mass. |
| Michigan | MI | Mich. |
| Minnesota | MN | Minn. |
| Mississippi | MS | Miss. |
| Missouri | MO | Mo. |
| Montana | MT | Mont. |

c.o.d.

| State or Territory | Two-Letter Postal Designation | Standard Abbreviation |
|---|---|---|
| Nebraska | NE | Nebr., Neb. |
| Nevada | NV | Nev. |
| New Hampshire | NH | N.H. |
| New Jersey | NJ | N.J. |
| New Mexico | NM | N. Mex. |
| New York | NY | N.Y. |
| North Carolina | NC | N.C. |
| North Dakota | ND | N. Dak. |
| Ohio | OH | — |
| Oklahoma | OK | Okla. |
| Oregon | OR | Oreg., Ore. |
| Pennsylvania | PA | Pa., Penn., Penna. |
| Puerto Rico | PR | P.R. |
| Rhode Island | RI | R.I. |
| South Carolina | SC | S.C. |
| South Dakota | SD | S. Dak. |
| Tennessee | TN | Tenn. |
| Texas | TX | Tex. |
| Utah | UT | — |
| Vermont | VT | Vt. |
| Virgin Islands | VI | V.I. |
| Virginia | VA | Va. |
| Washington | WA | Wash. |
| West Virginia | WV | W. Va. |
| Wisconsin | WI | Wis., Wisc. |
| Wyoming | WY | Wyo. |

## 5–13. Two-Letter Postal Designations for Canadian Provinces

| Canadian Province | Designation |
|---|---|
| Alberta | AB |
| British Columbia | BC |
| Labrador | LB |
| Manitoba | MB |
| New Brunswick | NB |
| Newfoundland | NF |
| Northwest Territories | NT |
| Nova Scotia | NS |
| Ontario | ON |
| Prince Edward Island | PE |
| Quebec | PQ |
| Saskatchewan | SK |
| Yukon Territory | YT |

c.o.d.

Abbreviations

5

# Contractions

### 5–14. Contractions

a. Contractions are similar to abbreviations in that they are shortened forms. Unlike most abbreviations, however, contractions always contain an apostrophe to indicate where letters have been omitted. The use of single-word contractions is generally limited to business forms and tables. Some common single-word contractions follow:

| | | | |
|---|---|---|---|
| ack'd | (acknowledged) | rec't | (receipt) |
| ass't | (assistant) | sec'y | (secretary) |
| gov't | (government) | cont'd | (continued) |
| nat'l | (national) | '99 | (1999) |

b. A second kind of contraction occurs with verb forms. By using an apostrophe to indicate where letters have been omitted, two words may be combined into one. The use of verb contractions is generally limited to informal business writing. A sampling of commonly used verb contractions follows:

| | | | |
|---|---|---|---|
| aren't | (are not) | weren't | (were not) |
| shouldn't | (should not) | I'll | (I will) |
| can't | (cannot) | what's | (what is) |
| should've | (should have) | I'm | (I am) |
| couldn't | (could not) | where's | (where is) |
| that's | (that is) | isn't | (is not) |
| didn't | (did not) | who's | (who is) |
| there's | (there is) | it's | (it is) |
| doesn't | (does not) | won't | (will not) |
| they're | (they are) | I've | (I have) |
| don't | (do not) | wouldn't | (would not) |
| wasn't | (was not) | let's | (let us) |
| hasn't | (has not) | you'd | (you would) |
| we'll | (we will) | she's | (she is) |
| haven't | (have not) | you're | (you are) |
| we're | (we are) | you've | (you have) |
| he's | (he is) | | |

# Symbols

### 5–15. Symbols on the Standard Computer Keyboard

a. Except for the dollar sign ($) in amounts of money, the asterisk (*) in unnumbered footnotes, and the ampersand (&) in company names, avoid using symbols in running copy. Limit the use of symbols to business forms, statistical material, tables, charts, graphs, and other documents or visuals where space is limited.

**dollar sign, asterisk, and ampersand in running copy**

Unauthorized charges of **$247.56**, **$153.29**, and **$73.20** appeared on our last month's credit card statement.

Use only **ASCII\*** characters to prepare your résumé for any on-line career centers.

We have retained **Leavitt, Kahn & Moss** to handle this legal matter for our firm.

**symbols in forms, statistical materials, and visuals**

3 @ $6.80     #507     23#     82%     5'2" tall     3:1

**b.** Use standard keys on the computer keyboard for the following commonly used symbols:

| Symbol | Description | Examples |
|---|---|---|
| / | abbreviated word separator | c/o, w/o |
| & | and (ampersand) | Johnson & Sons, Inc., AT&T |
| @ | at, each | 50 @ $39.95 |
| " | ditto, same as (quotation marks) | 30 unformatted floppy disks 40 IBM formatted  "    " |
| / | divided by (diagonal) | May Sales/Annual Sales, $4,500/3 |
| $ | dollar, dollars | $1,593.62 |
| = | equals | Price +Tax = Cost |
| ' | foot/feet (apostrophe) | 12' x 15' room, 5' 9" tall |
| / | fraction separator (diagonal) | 1/2, 2/3, 3/4 |
| > | greater than | 100 > 90 |
| " | inch/inches (quotation marks) | 8 1/2" x 11" paper |
| < | less than | 90 < 100 |
| ' | minute, minutes (apostrophe) | 60' sessions |
| − | minus | Price − Discount, 75 − 50 |
| × | multiplied by, by | 12 × 12 = 144, 4 × 6 card |
| * | multiplied by (asterisk) | 12 * 12 = 144 |
| # | number | #678452,  #3 pencil |
| % | percent | 43.5% |
| + | plus | Principal  +  Interest, 8 + 4 |
| # | pound, pounds | 24# paper |
| : | ratio (colon) | 3:1 ratio |
| " | second, seconds (quotation marks) | 5" intervals |
| * | unnumbered footnote (asterisk) | . . . for diacritical marks.* |
| / | word separator (diagonal) | and/or |

c.o.d.

Abbreviations

5

## 5–16. Symbols Not on the Standard Computer Keyboard

Many commonly used symbols do not appear on the standard computer keyboard. Contemporary word processing programs, though, have extended character sets and provide access to many of these symbols. With just a few keystrokes or mouse movements, you can access the following symbols:

| Symbol | Description | Examples |
|---|---|---|
| ¢ | cents | 85¢ |
| © | copyright | Copyright © 1998 by South-Western College Publishing |
| ° | degree, degrees | 72° |
| ÷ | divided by | 144 ÷ 12 = 12 |
| ≥ | greater than or equal to | x ≥ 10 |
| ≤ | less than or equal to | x ≤ 12 |
| é | letter with diacritical mark | résumé, La Cañada, Fraülein |
| ∓ | minus or plus | ∓ 4 |
| ¶ | paragraph, paragraphs | ¶23, ¶¶123–132 |
| ‖ | parallel to | Main Street ‖ Hill Street |
| ± | plus or minus | ± $2 |
| ® | registered | Kinko's®, Pentium® |
| § | section, sections | §12, §§56–59 |
| SM | service mark | The new way to office.SM |
| $\sqrt{\ }$ | square root | $\sqrt{4}$ = 2 |
| TM | trademark | The Computer Inside.TM |

# Grammar and Usage

noun

## Grammar and Usage Solution Finder

noun

## Grammar and Usage Solution Finder (*continued*)

noun

Grammar

6

# Sentences

## 6–1. Complete Sentences

**a.** Use complete sentences to express your ideas. A complete sentence (1) contains a verb (a word showing action or describing a condition), (2) has a subject (a noun or pronoun that interacts with the verb), and (3) makes sense (comes to a closure). A complete sentence is an independent clause.

Verbs appear by themselves or in a verb phrase. The last verb in a verb phrase is considered the main verb.

Subjects are either simple or compound. *Simple subjects* consist of a single noun or pronoun whereas *compound subjects* contain two or more nouns or pronouns linked by *and, or,* or *nor.*

### statements

(simple subject)
Last week several **employees** in our Production Department
  (verb)
**increased** their standard output by 10 percent.  (Makes sense)

(compound subject)                                                (verb phrase)
**Karen and Richard,** as a result of their hard work, **have been promoted** to senior analysts.  (Makes sense)

         (subject)                          (verb)
This latest **manuscript** by Kym Freeman **is** excellent.  (Makes sense)

### questions

When **may I expect** your reply?  (Simple subject, *I;* verb phrase, *may expect;* makes sense)

How many **members** of your staff **plan** to attend the convention? (Simple subject, *members;* verb, *plan;* makes sense)

### requests or commands

Please **return** the questionnaire by March 31.  (Simple subject, the word *you* understood; verb, *return;* makes sense)

**Do** not **litter** in the parks or on the highways.  (Simple subject, the word *you* understood; verb, *do* (not = adverb) *litter;* makes sense)

**b.** Simple sentences consist of a single independent clause that contains a subject and a verb or verb phrase. They express only one complete thought.

The **manager** of our Springfield branch **has been** in our employ for over ten years.  (Simple subject, *manager;* verb phrase, *has been*)

**Partnerships and corporations** in this state **are** not eligible for this tax deduction.  (Compound subject, *partnerships and corporations;* verb, *are*)

**c.** Compound sentences contain two independent clauses (each with a subject and a verb or verb phrase) that are usually separated by a coordinating conjunction—*and, but, or,* or *nor.*

Our regional **representative will call** on you next week, **and she will demonstrate** our new line of Creation III cosmetics. (Simple subjects, *representative* and *she*; verb phrases, *will call* and *will demonstrate*; coordinating conjunction, *and*)

**Neither** of our vice presidents **is** in the office this week, **but** our **general manager** for East Coast operations **will be able** to answer your questions. (Subjects, *neither* and *general manager*; verb and verb phrase, *is* and *will be able*; coordinating conjunction, *but*)

d. Other compound sentences contain two independent clauses (each with a subject and a verb or verb phrase) that are joined by either (1) a semicolon or (2) a semicolon combined with a transitional expression such as *therefore, however, nevertheless, for example*, or *of course*.

### joined by a semicolon

The **loan** on your home **has been transferred** to Certified Home Mortgage Corporation; **you should receive** a new payment booklet from Certified within the next ten days. (Simple subjects, *loan* and *you*; verb phrases, *has been transferred* and *should receive*)

### joined by a semicolon and a transitional expression

**Professors and administrators** at our college **are covered** under the same retirement program; **therefore, administrators** also **are** eligible for retirement at age 55. (Compound and simple subjects, *professors and administrators* and *administrators*; verb phrase and verb, *are covered* and *are*; transitional expression, *therefore*)

e. Complex sentences include an independent clause and a dependent clause, each of which contains both a subject and a verb or verb phrase. The independent clause can stand alone as a complete sentence because it makes sense, but the dependent clause cannot.

Dependent clauses begin with (1) relative pronouns such as *who, whom, that*, or *which* or (2) subordinating conjunctions such as *if, when, as, since, because, although, while,* and *whereas*. The dependent clause may begin, interrupt, or conclude the sentence.

### complex sentence with a relative pronoun clause

Mr. Johnson asked me **who won the grand prize in our drawing**.

None of the people **whom we interviewed** were willing to accept the position at the salary offered.

The book **that you recommended** is no longer available in our bookstore.

Michael is habitually absent, **which may be the reason for his dismissal**.

### complex sentence with a subordinating conjunction

**As soon as we receive your check**, we will begin processing your application.

In the future you may, **if you wish,** send all your orders directly to our Springfield office.

Our sales have increased substantially **since the new advertising campaign began.**

**f.** **Compound-complex sentences contain two independent clauses and one dependent clause.**

We are discontinuing our present line of mattresses **because deliveries from the manufacturer have been slow in reaching our customers,** but we expect to replace this line with one of equal or better quality.

We received nearly thirty applications for this opening; but **after I read all the résumés,** I realized that not one of the candidates was qualified for the position.

## 6–2.   Sentence Fragments

**a.** **Use only sentence fragments that *represent* a complete thought. Such usages should be confined to informal business writing.**

And now to the point.

If only I had known!

What a relief!

**b.** **For the most part, use concluding punctuation marks (periods, question marks, and exclamation marks) only after complete sentences. Avoid these marks after sentence fragments except in those instances in informal writing where the fragment represents a complete thought (Section 6-2a).**

Not: **In the near future.**
But: **In the near future** we will expand our operations.

Not: **Although the present contract has expired.**
But: **Although the present contract has expired,** both management and union are governed by its provisions until a new contract is negotiated.

Not: **The biggest money-saving event of the year.**
But: We look forward to seeing you at our annual clearance sale, **the biggest money-saving event of the year.**

# Nouns[1]

## 6–3.   Nouns

**a.** **Nouns are words that name something—for example, persons, animals, places, things, objects, time, feelings, qualities, actions, concepts, measures, and states of being.**

---

[1]The rules and spellings in this chapter are based on *Merriam Webster's Collegiate Dictionary*, 10th Ed. (Springfield, Mass.: Merriam-Webster, Incorporated, 1996).

### person

Please have your **attorney** call me.

Did you refer this **client** to me?

### animal

We have been interested in purchasing another **horse**.

This **fish** is too old to eat.

### place

The new **park** will be located in our **suburb**.

When will you visit our **city**?

### thing

All this **information** is stored on our **network**.

Have the **company** and the **union** reached an **agreement**?

### object

Did you find your **purse**?

Place the **computer** on this **table**.

### time

We signed the contract **yesterday**, and it will become effective in 30 **days**.

The balloon payment is due next **month**.

### feeling

Everyone in the room detected his **anger** as he spoke.

We can certainly sympathize with his **sorrow** and **grief**.

### quality

I appreciate your **thoughtfulness** and **generosity**.

Such **irresponsibility** cannot be tolerated.

### action

Do you enjoy **swimming**?

**Golfing** is an individual sport.

### concept

Our country was founded on **freedom** of **expression**.

Please report any **progress** you have made.

### measure

Our company's assets total nearly **$23 million**.

Three **yards** of fabric will be needed for each chair.

**state of being**

Her **illness** has not yet been properly diagnosed.

**Complacency** in this rapidly changing industry could easily lead to **bankruptcy.**

b. Any noun that names a particular entity is capitalized. These capitalized nouns are known as *proper nouns*. Nouns that do not name specific entities are known as *common nouns*, and they are not capitalized.

**proper nouns**

Last month the **Columbus City Council** approved a 4 percent increase in property taxes.

Repairs on the **Golden Gate Bridge** are still in progress.

We must make a decision by **December** 1.

Much of this information is available through the **Internet.**

**common nouns**

Last month the **city council** approved a 4 percent increase in property taxes.

Repairs on the **bridge** are still in progress.

We must make a decision by the **1st** of next **month.**

Much of this information is available through on-line network **resources.**

c. Although most common nouns consist of single words, many contain two or even three words. These *compound nouns* appear as regular entries in the dictionary and are defined as nouns. Some are hyphenated, but most are separate words without hyphens (*open compounds*).

**hyphenated compound nouns**

This business is operated by the mayor's **brother-in-law.**

The **vice-chancellor** must approve all faculty appointments.

**open compound nouns**

Please have the **vice president** sign this purchase order.

Our local **high school** is sponsoring this event.

## 6–4. Noun Plurals[2]

a. Most nouns form their plurals by adding *s*. However, nouns ending in *s*, *sh*, *ch*, *x*, or *z* form their plurals by adding *es*.

---

[2]Noun plurals, other than those regular ones ending in *s* or *es*, are shown in the dictionary immediately after the singular form of the word.

### nouns adding *s*

| | | | |
|---|---|---|---|
| account | accounts | executive | executives |
| letter | letters | message | messages |

### nouns adding *es*

| | | | |
|---|---|---|---|
| bus | buses | branch | branches |
| business | businesses | tax | taxes |
| wish | wishes | waltz | waltzes |

**b.** Common nouns ending in *y* form the plural in one of two ways. If the letter preceding the *y* is a vowel, just add *s*. However, if the letter preceding the *y* is a consonant, drop the *y* and add *ies*.

### *y* preceded by a vowel

| | | | |
|---|---|---|---|
| attorney | attorneys | money | moneys |
| delay | delays | valley | valleys |

### *y* preceded by a consonant

| | | | |
|---|---|---|---|
| company | companies | reply | replies |
| policy | policies | secretary | secretaries |

**c.** Musical terms ending in *o* form the plural by adding *s*. Other common nouns ending in *o* may form the plural by adding *s* or *es*; the correct plural forms are shown in the dictionary after the singular forms of the words.

### musical terms

| | | | | |
|---|---|---|---|---|
| sopranos | concertos | cellos | solos | pianos |

### common nouns ending in *os*

| | | | | |
|---|---|---|---|---|
| zeros | mementos | dynamos | portfolios | ratios |

### common nouns ending in *oes*

| | | | | |
|---|---|---|---|---|
| cargoes | heroes | potatoes | embargoes | vetoes |

**d.** Nouns ending in *ff* form the plural by adding *s*. Nouns ending in just *f* or *fe* may add *s*, or they may drop the *f* or *fe* and add *ves*. The plurals of those nouns taking the irregular form by adding *ves* are shown in the dictionary. If the dictionary does not show the plural form, just add *s*.

### plural nouns ending in *ffs*

| | | | |
|---|---|---|---|
| bailiff | bailiffs | plaintiff | plaintiffs |
| cliff | cliffs | sheriff | sheriffs |

### plural nouns ending in *fs* or *fes*

| | | | |
|---|---|---|---|
| belief | beliefs | roof | roofs |
| chief | chiefs | safe | safes |
| proof | proofs | strife | strifes |

noun

Grammar

6

**plural nouns ending in *ves***

| half | halves | shelf | shelves |
|------|--------|-------|---------|
| knife | knives | thief | thieves |
| self | selves | wife | wives |

**e.** The plurals of proper nouns are formed by adding *s* or *es*. Those proper nouns ending in *s*, *sh*, *ch*, *x*, or *z* form the plural by adding *es*. All others form the plural by adding *s*.

**proper noun adding *es* for plural form**

| Bendix | the Bendixes | Rodriguez | the Rodriguezes |
|--------|--------------|-----------|-----------------|
| Bush | the Bushes | Ross | the Rosses |
| Finch | the Finches | Winters | the Winterses |

**proper noun adding *s* for plural form**

| Dixon | the Dixons | Kelly | the Kellys |
|-------|-----------|-------|-----------|
| Griffin | the Griffins | Russo | the Russos |
| Halby | the Halbys | Wolf | the Wolfs |

**f.** Many nouns of foreign origin have both an English plural and a foreign plural. Consult your dictionary and use the one that appears first.

**foreign-derived nouns with preferred English plurals[3]**

| appendix | appendixes | hors d'oeuvre | hors d'oeuvres |
|----------|-----------|---------------|----------------|
| auditorium | auditoriums | index | indexes (book) |
| bureau | bureaus | memorandum | memorandums |
| formula | formulas | plateau | plateaus |
| gymnasium | gymnasiums | ultimatum | ultimatums |

**foreign-derived nouns with preferred foreign-derived plurals**

| alumna | alumnae | emphasis | emphases |
|--------|---------|----------|----------|
| alumnus | alumni | medium | media |
| analysis | analyses | parenthesis | parentheses |
| basis | bases | phenomenon | phenomena |
| crisis | crises | stimulus | stimuli |
| criterion | criteria | syllabus | syllabi |
| curriculum | curricula | synopsis | synopses |
| datum | data | synthesis | syntheses |
| diagnosis | diagnoses | terminus | termini |
| ellipsis | ellipses | thesis | theses |

---

[3]Preferences for English and foreign noun plurals are based upon entries shown in *Merriam-Webster's Collegiate Dictionary*, 10th Ed. (Springfield, Mass: Merriam-Webster, Incorporated, 1996).

**g.** Some nouns form their plurals by changing letters within the word or adding letters other than *s* or *es*. These irregular plurals are shown in the dictionary.

| | | | |
|---|---|---|---|
| child | children | mouse | mice |
| foot | feet | tooth | teeth |
| man | men | woman | women |

**h.** Some nouns have the same form in both the singular and the plural. Other nouns are used only with singular verbs while still others are used solely with plural verbs. These unusual constructions are explained in the dictionary in the entry that defines the word.

**nouns with the same singular and plural forms**

| | | | |
|---|---|---|---|
| Chinese | gross | mumps | series |
| cod | headquarters | odds | sheep |
| corps | Japanese | politics | species |
| deer | measles | salmon | vermin |
| fish | moose | scissors | Vietnamese |

**nouns always used with singular verbs**

| | | |
|---|---|---|
| aeronautics | genetics | news |
| economics (course) | mathematics | statistics (course) |

**nouns always used with plural verbs**

| | | | |
|---|---|---|---|
| belongings | earnings | premises | thanks |
| credentials | goods | proceeds | winnings |

**i.** Hyphenated or open compound nouns containing a main word form their plurals on the main words. Those hyphenated compounds not containing a main word and compound nouns consisting of only one word form the plural at the end.

**plural formed on main word**

| | | |
|---|---|---|
| attorneys-at-law | grants-in-aid | notaries public |
| bills of sale | graphic designs | personnel managers |
| co-owners | leaves of absence | sisters-in-law |
| goings-over | lieutenant colonels | vice-chancellors |

**plural formed at end**

| | | |
|---|---|---|
| bookshelves | get-togethers | stockholders |
| come-ons | go-betweens | teaspoonfuls |
| databases | printouts | trade-ins |
| follow-ups | stand-ins | workmen |

**j.** The plurals of numerals, most capital letters, words referred to as words, and abbreviations composed of initials are formed by adding *s* or *es*. For clarity, though, all isolated lowercase letters and the capital letters *A*, *I*, *M*, and *U* are made plural by adding an apostrophe before the *s*.

noun

Grammar

6

163

**plural formed with s or *es***

I have difficulty distinguishing between his **1s** and his **7s**.

Can you list the seven **Cs** of good letter writing?

Ms. Smith, our new copy editor, does not use her **whiches** and **thats** correctly.

On the last ballot the **noes** outnumbered the **yeses**.

Mr. Wilson wants this assignment completed without any further **ifs**, **ands**, or **buts**.

Make a list of **dos** and **don'ts** for the care and maintenance of these scanners.

There are two vacancies for **R.N.s** on our team.

How many of your graduates became **CPAs** last year?

All our **c.o.d.s** still need to be sent out.

Type the "**a.m.s**" and "**p.m.s**" in lowercase letters.

**plural formed with an apostrophe and *s***

We were asked to mind our **p's** and **q's** while the dignitaries were in the building.

To improve your penmanship, be sure to dot your **i's** and cross your **t's**.

Your son received three **A's** on his last grade report.

Why are the **M's** smudged on this document?

k. **When referring to two or more individuals with the same name and title, make either the name or the title plural, but never both.**

the **Messrs.** Johnson   *or*   the Mr. **Johnsons**

the **Drs.** Clark   *or*   the Dr. **Clarks**

the **Mses.** Smith   *or*   the Ms. **Smiths**

the **Mesdames** Jones   *or*   the Mrs. **Joneses**

the **Misses** Fry   *or*   the Miss **Frys**

## 6–5.   Noun Possessives[4]

a. **All nouns *not* ending with a pronounced *s*, whether singular or plural, form the possessive by adding *'s*.**

| | |
|---|---|
| office of the **attorney** | **attorney's** office |
| toys belonging to the **children** | **children's** toys |
| books belonging to **Judy** | **Judy's** books |
| lounge for **women** | **women's** lounge |

---

[4]See Section 1-55 for additional examples.

| state tax of **Illinois** | **Illinois's** state tax |
| countryside of **Des Moines** | **Des Moines's** countryside |
| tribal customs of the **Iroquois** | the **Iroquois's** tribal customs |
| paycheck of **Ms. DuBois** | **Ms. DuBois's** paycheck |
| restaurant belonging to **Francois** | **Francois's** restaurant |

(Note: The final *s* in words such as *Illinois, Des Moines, Iroquois, DuBois,* and *Francois* is not pronounced; therefore, *'s* is used with these possessive forms.)

**b.** Nouns ending with a pronounced *s* form the possessive by simply adding an apostrophe unless an additional syllable is pronounced in the possessive form. In the latter case, *'s* is added.

**no extra pronounced syllable**

| clothing for **girls** | **girls'** clothing |
| the efforts of two **cities** | two **cities'** efforts |
| the home belonging to the **Foxes** | the **Foxes'** home |
| the pen belonging to **Mr. Simons** | **Mr. Simons'** pen |

**extra pronounced syllable**

| grades of the **class** | the **class's** grades |
| the briefcase belonging to **Mr. Harris** | **Mr. Harris's** briefcase |
| testimony of the **witness** | the **witness's** testimony |

**c.** In the case of joint ownership, possession is shown only on the last noun. Where individual ownership exists, possession is shown on each noun.

**joint ownership**

Mary and **Alice's** office has been newly painted.

The Rodriguezes and the **Martinsons'** store is located on Sixth Avenue.

Mr. Stewart and **Ms. Ross's** partnership agreement was drawn up over two weeks ago.

Clark and **Clark's** handbook is required for this class.

**individual ownership**

My **mother's** and **father's** clothes were destroyed in the fire.

**Bob's** and **John's** payroll checks were lost.

**Mr. Granados'** and **Ms. Stone's** stores are both located on Tampa Avenue in Westfield.

All the **accountants'** and **secretaries'** desks have been moved into the new offices.

**d.** The possessive form of compound nouns is shown at the end.

| investments of my **father-in-law** | my **father-in-law's** investments |
| the report for **stockholders** | the **stockholders'** report |

noun

Grammar

6

165

convention of **attorneys-at-law**     **attorneys-at-law's** convention

report of the **systems manager**     **systems manager's** report

**e.**    **Use the possessive form before a gerund.**

We would appreciate **Lisa's helping** us with the audit.

There is no record of the **witness's being** subpoenaed.

**f.**    **Use an apostrophe with the possessives of nouns that refer to time—minutes, hours, days, weeks, months, and years.**

### time nouns—singular

| | |
|---|---|
| peace for a **minute** | a **minute's** peace |
| work for a **day** | a **day's** work |
| delay for a **week** | a **week's** delay |
| notice of a **month** | a **month's** notice |
| mail from this **morning** | this **morning's** mail |
| calendar for **tomorrow** | **tomorrow's** calendar |

### time nouns—plural

| | |
|---|---|
| work for four **hours** | four **hours'** work |
| interest for two **weeks** | two **weeks'** interest |
| trial for three **months** | three **months'** trial |
| experience for five **years** | five **years'** experience |

**g.**    **Use an apostrophe with the possessive of nouns that refer to distance.**

He lives just a **stone's** throw from the office.

The truck missed hitting our car by just an **arm's** length.

**h.**    **Do not use an apostrophe to form possessives for inanimate objects, except for time or distance. Instead, use a simple adjective or an _of_ phrase.**

### adjective

The **armchair** cushion needs repair. (Not: The armchair's cushion needs repair.)

The **computer** monitor was damaged in transit. (Not: The computer's monitor was damaged in transit.)

### _of_ phrase

The door **of the supply cabinet** is jammed. (Not: The supply cabinet's door is jammed.)

The stipulations **of the will** were presented by the attorney. (Not: The will's stipulations were presented by the attorney.)

**i.**    **In some possessive constructions the item or items owned do not directly follow the ownership word or are not named. The ownership word, however, still shows possession with an apostrophe.**

**item owned not directly following the ownership word**

The only desk to be refinished is **Mary's**.  (Mary's desk)

On Tuesday we will meet at the **Culleys'** to discuss the sale of their property.  (The Culleys' property)

**item owned not named**

Mr. Ardigo left the **attorney's** over an hour ago.  (The attorney's office)

Did you leave your briefcase at the **Galloways'**?  (The Galloways' home)

# Pronouns

## 6–6.    Pronouns

a.  Pronouns are noun substitutes; they take the place of nouns.  Business writers use pronouns to add variety and interest to their writing.

**sentence without pronouns**

When you see Mr. Lee, please ask Mr. Lee to sign Mr. Lee's time card for this week.

**sentence with pronouns**

When you see Mr. Lee, please ask **him** to sign **his** time card for this week.

b.  Pronouns perform one of four functions: they may (1) substitute for a person or thing, (2) refer back to a noun used previously in the sentence, (3) substitute for an unspecific person or thing, or (4) act as an adjective by modifying a noun.

**substitute for a person or thing (personal pronoun)**

**Michael** has been ill for three days; **he** should schedule an appointment with a doctor.

Because **Mrs. Scher-Padilla** is in charge of this program, please give the forms to **her**.

The board **members** can only blame **themselves** for this error.

Our **company** has attempted to expand operations to other states.  However, **it** still has been unable to increase sales significantly.

**reference to a noun named previously in the sentence (relative pronoun)**

Please send me the **book that** Tony recommended.

Brian interviewed three **students who** are enrolled at Fillmore College.

**substitute for an unspecific person or thing (indefinite pronoun)**

Do you know **someone** who meets these qualifications?

**Neither** of these plans is acceptable to the committee.

**personal pronoun used as an adjective**

**His** computer needs a new floppy disk drive.

This account is **hers**.

## 6–7. Personal Pronouns

a. Each personal pronoun may be expressed in three ways; these ways are referred to as *case forms*. The three case forms for personal pronouns are the *subjective*, the *objective*, and the *possessive*.

b. The subjective case[5] personal pronouns are the following:

| | | | |
|---|---|---|---|
| I | she | we | who |
| he | you | they | it |

Use a subjective case pronoun (1) for the subject of a sentence, (2) for the complement of a "being" verb (*am, is, are, was, were, be, been*), and (3) after the infinitive *to be* when this verb does not have a subject (a noun or pronoun) directly preceding it.

**subject of a verb**

**She** has applied for the position.

**They** will arrive at 10 a.m.

Mark, Ellen, and **I** have been appointed to the committee.

**complement of a "being" verb**

The person who answered the telephone was not **I**.

This is **she**.

The visitors could have been **they**.

**infinitive *to be* without a subject**

Deanna is often thought to be **I**.

The doctor on duty at that time had to be **he**.

c. The objective case personal pronouns are the following:

| | | | |
|---|---|---|---|
| me | her | us | whom |
| him | you | them | it |

The objective case is used when the pronoun is (1) the direct or indirect object of a verb (2) the object of a preposition, (3) the subject of any infinitive, (4) the object of the infinitive *to be* when it has a subject, and (5) the object of any other infinitive.

**direct object of a verb**

Mr. Reslaw will meet **her** at the airport tomorrow.

You may ask **him** for this information.

---

[5]The subjective case is also known as the *nominative case*.

noun

Ms. Orsini asked Ken and **me** to provide her with this information by June 15.

**indirect object of a verb**

Please mail **me** a receipt as soon as possible.

We will send Marie or **him** these copies before Friday.

**object of a preposition**

When was the shipment sent to **us**?

Two of the customers asked for **her**.

Between **you** and **me**, I do not believe the plan will be approved.

**subject of an infinitive**

Our department manager expects **her** to complete the audit by December 1.

We thought **them** to be somewhat overconfident.

**object of *to be* with a subject**

I wanted the **candidate** to be **her**.

Ms. Stapleton thought **them** to be **us**.

They expected **Mary** to be **me**.

**object of an infinitive other than *to be***

Our office will not be able to mail **them** until Monday.

We asked her to help **us** with the decorations.

**d.** The possessive case personal pronouns are the following:

| | | | |
|---|---|---|---|
| my | mine | their | theirs |
| his, her | his, hers | its | its |
| your | yours | whose | |
| our | ours | | |

All pronoun possessive case forms are written without apostrophes. They should not be confused with contractions.

**possessive pronouns—no apostrophes**

**Its** wrapping had been torn.

Is this **your** signature?

The idea was **theirs**.

**Whose** briefcase was left in the conference room?

**contractions—apostrophes**

**It's** (It is) still raining very heavily here on the West Coast.

Let us know if **you're** (you are) going to the convention.

noun

Grammar

6

169

If **there's** (there is) a logical reason for the delay, please inform the passengers.

**Who's** (Who is) in charge of ordering supplies for our computers?

e. **Use the possessive case immediately before a gerund.**

**His leaving** the company was quite a surprise.

We would appreciate **your returning** the enclosed card by Friday, March 18.

f. **A pronoun after *than* or *as* may be expressed in either the subjective or objective case, depending on whether the pronoun is the subject or object of the following stated or implied verb.**

**subjective case**

Are you as concerned about this matter as **I am**? (Stated verb *am*)

He has been with the company two years longer than **I**. (Implied verb *have*)

**objective case**

Our editor compliments my coauthor more than he compliments **me**. (Stated subject and verb *he compliments*)

She works for Mr. Reece more often than **me**. (Implied subject, verb, and preposition *she works for*)

g. **Pronouns used in apposition take the same case as those nouns or pronouns with which they are in apposition.**

**We**, Barbara and **I**, will appear in court tomorrow.

Barry told Ms. Larsen to submit her expenses to one of our accounting **supervisors**, John or **me**.

h. **Pronouns followed by an identifying noun (such as *we employees* or *us employees*) are treated as if the noun were not there in determining the proper case form. Therefore, mentally omit the noun in such pronoun-noun combinations (restrictive appositives) to select the correct form.**

**subjective case**

Within the next week **we** ~~employees~~ must decide whether or not we will move with the company to Columbus. (Subject of verb phrase *must decide*)

The victims in this case are **we** ~~students~~. (Complement of being verb *are*)

**objective case**

The company just gave **us** ~~employees~~ the opportunity to purchase company stock at prices below the market value. (Indirect object of verb *gave*)

None of **us** ~~students~~ have yet received any enrollment information. (Object of preposition *of*)

**i.** Pronouns ending in *self* or *selves* emphasize or reflect a noun or pronoun used previously. They should not be used in place of objective case pronouns.

**emphasizes previous noun or pronoun**

**Wendy herself** was not pleased with the results of the advertising campaign.

**They themselves** could not justify their exorbitant budget requests.

**reflects a previous noun or pronoun**

**Jim** addressed the envelope to **himself**.

The **council** voted **themselves** annual salary increases of $4,000.

**objective case pronoun used correctly**

None of these packages are for **me**. (Not: None of these packages are for *myself*.)

These contracts will be sent directly to **you** after they have been signed by our president. (Not: These contracts will be sent directly to *yourself* after they have been signed by our president.)

**j.** The same rules apply to the pronouns *who, whoever, whom, whomever,* and *whose* as apply to the other personal pronouns. *Who* and *whoever* are used for the subjective case; *whom* and *whomever,* for the objective case; and *whose,* for the possessive case.

To distinguish easily whether to use *who* or *whom,* use the following procedure. See how the model sentence leads to the correct choice. The model sentence for this example is *John is the person [who, whom] I believe Ms. Wilkes will hire.*

(1) Isolate the clause in which the pronoun appears. (*[who, whom] I believe Ms. Wilkes will hire*)

(2) Eliminate any extra clauses. (*[who, whom] Ms. Wilkes will hire*)

(3) Place the clause in subject-verb order if it does not already appear so. (*Ms. Wilkes will hire [who, whom]*)

(4) Apply the rules outlined for the subjective and objective case pronouns in Sections 6-7b and c. Mentally substitute *he* for *who* and *him* for *whom* to help you distinguish between the subjective and objective cases. (*Ms. Wilkes will hire him.* Thus the correct choice for the example sentence is *whom: John is the person whom I believe Ms. Wilkes will hire.*)

**subjective case— *who* or *whoever***

**Who** delivered these contracts to my office? (Subject of verb—*[he] delivered*)

Please give me a listing of **who** called while I was in New York. (Subject of verb—*[he]* called)

I do not know **who** the caller may have been. (Place clause in subject-verb order.) (Complement of "being" verb *been*—the caller may have been *[he]*)

Please let me know **who** the winner is. (Place clause in subject-verb order.) (Complement of "being" verb *is*—the winner is *[he]*)

**Who** do you think will be appointed to the board? (Omit extra clause *do you think*.) (Subject of verb phrase—*[he]* will be appointed)

The city council will ratify the appointment of **whoever** is selected. (Subject of verb phrase—*[he]* is selected)

The committee will allow you to select **whoever** you think is qualified. (Omit extra clause *you think*.) (Subject of verb—*[he]* is qualified)

### objective case— *whom* or *whomever*

**Whom** did Mr. Williams promote to the position of office manager? (Place clause in subject-verb order.) (Direct object—Mr. Williams did promote *[him]*)

He is a person with **whom** we have done business for over twenty-five years. (Place clause in subject-verb order.) (Object of preposition—we have done business with *[him]*)

Ask Mr. Robbins **whom** he selected to replace Jerome. (Place clause in subject-verb order.) (Direct object—he selected *[him]*)

We do not know **whom** to award the contract. (Place clause in subject-verb order.) (Object of an infinitive—to award *[him]*)

**Whom** do you think the Savoys will hire as their new manager? (Omit extra clause *do you think*.) (Place clause in subject-verb order.) (Direct object—the Savoys will hire *[him]*)

The committee will allow you to select **whomever** you wish. (Place clause in subject-verb order.) (Direct object—you wish *[him]*)

I'm sure the president will approve **whomever** you choose for the position. (Place clause in subject-verb order.) (Direct object—you choose *[him]*)

### possessive case— *whose*

**Whose** sales reports have not yet been submitted?

We do not know **whose** recommendations will be adopted to implement our new cost-saving plan.

**k.** **Pronouns must agree in gender and number with any nouns or other pronouns they represent.**[6]

---

[6]Refer to Section 6-18 for additional information on principles of agreement.

A **customer** must first register **his** or **her** complaint with an assistant manager.

Both **Ms. Greer** and **Mr. Baty** received **their** orders yesterday.

The **puppy** caught **its** tail in the door.

The **company** will conduct **its** annual inventory next week.

## 6–8. Relative Pronouns

**a.** Relative pronouns introduce dependent clauses that refer back (relate) to a noun in the main clause of the sentence. Relative pronoun forms are *who, whom, that,* and *which.*

**b.** Use *who* and *whom* to refer to a person or persons. To distinguish between *who* and *whom,* apply the procedures given in Section 6-7j.

### subjective case—*who*

Mr. Vasquez is the applicant **who** was selected for the position. (Refers back to *applicant*) (Subject of verb—*[he]* was selected)

The person **who** served as the seventh president of our college was Ms. Graham. (Refers back to *person*) (Subject of verb—*[she]* served)

Peter is the sales representative **who** I believe will be successful as an editor in the business area. (Refers back to *sales representative*) (Omit extra clause *I believe.*) (Subject of verb—*[he]* will be successful)

Next month our advertising manager, **who** has held this position for over twenty years, will retire. (Refers back to *advertising manager*) (Subject of verb—*[he]* has held)

### objective case—*whom*

Mr. Vasquez is the applicant **whom** Ms. Jones selected for the position. (Refers back to *applicant*) (Direct object of verb—Ms. Jones selected *[him]*)

Our new college president, **whom** the board assigned just yesterday, has already called a meeting of campus administrators. (Refers back to *president*) (Direct object of verb—the board assigned *[him]*)

You are a person **whom** I know Ms. Ferraro would be pleased to hire. (Refers back to *person*) (Omit extra clause *I know.*) (Object of infinitive—Ms. Ferraro would be pleased to hire *[him]*)

**c.** Use *that* or *which* to introduce a dependent clause that refers back to a thing or things in the main clause—any noun that does not represent a person or persons. Careful writers use *that* to introduce restrictive dependent clauses and *which* to introduce nonrestrictive dependent clauses.

*Restrictive dependent clauses* provide essential ideas that refine the information contained in the main clause; that is, they specify *which one. Nonrestrictive dependent clauses* provide extra information that does not alter the substance of the main clause; in other words, the

*noun*

Grammar

6

information is not needed to identify *which one*. Nonrestrictive clauses are separated from the main clause with a comma or a pair of commas.

**restrictive dependent clause requiring *that***

Be sure to include on the order form the catalog number of each item **that** you order. (Refers back to *item*) (Specifies only items that are ordered)

The prices **that** are listed in this catalog are guaranteed until June 30. (Refers back to *prices*) (Specifies which prices)

**nonrestrictive dependent clause requiring *which***

The Catalog No. 8731 lace-embroidered blouse, **which** you ordered last week, is no longer available. (Refers back to *blouse*) (Clause not needed to identify which blouse—provides extra idea)

Please credit my account for these items, **which** were charged in error to my account. (Refers back to *items*) (Clause not needed to identify which items—provides additional information)

## 6–9. Indefinite Pronouns

**a.** *Indefinite pronouns* are pronouns that do not represent a specific person, place, or thing.

**b.** Simple indefinite pronouns include the following words used as subjects or objects:

| | |
|---|---|
| each | every |
| either | neither |

**c.** Compound indefinite pronouns end with *-body*, *-one*, or *-thing*.

| ____body | ____one | ____thing |
|---|---|---|
| anybody | anyone | anything |
| everybody | everyone | everything |
| nobody | no one | nothing |
| somebody | someone | something |

**d.** Indefinite pronouns used as subjects require singular verbs.

**simple indefinite pronoun as subject**

**Each** of the candidates **has** been given an equal opportunity to address our audience.

**Neither** of the applicants **is** qualified for the position.

**compound indefinite pronoun as subject**

Nearly **everybody was** late for the meeting because of the unexpected snowstorm.

**Everything** in these files **is** outdated.

**e.** Any other pronouns representing an indefinite pronoun must agree in number and gender with the indefinite pronoun.

**Neither** of the winners has claimed **his** or **her** prize.

Would **everyone** please return **his** or **her** evaluation form by May 15.

## Verbs

### 6–10. Verbs

**a.** Verbs are often described as the motor of a sentence—they make a sentence "go." Verbs show action or describe a state of being at a certain point in time. Examples of action verbs are *run, swim, talk,* and *write.* Nonaction verbs, those that describe a state of being, include words such as *seem, feel,* and *smell.* The most commonly used nonaction verbs, however, are derived from the verb *be—am, is, are, was, were,* and *been.*

**b.** In their infinitive form, verbs are preceded by the preposition *to.*

| action verbs | nonaction verbs |
|---|---|
| to go | to be |
| to demonstrate | to appear |
| to apply | to taste |

**c.** Verbs appear alone or in phrases with helpers. The last word in a verb phrase is the main verb. Word groups must contain a verb or a verb phrase to be complete sentences.

**verb in sentence**

David **calls** his stockbroker daily.

Please **send** this order to the customer immediately.

Vista Industries **is** one of our best customers.

**verb phrase in sentence**

We **have received** several payments from this client.

Our company **has been involved** in two lawsuits during the past year.

Our office **is** presently **processing** your order.

How much money **did** you **spend** on this project?

**d.** Verbs require varied forms to signify tenses; that is, points in time. The principal forms or parts of a verb used to construct tenses include the present part, the past part, the past participle, and the present participle.

### 6–11. Formation of Parts for Regular Verbs

Most verbs, regular verbs, form their parts in the same way: (1) the present part has the infinitive form without the accompanying *to,*

*noun*

Grammar 6

175

(2) the past part adds *ed* to the present form, (3) the past participle uses the past part with at least one verb helper, and (4) the present participle adds *ing* to the present form and uses at least one verb helper.

| infinitive | present | past |
|---|---|---|
| to ask | ask | asked |
| to collect | collect | collected |
| to interview | interview | interviewed |

| past participle | present participle |
|---|---|
| (have, was) asked | (was, has been) asking |
| (has, had been) collected | (am, have been) collecting |
| (were, have been) interviewed | (are, will be) interviewing |

**sentence examples**

We need **to collect** more information for this report. (Infinitive)

Jeff **collects** stamps from countries all over the world. (Present part)

The courier **collected** all our mail for overnight delivery about an hour ago. (Past part)

My assistant **has collected** prospectuses from seven major suppliers of health insurance programs. (Past participle with a helping verb)

Our Research Department **is collecting** additional information from consumers. (Present participle with a helping verb)

## 6–12. Formation of Parts for Irregular Verbs[7]

a. Many verbs do not form their past part, past participle, and present participle in the usual manner. *All such irregular verb forms are shown in the dictionary; they are listed directly after the present form of the verb.* Any verbs without a listing are regular verbs, and their parts are formed in the regular way described in Section 6-11.

b. A number of irregular verbs form their parts in the same way. Most verbs ending in *e* form their past part and past participle by adding *d*. These same verbs form the present participle by dropping the *e* and adding *ing*.

Another group of verbs double the final consonant before adding the regular endings to the past part, past participle, and present participle.

**verbs ending in *e***

| Infinitive: | to change | to enclose | to complete |
|---|---|---|---|
| Present part: | change | enclose | complete |
| Past part: | changed | enclosed | completed |
| Past participle: | (has) changed | (have) enclosed | (have) completed |
| Present participle: | (is) changing | (are) enclosing | (is) completing |

---

[7]Parts for all irregular verbs are shown in the dictionary directly after the main entry.

## verbs that double the final consonant

| Infinitive: | to trim | to stir | to clip |
|---|---|---|---|
| Present part: | trim | stir | clip |
| Past part: | trimmed | stirred | clipped |
| Past participle: | (has) trimmed | (has) stirred | (have) clipped |
| Present participle: | (is) trimming | (are) stirring | (is) clipping |

c. Some irregular verb forms do not follow a particular pattern in form-ing the past part and the past participle. A list of parts for some such commonly used irregular verbs follows:

| Present Part | Past Part | Past Participle | Present Participle |
|---|---|---|---|
| am | was | been | being |
| arise | arose | arisen | arising |
| become | became | become | becoming |
| begin | began | begun | beginning |
| bite | bit | bitten | biting |
| blow | blew | blown | blowing |
| break | broke | broken | breaking |
| bring | brought | brought | bringing |
| burst | burst | burst | bursting |
| buy | bought | bought | buying |
| catch | caught | caught | catching |
| choose | chose | chosen | choosing |
| come | came | come | coming |
| dig | dug | dug | digging |
| do | did | done | doing |
| draw | drew | drawn | drawing |
| drink | drank | drunk | drinking |
| drive | drove | driven | driving |
| eat | ate | eaten | eating |
| fall | fell | fallen | falling |
| fight | fought | fought | fighting |
| fly | flew | flown | flying |
| forget | forgot | forgotten | forgetting |
| forgive | forgave | forgiven | forgiving |
| freeze | froze | frozen | freezing |
| get | got | got | getting |
| give | gave | given | giving |
| go | went | gone | going |
| grow | grew | grown | growing |
| hang | hung | hung | hanging |
| hide | hid | hidden | hiding |
| know | knew | known | knowing |
| lay | laid | laid | laying |
| lead | led | led | leading |
| leave | left | left | leaving |
| lend | lent | lent | lending |
| lie | lay | lain | lying |
| lose | lost | lost | losing |
| make | made | made | making |

| Present Part | Past Part | Past Participle | Present Participle |
|---|---|---|---|
| pay | paid | paid | paying |
| ride | rode | ridden | riding |
| ring | rang | rung | ringing |
| rise | rose | risen | rising |
| run | ran | run | running |
| see | saw | seen | seeing |
| set | set | set | setting |
| shake | shook | shaken | shaking |
| shrink | shrank | shrunk | shrinking |
| sing | sang | sung | singing |
| sink | sank | sunk | sinking |
| sit | sat | sat | sitting |
| speak | spoke | spoken | speaking |
| spring | sprang | sprung | springing |
| steal | stole | stolen | stealing |
| strike | struck | struck | striking |
| swear | swore | sworn | swearing |
| swim | swam | swum | swimming |
| take | took | taken | taking |
| tear | tore | torn | tearing |
| throw | threw | thrown | throwing |
| wear | wore | worn | wearing |
| write | wrote | written | writing |

**sentence examples**

Our holiday sale **begins** this Monday.

We **began** work on this construction project early last June.

Orders from our national television campaign **have begun** flooding our telephone lines.

These stocks **are beginning** to pay substantial dividends.

### 6–13. Simple Tenses

Verb parts are used to form tenses that place an action or a condition in a time frame. The verb part itself may express tense, or a verb part with helpers (a verb phrase) may be needed to specify the time frame. The most commonly used tenses are the simple tenses—the *present*, the *past*, and the *future*.

a. The *present tense* is used to indicate an ongoing action or a currently existing condition. Use the present part or a conjugation (changes in spelling to accommodate person) of the present part to form this tense.

Place an *s* at the end of the present part when it is used with any singular subject except *I* and *you*. For verbs ending in *s*, *sh*, *ch*, *x*, and *z*, add *es* instead of *s*.[8]

---

[8]The verbs *do* and *go* add *es* also; i.e., the singular form of *do* for *he*, *she*, and *it* is *does*. The corresponding form for *go* is *goes*.

noun

### present tense formations for most verbs

| to eat | to provide | to sit |
|---|---|---|
| I eat | I provide | I sit |
| you eat | you provide | you sit |

| | | |
|---|---|---|
| he eats | he provides | he sits |
| John eats | John provides | John sits |
| she eats | she provides | she sits |
| Mary eats | Mary provides | Mary sits |
| it eats | it provides | it sits |
| the cat eats | the company provides | the cat sits |

| | | |
|---|---|---|
| we eat | we provide | we sit |
| you eat (pl.) | you provide (pl.) | you sit (pl.) |
| they eat | they provide | they sit |
| the children eat | the parents provide | the patients sit |

### present tense formations for verbs ending in *s*, *sh*, *ch*, *x*, and *z*

| to wish | to teach | to relax |
|---|---|---|
| I wish | I teach | I relax |
| you wish | you teach | you relax |

| | | |
|---|---|---|
| he wishes | he teaches | he relaxes |
| John wishes | John teaches | John relaxes |
| she wishes | she teaches | she relaxes |
| Mary wishes | Mary teaches | Mary relaxes |
| it wishes | it teaches | it relaxes |
| the board wishes | the program teaches | the cat relaxes |

| | | |
|---|---|---|
| we wish | we teach | we relax |
| you wish (pl.) | you teach (pl.) | you relax (pl.) |
| they wish | they teach | they relax |
| the children wish | the schools teach | the travelers relax |

### use of present tense

Our purchasing agent **buys** most of his stock from local sources.

I **recognize** the person in this picture.

Our company **establishes** offices in all cities in which it **conducts** business.

Our cleaning crew **waxes** these floors weekly.

He **goes** to the doctor regularly for checkups.

**b.** The *past tense* describes a single past action or event. Simply use the past part of a verb to express the past tense.

The customer **selected** tan carpeting for his new offices.

I **received** these documents last week.

Our purchasing agent **bought** this stock from a local source.

c.  The *future tense* describes expected or anticipated occurrences. To form the future tense, use the present part with the helping verb *will*.

I **will call** you within the next few days to confirm your reservation.

The committee **will review** your proposal by March 1, and Mr. Rosen **will notify** you of the committee's decision by March 8.

Our company **will** not **participate** in the bidding for this contract.

## 6–14.  Perfect Tenses

The perfect tenses—the present, past, and future—use the past participle of the verb along with a helping verb derived from *have*.

a.  The *present perfect tense* describes an action or a condition that began in the past and has continued until the present. This tense is formed by using *has* or *have* with the past participle of the verb.

Mr. Randolf **has worked** in our Accounting Department since July 1990.

The company **has paid** heavy fines during the past three years for environmental-impact violations.

We **have** already **sent** you three reminders about your past-due account.

b.  The *past perfect tense* describes a past action that occurred before another past action. Use *had* as a helping verb with the past participle of the main verb to form this tense.

Our client **had signed** this will just three days before he **died**.

We **accepted** this offer only after we **had contacted** three other vendors.

Although we **had paid** for the merchandise, the manufacturer **did** not **ship** it in time for our spring sale.

c.  The *future perfect tense* describes an action that will take place before another future action. Use the helping verbs *will have* with the past participle of the main verb to form this tense.

By the time you submit the final manuscript, we **will have spent** over $50,000 in fees to freelance writers.

If allowed to continue, this project at its conclusion **will have cost** United States taxpayers over $3 billion.

## 6–15.  Progressive Tenses

The progressive tenses show action in progress during the present, past, and future. Use the present participle of the verb along with a being verb helper—*am*, *is*, *are*, *was*, *were*, or *be*.

a.  The *present progressive tense* describes an ongoing action during the present time. The being verb helpers *am*, *is*, and *are* are used with the present participle to form this tense.

I **am taking** several classes in computer applications this semester.

Our company **is sponsoring** a number of youth and adult programs in the community.

Several of our key employees **are relocating** to our main office in Boston.

b.  The *past progressive tense* relates an ongoing action that occurred in the past. The being verb helpers *was* and *were* with the present participle of a verb are used to form this tense.

I **was discussing** this problem with the vice president when her secretary interrupted us with an emergency message from the chairman of the board.

Until the end of last year, we **were** still **selling** more copies of the sixth edition than the seventh edition.

c.  The *future progressive tense* forecasts an ongoing future action. To form this tense, use the helping verbs *will* and *be* with the present participle of the verb.

We **will be staffing** this branch office about one month before construction is completed.

Our auditors **will be reviewing** this company's books for at least another two months.

## 6–16.  Passive Voice Constructions

Unlike other verb constructions, the passive voice does not necessarily identify who does what. Instead, the person or thing performing the action may be cloaked in ambiguity.

In business communications the passive voice is often used to soften the impact of a negative idea or to avoid placing blame for an oversight or error. It is also used simply to provide variety in sentence construction.

To form a passive voice construction, use the past participle of the verb with one of the following being verb helpers: *is, are, was, were, be,* or *been.*

Each order **is entered** into our computer when it arrives at our factory.

Our products **are sold** only through franchised retailers.

Unfortunately, the shipment **was damaged** in transit.

These eviction notices **were mailed** to the tenants on September 1.

The building **will be restored** within the next year.

All the depositors **have been notified** that the insured deposits of Universal Savings **have been assumed** by First Arizona Savings.

### 6–17. Use of *Lay* and *Lie*

**a.** Broadly defined, the verb *lay* means "to place or put" and the verb *lie* means "to recline." Forms of these two verbs are often confused in usage. The principal parts of *lie* and *lay* follow:

| present | past | past participle | present participle |
|---------|------|-----------------|--------------------|
| lie | lay | lain | lying |
| lay | laid | laid | laying |

**b.** Use a form of *lie* when the verb called for is intransitive (does not have a direct object) and a form of *lay* when the verb is transitive (has a direct object).[9] Always use a form of *lay* when the past participle appears with a "being" verb helper (*is, are, was, were, be, been*).

**intransitive**

The new shopping center **lies** at the base of the Flintridge Foothills.

He **lay** unconscious for nearly an hour before the doctor arrived.

Our mainframe computer **has lain** idle for nearly six hours.

Your packages **are lying** on the bottom shelf of the cupboard.

**transitive**

Please **lay** all new magazines on the table in the reception area.

Before leaving the office, she **laid** the contracts on your desk.

We **have** always **laid** these booklets horizontally in their packing boxes.

Retail stores throughout the country **are laying** plans to capture their share of holiday purchases.

**always a form of *lay* ("being" verb + past participle)**

These sandbags have **been laid** here because of impending flood damage.

The carpeting for our new building **was laid** yesterday.

### 6–18. Principles of Agreement

**a.** The verb of a sentence must agree in person and number with the subject. To identify a subject, omit any prepositional phrases that separate the subject and the verb.

The **legs** of the table **were damaged** in transit. (Omit prepositional phrase *of the table*.)

Our **stock** of ribbons for our IBM and Epson printers **is running** low. (Omit prepositional phrases *of ribbons* and *for our IBM and Epson printers*.)

---

[9]Use of the verb *lay* with three of its parts—*lay, laid*, and (has, have or had) *laid*—is often easily identified by substituting a form of the verb *put*. If *put* or one of its forms makes sense, then the use of *lay* or one of its forms is correct. Otherwise, a form of *lie* is more than likely correct.

**b.** **A pronoun that represents the subject must agree in number and gender with the subject.**

**Mr. Charles** was asked to prepare **his** report by the end of this week.

Would **every student** please be sure to submit **his** or **her** class schedule by February 5.

**Ellen** and **Margaret** were asked to resubmit **their** applications for employment.

The **company** filed for bankruptcy because **it** was unable to meet **its** obligations.

**c.** **Compound subjects joined by *and* generally require the use of a plural verb. When compound subjects are joined by *or* or *nor*, the form of the verb is determined by the part of the subject that is closer to the verb. If one part is plural and the other is singular, place the plural part, where possible, closer to the verb.**

**compound joined by *and***

My **son and daughter-in-law receive** monthly issues of *Business Forecast*.

Outgoing **letters and packages leave** our office on a regularly scheduled basis.

**Mr. Lopez and his two assistants** were requested to attend the board meeting.

**compound joined by *or* or *nor***

Neither Sharon nor **John was** available for comment to the press.

Either you or **I am** responsible for writing this section of the report.

Ms. Binder or her **assistants are** reviewing the manuscript.

Candy or **flowers are** typically given on this occasion. (Not: Flowers or *candy is* typically given on this occasion.)

**d.** **Subjects joined by *and* take singular verbs in only two cases: (1) when the parts separated by *and* constitute a single person or thing and (2) when the compound is preceded by *each*, *every*, or *many a (an)*.**

**single person or thing**

Our **accountant and tax attorney has** prepared all the reports for the Internal Revenue Service.

Her **nurse and companion works** six days a week.

**Bacon and eggs is** served in our coffee shop until 11 a.m. each day.

Luckily the **horse and carriage was** stolen after the scene had been shot.

**compound preceded by *each*, *every*, or *many a (an)***

**Each apartment and condominium was** inspected by our general manager before it was released for rental.

183

**Every man, woman, and child is** responsible for carrying his or her belongings during the tour.

**Many a student and instructor has** requested additional tickets to our Drama Department's production of *Picnic.*

e. Indefinite pronouns such as *each, every, everyone, everything, somebody, anybody, either,* and *neither* take singular verbs.

**Each** of the books **was** stamped with the company name.

**Everyone was** pleased with the hotel accommodations.

**Everything** in these files **needs** to be transferred to microfiche.

**Neither** of them **was** present at the meeting.

f. When the word *there* precedes the verb, select the singular or plural verb form on the basis of the number of the noun that follows. If the noun is singular, then use a singular verb; if it is plural, use a plural verb.

The same rule applies to those words such as *some, all, none, most, a majority, one fourth,* and *part* that indicate portions. When they function as subjects, the number of the noun that follows governs whether a singular or plural verb is correct.

**there preceding a singular verb form**

There **is** one **person** on the mailing list you may wish to call.

There **appears** to be only one **reason** why we did not receive the contract.

**there preceding a plural verb form**

There **are** three **people** on the reserve list.

There **appear** to be several **reasons** why our bid was not accepted.

**portion preceding a singular verb form**

**Some** of the **money has** been invested in U.S. Savings Bonds.

**Part** of your **order has** been shipped.

**One third** of our **equipment needs** to be replaced.

**portion preceding a plural verb form**

**All** the **materials were** shipped to you yesterday.

Only **one half** of the **packages have** been inspected.

**A majority** of our **employees receive** extra benefits from our incentive plan.

g. "A number" used as a subject requires a plural verb. "The number" used as a subject requires a singular verb. Keep in mind that descriptive adverbs and adjectives may separate the article *a* or *the* from the word *number.*

### "a number" subject, plural verb

Under the circumstances, **a number** of our customers **are** requesting a full refund.

**A** surprisingly small **number** of our students **have** registered late this semester.

### "the number" subject, singular verb

We believe that **the number** of employees selecting the DSE insurance option **has** increased.

**The** large **number** of responses received from our recent advertising campaign **was** far greater than we had anticipated.

**h.** To express the subjunctive mood (a situation or condition that is untrue or highly unlikely), use *were* instead of *was* after *if, as if, as though,* or *wish.* The verb *was* is used only if the situation after *if, as if,* or *as though* could be true.

### use of *were* instead of *was*

If I **were** you, I would submit another application before the deadline date. (A condition that is untrue—I cannot be you.)

Mr. Greeley took charge **as though** he **were** the owner of the store. (But Mr. Greeley is not the owner of the store.)

I **wish** I **were** able to answer that question for you. (But I cannot answer the question.)

### use of *was*

If Mary **was** here, she did not return the overdue library books. (Mary could have been there.)

The customer acted **as though** he **was** irritated with our credit policies. (The customer may have been irritated.)

**i.** Avoid splitting an infinitive, that is, placing any words between *to* and the verb form.

Unfortunately, I was unable **to follow logically** the speaker's train of thought. (Not *to logically follow*)

Were you able **to understand fully** the ramifications of this policy change? (Not *to fully understand*)

**j.** Collective nouns such as *committee, jury, audience, group, team, class, board, crowd,* and *council* may take either singular or plural verbs, depending upon the situation in which the verb is used. If the individual members of the collective noun are operating as a unit, use a singular verb; if the individual members are acting separately, use a plural verb.

In most cases the use of a plural verb with a collective noun results in an awkward-sounding construction. To avoid such situations, restructure the sentence to use a plural-noun subject.

**elements of collective noun acting as a unit**

When an **audience gives** a speaker a standing ovation, you may be sure that he or she has delivered an exceptional address.

**Has** the **committee** finished its report?

**elements of collective noun acting separately**

The **jury were** arguing violently. (Alternative: The jury members were arguing violently.)

The **board have** not yet reached a decision. (Alternative: The board members have not yet reached a decision.)

**restructured sentence with plural-noun subject**

Unfortunately, the **members** of the council **do** not agree on the purpose of the newly formed committee.

After the game the team **members were** seen arguing with one another on national television.

**k.** A relative pronoun clause (a clause commonly beginning with *who* or *that*) must agree in gender and number with the noun or pronoun it modifies.

Ms. Cohen is a **person** who **is** concerned about maintaining **her** good health.

Our manager is the kind of **man** who **is** always considerate of **his** subordinates.

All the **children** who **attend** this school must maintain **their** grade averages at or above the "C" level.

Have you read all the **papers** that **were** placed on your desk?

Our committee **meeting**, which **was** scheduled for next Monday, has been canceled.

**l.** Relative pronoun clauses (*who* and *that* clauses) preceded by such phrases as "one of those (or the) doctors," generally agree with the plural noun—in this case, *doctors*. Phrases such as "one of those (or the) executives," "one of those (or the) books," or "one of those (or the) secretaries" are in the same category. The entire group is described by the clause and, therefore, plural forms must be used.

In sentences where the "one of those (or the) _____" is limited by the word *only*, the relative clause does not refer to the entire group. Singular forms are correct in this instance.

**"one of those _____"—plural forms**

Mary is one of those business **executives** who **travel** extensively in **their** jobs.

He is one of the **salespersons** who regularly **visit** all **their** customers.

*Joshua's Travels* is one of those **books** that **have** a tragic ending.

She is one of the **employees** who **work** in Chicago.

**"one of those _____" limited by** *only*—**singular forms**

Mary is the **only one** of the business executives who **travels** extensively in **her** job.

He is the **only one** of thé salespersons who regularly **visits** all **his** customers.

*Joshua's Travels* is the **only one** of those books that **has** a tragic ending.

She is the **only one** of the employees who **works** in Chicago.

# Adjectives

## 6–19.  Adjectives Modify Nouns

Adjectives modify nouns or pronouns. They answer such questions as what kind? how many? which one?

**what kind?**

| | | |
|---|---|---|
| **damaged** merchandise | **laser** printers | **stylish** dresses |

**how many?**

| | | |
|---|---|---|
| **three** salespersons | **several** years | **two dozen** pencils |

**which one?**

| | | |
|---|---|---|
| **that** chair | **those** flight attendants | **this** idea |

## 6–20.  Use of the Articles *A* and *An*

Use the article *a* before a word that begins with a consonant sound, a long *u* sound, or an *h* that is pronounced. Use *an* before words that begin with a pronounced vowel sound (except long *u*) or before words that begin with a silent *h*.

**use of *a***

| | | |
|---|---|---|
| a newspaper | a uniform | a hillside development |
| a restaurant | a union | a history class |

**use of *an***

| | | |
|---|---|---|
| an answer | an unusual request | an honest person |
| an opportunity | an upper floor | an hour |

## 6–21.  Adjective Comparison

**a.**  Adjectives may be used to compare two or more nouns or pronouns. Use the comparative form for comparing two persons or things and the superlative form for comparing three or more.

noun

Grammar

6

**b.** Regular one-syllable adjectives ending in *e* add *r* for the comparative and *st* for the superlative. Regular one-syllable adjectives ending in consonants add *er* for the comparative and *est* for the superlative.

### one-syllable adjectives ending in *e*

He has a **fine** set of golf clubs.

He has a **finer** set of golf clubs than I.

He has the **finest** set of golf clubs I have ever seen.

### one-syllable adjectives ending in a consonant

This is a **short** letter.

This letter is **shorter** than the last one you dictated.

This is the **shortest** letter I have written today.

**c.** Most two-syllable adjectives and all adjectives containing three or more syllables use *more* or *less* and *most* or *least* to construct comparative and superlative forms. Forms for those two-syllable adjectives that do not follow this pattern are shown in the dictionary after their simple form. These words include *costly, friendly, happy, healthy, merry, lovely, pretty*—all ending in *y*.

### two- and three-syllable adjectives with *more, most, less,* or *least*

We interviewed an **outstanding** candidate yesterday.

This candidate is **more outstanding** than the one we interviewed yesterday.

This candidate is the **most outstanding** one we have interviewed so far.

We purchased an **expensive** scanner yesterday.

This phone system is **less expensive** than the one we evaluated yesterday.

This is the **least expensive** grade of carpeting we carry.

### two-syllable adjectives using *er* or *est*

We initiated a **costly** program.

The state's highway program is **costlier** than its conservation program.

Our welfare program is the **costliest** one in the nation.

**d.** Irregular forms for adjective comparison appear in the dictionary. They are listed after the simple forms. A list of commonly used irregular adjectives follows:

| simple | comparative | superlative |
| --- | --- | --- |
| bad, ill | worse | worst |
| good, well | better | best |
| far | farther, further | farthest, furthest |
| little | littler, less | littlest, least |
| many, much | more | most |

**e.** Use *other* or *else* when comparing one person or object with the other members of the group to which it belongs.

Our Dallas office earns more revenue than any of our **other** branch offices. (Not *any of our branch offices*)

John is more intelligent than anyone **else** in the class. (Not *anyone in the class*)

**f.** Some adjectives cannot be compared in the regular sense because they are absolute. A partial list of such adjectives follows:

| | | |
|---|---|---|
| alive | finished | round |
| complete | full | straight |
| dead | perfect | unique |

Absolute adjectives may show comparison by use of the forms "more nearly" or "most nearly."

This water cooler is **full**.

The water cooler in your office is **more nearly full** (not *fuller*) than the one in ours.

The water cooler in the Office of Human Resources is the **most nearly full** (not *fullest*) one on this floor.

The police report is **accurate**.

The *Daily News'* report of this incident was **more nearly accurate** (not *more accurate*) than the one appearing in the *Tribune*.

The *Daily News'* report was the **most nearly accurate** (not *most accurate*) account of this incident that appeared in the media.

## 6–22. Independent Adjectives[10]

When two or more adjectives appearing before a noun independently modify the noun, separate these adjectives with commas.

His **direct, practical** approach to problem-solving has created a high degree of respect for him among his staff.

We returned that **boring, poorly written** manuscript to its author.

She handled the problem in a **sure, calm, decisive** manner.

## 6–23. Adjectives With Linking Verbs

Use adjectives, not adverbs, after linking verbs. Common linking verbs include *feel*, *look*, *smell*, *sound*, and *taste*.

I **feel bad** that you were not elected. (Not *badly*)

Cakes from Federico's Bakery always **taste delicious**. (Not *deliciously*)

---

[10]See Section 1-8 for a detailed explanation of the use of the comma with independent adjectives.

After the fire the adjoining rooms **smelled terrible**. (Not *terribly*)

## 6–24. Compound Adjectives[11]

**a.** Adjectives containing two or more words that are shown hyphenated in the dictionary are known as *permanent compounds*.[12] These words are always hyphenated when they are used as adjectives.

Your **up-to-date** files have been very helpful in compiling this data.

My present job is only **part-time**, but I will begin looking for a **full-time** job in September.

As one of the oldest players in the league, Steve doesn't seem to know when he is **well-off**.

**b.** When two or more words appearing before a noun function as a single-thought modifier, place hyphens between the words, even though these words do not appear hyphenated in the dictionary. These compound adjectives are *temporary compounds* and are hyphenated only when they appear before the noun or pronoun they modify.

**temporary compound adjective before the modified noun**

Upon reading your **well-written** report, the committee members agreed to establish a new community center.

Very little of the **high-priced** merchandise was sold during our clearance sale.

Do not exceed the **65-mile-an-hour** speed limit.

You may advertise this opening as a **$30,000-a-year** position.

**temporary compound adjective following the modified noun**

Your report is certainly **well written**.

This merchandise is too **high priced** for our store.

The speed limit on this freeway is **65 miles an hour**.

Our manager's salary is at least **$30,000 a year**.

# Adverbs

## 6–25. Functions and Forms of Adverbs

Adverbs modify verbs, adjectives, or other adverbs. They answer such questions as when? where? why? how? to what degree?

---

[11]See Section 2-2 for detailed rules regarding the formation of compound adjectives.

[12]All hyphenations for compound adjectives in this manual are based on those shown in *Merriam Webster's Collegiate Dictionary*, 10th Ed. (Springfield, Mass.: Merriam-Webster, Incorporated, 1996).

a. Most adverbs end in *ly*.

| | | |
|---|---|---|
| accidentally | daily | finally |
| carefully | definitely | steadily |
| cautiously | diligently | usually |

b. **Some adverbs may either end in *ly* or take the adjective form of the word.[13]**

Please drive **slowly** (or **slow**) on this icy road.

Your order will be processed as **quickly** (or **quick**) as possible.

You may call **directly** (or **direct**) to Chicago on this line.

c. **Other adverbs do not take an *ly* form. Such adverbs include the following:**

| | | | |
|---|---|---|---|
| again | late | not | there |
| almost | never | now | very |
| here | no | soon | well |

## 6–26. Adverb Comparison

a. **One-syllable adverbs and some two-syllable adverbs are compared by adding *er* or *est*. For comparisons between two items, use *er*; for comparisons among more than two items, use *est*.[14]**

**comparison of two**

You live **closer** to the library than I.

My assistant left **earlier** than I.

**comparison of more than two**

Of all the students in the study group, you live **closest** to the library.

Who is scheduled to arrive the **earliest**—Bill, Paula, or Bob?

b. **Most adverbs containing two syllables and all adverbs containing more than two syllables form the comparison by adding *more* or *most* (or *less* or *least*) to the positive form. Use *more* (or *less*) in comparing two items and *most* (or *least*) in comparing more than two items.**

**comparison of two**

This conveyer belt travels **more slowly** than the one next to it.

Please pack these items **more carefully** than you have done in the past.

This brand of soap is **less widely** used on the East Coast than in the South.

---

[13]Both forms of those adverbs that may end in *ly* or just take the adjective form are shown in the dictionary.

[14]Two-syllable adverbs that show comparison by adding *er* or *est* are considered irregular. Therefore, these forms are shown in the dictionary following the simple form.

### comparison of more than two

Denver has been mentioned **most often** as the likely site for our next convention.

This conference is the **most unusually** conducted one I have ever attended.

This brand of soap is the **least widely** used of all the major brands.

## 6–27.  Adverb Placement

**a.**  **Place adverbs as closely as possible to the words they modify. The misplacement of an adverb can change the meaning of a sentence or result in an awkward-sounding sentence.**

### changed meaning

**Only** Beverly and I were invited to attend the seminar on human relations.

Beverly and I were invited to attend **only** the seminar on human relations.

### awkward construction

Our costs have **nearly** risen 20 percent this year.  (Awkward)

Our costs have risen **nearly** 20 percent this year.  (Correct)

**b.**  **Avoid splitting an infinitive with an adverb; place the adverb after the infinitive.**

We will need **to scrutinize carefully** all applicants for this position.

If you wish **to discuss** this situation **further,** please call me.

## 6–28.  Adverbs vs. Adjectives

**Use an adverb after a verb that shows action; use an adjective, however, after a nonaction (or linking) verb.**

### action verb

You **did well** on your six-month evaluation.

The pedestrian **crossed** the street **cautiously.**

Most of the committee **opposed bitterly** the controversial measure.

The professional soccer team **was beaten badly** in yesterday's game.

### nonaction or linking verb

The employees' lounge **smells terrible.**

If we do not brew fresh coffee every two hours, it begins to **taste bitter.**

I **feel bad** about Mr. Johnson's predicament.

The entrée at the Sunday evening banquet **was delicious.**

## 6–29. Double Negatives

Use only one negative word or limiting adverb to express a single idea.

Do **not** release this information to **anybody**. (Not *nobody*)

I did **not** receive **anything** from our insurance agent. (Not *nothing*)

I **can** (not *can't* or *cannot*) **scarcely** believe that our president would make such a foolish statement.

We **were** (not *weren't* or *were not*) **hardly** in the office when Ms. Kawamura gave us the disappointing news.

He **had** (not *hadn't* or *had not*) **barely** finished computing the results when the Board of Directors requested him to report his findings.

# Prepositions

## 6–30. Prepositions as Connectors

**a.** Prepositions link descriptive words to other words or ideas in a sentence. The most commonly used prepositions are *of* and *for*. Occasionally used ones are *about, during, except,* and *but* (meaning *except*). Other commonly used prepositions, those listed below, can easily be identified by picturing what an airplane can do in relation to clouds: the airplane can fly _____ the clouds.

| | | |
|---|---|---|
| above | down | over |
| after | from | through |
| alongside | in | to |
| among | inside | toward |
| around | into | under |
| at | near | up |
| before | off | upon |
| behind | on | with |
| below | opposite | within |
| between | outside | without |

**b.** Prepositions begin a phrase that ends with a noun or pronoun. This phrase is related to another word in the sentence—it describes, limits, or modifies the word in some way by clarifying who, what, when, where, how, why, or to what degree.

Our staff **of accountants** is available to assist you at any time. (*Of accountants* is related to *staff*—specifies what.)

You may park your car **behind the building**. (*Behind the building* is related to *park*—specifies where.)

## 6–31. Prepositional Phrases

In determining subject-verb agreement, generally ignore any prepositional phrases that separate the subject and the verb. See

Section 6-18 I for subject-verb agreement principles related to prepositional phrases appearing before relative pronoun clauses (clauses beginning with *who* or *that*).

**One** of your brothers **is** waiting in your office. (Omit *of your brothers* to match "One . . . is.")

A large **quantity** of goods **has** been ordered for the sale. (Omit *of goods* to match "quantity . . . has.")

Last Monday our **supply** of paper goods and kitchen utensils **was** destroyed. (Omit *of paper goods and kitchen utensils* to match "supply . . . was.")

## 6–32. *In, Between,* or *Among*?

When a preposition has a single object, use *in*. For two separate objects, use *between*; for three or more objects, use *among*.

**in**

There are several discrepancies **in** the auditor's report.

The prosecution noted several discrepancies **in** the witness's testimony.

**between**

**Between** you and me, I believe our company stock will split within the next several months.

There were several discrepancies **between** the two witnesses' reports.

**among**

Please distribute these supplies **among** the various branch offices.

**Among** themselves the Board of Directors had consented previously to withdraw that motion.

## 6–33. Prepositions Used With Certain Words

Certain words require particular prepositions, depending upon the meaning to be conveyed. Other words often acquire prepositions incorrectly. A list of commonly used correct combinations follows:

Agree **on** or **upon** (mutual ideas or considerations—to reach an understanding)
Agree **to** (undertake an action)
Agree **with** (a person or his or her idea)

All **of** (Use *of* when followed by a pronoun; omit *of* when followed by a noun. *All of us . . . . All the people . . . .*)

Angry **about** (a situation or condition)
Angry **at** (things)
Angry **with** (a person or a group of persons)

Both **of** (Use *of* when followed by a pronoun; omit *of* when followed by a noun. *Both of them . . . . Both the managers . . . .*)

Buy **from** (Not *off* or *off of*)

Comply or compliance **with** (Not *to*)

Conform **to** (to act in accordance with prevailing standards)
Conform **with** (to be similar or in agreement)

Convenient **to** (a location)
Convenient **for** (a person)

Correspond **with** (a person—by writing)
Correspond **to** (a thing)

Discrepancy **in** (one thing)
Discrepancy **between** (two things)
Discrepancy **among** (three or more things)

Different **from** (Not *than*)

From (a person) (Not *off* a person)

Help (doing something) (Not *help from. He could not help laughing at . . . .*)

Identical **with** (Not *to*)

Inside (Not *inside of*)

Off (a thing) (Not *off of*)

Opposite (Not *opposite to* or *opposite of*)

Outside (Not *outside of*)

Plan **to** (Not *plan on*)

Retroactive **to** (Not *retroactive from*)

Take **off** (a thing)
Take **from** (a person)

# Conjunctions

Conjunctions join words or groups of words within a sentence. While some conjunctions join equal ideas, others join contrasting ideas or introduce dependent clauses.

## 6–34. Coordinating Conjunctions

a. The most commonly occurring coordinating conjunctions—*and, but, or,* and *nor*—are used to join like or equal ideas within a sentence. These ideas may be words, phrases, or clauses.

**words**

Please place copies of the **proposal** and **contract** in each client's file.

You may obtain additional information from **Mr. Phelps, Ms. Dow,** or **me.**

**phrases**

Please post these notices **on all campus bulletin boards** and **in student gathering places throughout the campus.**

Ms. Ross has agreed to **edit the manuscript** and **follow it through all the production stages.**

**clauses**

If you accept our offer, **we will sign a guarantee of completion by May 1** and **you will be protected against any losses beyond this date.**

**Our advertising funds for this year have been depleted,** but **we are interested in considering your proposal for our next year's budget.**

**b.** Because coordinating conjunctions join equal ideas, the ideas they join must be expressed in the same way; that is, they must have *parallel structure*. Parallel structure requires that the connected ideas have the same format. For example, if the first idea begins with a noun or pronoun, so must any others. If the first idea begins with an infinitive, then all others must begin with an infinitive. Be sure to match each idea—gerund with gerund, verb with verb, prepositional phrase with prepositional phrase, and so forth.

**parallel structure with gerunds**

You may obtain your free trial subscription by **calling** or **writing** our main office.

We would appreciate your **paying** this bill as soon as possible and **sending** us a copy of the receipt issued at the time of payment.

**parallel structure with verb phrases (past participles)**

The contractor has already **leveled** the construction site and **poured** the foundation.

As you requested, we have **notified** our delinquent customers of their status, **requested** immediate payment of all overdue amounts, and **halted** any charge orders in progress.

**parallel structure with clauses (subject and verb)**

As soon as we receive your credit application, **we will check** your credit rating and our **Credit Department will contact** you.

Our local **chamber of commerce has endorsed** this proposal, but other **chambers of commerce** in the county **are opposed** to it.

## 6–35. Conjunctions Used in Pairs

**a.** Use *either . . . or* for positive statements; use *neither . . . nor* for negative statements. The same grammatical construction should be used after each part.

**positive statements,** *either . . . or*

**Either** Ms. Saunders **or** Mr. Ramirez will inspect the property.

You may specify **either** black **or** brown on your order.

**negative statements, *neither . . . nor***

**Neither** a Toyota **nor** a Datsun is available for rental this week.

I could not believe that **neither** Larry **nor** Debbie would accept the assignment.

b. **Use the same grammatical construction after each part of the conjunctive pair *not only . . . but also.***

Our company manufactures **not only** furniture **but also** major appliances. (Not: Our company *not only* manufactures furniture *but also* major appliances.)

Our company **not only** manufactures and services major appliances **but also** services small appliances.

c. **In comparisons use *as . . . as* for positive ideas and *so . . . as* for negative ideas.**

**positive ideas, *as . . . as***

Our Model 874 cellular phone has become **as** popular **as** our Model 923.

I believe that her understudy is **as** talented **as** Ms. Saito.

**negative ideas, *so . . . as***

Our Model 874 cellular phone is not **so** popular **as** our Model 923.

Avocados are not **so** expensive **as** they were last year.

**6–36. Subordinating Conjunctions**

**Subordinating conjunctions may be used to introduce dependent clauses. A partial listing of subordinating conjunctions follows:**

| | | |
|---|---|---|
| if | because | while |
| as | since | before |
| when | although | after |

a. **When a subordinating conjunction with its corresponding clause introduces a sentence, place a comma after the introductory clause.**

**If you wish any additional information,** Mr. Johnson will be pleased to supply it.

**Before you sign these contracts,** you should speak with some of this company's former clients.

b. **When a subordinating conjunction with its corresponding clause follows a main clause, separate the two clauses with a comma only if the subordinating conjunction introduces a nonrestrictive idea.**

**no comma separating clauses—restrictive idea**

We will ship your merchandise **when we receive your authorization.**

You may wish to verify this information **before you make any further payments.**

197

**comma separating clauses—nonrestrictive idea**

Mr. Johnson would be pleased to supply you with any additional information, **if you need it.**

My clients have agreed to settle this matter out of court, **although I advised them against doing so.**

### 6–37. As vs. Like

*As* is a conjunction and is used when the following construction is a clause (a word group containing a subject and a verb). *Like* is a preposition and is used when the following construction is a prepositional phrase (a phrase ending with a noun or pronoun).

**as with a clause**

They did not package the order **as** (not *like*) **he expected they would.**

**As** (not *like*) **you indicated in your letter,** we cannot expect to make a profit during our first year of operation.

**like with a prepositional phrase**

We need more qualified agents **like you.**

Please order another desk **like the one** you have in your office.

## Interjections

### 6–38. Use of Interjections

Interjections impart sudden emotion or strong feeling, but they do not contribute substantially to the meaning of the sentence. When used alone, interjections are followed by an exclamation mark. When they are used within a sentence, the sentence is generally concluded with an exclamation mark. Examples of interjections used alone follow:

| | | |
|---|---|---|
| Absolutely not! | Never! | Well! |
| Ah! | No! | Whew! |
| Great! | Oh! | Wow! |
| Indeed not! | Terrific! | Yes! |

**interjections used alone**

**Whew!** I'm certainly glad the work for this tax period is behind us.

**Absolutely not!** Only employees with security clearances are permitted in this area.

**interjections in sentences**

**Oh,** you can't expect us to have these photographs developed by tomorrow!

**No,** we cannot make any exceptions to this company policy!

# Chapter 7

# Words Often Confused and Misused

a/an

# Words Often Confused and Misused Solution Finder

All entries in this chapter appear in alphabetical order.

### A/An

**A** (ARTICLE; used before a word beginning with a consonant sound or a long $\bar{u}$ sound)—Please call *a* technician to service the photocopier. *A u*nion representative met with us yesterday.

**An** (ARTICLE; used before a word beginning with a vowel sound other than long $\bar{u}$)—Please make *an a*ppointment for me to meet with Mr. Barrett on Monday.

### A lot/Allot/Alot

**A lot** (ARTICLE + NOUN; combination meaning "many" or "much")—*A lot* of our customers have requested us to extend our hours. We have spent *a lot* of time investigating your proposal.

**Allot** (VERB; to allocate, assign)—How much money will we *allot* for advertising next year?

**Alot** (misspelling of *a lot*)

### A while/Awhile

**A while** (ARTICLE + NOUN; combination meaning "a short time")—He will be here in *a while*.

**Awhile** (ADVERB; meaning "*for* a short time")—Exercise *awhile* each day to maintain your good health.

### Accede/Exceed

**Accede** (VERB; to agree or consent)—I will *accede* to this request only if the tenants sign a one-year lease.

**Exceed** (VERB; to surpass a limit)—Many accidents occur when drivers *exceed* the posted speed limit.

### Accelerate/Exhilarate

**Accelerate** (VERB; to speed up)—We must *accelerate* our progress in developing new software if we expect to stay ahead of our competition.

**Exhilarate** (VERB; to make cheerful; to refresh or stimulate)—The entire staff was *exhilarated* by the news that our office was No. 1 in sales. All of us attending the retreat at Blue Pines were *exhilarated* by the crisp, fresh air.

### Accept/Except

**Accept** (VERB; to take or receive)—We do not *accept* checks written on out-of-state banks.

**Except** (CONJUNCTION; with the exclusion of, but)—No one outside the company *except* you knows about the proposed merger.

### Access/Excess

**Access** (NOUN; admittance or approachability)—Everyone in the office should have *access* to these files.

**Excess** (ADJECTIVE; beyond ordinary limits; a surplus)—You may return all *excess* flooring materials for full credit within 60 days of purchase.

## Ad/Add

**Ad** (NOUN; abbreviated form of *advertisement*)—We fill most of our personnel needs by running an *ad* in the local newspaper.

**Add** (VERB; to increase by uniting or joining)—This new computer will *add* to the efficiency of our office staff.

## Adapt/Adept/Adopt

**Adapt** (VERB; to adjust or modify)—We must readily *adapt* ourselves to new situations in this rapidly changing market.

**Adept** (ADJECTIVE; skilled)—The person hired for this position must be *adept* at dealing with customer complaints.

**Adopt** (VERB; to take and follow as one's own)—We will *adopt* Mrs. Williams' proposal to computerize our accounting system.

## Add: see Ad.

## Addict/Edict

**Addict** (NOUN; one who is habitually or obsessively dependent; devotee)—Our clinic has noted success with the rehabilitation of drug *addicts*. Many of today's teenagers are rock music *addicts*.

**Edict** (NOUN; order or command)—When did our manager issue this *edict*?

## Addition/Edition

**Addition** (NOUN; the process of uniting or joining; an added part)—The increased production quotas require the *addition* of factory floor space in all our facilities.

**Edition** (NOUN; a particular version of printed material)—Only the second *edition* of this book is now available.

## Adept: see Adapt.

## Adherence/Adherents

**Adherence** (NOUN; a steady attachment or loyalty)—A strict *adherence* to all safety procedures is required of all personnel.

**Adherents** (NOUN; loyal supporters or followers)—The many *adherents* to the space program believe in its importance to the human race.

## Adopt: see Adapt.

## Adverse/Averse

**Adverse** (ADJECTIVE; opposing; antagonistic)—Rising interest rates have had an *adverse* effect on real estate sales and new home developments.

**Averse** (ADJECTIVE; unwilling; reluctant)—One of Carol's many attributes is that she is not *averse* to working long hours to meet specific production schedules.

## Advice/Advise

**Advice** (NOUN; a suggestion, an opinion, or a recommendation)—He would have avoided the problem if he had followed his attorney's *advice*.

**Advise** (VERB; to counsel or recommend)—We had to *advise* her not to sign the contract in its present form.

## Affect/Effect

**Affect** (VERB; to influence)—Large pay increases throughout the country will *affect* the rate of inflation. Increased costs will *affect* our pricing policy on all merchandise.

**Effect** (VERB; to bring about or cause to happen; to create)—Our government plans to *effect* a change in the rate of inflation by tightening bank credits. Rising costs of raw materials will *effect* large price increases in May.

**Effect** (NOUN; a result or consequence)—Inflation usually has a negative *effect* on our economy. The new vacation policy had no apparent *effect* on company morale.

### Aggravate/Irritate

**Aggravate** (VERB; to exacerbate; to make something worse)—To bring in legal counsel at this time would only *aggravate* the situation further. By scratching the infected area, you will only *aggravate* the itching and puffiness.

**Irritate** (VERB; to create an annoying condition)—If you do not refund the full purchase price, you will surely *irritate* the customer.

### Aid/Aide

**Aid** (VERB, to help or assist; NOUN, assistance)—The United States *aids* many foreign countries. Your application for financial *aid* is currently being processed.

**Aide** (NOUN; a person who assists another)—Please ask your *aide* to deliver these papers to Dr. Powell's office by Friday afternoon.

### Aisle/Isle

**Aisle** (NOUN; a passageway for inside traffic)—After the show the *aisles* of the theater were littered with empty popcorn containers and candy wrappers.

**Isle** (NOUN; a piece of land surrounded by water; island)—This script centers around two teenagers marooned on a tropical *isle*.

### All ready/Already

**All ready** (ADJECTIVE; prepared)—We are *all ready* to initiate the new procedures as soon as the equipment arrives.

**Already** (ADVERB; by or before this time)—Orders for our August sale have *already* been placed with the suppliers.

### All right/Alright

**All right** (ADJECTIVE; satisfactory or agreeable)—Changing your vacation dates from June to July seems to be *all right* with our supervisor.

**Alright** (An informal spelling of *all right* that is not appropriate for business writing.)

### All together/Altogether

**All together** (ADVERB + ADVERB; wholly as a group; counted or summed up)— We must work *all together* if the company is to survive this crisis. *All together*, 87 families signed up for the company picnic.

**Altogether** (ADVERB; entirely or completely; in all; on the whole)—This problem is *altogether* different from the one we faced last year. We believe he has embezzled over $200,000 *altogether*. Although we did not reach our goal of $3 million in sales, our result may *altogether* be considered successful.

### All ways/Always

**All ways** (ADJECTIVE + NOUN; by all methods)—We must try *all ways* possible to solve the problem.

**Always** (ADVERB; at all times; continually)—Our company is *always* looking for qualified office personnel.

a/an

**Allot:** see A lot.

### Allowed/Aloud

**Allowed** (VERB; permitted)—We are *allowed* to sell our products only through contracted retail outlets.

**Aloud** (ADVERB; audibly)—The president's resignation was read *aloud* to all board members present.

### Allude/Elude

**Allude** (VERB; to mention or refer to)—As proof of Americans' concern for economy, I *allude* to the increased popularity of small cars during recent years.

**Elude** (VERB; to evade or escape)—The senator has been able to *elude* severe criticisms of his program by anticipating and counteracting objections.

### Allusion/Delusion/Illusion

**Allusion** (NOUN; an indirect reference)—Several *allusions* were made to Mr. Reed's apparent laziness.

**Delusion** (NOUN; a false belief instilled through purposeful deception)—Many people invested heavily in these oil stocks because they operated under the *delusion* that its wells were active producers.

**Illusion** (NOUN; a misconception or misapprehension)—Many of our employees originally had the *illusion* that this new equipment would reduce our staff by one half, but they were pleased to learn that it would only increase their productivity.

### Almost/Most

**Almost** (ADVERB; nearly)—By the end of the third quarter, our company had *almost* reached its sales quota for the year.

**Most** (ADJECTIVE; the greatest in amount or number)—Patricia Lynn received the *most* votes in the election for faculty senate treasurer.

**Alot:** see A lot.

**Aloud:** see Allowed.

**Already:** see All ready.

**Alright:** see All right.

### Altar/Alter

**Altar** (NOUN; a structure used for worship)—The wedding flowers are to be placed on the *altar* by 6 p.m.

**Alter** (VERB; to change)—Please *alter* your schedule so that you will be able to attend the monthly committee meetings.

### Alternate/Alternative

**Alternate** (VERB, ['öl-tər-‚nāt], to change from one to another repeatedly; NOUN, ['öl-tər-nət], one that substitutes for another; ADJECTIVE, ['öl-tər-‚nət], separate and distinct)—Our conferences *alternate* between the northern and southern parts of the state. Jack Smith has agreed to serve as my *alternate* on the budget committee. For the next few months, motorists will be required to use an *alternate* route to the downtown area.

**Alternative** (NOUN; a choice between two or among several)—We were left with only two *alternatives*—either accept the lease conditions or find another location. None of the *alternatives* presented by the committee were acceptable to the Board of Directors.

**Altogether: see All together.**

**Always: see All ways.**

**Among/Between**
**Among** (PREPOSITION; refers to more than two persons or things)—Distribute the supplies equally *among* the three departments.
**Between** (PREPOSITION; refers to two persons or things)—The final selection for the position is *between* Ms. Claffey and Mr. Thompson.

**Amount/Number**
**Amount** (NOUN; used with singular nouns and mass items that cannot be counted)—Only a small *amount* of the cake was eaten. The store manager has not yet determined the *amount* of money that was stolen. Because of the power failure, a significant *amount* of the frozen food had deteriorated and was discarded.
**Number** (NOUN; used with plural nouns and items that can be counted)—Only a small *number* of spaces have been allotted for visitor parking. This year the *number* of children in each classroom has been reduced by three.

**An: see A.**

**Anecdote/Antidote**
**Anecdote** (NOUN, ['a-nik-,dōt]; a story or a brief account of an event)—We all had to laugh at Tom's *anecdote* about the customer who insisted upon returning a product our store doesn't even sell.
**Antidote** (NOUN, ['an-ti-,dōt]; a remedy that counteracts a harmful substance or circumstance)—Dr. Martin has consented to write an article about the new *antidote* he developed to counteract five different household poisons.

**Annual/Annul**
**Annual** (ADJECTIVE; yearly)—The company's *annual* report will be mailed to all stockholders of record next week.
**Annul** (VERB; to void or abolish)—We had to *annul* the contract because of unexpected legal complications.

**Antidote: see Anecdote.**

**Anxious/Eager**
**Anxious** (ADJECTIVE; worried or apprehensive)—Donna is *anxious* about taking the upcoming real estate brokers' examination.
**Eager** (ADJECTIVE; anticipating with enthusiasm)—Mr. Adams is *eager* to begin his new job with Girard Enterprises next week.

**Any one/Anyone**
**Any one** (ADJECTIVE + PRONOUN; any one person or thing in a group [always followed by *of* ])—You may assign me to assist *any one* of the new students.
**Anyone** (PRONOUN; any person at all)—If you know of *anyone* who has these qualifications, please have that person contact our manager of human resources.

**Any time/Anytime**
**Any time** (ADJECTIVE + NOUN; an unspecified *point* in time; an amount of time)—Please let us know *any time* you have questions about our products or

services. *Any time* we can be of service, just call our toll-free number and a telephone representative will assist you. We do not have *any time* to review this case.
**Anytime** (ADVERB; at any time *whatsoever*)—Drop by our offices *anytime*. For an emergency you may call Dr. Mulcahy *anytime*, day or night. During the last quarter of the year, you may take your vacation *anytime*.

## Any way/Anyway

**Any way** (ADJECTIVE + NOUN; any method)—Is there *any way* we can step up production to advance our July 1 release date?
**Anyway** (ADVERB; in any case)—Considering the low bids of our competitors, I don't believe we would have received the contract *anyway*.
**Anyways** (An informal form of *anyway* that is not appropriate for business writing.)

## Appraise/Apprise

**Appraise** (VERB; to estimate the value or nature)—Before we can liquidate this company, we must hire an outside firm to *appraise* its assets.
**Apprise** (VERB; to inform or notify)—Please *apprise* all employees immediately of this change in policy.

## As/Like

**As** (CONJUNCTION; used at the beginning of a clause)—I will get the material to you by Friday, *as* (not *like*) I promised. Our manager always acts *as if* (not *like*) he knows more than anyone else.
**Like** (PREPOSITION; used when the sentence requires a preposition meaning "similar to" [followed by a noun or pronoun and its modifiers])—This new adhesive feels *like* wet cement. I have never met anyone else *like* him. These cookies taste *like* the chocolate chip cookies my mother used to make.

## Ascent/Assent

**Ascent** (NOUN; rising or going up)—The recent *ascent* of stock market prices has encouraged more small investors to enter the market.
**Assent** (VERB; to agree or consent)—Everyone at the meeting will surely *assent* to the plan you have outlined in this report.

## Assistance/Assistants

**Assistance** (NOUN; help or aid)—The project could not have been completed on time without your *assistance*. If you need financial *assistance*, please fill out these forms.
**Assistants** (NOUN; people who aid or help a superior)—The consultant's staffing report indicates that our general manager should have three *assistants*.

## Assume/Presume

**Assume** (VERB; to take for granted as true; to take on)—I *assumed* these sales figures had been corrected before they were submitted to the general manager. Who will be assigned to *assume* these extra duties?
**Presume** (VERB; to anticipate with confidence)—After this episode we can no longer *presume* that this vendor will stand behind its products or fulfill the conditions of its warranties.

## Assure/Ensure/Insure

**Assure** (VERB; to promise; to make a positive declaration)—I *assure* you that the loan will be repaid according to the terms specified in the note. Please *assure* the patient that this procedure is not painful.

205

**Ensure** (VERB; to make certain)—To *ensure* the timely completion of this project, please hire additional qualified personnel.

**Insure** (VERB; to protect against financial loss)—We *insure* all our facilities against earthquake damage.

## Attendance/Attendants

**Attendance** (NOUN; being present or attending)—At least two thirds of the members of this committee must be in *attendance* before the meeting can be called to order.

**Attendants** (NOUN; those who attend with or to others)—The *attendants* had difficulty parking all the cars for such a large crowd.

### Averse: see Adverse.

### Awhile: see A while.

## Bad/Badly

**Bad** (ADJECTIVE; an adjective or subject complement used after such intransitive or nonaction verbs as *is, was, feel, look,* or *smell*)—I feel *bad* that your transfer request was denied.  Profits for the first quarter of this year look *bad* in view of the additional expenses incurred by our sales staff.  The air in this office smells *bad*.

**Badly** (ADVERB; used with transitive or action verbs)—We *badly* need the advice of a tax attorney before we invest further in this project.  The defeated candidate behaved *badly* before thousands of television viewers.

## Bail/Bale

**Bail** (NOUN; guarantee of money necessary to set a person free from jail until the trial)—*Bail* in your client's case has been set at $25,000.

**Bale** (NOUN; a large bundle)—One *bale* of used clothing was lost in transit.

## Bare/Bear

**Bare** (ADJECTIVE; uncovered, empty, plain, or mere)—The paint had chipped and peeled so badly that the *bare* wood was showing.  After the break-in the two outer offices were *bare* of furniture and equipment.  Every year our work group retreats for three days to a *bare* wooden cabin in the mountains.  I had time to cover only the *bare* facts involved in this issue.

**Bear** (VERB; to support, carry, or bring forth)—Unfortunately, he had to *bear* the brunt of the losses.  Our travel agency will secure for you guides who have donkeys to *bear* the luggage and provisions.  As a result of the surgery, the patient was able to *bear* children.

## Base/Bass

**Base** (NOUN; bottom part of something; foundation)—When did the *base* of this marble column crack?

**Bass** (ADJECTIVE; a low-pitched sound; musical instrument having a low range)—We could use his *bass* voice in our quartet.  Do you play the *bass* violin?

## Bazaar/Bizarre

**Bazaar** (NOUN; a fair for the sale of articles)—Our Lady of Lourdes Church will hold its annual *bazaar* during the Memorial Day weekend.

**Bizarre** (ADJECTIVE; strikingly out of the ordinary)—Floyd's Fashions has often been described as carrying *bizarre* clothing lines and accessories.

### Bear: see Bare.

## Berth/Birth

**Berth** (VERB, to bring into a berth; NOUN, the place where a ship lies at anchor; place to sit or sleep on a ship or vehicle)—When will the Song of Norway next *berth* in Puerto Rico? How many *berths* does your port have for ships from major cruise lines? The only sleeping accommodations not yet reserved are upper *berths*.

**Birth** (NOUN; the emergence of a new individual from the body of its parent)—Hospital policy permits only the father and one other family member to be present during the *birth* of a child.

## Beside/Besides

**Beside** (PREPOSITION; by the side of)—Please place the new file cabinet *beside* the one in the corner.

**Besides** (PREPOSITION; in addition to)—Who else *besides* Ms. Graham was awarded a bonus?

## Between: see Among.

## Bi-/Semi-

**Bi-** (PREFIX; two)—Our newsletter is published *bi*monthly: January, March, May, July, September, and November.

**Semi-** (PREFIX; half)—Bulletins to the staff are issued *semi*monthly, the 1st and 15th of each month.

## Biannual/Biennial

**Biannual** (ADJECTIVE; occurring twice a year)—The stockholders' *biannual* meetings are held in January and July.

**Biennial** (ADJECTIVE; occurring once every two years)—According to our society's constitution, the *biennial* election of officers should be held in November.

## Bibliography/Biography

**Bibliography** (NOUN; a list of works consulted by an author for a production)—Be sure to include in the *bibliography* all the sources—books, magazines, newspapers, compact disks, Internet resources, etc.—you used for this report.

**Biography** (NOUN; history of a person's life written by someone else)—This *biography* of Henry Ford is exceptionally well written.

## Billed/Build

**Billed** (VERB; charged for goods or services)—You will be *billed* on the 10th of each month.

**Build** (VERB; to construct)—We plan to *build* a new plant in Texas.

## Biography: see Bibliography.

## Birth: see Berth.

## Bizarre: see Bazaar.

## Boarder/Border

**Boarder** (NOUN; one who is provided with regular meals and lodging)—Owners of homes in residential areas are limited in the number of *boarders* they may solicit for commercial purposes.

**Border** (NOUN; an outer part or edge; boundary)—Which *border* did you select for the cover page of the report? If you plan to cross the *border* into Mexico, be sure to take your passport with you.

a/an

Misused Words

7

## Bolder/Boulder

**Bolder** (ADJECTIVE; more fearless or daring)—Perhaps we need a *bolder* person as president of the university.

**Boulder** (NOUN; a large rock)—Damage to the insured's left-front tire was apparently caused by a *boulder* in the road.

## Born/Borne

**Born** (ADJECTIVE; brought forth by birth; originated)—This patient was *born* on February 14, 1943. One can hardly believe that this multibillion-dollar industry was *born* in a garage fewer than three decades ago.

**Borne** (VERB; past participle of *bear*)—Mrs. Talbert has already *borne* six children, and she is currently expecting her seventh. Our school district has *borne* these financial burdens for over six years.

## Bouillon/Bullion

**Bouillon** (NOUN; a clear soup)—For the first course I have ordered *bouillon*.

**Bullion** (NOUN; uncoined gold or silver in bars or ingots)—Mr. Reece had hidden in his home nearly $45,000 in gold *bullion*.

## Boulder: see Bolder.

## Breach/Breech

**Breach** (NOUN; a violation of a law or agreement; a hole, gap, or break)—The judge ruled that a *breach* of contract transpired when the building was not finished by the date agreed upon. If contract negotiations are to continue, we must narrow the *breach* between union and management negotiators.

**Breech** (NOUN; part of a firearm or cannon that is located behind the barrel)—They had difficulty firing the old cannon because the *breech* would not work properly.

## Bring/Take

**Bring** (VERB; to carry toward [a place])—Please *bring* (not *take*) all your receipts when you meet with our accountant.

**Take** (VERB; to carry away; to carry from one place to another)—You may *take* any one of these samples. Please *take* these brochures to our Springfield office.

## Build: see Billed.

## Bullion: see Bouillon.

## Calendar/Colander

**Calendar** (NOUN; a schedule of days and months for a period of time)—Please order a supply of desk *calendars* for the new year.

**Colander** (NOUN; a strainer)—Use a *colander* to drain the pasta before placing it in the sauce.

## Callous/Callus

**Callous** (ADJECTIVE; insensitive; without feeling)—Everyone on the committee agreed that Mr. Bush's *callous* remark concerning Ms. Wright's attire was in poor taste.

**Callus** (NOUN; hard, thick skin)—Pointed-toe shoes can cause permanent *calluses* on your feet.

## Can/May

**Can** (VERB; to have the ability to do something)—Pauline *can* convert our manual accounting system to a computerized one.

**May** (VERB; to express permission or possibility)—Yes, you *may* take a day's vacation tomorrow. *May* we have these files translated into ASCII files by next Wednesday?

## Canvas/Canvass

**Canvas** (NOUN; a firm, closely woven cloth)—Use these *canvas* coverings to protect the new cars as they arrive.

**Canvass** (VERB; to survey or solicit in an area)—Do you have a volunteer who will *canvass* the residences on Jersey Street?

## Capital/Capitol

**Capital** (NOUN; a city in which the official seat of government is located; the wealth of an individual or firm)—The *capital* of Wisconsin is Madison.  Much of our *capital* is tied up in equipment.

**Capital** (ADJECTIVE; punishable by death; foremost in importance)—Treason is a *capital* crime in many countries.  The forthcoming election is *capital* in the minds of the school board members.

**Capitol** (NOUN; a building used by the U.S. Congress [always capitalized])—Senator Cano must be in the *Capitol* by 9 a.m. for the hearings.  The United States *Capitol* is a major tourist attraction in Washington, D.C.

**Capitol** (NOUN; a building in which a state legislature convenes [capitalized only when used in full name of building])—The *capitol* was surrounded by angry pickets waving placards. Is this office located in the California State *Capitol*?

## Carat/Caret/Carrot/Karat

**Carat** (NOUN; a unit of weight for gems)—The total weight of this diamond ring is 2.17 *carats*.

**Caret** (NOUN; a proofreading symbol similar to an inverted *v* that is placed at the bottom of a line to show insertions in edited copy)—Our editor placed a *caret* between the two words where the company name is to be inserted.

**Carrot** (NOUN; a vegetable)—A *carrot* can be just as delicious raw as it is cooked.

**Karat** (NOUN, GENERALLY USED AS ADJECTIVE; a unit of weight for gold)—This Italian chain is made of 18-*karat* gold.

## Cease/Seize

**Cease** (VERB; to come to an end or stop)—Please *cease* shipment of any further orders to the Hogan Company until its current balance has been paid.

**Seize** (VERB; to take possession of; to take)—Will the Internal Revenue Service *seize* all the company's assets for the payment of back taxes?  You may wish to *seize* this opportunity to ask Mr. Rodriguez for a salary increase.

## Ceiling/Sealing

**Ceiling** (NOUN; overhead inside lining of a room; upper limit)—Have you checked all the acoustical *ceilings* in this apartment complex to ensure they are free from asbestos? *Ceilings* on rent increases are controlled by the city council.

**Sealing** (NOUN; closing with a coating to make secure)—These glue sticks are used mostly for *sealing* envelopes.

## Censor/Censure

**Censor** (VERB, to examine materials and delete objectionable matter; NOUN, one who censors)—We will need to *censor* scenes from this movie for television viewing.  When will the *censor* finish reviewing the script?

**Censure** (VERB, to criticize or condemn; NOUN, condemnation)—The city council *censured* the mayor for awarding the contract to his brother-in-law's firm. After the facts were disclosed, Senator Dillon was subjected to public *censure*.

### Census/Senses

**Census** (NOUN; an official count of population within a specified geographical area)—The United States undergoes an official *census* every ten years.

**Senses** (NOUN; the specialized functions of sight, hearing, smell, taste, and touch)—Our client's *senses* of hearing and touch were impaired as a result of the accident.

### Cent/Scent/Sent

**Cent** (NOUN; a coin known as a *penny*)—Your tallies always balance to the last *cent*.

**Scent** (NOUN; a distinctive smell or odor)—Because Webby Bakery is located in our industrial complex, the *scent* of freshly baked bread permeates the area each morning.

**Sent** (VERB; the past tense and past participle of *send*)—Your order was *sent* by United Parcel Service yesterday.

### Cereal/Serial

**Cereal** (NOUN; a breakfast food made from grain)—Your diet calls for a daily serving of wheat *cereal*.

**Serial** (ADJECTIVE; arranged in a series)—The *serial* numbers of all our equipment should be on file in your office.

### Choose/Chose

**Choose** (VERB; to select or make a choice)—We do not know whom he will *choose* for his executive assistant.

**Chose** (VERB; past tense of *choose*)—The new president *chose* Ms. Randall to be his executive assistant.

### Cite/Sight/Site

**Cite** (VERB; to quote or mention; to summon to a court appearance)—Dr. Rosenthal can *cite* many authorities who have studied the problem of pollution in major United States cities. Did the police officer *cite* you for speeding in a company vehicle?

**Sight** (VERB, to see; NOUN, a view or spectacle)—Unfortunately, the salesperson did not *sight* Ms. Brown leaving the office. The Statue of Liberty is a frequently visited tourist *sight* in New York City.

**Site** (NOUN; a location)—This 20-acre land parcel is a perfect *site* for the proposed housing project.

### Close/Clothes/Cloths

**Close** (VERB; to shut; to stop or end)—We *close* the safe at 5 p.m. every afternoon. Our accountant *closes* our books at the end of each month.

**Clothes** (NOUN; wearing apparel)—The previous tenant still needs to remove his *clothes* from the apartment.

**Cloths** (NOUN; pieces of fabric)—Use these *cloths* to clean the glass showcases.

### Coarse/Course

**Coarse** (ADJECTIVE; rough texture)—This material is too *coarse* for our use.

a / an

**Course** (NOUN; a particular direction or route; part of a meal; a unit of learning)—We are now committed to a *course* of action that we hope will increase our sales volume. Which menu item have you selected for the main *course*? You need only three more *courses* to graduate.

### Colander: see Calendar.

### Collision/Collusion
**Collision** (NOUN; a crash)—Fortunately, no one was hurt in the *collision*.
**Collusion** (NOUN; an agreement to defraud)—No one suspected the seller, broker, and escrow officer of *collusion* in the sale of this unstable hillside property.

### Command/Commend
**Command** (VERB, to order or direct; NOUN, an order)—The sergeant *commanded* his troops to return to base by 0600. This dog has been trained to obey only its owner's *commands*.
**Commend** (VERB; to praise or compliment)—Please *commend* the staff for the fine job it did in promoting our line at the San Francisco convention.

### Complement/Compliment
**Complement** (VERB; to complete or make perfect)—The paintings you have selected for the office reception area will *complement* the remainder of the decor. You may wish to select one of our fine wines to *complement* your meal.
**Compliment** (VERB; to praise or flatter)—Mr. Rose did *compliment* me on the fine job I had done.

### Complementary/Complimentary
**Complementary** (ADJECTIVE; serving mutually to blend, fill out, or complete)—Both these wall coverings are *complementary* to the carpeting you have selected.
**Complimentary** (ADJECTIVE; favorable; given free)—We appreciate receiving your *complimentary* letter about the service you received in our Fifth Avenue store.
To receive your *complimentary* copy of this textbook, merely fill out and return the enclosed postcard.

### Confidant/Confident
**Confidant** (NOUN; a trusted friend)—He has been his closest *confidant* for years.
**Confident** (ADJECTIVE; sure of oneself)—Mrs. Allen was *confident* she would get the position.

### Conscience/Conscious
**Conscience** (NOUN; the faculty of knowing right from wrong)—In the last analysis, his *conscience* required him to release the funds.
**Conscious** (ADJECTIVE; aware or mentally awake)—Yes, we are *conscious* of the new global marketing opportunities available to our firm. Most of our patients are *conscious* during this type of surgery.

### Console/Consul
**Console** (NOUN; a cabinet)—The popularity of our Model 4750 stereo may be attributed to its attractive *console*.

a/an

Misused Words

7

211

**Consul** (NOUN; an official representing a foreign country)—Travel information can often be obtained by contacting the *consul* of the country one wishes to visit.

## Continual/Continuous
**Continual** (ADJECTIVE; a regular or frequent occurrence)—The *continual* complaints from customers in the Vancouver area warrant inquiry into the activities of our Seattle office.
**Continuous** (ADJECTIVE; without interruption or cessation)—The *continuous* humming of the new air-conditioning system is disturbing everyone in the office.

## Convince/Persuade
**Convince** (VERB; to bring a person to your point of view)—Do you think you will *convince* the board that these proposed policies will increase our profits?
**Persuade** (VERB; to induce a person to do something)—An effective sales letter will *persuade* the reader to purchase a service or commodity.

## Cooperation/Corporation
**Cooperation** (NOUN; working together)—The full *cooperation* of all employees is needed to reduce our high rate of absenteeism.
**Corporation** (NOUN; one type of business organization)—We are looking into the possibility of forming a *corporation*.

## Corespondent/Correspondence/Correspondents
**Corespondent** (NOUN; person named as guilty of adultery with the defendant in a divorce suit)—Who was named as *corespondent* in this divorce case?
**Correspondence** (NOUN; letters or other written communications)—When did we receive the last *correspondence* from Mr. Flores?
**Correspondents** (NOUN; message writers or news reporters)—Be sure to have one of our *correspondents* answer these customers' letters within the next three days. African *correspondents* have reported that several countries are now suffering severe food shortages.

**Corporation: see Cooperation.**

## Corps/Corpse
**Corps** (NOUN, ['kōr]; a body of persons having a common activity or occupation)—A *corps* of students have been soliciting funds for the stadium lights. Representatives from the Marine *Corps* will visit our campus next week.
**Corpse** (NOUN, ['kȯrps]; a dead body)—The identity of the *corpse* is still unknown.

**Correspondence: see Corespondent.**

**Correspondent: see Corespondent.**

## Council/Counsel
**Council** (NOUN; a governing body)—We will present the proposal to the city *council* in the morning.
**Counsel** (VERB, to give advice; NOUN, advice)—Our staff *counsels* at least eighty students each day. In this situation the president received good *counsel* from his advisors.

**Course: see Coarse.**

## Credible/Creditable

**Credible** (ADJECTIVE; believable or reliable)—The excuses offered by Ms. Day for her many absences are hardly *credible*.

**Creditable** (ADJECTIVE; bringing honor or praise)—Ms. Kawakami's perfect attendance record is certainly *creditable*.

## Deceased/Diseased

**Deceased** (ADJECTIVE; dead)—Two of the company founders are already *deceased*.

Diseased (ADJECTIVE; sick)—Spray all these *diseased* rose bushes with insecticide.

## Decent/Descent/Dissent

**Decent** (ADJECTIVE; in good taste; proper)—The *decent* solution to the problem would have been for the salesperson to apologize for his rude behavior.

**Descent** (NOUN; moving downward; ancestry)—The view of the city from the sky was breathtaking as the plane began its *descent* into the Denver airport. Mr. Sirakides is of Greek *descent*.

**Dissent** (NOUN; differences or disagreement)—There was no *dissent* among the council members concerning the resolution to expand our city's parking facilities.

## Defer/Differ

**Defer** (VERB; to put off or delay)—Our company has decided to *defer* this project until next spring.

**Differ** (VERB; to vary or disagree)—Doctors *differ* in their views as to the optimum treatment for this particular virus.

## Deference/Difference

**Deference** (NOUN; yielding to someone else's wishes)—In *deference* to many shoppers' requests, the store remained open until 9 p.m. during the summer months.

**Difference** (NOUN; state of being different; dissimilarity)—There is very little *difference* between these two product brands.

## Delusion: see Allusion.

## Deprecate/Depreciate

**Deprecate** (VERB; to disapprove or downgrade)—His speech did nothing but *deprecate* the present zoning system.

**Depreciate** (VERB; to lessen the value)—The tax code allows us to *depreciate* this new equipment over a five-year period.

## Descent: see Decent.

## Desert/Dessert

**Desert** (NOUN; an arid, barren land area)—Palm Springs was once a *desert* area occupied only by Agua Caliente Indians.

**Dessert** (NOUN; a sweet course served at the end of a meal)—Apple pie and ice cream is a traditional American *dessert*.

## Device/Devise

**Device** (NOUN; an invention or mechanism)—The *device* worked perfectly during the demonstration.

a/an

Misused Words

7

**Devise** (VERB; to think out or plan)—Were you able to *devise* an overtime plan that would be equitable to all employees?

### Dew/Do/Due

**Dew** (NOUN; drops of moisture)—The heavy morning *dew* forecast for this morning was instead a heavy layer of fog, which caused the airport officials to delay all flights.

**Do** (VERB; to perform or bring about)—We must *do* everything possible to ship the order by June 17.

**Due** (ADJECTIVE; immediately payable)—Your payments are *due* by the 10th of each month.

### Die/Dye

**Die** (VERB; to pass from physical life)—During the summer months water your grass twice daily so that it will not *die*.

**Dye** (VERB; to change a color with a coloring substance)—We can custom *dye* this carpeting to your color choice.

### Differ: see Defer.

### Difference: see Deference.

### Disapprove/Disprove

**Disapprove** (VERB; to withhold approval)—Our manager will *disapprove* any plan that is not properly justified.

**Disprove** (VERB; to prove false)—We must *disprove* the rumor that we are cutting back production next month.

### Disburse/Disperse

**Disburse** (VERB; to pay out; to distribute methodically)—A new system has been devised to *disburse* commissions more rapidly. The property will be *disbursed* according to the provisions set forth in Mr. Williams' will.

**Disperse** (VERB; to scatter; to cause to become spread widely)—The crowd *dispersed* rapidly after the ball game. Those factories that *disperse* pollutants into the environment will continue to be subject to heavy fines. Please *disperse* this information to consumers nationwide.

### Discreet/Discrete

**Discreet** (ADJECTIVE; showing good judgment in conduct and speech)—Ms. Harris is *discreet* in discussing patients' cases with other hospital personnel.

**Discrete** (ADJECTIVE; separate)—There are several *discrete* possibilities for distributing our products in Europe and parts of Asia.

### Diseased: see Deceased.

### Disinterested/Uninterested

**Disinterested** (ADJECTIVE; impartial)—All the judges for this competition have been certified to be *disinterested* parties.

**Uninterested** (ADJECTIVE; indifferent)—Those employees who are *uninterested* in the success of the company are certainly not candidates for promotion.

### Disprove: see Disapprove.

### Dissent: see Decent.

### Do: see Dew.

a / an

### Done/Dun

**Done** (VERB; past participle of *do*)—Our company has not **done** any further research in this area.

**Dun** (VERB, to make persistent demands for payment; NOUN, OFTEN USED AS ADJECTIVE, a variable drab color, usually a neutral brownish gray)—Ms. Green's main responsibility is to **dun** slow-paying customers. One of our tasks is to repaint these **dun**-colored walls to achieve a more cheerful atmosphere.

**Due: see Dew.**

**Dun: see Done.**

**Dye: see Die.**

**Edict: see Addict.**

**Edition: see Addition.**

**Effect: see Affect.**

### E.g./I.e.

**E.g.** (PREPOSITION + NOUN; Latin abbreviation meaning *for example*)—Our company specializes in office furniture; **e.g.**, desks, cabinets, bookcases, chairs, and reception area furniture.

**I.e.** (PRONOUN + VERB; Latin abbreviation meaning *that is*)—You may telephone your order to us at any time; **i.e.**, we have operators on duty 24 hours a day every day.

### Elicit/Illicit

**Elicit** (VERB; to draw out or bring forth)—Was the speaker able to **elicit** questions from the audience?

**Illicit** (ADJECTIVE; unlawful)—One of our agents was cited for **illicit** business practices.

### Eligible/Illegible

**Eligible** (ADJECTIVE; qualified to be chosen)—To be **eligible** for these employment opportunities, applicants must be at least 21 years of age.

**Illegible** (ADJECTIVE; unreadable)—The handwriting on this student's paper is **illegible**.

### Elude: see Allude.

### Emigrate/Immigrate

**Emigrate** (VERB; to move from a country)—The Johnsons **emigrated** from Norway in 1987.

**Immigrate** (VERB; to enter a country)—How many Canadians were permitted to **immigrate** to the United States last year?

### Eminent/Imminent

**Eminent** (ADJECTIVE; prominent, distinguished)—Mr. Mendez is an **eminent** authority on labor relations.

**Imminent** (ADJECTIVE; impending, likely to occur)—There is **imminent** danger of equipment breakdown unless periodic service checks are made.

### Ensure: see Assure.

215

### Envelop/Envelope

**Envelop** (VERB; to wrap, surround, or conceal)—Each tamale is *enveloped* in a corn husk before it is boiled. The chief said his fire fighters would *envelop* the fire by morning. Each day a layer of early morning fog *envelops* the city.

**Envelope** (NOUN; a container for a written message)—Please send me your answer in the return *envelope* provided for your convenience.

### Every day/Everyday

**Every day** (ADJECTIVE + NOUN; each day)—I will call you *every day* and give you a status report on the new project.

**Everyday** (ADJECTIVE; ordinary)—Sales meetings seem to be an *everyday* occurrence in this office.

### Every one/Everyone

**Every one** (ADJECTIVE + PRONOUN; each person or thing in a group [always followed by *of*])—*Every one* of our staff is proficient in the use of our word processing and spreadsheet programs.

**Everyone** (PRONOUN; all people in a group)—*Everyone* on the staff is expected to be present for the stockholders' meeting.

### Example/Sample

**Example** (NOUN; something serving as a pattern to be imitated)—Please illustrate each of these principles with a meaningful *example*.

**Sample** (NOUN; a representative part or a single item from a larger whole)—When purchasing See's candy, each customer is offered a *sample*. How large of a *sample* population do you need to validate the results of the proposed study?

### Exceed: see Accede.

### Except: see Accept.

### Excess: see Access.

### Executioner/Executor

**Executioner** (NOUN; one who puts others [usually criminals] to death)—The *executioner*-style murders still remain unsolved.

**Executor** (NOUN; person appointed to carry out the provisions of a will)—Whom have you named as *executor* of your will?

### Exhilarate: see Accelerate.

### Expand/Expend

**Expand** (VERB; to enlarge)—The plan to *expand* our storage facilities was approved.

**Expend** (VERB; to use up or pay out)—Ms. Smith *expends* too much time dealing with insignificant matters. If you do not *expend* these moneys by June 30, they will revert to the general fund.

### Expansive/Expensive

**Expansive** (ADJECTIVE; capable of expanding; extensive)—An *expansive* commercial development is planned for this area.

**Expensive** (ADJECTIVE; costly)—The consultant's recommendations were too *expensive* to implement.

### Expend: see Expand.

**Expensive: see Expansive.**

### Explicit/Implicit

**Explicit** (ADJECTIVE; expressed clearly)—The accompanying booklet gives *explicit* instructions for assembling this piece of equipment.

**Implicit** (ADJECTIVE; implied)—By reading between the lines, one can discern an *implicit* appeal for additional funds.

### Extant/Extent

**Extant** (ADJECTIVE; currently or actually existing)—Please provide me with a three-year budget for all *extant* and projected programs.

**Extent** (NOUN; range, scope, or magnitude)—Unfortunately, we will be unable to assess the *extent* of the damage until next week.

### Facetious/Factious

**Facetious** (ADJECTIVE; humorous or witty, often in an inappropriate manner)—His seemingly *facetious* remark contained a kernel of truth.

**Factious** (ADJECTIVE; creating a faction or dissension)—A series of *factious* disputes eventually led to the dissolution of the partnership.

### Factitious/Fictitious

**Factitious** (ADJECTIVE; artificial)—One manufacturer created a *factitious* demand for copper alloy by spreading rumors of shortages.

**Fictitious** (ADJECTIVE; nonexistent; imaginary; false)—Many people believe that the reported UFO sightings are *fictitious*. This suspect has been known to operate under a number of *fictitious* names.

### Fair/Fare

**Fair** (NOUN, an exhibition; ADJECTIVE, marked by impartiality and honesty; mediocre)—Our annual county *fair* is usually held during the first week of September. Further legislation was passed recently to enforce *fair* employment practices. He did a *fair* job.

**Fare** (VERB, to get along or succeed; NOUN, price charged to transport a person)—Our company did not *fare* well in its last bidding competition. How much is the first-class airline *fare* from Chicago to New York?

### Farther/Further

**Farther** (ADJECTIVE; a greater distance [always a measurable amount of space])—The trip from the warehouse to the plant is *farther* than I thought.

**Further** (VERB, to help move forward; ADVERB, to a greater degree or extent; ADJECTIVE, additional)—The Truesdale Foundation has contributed $5 million to *further* research in spinal cord injuries. Stock market prices declined even *further* after the president's announcement. Refer to my July 8 memo for *further* details.

### Feasible/Possible

**Feasible** (ADJECTIVE; capable of being done or carried out)—Installing tape backup systems in all our computers is certainly *feasible*, but budget restraints prohibit our doing so at this time.

**Possible** (ADJECTIVE; being within the limits of realization)—Although networking all our computers would increase productivity, such a plan will not be *possible* until next year.

a/an

Misused Words | 7

### Feat/Fete

**Feat** (NOUN, ['fēt]; an act of skill, endurance, or ingenuity)—Human beings under stress have been known to perform *feats* beyond their normal capabilities. **Fete** (VERB, ['fāt]; to honor or commemorate; NOUN, a large elaborate party)—A banquet is being planned to *fete* our company president upon his retirement in September. The *fete* to honor our company president will be held on August 19.

### Fever/Temperature

**Fever** (NOUN; a rise of body temperature above the normal)—When the child was brought into the emergency room, he had a *fever.* **Temperature** (NOUN; degree of hotness or coldness measured on a definite scale)—Normal body *temperature* is 98.6 degrees. Be sure to record patients' *temperatures* in their charts.

### Fewer/Less

**Fewer** (ADJECTIVE; used with items that can be counted and plural nouns)—We had *fewer* sales this month. Reserve this checkout for customers with ten or *fewer* items. *Fewer* than half the employees elected to purchase stock options. **Less** (ADJECTIVE; used with mass items that cannot be counted and singular nouns)—You will get by with *less* work if you follow my suggestions. *Less* than half the cake had been eaten.

### Fictitious: see Factitious.

### Finally/Finely

**Finally** (ADVERB; in the end)—The missing part was *finally* delivered. **Finely** (ADVERB; elegantly or delicately; in small parts)—We all admired the *finely* embroidered tapestry. This engine has been *finely* tuned by our expert mechanics. You may purchase these *finely* chopped nuts in 8- and 16-ounce packages.

### Fiscal/Physical

**Fiscal** (ADJECTIVE; relating to financial matters)—The *fiscal* year for our school district begins on July 1 and ends on June 30. **Physical** (ADJECTIVE; concerned with the body and its needs)—Every individual should do a minimum amount of *physical* exercise daily.

### Flagrant/Fragrant

**Flagrant** (ADJECTIVE; glaring, scandalous)—His behavior was a *flagrant* violation of company policy. **Fragrant** (ADJECTIVE; sweet smelling)—She received a *fragrant* bouquet of flowers from the staff.

### Flair/Flare

**Flair** (NOUN; a natural talent or aptitude)—Ms. Strehike has a *flair* for making people feel at ease when they enter the office. **Flare** (VERB, to blaze up or spread out; NOUN, a signal light)—The gusty winds could easily cause the fire to *flare* out of control. *Flares* in the road guided motorists around the accident.

### Flaunt/Flout

**Flaunt** (VERB; to make a gaudy or defiant display)—Although Mrs. Paige is recognized as one of the most affluent Hartford residents, she does not *flaunt* her wealth.

a / an

**Flout** (VERB; to mock or show contempt for; to defy)—As a new driver, the young man continued to *flout* the posted speed limit.

### Flew/Flu/Flue

**Flew** (VERB; past tense of *fly*)—Our plane *flew* to the West Coast in record time.
**Flu** (NOUN; abbreviated form of *influenza*)—Nearly 30 percent of our employees are absent because of the *flu*.
**Flue** (NOUN; a duct in a chimney)—If the *flue* is closed, smoke from a burning fire cannot escape through the chimney.

**Flout: see Flaunt.**

**Flu: see Flew.**

**Flue: see Flew.**

### Foreword/Forward

**Foreword** (NOUN; prefatory comments, as for a book)—Thomas S. Healy, president of the New York Public Library, wrote the *foreword* for the 1992 publication of *The New York Public Library Book of Twentieth-Century American Quotations.*
**Forward** (ADVERB; to or toward what is ahead)—Since its beginnings our company has moved *forward* in research and development at a rapid pace.

### Formally/Formerly

**Formally** (ADVERB; in a formal manner)—At our next meeting you will be *formally* initiated into the organization.
**Formerly** (ADVERB; in the past)—Marie Martin was *formerly* the president of a large metropolitan area community college.

### Former/Latter

**Former** (ADJECTIVE; first of two things or belonging to an earlier time)—Your *former* suggestion appears to be the better one. As a *former* employee, Lois Oliver is always invited to all the company social functions.
**Latter** (ADJECTIVE; second of two things or nearer to the end)—Of the two proposals the *latter* one seems to be more economical. Mail deliveries in your area are scheduled for the *latter* part of the day.

### Forth/Fourth

**Forth** (ADVERB; forward)—The president requested that any objections to his plan be brought *forth* at this time.
**Fourth** (a numeric term; the ordinal form of *four*)—The *fourth* member of our group never arrived.

### Fortunate/Fortuitous

**Fortunate** (ADJECTIVE; having good luck)—We were *fortunate* to obtain the contract to rebuild the Northridge Mall.
**Fortuitous** (ADJECTIVE; accidental; happening by chance)—Only through *fortuitous* circumstances were we able to purchase these airline tickets at such a reduced price.

**Forward: see Foreword.**

**Fourth: see Forth.**

**Fragrant: see Flagrant.**

219

**Further: see Farther.**

### Good/Well

**Good** (ADJECTIVE; meaning *of favorable quality* in describing a noun or pronoun; meaning *fit, wholesome* in describing a person's well-being)—Mr. Collins writes **good** letters. I always feel **good** after finishing my exercises at the gym.
**Well** (ADVERB; meaning *properly, skillfully* in describing an action; ADJECTIVE, meaning *fit, healthy* in describing a person's health)—The majority of our nursing graduates do **well** on their state board examinations. My assistant did not look **well** today.

### Grate/Great

**Grate** (VERB, to reduce to small particles by rubbing on something rough; to cause irritation; NOUN, a frame of parallel or crossed bars blocking a passage)—In the future please use a food processor to **grate** the cheese for our pizzas. His continual talking could **grate** on anyone's nerves. Be sure to place a **grate** over this excavation when you have finished removing the dirt.
**Great** (ADJECTIVE; large in size; numerous; eminent or distinguished)—From the cruise ship we often sight a **great** white shark. A **great** many people have expressed an interest in purchasing our Model No. 47A videocassette recorder. Many **great** performers from stage and screen will be present at our annual benefit.

### Guarantee/Guaranty

**Guarantee** (VERB, to assure the fulfillment of a condition; NOUN, assurance of the quality or length of service of a product)—I **guarantee** that your children will enjoy immensely the adventures Disneyland has to offer. All our cars have a one-year or 50,000-mile **guarantee**.
**Guaranty** (VERB, to agree to pay the debt of another in case of default; NOUN, an assurance to pay the debt of another in case of default)—The federal government will **guaranty** all loans made under this new student loan program. John Fletcher's car loan will be approved as soon as we receive his parents' signed **guaranty**.

### Hail/Hale

**Hail** (VERB, to greet or summon; NOUN, rain that falls in the form of small ice balls)—On rainy afternoons you may find it difficult to **hail** a taxi in New York City. Unfortunately, the unexpected **hail** this season has damaged our strawberry crops.
**Hale** (ADJECTIVE; healthy)—Let's hope you will return from this adventuresome vacation **hale** and hearty.

### He/Him/Himself

**He** (PRONOUN; the subject of a clause or a complement pronoun)—**He** is the one I interviewed for the job. The person in our group with the best singing voice has always been **he**.
**Him** (PRONOUN; a direct object, an indirect object, or an object of a preposition)—The president asked **him** to head the project. Doris Waters gave **him** the results of the study yesterday. The choice is between you and **him**.
**Himself** (PRONOUN; a reflexive pronoun used to emphasize or refer back to the subject)—He **himself** had to solve the problem. Rick Bogart addressed the envelope to **himself**.

a/an

### Healthful/Healthy

**Healthful** (ADJECTIVE; beneficial to health of body or mind; promotes one's well-being or good health)—Millions of Americans consider vitamin supplements to be *healthful*. Mary tries to eat only *healthful* foods. Many doctors recommend daily exercise as a *healthful* activity.

**Healthy** (ADJECTIVE; being well or fit; enjoying health and vigor of body, mind, or spirit)—Be sure to keep only *healthy* plants in our nursery section. Most of our clients have selected the one-year membership program to remain *healthy* and maintain their physical fitness.

### Hear/Here

**Hear** (VERB; to perceive by the ear)—Yes, I can *hear* you clearly.

**Here** (ADVERB; in this place or at this point)—Install the telephone *here*.

### Her/Herself/She

**Her** (PRONOUN; a direct object, an indirect object, or an object of a preposition)—When Paulette arrived, Mr. Schultz asked *her* for the information. Barbara offered *her* a chair. The check is for *her*.

**Herself** (PRONOUN; a reflexive pronoun used to emphasize or refer back to the subject)—Wendy *herself* wrote and dictated the entire audit report. Kristen often talks to *herself*.

**She** (PRONOUN; the subject of a clause or a complement pronoun)—*She* went to lunch about 15 minutes ago. The person who designed this spreadsheet was *she*.

### Here: see Hear.

### Herself: see Her.

### Hew/Hue

**Hew** (VERB; to cut with blows of a heavy cutting instrument)—Which famous faces have been *hewed* on Mount Rushmore?

**Hue** (NOUN; color or gradation of color; aspect)—The *hues* of the rainbow glistened in the sunlight. Persons from every political *hue* criticized the president for not informing the American public of his actions.

### Him: see He.

### Himself: see He.

### Hoard/Horde

**Hoard** (VERB; to store or accumulate for future use)—Please do not *hoard* stationery and other supplies.

**Horde** (NOUN; a multitude)—A *horde* of people were waiting for the doors to open.

### Hoarse/Horse

**Hoarse** (ADJECTIVE; low, husky sound)—Your voice is too *hoarse* to make these telephone calls today.

**Horse** (NOUN; a large animal)—For this commercial we will need at least eight *horses*.

### Hole/Whole

**Hole** (NOUN; an opening or open place)—Burglars had entered the jewelry store by cutting a *hole* through the outer wall.

a/an

Misused Words | 7

**Whole** (ADJECTIVE; complete, entire)—Too many inexperienced managers make decisions before knowing the *whole* story.

### Holy/Wholly

**Holy** (ADJECTIVE; sacred)—Visitors continually flock to Jerusalem's *holy* shrines.

**Wholly** (ADVERB; completely)—Do you agree *wholly* with the committee's plan to invest additional funds in the proposed shopping center?

**Horde:  see Hoard.**

**Hue:  see Hew.**

### Human/Humane

**Human** (ADJECTIVE; characteristic of people)—Please remember that all of us are guilty of possessing *human* frailties.

**Humane** (ADJECTIVE; marked by compassion, sympathy, or consideration)— The treatment of elderly people in this convalescent home is certainly less than *humane*.

### Hypercritical/Hypocritical

**Hypercritical** (ADJECTIVE; excessively critical)—Many of his coworkers believe Mr. Reed to be *hypercritical* of new employees.

**Hypocritical** (ADJECTIVE, [ˌhi-pə-ˈkri-ti-kəl]; falsely pretending)—Because Jodi pretended to be friendly to other staff members and then gossiped about their shortcomings, she was eventually fired for her *hypocritical* behavior.

### I/Me/Myself

**I** (PRONOUN; a subject of a clause or a complement pronoun)—*I* finished the sales report last night.  If you were *I*, what would you do under these circumstances?

**Me** (PRONOUN; a direct object, an indirect object, or an object of a preposition)—Jolene Mack telephoned *me* this morning.  Pat gave *me* the sales report this morning.  None of this material is for *me*.

**Myself** (PRONOUN; a reflexive pronoun used to emphasize or refer back to the subject)—I wrote the entire report *myself*.  I can blame only *myself* for losing this sale.

### Ideal/Idle/Idol

**Ideal** (ADJECTIVE; perfect, model)—Your proposal outlines an *ideal* solution to the problem.

**Idle** (ADJECTIVE; doing nothing)—The production line was *idle* for almost a week.

**Idol** (NOUN; an object for religious worship; a revered person or thing)—One of the church *idols* had been vandalized.  Money is often the *idol* of ambitious, greedy people.

**I.e.:  see E.g.**

**Illegible:  see Eligible**

**Illicit:  see Elicit.**

**Illusion:  see Allusion.**

**Immigrate:  see Emigrate.**

a / an

**Imminent:** see Eminent.

**Implicit:** see Explicit.

### Imply/Infer
**Imply** (VERB; to suggest without stating)—Does that statement *imply* that I have made a mistake?

**Infer** (VERB; to reach a conclusion)—From the results of this independent survey, we can only *infer* that our advertising campaign in the Pittsburgh area was ineffective.

### In behalf of/on behalf of
**In behalf of** (PREPOSITION + NOUN + PREPOSITION; speak for or represent; in the interest or benefit of)—Because Ms. Shields was scheduled to be out of town, she requested Mary Ann to present the award *in behalf of* the company.

**On behalf of** (PREPOSITION + NOUN + PREPOSITION; plead a person's case; in support, defense)—Dr. Phillips spoke *on behalf of* Ms. Jones at the hearing.

### Incidence/Incidents
**Incidence** (NOUN; occurrence; rate of occurrence)—There has yet to be an *incidence* of theft within the company. The low *incidence* of traffic accidents over this holiday weekend may be attributed to our television safety campaign.

**Incidents** (NOUN; events or episodes)—Several *incidents* have occurred recently that require us to review our safety policies and practices.

### Incite/Insight
**Incite** (VERB; to urge on or provoke action)—The speaker attempted to *incite* the audience to take action. Poverty, depression, and starvation *incited* riots throughout the country.

**Insight** (NOUN; keen understanding)—Bob's *insight* and patience prevented the situation from developing into a major problem.

### Indigenous/Indigent/Indignant
**Indigenous** (ADJECTIVE; native of a particular region)—I believe that this tree is *indigenous* only to the Northwest.

**Indigent** (ADJECTIVE; poor, needy)—He began as an *indigent* refugee from war-torn Europe.

**Indignant** (ADJECTIVE; insulting, angry)—Successful store managers must know how to deal with *indignant* customers.

**Infer:** see Imply.

### Ingenious/Ingenuous
**Ingenious** (ADJECTIVE; marked by originality, resourcefulness, and cleverness)—This *ingenious* plan could save our company thousands of dollars annually.

**Ingenuous** (ADJECTIVE; showing innocent or childlike simplicity; natural)—Mr. Warren's *ingenuous* smile and warm personality have contributed immeasurably to his successful political career.

**Insight:** see Incite.

**Insure:** see Assure.

a/an

Misused Words

7

### Interstate/Intrastate

**Interstate** (ADJECTIVE; between states)—Since expanding operations to New Jersey, we must abide by all laws governing **interstate** commerce.

**Intrastate** (ADJECTIVE; within a state)—This firm, an Illinois corporation, is primarily concerned with **intrastate** product sales.

### Irregardless/Regardless

**Irregardless** (an incorrect usage for *regardless* that is not acceptable for speaking or writing).

**Regardless** (ADVERB; despite everything)—We must vacate these premises by July 31 *regardless*!

**Regardless of** (PREPOSITION; without taking into account; in spite of)—***Regardless of*** price, which one of these models has the best performance record? We have opened an account for Ritter's Clothing Store ***regardless of*** its slow-pay payment record.

### Irritate: see Aggravate.

### Isle: see Aisle.

### It's/Its

**It's** (PRONOUN + VERB; contraction of *it is*)—Although this model microwave oven has become very popular, *it's* not our best-seller.

**Its** (PRONOUN USED AS ADJECTIVE; possessive form of *it*)—The company had *its* stockholders' meeting in Atlanta last week.

### Karat: see Carat.

### Later/Latter

**Later** (ADVERB; after the proper time)—The shipment arrived *later* than we had anticipated.

**Latter** (ADJECTIVE; the second thing of two things mentioned)—Your *latter* suggestion is more likely to be adopted. [See also *Former.*]

### Lay/Lie

**Lay** (VERB; to put or place; a transitive verb that needs an object to complete its meaning; *lay, laid, laid,* and *laying* are the principal parts of this verb)—Please *lay* the message on my desk. I *laid* the message on your desk. I have *laid* several messages on your desk from Fred Obermiller. We are *laying* the foundation for the new building today.

**Lie** (VERB; to recline; an intransitive verb that does not have an object; *lie, lay, lain,* and *lying* are the principal parts of this verb)—May I *lie* down? He *lay* in the hospital waiting room for over three hours before a doctor saw him. These papers have *lain* on your desk since Monday. Mrs. Hartman is *lying* down.

### Lead/Led

**Lead** (NOUN USED AS ADJECTIVE, ['led]; a metallic element)—How many feet of *lead* pipe did the contractor order for this apartment house complex?

**Led** (VERB, past tense of *lead* ['lēd], meaning *to provide direction*)—Before his retirement Mr. Andrews *led* this company from a $3 million deficit to a $6 million annual profit.

a/an

## Lean/Lien

**Lean** (VERB, to rest against; to be inclined toward; ADJECTIVE, not fat)—Do not *lean* against these railings. I believe that most of our employees *lean* toward accepting increased medical benefits rather than greater salaries. We use only first-quality *lean* ground beef in our hamburgers.

**Lien** (NOUN; a legal right or claim to property)—If he refuses to pay, we will be forced to place a *lien* against his property.

## Leased/Least

**Leased** (VERB; property rented for a specified time period)—This suite of offices has been *leased* by our company for the past eight years.

**Least** (ADJECTIVE; smallest, slightest, lowest)—This year we showed the *least* profit since our company was founded in 1969.

## Led: see Lead.

## Lend/Loan

**Lend** (VERB; to give for temporary use with the understanding that the same or equivalent will be returned)—Has the bank agreed to *lend* us additional funds for expansion?

**Loan** (NOUN; something given for a borrower's temporary use)—Your $3,000 *loan* will be fully paid with your October 1 payment.

## Less: see Fewer.

## Lessee/Lesser/Lessor

**Lessee** (NOUN; one to whom a lease is given)—As specified in the lease agreement, the *lessee* must pay a monthly rent of $650 to the landlord.

**Lesser** (ADJECTIVE; smaller or less important)—Although the judge ruled in favor of the defendant, he awarded a *lesser* amount than we had anticipated.

**Lessor** (NOUN; one who grants a lease)—The *lessor* for all our company cars is Allied Car Rental Service.

## Lessen/Lesson

**Lessen** (VERB; to make smaller)—Chris Timmins recommended that we *lessen* our efforts in the manufacturing area.

**Lesson** (NOUN; a unit of study; something from which one learns)—The experience was a good *lesson* in how miscommunication can cause problems.

## Lesser: see Lessee.

## Lessor: see Lessee.

## Levee/Levy

**Levee** (NOUN; the bank of a river or a boat landing)—The river overflowed the *levee*.

**Levy** (NOUN; an order for payment)—To pay for the flood damage, the governor ordered a 1 percent *levy* on gasoline sales.

## Liable/Libel/Likely

**Liable** (ADJECTIVE; legally responsible, obligated)—The court ruled that the company was *liable* for all damages resulting from the accident.

**Libel** (NOUN; a false or damaging written statement about another)—Don refused to include the statement in his article because he feared he would be sued for *libel*.

**Likely** (ADJECTIVE or ADVERB, probable; probably)—He is a *likely* candidate for the position. If you break a law, you are *likely* (not *liable*) to be arrested.

**Lie:** see Lay.

**Lien:** see Lean.

**Lightening/Lightning**
**Lightening** (VERB [GERUND]; illuminating or brightening; lessening or alleviating)—Please select colors that will result in *lightening* the reception area. Only by *lightening* her workload can we expect to retain Ms. Burton.
**Lightning** (NOUN; the flashing of light produced by atmospheric electricity)—During the storm flashes of *lightning* streaked across the sky.

**Like:** see As.

**Likely:** see Liable.

**Loan:** see Lend.

**Local/Locale**
**Local** (ADJECTIVE; limited to a particular district)—Only persons living in the *local* area were interviewed.
**Locale** (NOUN, [lō'kal]; a particular location)—This parcel of land is an ideal *locale* for a shopping center.

**Loose/Lose**
**Loose** (ADJECTIVE; not fastened, not tight or shut up)—A *loose* connection was the probable cause of the power failure on the fifth floor of the Fisher Building.
**Lose** (VERB; to fail to keep; to mislay)—We do not want to *lose* any of our accounts in the Philippines. If you *lose* your keys, please call Mr. Drew in Plant Facilities.

**Magnate/Magnet**
**Magnate** (NOUN; a powerful or influential person)—As the first *magnate* of the automobile industry, Henry Ford changed the lifestyle of many Americans.
**Magnet** (NOUN or ADJECTIVE; something that has the ability to attract)—Picking up the spilled paper clips with a *magnet* was an easy task. This *magnet* school has many talented musicians.

**Main/Mane**
**Main** (ADJECTIVE; principal or most important part)—Our *main* selling feature is still customer service.
**Mane** (NOUN; the heavy hair on the neck of a horse or lion)—The horse's *mane* had become entangled in the wire fence.

**Manner/Manor**
**Manner** (NOUN; method; a customary or particular way)—Unless the company changes its *manner* of doing business, it will lose many more customers. Chancellor Phelps' congenial *manner* has endeared him to both faculty and students alike.
**Manor** (NOUN; a main house or mansion)—Although the decor of the *manor* dates back to the early years of the twentieth century, it is still well maintained and elegant.

## Marital/Marshal/Martial

**Marital** (ADJECTIVE; pertaining to marriage)—Use "*marital* bliss" as the primary appeal in your advertising copy for this client.
**Marshal** (NOUN; a military or law enforcement rank; the head of a ceremony)—If you wish to have a *marshal* serve these papers, there is an additional $25 fee. Jack Ritter was asked to act as honorary *marshal* of the parade.
**Martial** (ADJECTIVE; warlike, military)—Several bands played *martial* music at the Veterans Day commemoration.

## May: see Can.

## May be/Maybe

**May be** (VERB; a verb phrase [a helping verb and a main verb] derived from the infinitive *to be*)—This *may be* the last year we will be able to lease these facilities.
**Maybe** (ADVERB; perhaps)—*Maybe* the new carpeting will reduce the noise level in the office.

## Me: see I.

## Medal/Meddle

**Medal** (NOUN; a metal disk; an award in the form of a metal disk)—This gold religious *medal* was found lying on the sidewalk outside the church. He should receive a *medal* for his heroic efforts.
**Meddle** (VERB; to interfere)—This argument was one in which he dared not *meddle*.

## Miner/Minor

**Miner** (NOUN; a person who works in a mine)—He listed his last job as that of coal *miner*.
**Minor** (NOUN, a person under legal age; ADJECTIVE, a lesser thing)—Please post a sign that reads "No *minors* allowed." Your forgetting to mail the proposal proved to be only a *minor* error.

## Mode/Mood

**Mode** (NOUN; style or preferred method)—What *mode* of transportation will you use to reach the airport?
**Mood** (NOUN; feeling or disposition)—Before you ask Mr. Smith for a salary increase, be sure he is in a good *mood*.

## Moral/Morale

**Moral** (ADJECTIVE; pertaining to right and wrong; ethical)—She made the decision on a *moral* basis rather than on a practical basis.
**Morale** (NOUN; a mental condition)—Announcement of an across-the-board 7 percent pay increase instantly boosted employee *morale*.

## Morning/Mourning

**Morning** (NOUN; the time from sunrise to noon)—Would you be able to schedule an appointment Friday *morning* for me to see Dr. Rose?
**Mourning** (NOUN; showing signs of grief)—Please allow the family to observe this period of *mourning* without any interruptions concerning business matters.

## Most: see Almost.

## Mourning: see Morning.

a/an

Misused Words

7

227

**Myself:  see I.**

**Naval/Navel**

**Naval** (ADJECTIVE; relating to a navy)—Last week Mr. Marsh's son accepted an assignment with *naval* intelligence.

**Navel** (NOUN; a depression in the middle of the abdomen)—According to the doctor, the incision will leave a small scar directly below the *navel*.

**Number:  see Amount.**

**On behalf of:  see In behalf of.**

**Ordinance/Ordnance**

**Ordinance** (NOUN; a local regulation)—The city has an *ordinance* banning excessive noise after 10 p.m.

**Ordnance** (NOUN; military weapons)—We should know by the end of the month whether we will receive the army *ordnance* contract.

**Overdo/Overdue**

**Overdo** (VERB; to exaggerate; to do in excess)—Exercise is healthful if one does not *overdo* it.

**Overdue** (ADJECTIVE; late)—Your payment is 15 days *overdue*.

**Pair/Pare/Pear**

**Pair** (NOUN; two of a kind; made of two corresponding parts)—The *pair* of shoes the customer attempted to return showed signs of considerable wear.

**Pare** (VERB; to reduce in size or trim; to peel)—I hope you can *pare* this budget at least 15 percent.

**Pear** (NOUN; a fruit)—Our market carries three brands of canned *pears*.

**Partition/Petition**

**Partition** (NOUN; something that divides)—Office efficiency increased substantially after each computer station was separated by a *partition*.

**Petition** (NOUN; a formal written request)—Have you signed the *petition* to create curb cutouts at major intersections in the downtown business district?

**Passed/Past**

**Passed** (VERB; past tense or past participle of *pass*, meaning *to go by* or *to circulate*)—Once you have *passed* the intersection, look for our store on the right side of the street.  Lisa *passed* out copies of the job announcement to all eligible employees in the company.

**Past** (NOUN OR ADJECTIVE; time gone by or ended)—Our weak profit picture is all in the *past*. From *past* experience we have learned not to extend credit to this company.

**Patience/Patients**

**Patience** (NOUN; calm perseverance)—Your *patience* in working with these handicapped children is certainly to be admired.

**Patients** (NOUN; people undergoing medical treatment)—George Allison is one of Dr. Hedge's *patients*.

**Peace/Piece**

**Peace** (NOUN; truce; tranquillity)—As long as the hostilities exist, there can be no *peace* among these nations.  Since Ms. Seraydarian began the project, she has not had a moment's *peace*.

**Piece** (NOUN; a part of a defined quantity)—Each of the three beneficiaries inherited a *piece* of the prime property.

## Peak/Peek

**Peak** (ADJECTIVE OR NOUN; highest point; top)—Our *peak* sales period is from September through November. KLAC's transmitter is located at the *peak* of Mount Baldy.

**Peek** (VERB; to glance)—Some of the buyers have already had a *peek* at the new fall fashions by major designers.

## Peal/Peel

**Peal** (VERB; to give out a loud sound or succession of sounds)—The bells *pealed* from the church tower.

**Peel** (VERB, to remove by stripping; NOUN, skin or rind)—Ask the customer to *peel* off the mailing label and affix it to the enclosed postcard. Do any of these recipes require the use of lemon *peel*?

**Pear:** see Pair.

**Peek:** see Peak.

**Peel:** see Peal.

## Peer/Pier

**Peer** (VERB, to gaze; NOUN, one belonging to the same societal group)—Do customers often *peer* into the bakery shop window before entering the store? Most teenagers imitate the behavior of their *peers*.

**Pier** (NOUN; a structure extending into navigable waters)—No fishing is allowed from this *pier*.

## Persecute/Prosecute

**Persecute** (VERB; to harass persistently)—If your supervisor continues to *persecute* you, please contact your union representative at Ext. 3543.

**Prosecute** (VERB; to conduct legal proceedings against someone)—We are not sure whether the district attorney will *prosecute* the case.

## Personal/Personnel

**Personal** (ADJECTIVE; private; individual)—Each full-time employee has been assigned a *personal* parking place.

**Personnel** (NOUN, employees; ADJECTIVE, relating to employment)—All *personnel* are requested to work overtime until the inventory has been completed. Your annual performance evaluation will be placed in your *personnel* file.

## Perspective/Prospective

**Perspective** (NOUN; a mental picture or outlook)—His *perspective* is distorted by greed.

**Prospective** (ADJECTIVE; likely, expected)—Last week we interviewed several *prospective* candidates for our Accounting Department.

**Persuade:** see Convince.

## Peruse/Pursue

**Peruse** (VERB; to read hastily or casually)—Each morning at breakfast I *peruse* the newspaper for any items of interest to our industry.

**Pursue** (VERB; to follow; to proceed with a course of action)—May I suggest you *pursue* this sales lead further.

**Petition:** see Partition.

**Physical:** see Fiscal.

**Piece:** see Peace.

**Pier:** see Peer.

### Plaintiff/Plaintive

**Plaintiff** (NOUN; one who initiates a lawsuit to obtain a remedy for injury to his or her rights)—Who is the attorney for the *plaintiff*?

**Plaintive** (ADJECTIVE; expressive of suffering or woe)—In a *plaintive* voice the witness described how the gunmen carried out the robbery.

### Pole/Poll

**Pole** (NOUN; a long, slender object that is usually cylindrical)—The teachers will need a *pole* to open the top row of windows in these classrooms.

**Poll** (NOUN; counting of opinions or votes cast; place where votes are cast [usually *polls*])—Our latest *poll* shows that consumers prefer Revel toothpaste over any other. Be sure to urge all registered voters to go to the *polls* next Tuesday.

### Populace/Populous

**Populace** (NOUN; the masses; population of a place)—The winning candidate must have the support of the *populace*. During the flood the *populace* of Evansville was evacuated.

**Populous** (ADJECTIVE; densely populated)—At present we have restaurants only in *populous* areas.

### Pore/Pour

**Pore** (VERB, to read studiously or attentively; NOUN, a small opening in a membrane)—How long did the auditors *pore* over these books? Hot water will open the *pores* of your skin, and cold water will close them.

**Pour** (VERB; to dispense from a container; to move with a continuous flow)—Please ask the servers to *pour* the water before the guests are seated. Even before the game ended, spectators began to *pour* out of the stadium.

### Possible: see Feasible.

### Practicable/Practical

**Practicable** (ADJECTIVE; describes an idea or plan that in theory seems to be feasible or usable; capable of being put into practice)—The plan to build cars that run on electricity seems to be *practicable*.

**Practical** (ADJECTIVE; describes an idea or plan that is feasible or usable because it has been successfully tried or proved by past experience; fit for actual practice)—Once gasoline prices began to rise, many people found small cars to be the *practical* solution to reducing transportation costs.

### Pray/Prey

**Pray** (VERB; to make a request in a humble manner; to address a god)—I *pray* that these bureaucrats will listen to my request. Children may not be required to *pray* in public schools.

**Prey** (VERB, to have an injurious or destructive effect; NOUN, victim)—Ms. Rice should not let this experience constantly *prey* on her thoughts. Do not become *prey* to the quick-rich schemes of such con artists.

## Precede/Proceed

**Precede** (VERB, [pri-'sēd]; to go before)—Mrs. Andrews' presentation will directly *precede* the convention's first general session.

**Proceed** (VERB, [prō-'sēd]; to go forward or continue)—Please *proceed* with your analysis of the financial statements.

## Precedence/Precedents

**Precedence** (NOUN, ['pre-cə-dən(t)s]; priority)—He will certainly give *precedence* to Mr. Wilson's application for funds.

**Precedents** (NOUN, ['pre-cə-dənts]; things done or said that can be used as an example)—There are no legal *precedents* in our state for this particular case.

## Presence/Presents

**Presence** (NOUN; condition of being present; stately or distinguished bearing of a person)—Please ensure the *presence* of all supervisors and managers at this meeting. Everyone was impressed by the confidence and *presence* with which the new president addressed the faculty.

**Presents** (NOUN; gifts or things given)—Company employees donated a record number of *presents* to needy children this year.

## Presume: see Assume.

## Prey: see Pray.

## Principal/Principle

**Principal** (NOUN; a capital sum; head of a school)—Both the *principal* and the interest paid are shown on your loan statement each month. As *principal* of Lindberg High School, Mrs. Brereton was proud that so many seniors attended college upon graduation.

**Principal** (ADJECTIVE; highest in importance)—The *principal* reason for changing our promotion procedures was to encourage all employees within the company to upgrade their skills.

**Principle** (NOUN; an accepted rule of action; a basic truth or belief)—Her knowledge of accounting *principles* is questionable. Our country was founded on the *principle* that all persons are created equal.

## Proceed: see Precede.

## Propose/Purpose

**Propose** (VERB; to suggest)—I *propose* that we borrow sufficient funds to purchase all the new equipment at once.

**Purpose** (NOUN; a desired result)—The *purpose* of this meeting is to discuss ways of increasing our productivity and sales.

## Prosecute: see Persecute.

## Prospective: see Perspective.

## Purpose: see Propose.

## Pursue: see Peruse.

## Quiet/Quite

**Quiet** (ADJECTIVE; peaceful; free from noise)—Our client wishes to purchase a home in a *quiet* neighborhood. The *quiet* operation of this printer is one of its main sales features.

a/an

Misused Words

7

**Quite** (ADVERB; completely or actually)—Our salespeople seem to be *quite* satisfied with the new commission plan.

### Raise/Raze/Rise

**Raise** (VERB; to lift something up, increase in amount, gather together, or bring into existence; a transitive verb that needs an object to complete its meaning; *raise*, *raised*, *raised*, and *raising* are the principal parts of this verb)—Please do not *raise* your voice.  The company *raised* our sales quota 30 percent last month.  We have *raised* $200 for Mrs. Morgan's retirement gift.  A number of our stockholders are *raising* questions about the proposed merger.

**Raze** (VERB; to tear down to the ground)—When does your company plan to *raze* this old warehouse?

**Rise** (VERB; to go up or to increase in value; an intransitive verb that does not have an object; *rise*, *rose*, *risen*, and *rising* are the principal parts of this verb)—Our sales should *rise* beyond the $1 million mark this quarter.  The rocket *rose* 30,000 feet before it exploded.  Our sales have *risen* for the third month in a row.  Production has been *rising* steadily since the new equipment was installed.

### Real/Really

**Real** (ADJECTIVE; actual, true; genuine)—The new accounting program was a *real* help in getting out our monthly statements.

**Really** (ADVERB; very, certainly)—Susan was *really* disappointed that Robert did not accept the position.

### Reality/Realty

**Reality** (NOUN; that which is real, that which exists)—Our problems began when the general plant manager would not face *reality* in negotiating with the employees' representatives.

**Realty** (NOUN OR ADJECTIVE; real estate)—The last *realty* company that tried to sell my property could not find a qualified buyer.

### Receipt/Recipe

**Receipt** (NOUN; a written acknowledgment of receiving goods or money)—No refunds can be made without a *receipt*.

**Recipe** (NOUN; a set of instructions)—Mama Lucia's has always kept secret the *recipe* for its delicious spaghetti sauce.

### Regardless:  See Irregardless.

### Residence/Residents

**Residence** (NOUN; place where one lives)—This house has been Mrs. Scott's *residence* for the past twenty years.

**Residents** (NOUN; people who live in a place)—One of the retirement home *residents* reported that the heater in her room emits only cold air.  The *residents* of Nashville have elected a new mayor.

### Respectably/Respectfully/Respectively

**Respectably** (ADJECTIVE; in a correct or decent manner)—The vagrant was dressed *respectably* for his court appearance.

**Respectfully** (ADVERB; a manner denoting high regard; word used in the body or complimentary close of a letter to show high regard or respect for the addressee)—Please remember to treat all our customers *respectfully*.

a/an

**Respectively** (ADVERB; each in turn or in order)—Janice Jackson, John Zelinsky, and Al Turnbull were first-, second-, and third-prize winners, *respectively*.

## Ring/Wring

**Ring** (VERB; to give out a resounding sound)—Remind all patients to *ring* their bells if they need any assistance.

**Wring** (VERB; to squeeze or twist)—For each of these garments, make sure that the care instructions caution consumers to "Hand wash only. Do not *wring* dry; blot dry with towel."

## Rise: see Raise.

## Role/Roll

**Role** (NOUN; proper function of a person or thing; a part or character assumed)—Mr. Hayworth is very successful in his *role* as mediator for grievances within the company. What *role* will you play in this theater production?

**Roll** (VERB, to move by turning or rotating; NOUN, something wound around a core; a list of names)—Be sure to *roll* back the bathroom carpeting before attempting any plumbing repairs. Please order 3 dozen *rolls* of transparent packaging tape from Hillsdale Stationers. How many students are on your *roll*?

## Rote/Wrote

**Rote** (NOUN; mechanical or repetitious procedure)—All fourth-grade children are expected to learn the multiplication tables *one* through *ten* by *rote*.

**Wrote** (VERB; past tense of *write*)—We *wrote* to all our clients last week informing them of our merger with American Financial Corporation.

## Rout/Route

**Rout** (NOUN, ['raůt—sounds like *out*]; a disorderly assembly or disastrous defeat)—The game turned into a *rout* after the opposing team scored 30 points during the first quarter.

**Route** (NOUN, ['rüt]; a course taken in traveling from one point to another)—Most of our delivery *routes* were changed based upon the consultant's recommendations.

## Sample: see Example.

## Scene/Seen

**Scene** (NOUN; place of an occurrence; an exhibition of anger)—The police arrived at the *scene* of the robbery shortly after the security guard telephoned them. How would you handle a hostile customer who was creating a *scene*?

**Seen** (VERB; past participle of *to see*)—I have not *seen* our sales manager for three days.

## Scent: see Cent.

## Sealing: see Ceiling.

## Seize: see Cease.

## Semi-: see Bi-.

## Senses: see Census.

## Sent: see Cent.

## Serial: see Cereal.

a/an

Misused Words

7

## Set/Sit

**Set** (VERB; to place, position, or arrange; a transitive verb that generally needs an object to complete its meaning; *set, set, set,* and *setting* are the principal parts of this verb)—Please *set* the calculator on my desk. He *set* the clocks ahead one hour for daylight saving time. I have *set* the times for all your medical appointments this week. We are *setting* higher quotas for all our sales personnel this year.

**Sit** (VERB; to be seated or occupy a seat; an intransitive verb that does not have an object; *sit, sat, sat,* and *sitting* are the principal parts of this verb)—*Sit* here, Ms. Brown. I *sat* for over an hour awaiting his return. He has *sat* in that chair all day watching television. If Mr. Weaver calls, tell him I am *sitting* in on a meeting of the department heads.

## Sew/So/Sow

**Sew** (VERB; to fasten by stitches with thread)—Please have someone in the Alterations Department *sew* a button on this coat.

**So** (ADVERB, to that degree; CONJUNCTION, in a way indicated; in order that; therefore)—We are *so* interested in entering the Brazilian market that we have set up an office in Rio. *So* that we may update our files, please complete the enclosed form and mail it to us in the return envelope. Our company is moving its offices to Columbus, Ohio; *so* now we are in the process of recruiting new personnel in this city.

**Sow** (VERB; to scatter seed)—This machine can *sow* more seed in a day than any 15 farmhands.

## Shall/Will

**Shall** (HELPING VERB; denotes future time in the first person in formal writing)—I *shall* give your request the utmost consideration. We *shall* initiate legal proceedings on November 1.

**Will** (HELPING VERB; used with all three persons in business style)—I (or We) *will* call you tomorrow. You *will* receive your refund when you return the merchandise. He (or She or They) *will* finish the project according to schedule unless he (or she or they) encounter(s) bad weather conditions.

## She: see Her.

## Shear/Sheer

**Shear** (VERB; to cut, strip, or remove)—We had to *shear* off the bolts before we could remove the wheel.

**Sheer** (ADJECTIVE; transparently thin; utterly; steep)—None of the *sheer* fabrics are suitable for the kind of draperies we have in mind. This conference was a *sheer* waste of time. Did any of the prisoners attempt to scale the *sheer* cliffs?

## Shone/Shown

**Shone** (VERB; past tense and past participle of *shine*)—If flashing red lights had been *shone* through the dense fog, the accident might have been avoided.

**Shown** (VERB; past participle of *show*)—The computer-generated slide presentation describing our new products has been *shown* to all our salespeople.

## Should/Would

**Should** (HELPING VERB; denotes future time in the first person in formal writing)—We *should* appreciate your returning the signed contracts by Friday, March 23.

a/an

**Would** (HELPING VERB; used with all three persons in business style)—I (or We) *would* appreciate receiving a copy of that report. She (or He or They) said that she (or he or they) *would* be willing to work overtime if the report isn't finished by 5 p.m. Did you say that you *would* be interested in having a demonstration of our new Model 1100 facsimile?

**Shown:** see Shone.

**Sight:** see Cite.

**Sit:** see Set.

**Site:** see Cite.

**So:** see Sew.

**Soar/Sore**

**Soar** (VERB; to fly aloft or about; to rise or increase dramatically)—These miniature aircraft are built to *soar* through the sky without motor or battery power. News of the merger will cause the price of our stock to *soar*.
**Sore** (ADJECTIVE; painfully sensitive)—If you overdo an exercise program, your muscles will become *sore*. Last year's financial losses have become a *sore* point for our company president.

**Sole/Soul**

**Sole** (NOUN, the undersurface of a foot; ADJECTIVE, being the only one)—Distribute your weight evenly between the *sole* and the heel of your foot. John is the *sole* heir to his father's fortune.
**Soul** (NOUN; the immaterial essence of an individual; living example of moral principle)—Most contemporary religions believe that the *soul* of an individual continues on after his or her physical death. Mr. Perry is the *soul* of honesty and integrity.

**Some/Somewhat**

**Some** (ADJECTIVE; an indefinite amount)—The report revealed that we will have to make *some* structural changes when we move into our new offices.
**Somewhat** (ADVERB; to some degree)—Most members of our sales force feel that your sales projections for next year are *somewhat* optimistic.

**Some time/Sometime/Sometimes**

**Some time** (ADJECTIVE + NOUN; a period of time)—Our staff will need *some time* to review your proposal before we can make a decision.
**Sometime** (ADVERB; an indefinite time; anytime)—Your order should be delivered *sometime* during the early part of next week.
**Sometimes** (ADVERB; occasionally)—We are *sometimes* forced to hire personnel from temporary agencies.

**Somewhat:** see Some.

**Sore:** see Soar.

**Soul:** see Sole.

**Sow:** see Sew.

a/an

Misused Words

7

235

### Staid/Stayed

**Staid** (ADJECTIVE; sedate, composed)—A more *staid* individual is needed to fill this position.

**Stayed** (VERB; past tense and past participle of *stay*)—She *stayed* long after regular hours to finish the report.

### Stationary/Stationery

**Stationary** (ADJECTIVE; not movable)—Only two of the interior walls in this suite are *stationary.*

**Stationery** (NOUN OR ADJECTIVE; writing material)—Mr. Troy wants this letter prepared on his personal *stationery.* Our order for additional *stationery* supplies was placed last week.

### Statue/Stature/Statute

**Statue** (NOUN; a carved or molded image of someone or something)—Meet me in front of the *statue* of Lincoln at 2 p.m.

**Stature** (NOUN; the height of an object or a body; status gained by attainment)—The *stature* alone of the pyramids is overwhelming. Dr. Sunayama is a person of great *stature* within the community.

**Statute** (NOUN; law enacted by a legislature)—There is a *statute* in this state that prohibits gambling in any form.

### Stayed: see Staid.

### Straight/Strait

**Straight** (ADJECTIVE, free of bends, curves, or angles; ADVERB, in a direct manner)—Use a ruler with a *straight* edge to draw these lines. Ms. Torti always seems to be able to go *straight* to the source of the problem.

**Strait** (NOUN; a narrow space or passage connecting two bodies of water)—The ship and its cargo were damaged while going through the *strait.*

### Suit/Suite

**Suit** (NOUN, ['süt]; an action filed in court; a set of garments)—A & Z Computer Corporation has already filed *suit* against Compco for patent infringements. Be sure to wear a gray business *suit* for the interview.

**Suite** (NOUN, ['swēt]; a group of things forming a unit; a set)—Were you able to reserve a *suite* for the week of March 25 at the Americana Hotel? (refers to a group of rooms) How many pieces are featured in this bedroom *suite*? (refers to pieces of furniture in a set)

### Sure/Surely

**Sure** (ADJECTIVE; an adjective or subject complement meaning *certain* or *positive*)—Nancy was *sure* she had made the right decision.

**Surely** (ADVERB; certainly or undoubtedly)—The employees believed that they would *surely* get a raise this year.

### Take: see Bring.

### Tare/Tear/Tier

**Tare** (NOUN, ['tar—sounds like *care*]; a deduction from the gross weight of goods and their container made to allow for the weight of the container)—The *tare* on this shipment has been estimated to be 210 pounds.

**Tear** (VERB, ['tar], to pull apart or rip; NOUN, ['tar], a rip)—When you open the envelope, be careful not to *tear* the contents. The customer complained about a *tear* in the sweater she had purchased yesterday.

**Tier** (NOUN, ['tir]; placed one above or behind the other)—Our company's season tickets are on the first *tier* of the stadium.

**Temperature: see Fever.**

**Than/Then**

**Than** (CONJUNCTION; used to show comparison)—Ms. Espinoza has more experience *than* I in writing contract proposals.

**Then** (ADVERB; at that time)—Once all the data has been gathered, *then* you may begin organizing the report.

**That/Which**

**That** (PRONOUN; refers to animals or things; introduces a restrictive or essential subordinate clause)—We have in stock, Mr. Harrington, all the merchandise *that* you requested. All dogs *that* are found wandering in the streets will be impounded. This is the telephone *that* has been out of order since this morning.

**Which** (PRONOUN; refers to animals or things; introduces a nonrestrictive or nonessential subordinate clause)—The security staff recommended that we acquire a watchdog, *which* would be kept inside the plant at night. Our new credit system, *which* will be installed next week, will cost over $50,000.

**Their/There/They're**

**Their** (PRONOUN USED AS ADJECTIVE; the possessive form of *they*)—As a result of *their* recommendation, we installed an Apex Security System in our main warehouse.

**There** (ADVERB; at that place or at that point)—Please be *there* promptly at ten o'clock in the morning.

**They're** (PRONOUN + VERB; contraction of *they are*)—Although the union representatives rejected our first offer, *they're* willing to consider our second proposal.

**Theirs/There's**

**Theirs** (PRONOUN; possessive form of *they*)—This copy of the contract is *theirs*.

**There's** (PRONOUN + VERB; contraction of *there is* or *there has*)—*There's* still much to be done before we can open our new store. *There's* been too much time lost in attempting to install this new operating system on our network.

**Them/They**

**Them** (PRONOUN; a direct object, an indirect object, or an object of a preposition)—I asked *them* to please wait outside. I sent *them* a bill last week. I waited for *them* all morning.

**They** (PRONOUN; subject of a clause or a complement pronoun)—*They* are meeting with the Board of Directors this afternoon. The two persons who cochaired the committee were *they*.

**Then: see Than.**

**There: see Their.**

**There's: see Theirs.**

**They: see Them.**

237

**They're:** see Their.

**Threw/Through/Thru**

**Threw** (VERB; past tense of *throw*)—Mr. Samuels accidentally *threw* away the report on equipment purchases for the current year.

**Through** (PREPOSITION; in one end and out the other; movement within a large expanse; during the period of; as a consequence of)—May I give you a tour *through* our plant? The messenger pigeons flew gracefully *through* the air. This sale will be in progress *through* June. You may order this software at a 15 percent discount from June 15 *through* June 30. We have retained this account *through* your diligent efforts.

**Thru** (A variation of *through* that is not acceptable for business writing.)

**Tier:** see Tare.

**To/Too/Two**

**To** (PREPOSITION, function word to indicate direction toward; THE SIGN OF AN INFINITIVE, for example, *to go*)—Please return these materials *to* me when you have finished reviewing them. She wanted *to* see for herself the condition of the plant cafeteria.

**Too** (ADVERB; also; to an excessive extent)—I was there *too*. Because the office was *too* noisy, I had difficulty hearing you on the telephone.

**Two** (NOUN; the number between *one* and *three*)—There was just too much work for the *two* of us to finish by five o'clock.

**Tortuous/Torturous**

**Tortuous** (ADJECTIVE; winding, twisting)—The *tortuous* road leading to Hana Bay has been the scene of many automobile accidents.

**Torturous** (ADJECTIVE; causing pain)—Filling out all these reports is a *torturous* task.

**Toward/Towards**

**Toward** (PREPOSITION; in the direction of)—Set up these workstations so that all the screens on the computer monitors face *toward* the west wall.

**Towards** (Secondary form of *toward*; use *toward* instead of *towards* in business writing.)

**Uninterested:** see Disinterested.

**Us/We**

**Us** (PRONOUN; a direct object, an indirect object, or an object of a preposition)—The vice president took *us* on a tour of the plant. The manager gave *us* a copy of the report. The reception was planned for *us*.

**We** (PRONOUN; the subject of a clause or a complement pronoun)—*We* must decide upon a definite course of action by 3 p.m. The singers selected to perform for this special broadcast were *we*.

**Vain/Van/Vane/Vein**

**Vain** (ADJECTIVE; unduly proud or conceited)—Tom would be more popular with his fellow workers if he were not so *vain*.

**Van** (NOUN; a covered truck)—Our hospital *van* is used primarily for transporting patients.

**Vane** (NOUN; a thin object used to show wind direction)—The weather *vane* indicated that the wind was coming from a westward direction.

**Vein** (NOUN; a tubular vessel that carries blood to the heart; mode or style)—The laboratory technician had difficulty finding a *vein* from which to obtain a blood sample. Although Mr. Bates had been warned about his unfriendly attitude toward other employees, he continued to behave in that *vein*.

## Vary/Very

**Vary** (VERB; to change)—The new advertising manager said that for the time being he would not request us to *vary* any procedures.

**Very** (ADVERB; extremely)—These figures are *very* difficult to verify from the information available.

**Vein: see Vain.**

## Vice/Vise

**Vice** (NOUN; immoral habit; personal fault)—Drug abuse by America's populace is a *vice* that must be curtailed. Cigar smoking is his only *vice*.

**Vise** (NOUN, a clamp; ADJECTIVE, strong hold or squeeze)—Please order a *vise* for our new carpenter. He shook my hand with a *vise*-like grip.

## Waive/Wave

**Waive** (VERB; to relinquish; to refrain from enforcing)—Do you *waive* your right to a jury trial? You must petition the dean of academic affairs to *waive* this requirement.

**Wave** (VERB; to swing something back and forth or up and down)—The angry customer was determined to *wave* his bill in everyone's face.

## Waiver/Waver

**Waiver** (NOUN; the relinquishment of a claim)—Please sign the enclosed *waiver* to release our company from any further responsibility for your injury.

**Waver** (VERB; to shake or fluctuate)—I believe he is beginning to *waver* concerning my request for an early vacation.

**Wave: see Waive.**

**Waver: see Waiver.**

**We: see Us.**

## Weather/Whether

**Weather** (VERB, to bear up against; NOUN, the state of the atmosphere)—We are glad to learn that you were able to *weather* the high rate of employee turnover during the summer months. Today's *weather* forecast was for a cold, rainy day.

**Whether** (CONJUNCTION; an introduction of alternatives)—We will not know until next week *whether* our company or Artistry in Motion will be awarded the contracts.

**Well: see Good.**

**Whether: see Weather.**

**Which: see That.**

## Who/Whom

**Who** (PRONOUN; the subject of a subordinate clause or a complement pronoun)—I was the one *who* asked you to attend. I cannot tell you *who* the person at the door was.

**Whom** (PRONOUN; a direct object or an object of a preposition)—***Whom*** have you hired as my assistant? Here is the address of the person with ***whom*** we met for legal assistance. (See Section 6-7j for a further explanation of how to use *who* and *whom*.)

Whole: see Hole.

Wholly: see Holy.

Whom: see Who.

Who's/Whose
**Who's** (PRONOUN + VERB; a contraction of *who is*)—Please let me know ***who's*** taking over for you during August.
**Whose** (PRONOUN USED AS ADJECTIVE; possessive form of *who*)—He is the fellow ***whose*** position was abolished.

Will: see Shall.

Would: see Should.

Wring: see Ring.

Wrote: see Rote.

Your/You're
**Your** (PRONOUN USED AS ADJECTIVE; possessive form of *you*)—***Your*** assistant told me that you had invited the mayor to the reception.
**You're** (PRONOUN + VERB; contraction of *you are*)—If ***you're*** still interested in the position, please call me at (818) 555-3465.

a/an

# Chapter 8

# Spelling, Proofreading, and Editing

## Spelling, Proofreading, and Editing Solution Finder

### Editing

### Proofreading

### Spelling

# Spelling

## 8–1. Words Commonly Misspelled in Business Writing

a. Some frequently used words in business writing are often misspelled because they are mispronounced, contain double-letter combinations, or have silent letters. Since these words appear repeatedly in letters, memorandums, and reports, anyone involved with the preparation of business documents should be able to spell these words correctly.

**commonly misspelled words**

| | | |
|---|---|---|
| absence | consistent | government |
| accommodate | convenient | grammar |
| acknowledgment | correspondence | grateful |
| acquire | courteous | handicapped |
| adequate | creditor | harass |
| advantageous | currency | height |
| advertisement | decision | independent |
| advisable | deductible | interest |
| allotted | defendant | interrupt |
| among | deferred | itinerary |
| analysis | definitely | judgment |
| analyze | dependent | knowledgeable |
| appointment | describe | laboratory |
| argument | desirable | library |
| assistance | development | license |
| attorney | dissatisfied | maintenance |
| awkward | division | manageable |
| bankruptcy | efficient | manufacturer |
| becoming | embarrass | mileage |
| beginning | emphasis | miscellaneous |
| beneficial | emphasize | mortgage |
| benefit | employee | necessary |
| budget | endorsement | nevertheless |
| bureau | envelope | nineteenth |
| business | equipped | ninety |
| calendar | especially | ninth |
| canceled | evidently | noticeable |
| catalog | excellent | occasionally |
| clientele | exempt | occurred |
| column | exorbitant | offered |
| commission | extraordinary | omission |
| committee | familiar | omitted |
| competition | feasible | opposite |
| competitor | fiscal | ordinarily |
| congratulate | foreign | paid |
| conscientious | forty | pamphlet |
| conscious | fourth | permanent |
| consecutively | genuine | permitted |

| | | |
|---|---|---|
| pertinent | recognize | thank you |
| physician | recommendation | therefore |
| possession | regarding | thorough |
| postpaid | remittance | though |
| practical | restaurant | through |
| prevalent | schedule | truly |
| privilege | separate | undoubtedly |
| procedure | serviceable | unnecessarily |
| professor | severely | usable |
| profited | similar | usage |
| prominent | sincerely | using |
| quantitative | succeed | valuable |
| quantity | sufficient | volume |
| questionnaire | superintendent | weekday |
| receipt | supervisor | |
| receive | tenant | |

**b.** Some common words used in business writing are misspelled because they are confused with other words. Combinations such as *affect–effect, loose–lose, pole–poll, realty–reality, their–there,* and others are clarified in Chapter 7.

## 8–2.  General Rules to Improve Spelling

**a.** For one-syllable words ending with a single consonant that is preceded by a single vowel, repeat the consonant before adding the suffix *y* (bag + y = baggy).  Also repeat the consonant when adding a suffix beginning with a vowel (bag + age = baggage). Exceptions to this rule are many words ending in *s* and all words ending in *w, x,* and *y.*

**final consonant doubled**

| | | | | | | | | |
|---|---|---|---|---|---|---|---|---|
| can | canned | | skin | skinny | | pad | padding |
| stop | stopped | | trim | trimmed | | ship | shipped |
| big | bigger | | sit | sitting | | slip | slippage |

**exceptions**

| *s* | | *w* | | *x* | | *y* | |
|---|---|---|---|---|---|---|---|
| bus | buses | sow | sowing | tax | taxes | pay | payable |
| yes | yeses | tow | towing | box | boxed | say | saying |
| gas | gases | snow | snowy | wax | waxy | buy | buyer |

**b.** Do not repeat the final consonant for those one-syllable words that add a suffix beginning with a consonant (ship + ment = shipment).

| | | | | | | |
|---|---|---|---|---|---|---|
| sad | sadness | | bad | badly | | cup | cupful |
| glad | gladly | | star | stardom | | hat | hatless |

**c.** For multisyllable words ending with a consonant preceded by a single vowel (e.g., *prefer*), repeat the final consonant (*r*) before adding a suffix beginning with a vowel (*ed*) if the resulting word places the accent on the final syllable of the root word (*-fer* in *preferred*). If, however, the resulting word (e.g., *preference*) places the accent on the first syllable of the root word (*pref-*), do not repeat the final consonant (*r*) before adding the suffix (*ence*). There are exceptions to this rule.

**accent on final syllable of root word, final consonant repeated**

| | |
|---|---|
| occurred | occur + r + ed |
| beginning | begin + n + ing |
| referring | refer + r + ing |
| transferred | transfer + r + ed |
| unforgettable | un + forget + t + able |
| preferred | prefer + r + ed |

**accent on first syllable of root word, final consonant not repeated**

| | | | |
|---|---|---|---|
| canceled | cancel + ed | profitable | profit + able |
| credited | credit + ed | benefited | benefit + ed |
| reference | refer + ence | preferable | prefer + able |

**exceptions**

programmed     handicapped     formatted

**d.** The prefix *fore-*, which means "before," is used to precede whole words to form another word (fore + thought = forethought); the prefix *for-*, on the other hand, is generally used with letter combinations that by themselves are not separate words (for + tunate = fortunate).

**prefix *fore-***

| | | | |
|---|---|---|---|
| forego | fore + go | foreclose | fore + close |
| foresight | fore + sight | foreground | fore + ground |

**prefix *for-***

| | | | |
|---|---|---|---|
| forceps | for + ceps | formative | for + mative |
| forfeit | for + feit | formerly | for + merly |

**exceptions**

forgive     forget     forsake     forswear

**e.** For words ending with a silent *e*, generally drop the *e* before adding a suffix that begins with a vowel.

**silent *e* dropped**

| | | | |
|---|---|---|---|
| desire | desirable | approve | approval |
| file | filing | sense | sensible |
| finance | financial | execute | executive |

**exceptions**

| | | | |
|---|---|---|---|
| dye | dyeing | mile | mileage |
| acre | acreage | Europe | European |

**f.** Retain the silent *e* when adding suffixes beginning with *a* or *o* to words ending in *ce* and *ge*.

### silent *e* retained

| | | | |
|---|---|---|---|
| notice | noticeable | manage | manageable |
| service | serviceable | knowledge | knowledgeable |
| replace | replaceable | advantage | advantageous |
| enforce | enforceable | courage | courageous |

### exception

mortgage    mortgagor

**g.** For words ending with a silent *e*, generally retain the *e* when adding a suffix that begins with a consonant.

### silent *e* retained

| | | | |
|---|---|---|---|
| manage | management | achieve | achievement |
| sure | surely | precise | precisely |
| sincere | sincerely | nine | ninety |
| whole | wholesome | home | homeless |

### exceptions

| | | | |
|---|---|---|---|
| nine | ninth | true | truly |
| judge | judgment | acknowledge | acknowledgment |
| wise | wisdom | whole | wholly |
| argue | argument | gentle | gently |

**h.** For words ending with *y* preceded by a consonant, generally change the *y* to *i* before adding any suffix except one beginning with *i*.

### final *y* changed to *i*

| | | | |
|---|---|---|---|
| penny | pennies | easy | easiest |
| likely | likelihood | twenty | twentieth |
| cloudy | cloudiness | vary | variable |
| carry | carried | ordinary | ordinarily |

### final *y* retained before suffix beginning with *i*

| | | | |
|---|---|---|---|
| fly | flying | lobby | lobbyist |
| try | trying | thirty | thirtyish |

### exception

shy    shyly

**i.** When adding any suffix, retain the final *y* if it is preceded by a vowel.

### final *y* retained

| | | | |
|---|---|---|---|
| money | moneyed | display | displaying |
| employ | employable | pay | payment |
| convey | conveyer | okay | okayed |

**exceptions**

| | | | |
|---|---|---|---|
| pay | paid | day | daily |
| lay | laid | say | said |

**j.** Place *i* before *e* except after *c* or when the combination is pronounced like the *a* in "neighbor" or "weigh."

**ie combination**

| | | | |
|---|---|---|---|
| believe | relief | niece | chief |
| thief | achieve | yield | piece |

**ei combination after c**

| | | | |
|---|---|---|---|
| receive | receipt | ceiling | perceive |

**ei combination pronounced like a**

| | | | |
|---|---|---|---|
| weight | freight | sleigh | vein |

**exceptions**

| | | |
|---|---|---|
| either | neither | leisure |
| financier | species | weird |

**k.** For words ending with the syllable pronounced "seed," only one word is spelled *sede*, three words are spelled *ceed*, and the rest are spelled *cede*.

**word ending in sede**

supersede

**words ending in ceed**

| | | |
|---|---|---|
| exceed | proceed | succeed |

**words ending in cede**

| | | |
|---|---|---|
| accede | precede | concede |
| intercede | recede | secede |

## 8–3. Use of the Dictionary to Locate Correct Spellings

**a.** Use a recognized up-to-date collegiate, desk, or unabridged dictionary to locate any spellings of words you do not know or about which you are unsure. The dictionary used for all spellings in this manual is the 1996 printing of *Merriam-Webster's Collegiate Dictionary,* Tenth Edition, published by Merriam-Webster, Incorporated.

**b.** When the dictionary offers two spellings for a word in the same entry, use the *first* spelling.

**judgment** *not* judgement      **canceled** *not* cancelled

**c.** When verifying the spelling of words, match the word with its correct counterpart in the dictionary. For example, if the word is used as a noun in the sentence, then compare it with the noun spelling of this

247

word in the dictionary. As an illustration of differences in spellings, note that *under way* used as an adverb is two words but *underway* as an adjective is one. Similar situations occur with many other words.

| | |
|---|---|
| mark down (verb) | markdown (noun) |
| set up (verb) | setup (noun) |
| double-space (verb) | double space (noun) |

**d.** The spellings of irregular plural nouns and irregular verb forms appear in the dictionary directly after the root word in the entry. Therefore, when in doubt about the formation of these words, consult your dictionary for their spellings.

**irregular plural nouns**

| | | | |
|---|---|---|---|
| secretary | secretaries | tomato | tomatoes |
| half | halves | child | children |
| analysis | analyses | alumnus | alumni |

**irregular verb forms**

| | | |
|---|---|---|
| bring | brought | brought |
| sing | sang | sung |
| run | ran | run |
| lie | lay | lain |
| see | saw | seen |

**e.** The spellings of irregular adjective and adverb comparisons appear in the dictionary directly after the root word in the entry. Check your dictionary to verify these spellings. (See Sections 6-21 and 6-26 for rules on adjective and adverb comparisons.)

**irregular adjective comparisons**

| | | |
|---|---|---|
| costly | costlier | costliest |
| good | better | best |

**irregular adverb comparisons**

| | | |
|---|---|---|
| early | earlier | earliest |
| far | farther | farthest |

**f.** To locate easily the spellings of unfamiliar words in the dictionary, acquaint yourself with the various letter combinations that represent sounds in the written English language. Both consonants and vowels may have different letter combinations that represent the same sound. The chart below presents just a few of the sounds and combinations with which you should become familiar.

| Sound | Letter Combinations to Represent the Sound |
|---|---|
| ā | *a*lien*a*te, *ai*de, ga*u*ge, st*ea*k, f*eig*n, w*eigh*t |
| ak | *ac*tual, *acc*olade, *ack*nowledgment, *acq*uiesce, *aq*ueduct |
| ar | *aer*osol, *air*borne, *ar*eas, *arr*ogant |
| as | *as*piration, *asc*ending, *ass*ertive |
| aw | f*a*ther, *au*dacity, t*augh*t, *aw*esome, *o*stracize, *ough*t |
| ē | *e*dict, *ea*sement, d*ee*m, rec*ei*pt, p*eo*ple, f*ia*sco, p*ie*ce |
| er | simil*ar*, *er*adicate, *ear*nings, *err*oneous, f*ir*mly, w*or*risome, t*our*nament, *ur*banization |
| f | *f*elony, ef*f*icient, *ph*onetic, rou*gh*age |
| g | *g*rimace, *gh*astly, *gu*ardian |
| h | *h*azardous, *wh*olly |
| ī | *ai*sle, h*eigh*t, *i*dentify, t*ie*d, th*igh*, *hy*draulic |
| j | ju*dg*ment, *g*ermane, exa*gg*eration, *j*eopardize |
| k | *c*oincide, a*cc*ountant, *ch*emistry, *k*ilometer, *q*uandary |
| m | *m*iraculous, pa*lm*istry |
| n | *gn*aw, *kn*otty, *mn*emonic, *n*arrative, *pn*eumonia |
| ō | b*eau*, *o*dor, fl*oa*t, d*oe*skin, p*ou*ltry, d*ough*nut, sn*ow* |
| oi, oy | sp*oi*l, anno*y*ance |
| oo | n*eu*tral, fl*ew*, ad*ieu*, t*o*mb, l*oo*se, l*ou*ver, thr*ough*, n*u*trition, tr*ue*, s*ui*t |
| ow | ann*ou*nce, fl*ow*er |
| r | *r*etrieve, *rh*ythm, *wr*est |
| s | *c*ertainty, *s*alable, *ps*ychologist, *sc*intillate |
| sh | ma*ch*inery, espe*ci*ally, *s*urely, con*sc*ience, *sch*nauzer, nau*se*ous, *sh*rewd, preci*si*on, substan*ti*al |
| t | *pt*omaine, *t*ranslate |
| ū | b*eau*tiful, f*eu*d, sk*ew*ed, *u*niform, f*ue*l, *yu*letide |
| w | *ch*oir, *q*uarterly, *w*asteful, *wh*imsical |

# Proofreading

## 8–4.  Procedures for Proofreading Documents

Proofreading is the process of checking one document against another to ensure that it conforms with the original in all respects. Use these guidelines to proofread a document:

**a.**  Use the spell check feature of your word processing program before printing the document and/or beginning the proofreading process.

**b.**  Check for consistency of style throughout the document before actually beginning to read the text.

(1)  Assess the appropriateness of margins (top, bottom, left, and right).

(2)  Check the line spacing between paragraphs, before and after main or text headings, within letter closing lines, etc.

(3)  Inspect to ensure that the document contains no widow or orphan lines (single lines of a paragraph at the top or bottom of a page).

(4)  Evaluate the general appearance of the document.

c.  Read the text initially for content.

(1)  Does the material make sense?

(2)  Are there any missing words?

(3)  Are any words or groups of words repeated?

d.  Read the text again for accuracy. Check it carefully against the original copy.

(1)  Are any letters transposed or omitted? Are all words spelled correctly? The spell check feature of your word processing program will locate most spelling errors, but it will not detect such errors as using *form* for *from*, *an* for *and*, or *effect* for *affect*.

(2)  Have any letters, words, sentences, or paragraphs been omitted? Pay close attention to ensure that no *s*'s have been dropped from plural nouns and that no words, sentences, or paragraphs have been skipped.

(3)  When proofreading names and unfamiliar words or terminology, check each spelling meticulously—letter by letter.

(4)  Double-check all figures carefully with the original source. For long numbers verify the number of digits and then compare the digits in groups of three. If the numbers are in a column with a total, the easiest method of proofreading is to use a calculator to check the total in the original document and then check the same total in the document being proofread.

e.  When proofreading hard copy, use the pen-and-forefinger technique to maintain attention and keep the eyes focused on the line being proofread. To use this technique, hold the pen in the hand with which you will be making corrections and place the copy to be proofread on that side. Place the original on the opposite side and use the forefinger of that hand to follow along as you compare the two copies.

f.  When proofreading hard copy, use the standardized proofreaders' marks shown in Section 8-5 and also on the inside back cover to show your corrections. If possible, double-space your copy for proofreading purposes so that any corrections will be clearly visible.

## 8–5.  Standardized Proofreaders' Marks to Show Corrections

a.  Standardized proofreaders' marks are used to show corrections in handwritten, typewritten, computer-generated, or printed copy. These symbols are used so that anyone who reads the document will interpret the corrections in the same way. Use the following marks and symbols to make changes in words or word groups:

| Instruction | Mark or Symbol | Example | Marginal Note |
|---|---|---|---|
| Boldface word(s). | ~~~~ | received by <u>November 1</u> | (bf) |
| Capitalize letter. | ≡ | to the Retailers association | (cap) |
| Capitalize letters. | ≡≡ | from Unesco | (caps) |
| Change word(s). | —— | ~~In view of the fact that~~ you have *(Because)* | |
| Close up space. | ⌒ | You can, never the less, receive | |
| Delete stroke. | / | occassion | |
| Delete stroke. | ୫ | policyand send us | |
| Delete word(s). | ⌒୫ | a ~~postal~~ money order for $50 | |
| Hyphenate word(s). | = | up=to=date records | |
| Insert a space. | # | Inaddition, you will be | |
| Insert apostrophe. | ⌄ | its a good deal | |
| Insert colon. | ⊙ | followspen, ink, and paper. | |
| Insert comma. | ⋏ | On Tuesday, May 23we | |
| Insert em dash. | ⊥M̅ | comments—all are welcome! | |
| Insert en dash. | ⊥N̅ | January 14–16 | |
| Insert here (caret). | ⋀ | Insert at place. *(this)* | |
| Insert parentheses. | ⨍ ⨎ | end of this monthApril 30 | |
| Insert period. | ⊙ | by 10 amtomorrow | |
| Insert question mark. | ? | Do you agree? | |
| Insert quotation marks. | ⌄ ⌄ | article, Access on the Web, that | |
| Insert semicolon. | ⋏ | nowtherefore, you | |
| Insert word(s). | ⋀ | your latest form *(income tax)* | |
| Italicize word(s). | ———— | <u>The Wall Street Journal</u> | (ital) |
| Join to word. | ⌒ | in our computer laboratory *(micro)* | |
| Lowercase letter. | / | of the Association | (lc) |

| Instruction | Mark or Symbol | Example | Marginal Note |
|---|---|---|---|
| Lowercase letters. | / | the UNITED STATES OF AMERICA | lc |
| Restore word(s). | …… | our ~~furniture~~ warehouse in Toledo | stet |
| Roman type. | ___ | book titles in *italic* type | rom |
| Small capital letters. | = | our red tag sale on | sm caps |
| Spell out word or number. | ○ | ③ stores on Fifth Ave. | sp |
| Transpose letters. | ∽ | all thier profits. | tr |
| Transpose words. | ⌐⌐ | to legibly print your name | tr |
| Underscore word(s). | ___ | We <u>cannot</u> overemphasize | u'score |

**b.** Use the following symbols to move words or word groups:

| Instruction | Mark or Symbol | Example | Marginal Note |
|---|---|---|---|
| Align horizontally. | = | In the past two years | |
| Align vertically. | ‖ | ‖(1) New courses (2) New curriculum | |
| Center. | ] [ | ]PROOFREADERS' MARKS[ | |
| Combine paragraphs. | no ¶ | no ¶ You may also wish to | |
| Double-space copy. | | As a result of this investigation, we have decided to reduce expenses. | ds |
| Indent 0.5". | .5" | .5" During the last month | |
| Insert line space. | > | COMPUTER SALES SUMMARY February 1998 | +1 l# |
| Move as shown. | ○ | for the next year | |
| Move to next line. | ⌐ | give the contract to Mr. | |
| Move to the left. | ⌐ | You may wish to | |
| Move to the right. | ⌐ | You may wish to | |
| New paragraph. | ¶ | ¶Many customers do not | |
| Single-space copy. | | As a result of this investigation, we have decided to reduce expenses. | ss |

# Editing

## 8–6. Preparing to Edit

**a.** The proofreading process involves the comparison of one document with another to assess the correctness of the prepared copy. Editing, on the other hand, is a more challenging process since editors do not have "correct" copies upon which they may rely to determine if the copy they are reading has been prepared properly. Editors themselves are responsible for determining the accuracy and appropriateness of all language and format applications.

**b.** Assemble all the materials you will need to edit a document:

(1) An up-to-date (printed within the last three years) collegiate, desk, or unabridged dictionary, e.g., *Merriam-Webster's Collegiate Dictionary,* Tenth Edition

(2) An up-to-date (published within the last three years) reference manual, e.g., *HOW 8: A Handbook for Office Workers,* Eighth Edition

(3) An up-to-date (published within the last five years) thesaurus, e.g., *Roget's II: The New Thesaurus*

(4) Reference sources from which the document was created; e.g., rough drafts, authorization letters, file copies, meeting notes, etc.

(5) Any other published references that may relate to the document; e.g., mailing lists, telephone directories, zip code directories, maps, encyclopedias, books, magazines, newspapers, etc.

## 8–7. Editing the Document

**a.** Work from printed copy to edit a document. Because the editor does not just "check" a document against another source, you will probably need to read the material several times. As an editor you must evaluate the overall effectiveness of a document in terms of its attaining the goal for which it was written. Therefore, you will wish to read the material critically with several criteria in mind.

(1) Are there any omissions in ideas or content? All important ideas should be included in the document as well as any information to substantiate the ideas. Check to make sure the document is complete in every respect.

(2) Is the document well organized so that the reader can easily follow the ideas as they are presented? Coherent writing results in clarity and allows the reader to understand easily the purpose and contents of the document. The editor needs to make sure that ideas are placed in logical order and that each sentence flows smoothly and lucidly from the previous sentence.

(3) Is the document correct in every way—content, format, grammar, spelling, punctuation, capitalization, and number expression? Be sure to check the accuracy of all the data. In addition, make sure

that all the conventions of correct language usage have been observed and that the document has been formatted appropriately.

(4) Is the content easily understood? Examine the document to ensure that the ideas are presented vividly and with ample illustrations so that the reader can picture concretely what the writer had in mind.

(5) Have all the ideas been expressed in as few words as possible? Look at each sentence to make sure that it does not contain extra wording. Evaluate sentences and paragraphs to see if they contribute to achieving the overall purpose of the document. Any excess words, sentences, or paragraphs should be deleted.

(6) Are all abbreviations, number expressions, and other format considerations handled in the same way? Check for inconsistencies in these areas and in the contents of the document.

(7) Are the tone and language appropriate for accomplishing the purpose of the document? Check to make sure that letters are written in a friendly and courteous manner. Reports, on the other hand, should have a more formal tone. Match the formality of tone and language with the purpose of the document.

**b.** Use proofreaders' marks and symbols to indicate changes made during the editing process. These marks and symbols are explained and illustrated in Section 8-5 and on the inside back cover.

**c.** Double-space rough drafts of documents that are to be edited. Double spacing not only makes the document easier to read but also makes changes easier to interpret.

# Chapter 9

# Address Format and Forms of Address

Mr./Ms.

## Address Format and Forms of Address Solution Finder

**Mr./Ms.**

# General Address Format

## 9–1. General Address Format

**a.** Use combinations of the following to address general business correspondence: full name of person with appropriate courtesy title, professional title, company name, street address, city, state, and zip code (5 digits or 9 digits, depending upon the availability of the 9-digit code).

Coordinate the person's name, titles, and company name so that line endings in the inside address are as nearly even as possible. Use the two-letter postal state abbreviation or spell out the state name to achieve further a balanced appearance. (See Section 5-9c.)

Use the same format for both the inside address and the envelope, unless the company uses the envelope format recommended by the U.S. Postal Service described in Section 10-29.

**addressed to individual**

Mr. Anthony L. Caruana
2231 Washington Avenue
Des Moines, Iowa 50310

Dear Mr. Caruana:

Ms. Margaret Costellano
9240 Balboa Boulevard, Apt. 2
San Clemente, CA 92672-2036

Dear Ms. Costellano:

**addressed to individual within company**

Mrs. Marcelyn Scott-Beckwith
Vice President of Operations
Nation's Bank
5420 Bayshore Boulevard
Tampa, Florida 33611-4122

Dear Mrs. Scott-Beckwith:

Mr. Jay V. Berger, Manager
Policy Issue Department
General Insurance Company of
America
600 Prospect Avenue, Suite 600
Hartford, Connecticut 06105-2920

Dear Mr. Berger:

**addressed to company**

F. M. Tarbell Company
2740 S.W. Troy Street
Portland, OR 97219-2553

Ladies and Gentlemen:

Cinamerica
Post Office Box 20077
Encino, CA 91416-0077

Ladies and Gentlemen:

**b.** An address may have a maximum of six lines and a minimum of two lines.

**maximum six-line address**

Ms. Stephanie R. Whitaker
Chief Operations Manager
Quality Control Department
Neware Aluminum Accessories
3600 Chelwood Park Blvd., N.E.
Albuquerque, NM 87111-5416

**minimum two-line address**

Phillips Foods, Inc.
Morristown, NJ 07960-3305

## Names and Titles

### 9–2. Courtesy Titles

a. Abbreviate the courtesy titles *Mr.* and *Mrs.* when they are used with the names of individuals. The courtesy title *Ms.* ends with a period, although it is not an abbreviation. Always spell out the courtesy title *Miss*.

In the salutations of business letters, use the courtesy title with the last name only.

**courtesy title with full name**

**Mr.** Stanley Hutchinson          **Ms.** Frances Cates
**Mrs.** Charlene Carnachan          **Miss** Natalia Granados

**courtesy title in salutation**

Dear **Mr.** Hutchinson:          Dear **Ms.** Cates:
Dear **Mrs.** Carnachan:          Dear **Miss** Granados:

b. When the name of an individual does not signify whether the person is a man or a woman, omit the courtesy title. Use the same format for the salutation in a business letter.

**name does not signify gender**

| | | |
|---|---|---|
| Lynn Sebastian | Cory Williams | B. Kelly Clemens |
| T. R. Najjar | Cary Antonovich | Jaime Bennett |
| Chris V. Stauber | Casey R. Elliott | |

**salutation for name that does not signify gender**

Dear T. R. Najjar:          Dear Chris V. Stauber:
Dear Cory Williams:          Dear B. Kelly Clemens:

c. When addressing a woman, use the courtesy title *Ms.* unless *Mrs.* or *Miss* is specified by the addressee. For young girls under the age of thirteen, use the courtesy title *Miss*.

**woman does not indicate a title preference**

**Ms.** Laura Rankin          **Ms.** Ellen Togo

**girl under age thirteen**

**Miss** Kristen Fielding          **Miss** Claudia Martinez

Mr./Ms.

**d.** The courtesy title *Master* is used for addressing young boys, usually below the age of thirteen.

    **Master** William J. Clark          **Master** Charles Bentley

**e.** The abbreviated courtesy title *Esq.* (*Esquire*) is sometimes used after the surname of a lawyer. In such cases no courtesy title precedes the name.

    Murray T. Silverstein, **Esq.**         Lorraine H. Clark, **Esq.**

**f.** Female correspondents who have a courtesy title preference other than *Ms.* should indicate this preference in the signature lines of their correspondence by enclosing the preferred title in parentheses before their names. Correspondents who have names that do not indicate gender may also wish to indicate a courtesy title preference by enclosing it in parentheses before their names in a signature line.

**female with courtesy title preference other than *Ms.***

    (Mrs.) Nancy Willett          (Dr.) Karen L. Butler

**male or female whose name does not indicate gender**

    (Ms.) J. T. Robinson          (Ms.) Lonnie Abrams
    (Mrs.) Chris Dobrian         (Mrs.) Lee Haberman
    (Mr.) Dana Andrews          (Mr.) Leslie Mitchell

## 9–3. Professional Titles

**a.** Except for *Dr.* and long professional titles consisting of more than one or two words, write out and capitalize all professional titles when they precede the names of individuals. *Professor, Dean, The Reverend, Governor, Senator, Colonel, Lieutenant,* and *The Honorable* are examples of titles that are capitalized and written in full.

**Doctor abbreviated**

    **Dr.** Allen Wiedmeyer          **Dr.** Shannon T. Goar

**professional title written out**

    **Professor** Marly Bergerud       **The Honorable** Victor S. Ryan

**long professional title abbreviated**

    **Lt. Col. Ret.** Maurice P. Wiener  (Lieutenant Colonel Retired)

**b.** In addressing business correspondence or completing signature lines, capitalize and write out professional titles that follow an individual's name.

**single-line address format**

    Mr. Ray Johnson, **Dean**       Ms. Patricia A. Wilson, **Vice President**

**two-line address format**

    Ms. Margaret M. Fielding        Mr. Michael T. Livingston Jr.
    **Plant Superintendent**          **Assistant Vice President**

**single-line signature format**

(Dr.) Jean Loucks, **Dean**

William A. Murillo, **Manager**

(Mrs.) Joyce Moore, **President**

Rebecca L. Roberts, **Supervisor**

**two-line signature format**

John S. Minasian
**Plant Superintendent**

(Ms.) Orolyn L. Ruenz-Clark
**Vice President of Operations**

(Mrs.) Brenda Browning
**Collections Manager**

Thomas C. Johnson
**Customer Service Representative**

c. Capitalize professional titles *not* appearing in address format or signature lines only when they precede and are used directly with an individual's name in place of a courtesy title. Do not capitalize titles following an individual's name.

**title preceding name**

**President** Lloyd W. Bartholome will deliver the main address.

One of the senators from Wyoming, **Senator** Alan K. Simpson, will be the luncheon speaker.

**title following name**

Lloyd W. Bartholome, **president** of A & P Enterprises, will deliver the main address.

The Honorable Scot Ober, **senator** from Michigan, has agreed to deliver the main address.

d. Only one courtesy or professional title with the same meaning should appear with a single name. Use *Dr.* or *M.D.*, but not both titles, with the same name.

**titles with the same meaning**

**Dr.** James V. Glaser    *or*    James V. Glaser, **M.D.**

**Dr.** Cheng Wong    *or*    Cheng Wong, **D.D.S.**

**titles with different meanings**

**Dr.** Sue Rigby, **Professor**

e. Do not capitalize professional titles that substitute for individuals' names.

The **general** scheduled a staff meeting for Thursday afternoon.

Did the **governor** appear for the press conference?

## 9–4. Company Names

Spell out company names in full unless the company itself uses abbreviations in its official name.[1] *Inc.* and *Ltd.* usually appear in abbreviated form, but some companies write these words in full.

**company name written in full**

Pacific Mutual Life Insurance Company        Richter and Sons

Merriam-Webster, Incorporated        Watson Corporation

**company name containing abbreviation**

Consolidated Factors, **Ltd.**        McKnight, Fisher **&** Donovan

International Computer **Corp.**        Lyons Investment Group **Inc.**

## Places

### 9–5.  Buildings and Units

Capitalize the names of buildings and the names of any units **therein.** Place the unit, suite, or apartment location after the building **name,** but separate the two with a comma.

If an address contains a unit location without a building name, place it after the street address. Separate the street address and **the** unit location with a comma.

Use figure form for all unit numbers.

**building name with unit location**

Tishman Building, **Suite 103**

Medical Arts Center, **Suites 680–681**

California State Capitol, **Office 243F**

Greenwich Apartments, **Unit 3**

**unit location without building name**

140 Willow Street, **Suite 103**        18564 Clark Street, **Apt. 4**

9830 Grand Oaks Avenue, **Unit 22**        5426 S.W. 43rd Street, **#105**

### 9–6.  Street Addresses

a.  Use figures to express house or building numbers. Only the **house or** building number *one* is written in word form.

**house or building number *one***

**One** Lakeview Terrace        **One** Riverwalk Place

**house or building number in figures**

**8** Burbank Lane        **210** Third Avenue, Apt. 303

**17225** Lassen Street        **10239-3** White Oak Avenue

---

[1]The official name of a company may be determined from its printed letterhead or from any of its contracts. Official company names are also listed in the directories referenced in Chapter 15, copies of which may be found in most public libraries.

**b.** Spell out simple compass directions (*North, South, East* and *West*) that appear in a street address. Compound compass points (*Northeast, Northwest, Southeast*, and *Southwest*) in an address are abbreviated. Any compound compass directions following the street address are preceded by a comma.

**simple compass point in street address**

1864 **East** 37th Street                2160 Century Park **East**

1040 **North** Brand Boulevard          240 Manchester Street **West**

**compound compass point within street address**

2830 **N.E.** 17th Street                121 **S.W.** Morrison Street

**compass point following street address**

1301 K Street, **N.W.**                 4210 Broxten Street, **S.E.**, Apt. 23

**c.** All street number names *ten* and below are written in words using ordinal numbers—*first, second, third*, etc. Street number names above *ten*, however, are written in figures. Use ordinal numbers (*11th, 12th, 13th*, etc.) when expressing these street names.

**street number name *ten* or below**

1183 **Fifth** Avenue                   983 West **First** Street

**street number name above *ten***

980 North **81st** Street               3624 West **59th** Place

2036 **42nd** Street                    1843 **123rd** Street

**d.** Spell out street designations such as *Boulevard, Avenue, Street, Place, Drive*, and *Lane*. Only the street designation *Boulevard* may be abbreviated (*Blvd.*) with exceptionally long street names.

**street designation spelled out**

18394 Lankershim **Boulevard**

**street designation abbreviated**

9263 North Coldwater Canyon **Blvd.**

**e.** Spell out where possible mailing designations such as *Rural Route* or *Post Office Box* that are used in the place of street addresses. Abbreviate the mailing designation only with long addresses.

**postal designation spelled out**

Post Office Box 207                     **Rural Route** 2, Box 1620

**postal designation abbreviated**

**P.O. Box** 1269, Terminal Annex

**f.** Apartment, suite, and unit numbers are expressed in figures and are generally included on the same line as the building name. In addresses without building names, these numbers appear on the same line with the street address. The term *Apartment* may be abbreviated when it appears on the same line as the street address.

With long street addresses, apartment numbers may be placed on the following line. The term *Apartment* in these cases is spelled out.

**apartment, suite, or unit number with building**

Richmond Medical Plaza, **Suite 540**

**unit number with street address**

6176 Arroyo Road, **Unit 2**

**apartment number with street address**

3964 West 81st Street, **Apt. 3**

**no specific designation with street address**

16932 Wilshire Boulevard, **C-110**

**apartment number on line following street address**

8564 Kensington Street, S.W.
**Apartment 230**

## 9–7. City, State, and Zip Code

**a.** Spell out in full the names of cities.

Saint Louis        New York        Fort Worth        Los Angeles

**b.** Use the two-letter post office designation for state names or spell out in full the state name. Select either mode based upon (1) the degree of formality of the correspondence or (2) the one that provides better balance for setting up the entire address. Should both be equally suitable, use the two-letter postal designation. Use the same form for both the inside address and the envelope address unless the company chooses to use the U.S. Postal Service recommendations for addressing envelopes described in Section 10-29.

**state two-letter zip code designation**

Ms. Jessica Morton            Mr. Richard A. Chui
108 Academy Avenue           9540 Barr Drive, Apt. 204
Weymouth, MA 02188-4204      Indianapolis, IN 46229-1214

**state name written in full**

Mr. William R. Stephenson        Mrs. Shirley Schnair-Goldman
257 American Legion Highway      1124 Jefferson Boulevard
Revere, Massachusetts 02151      Flint, Michigan 48507-4201

**c.** Zip codes are typed a single space after the state.

Atlanta, GA 30331-8732      *or*      Atlanta, Georgia 30331

# Address Format for Foreign Correspondence

## 9–8.  Address Format for Foreign Correspondence

**a.**  Addresses for foreign correspondence contain combinations of the following: (1) full name of addressee with appropriate courtesy title, (2) professional title of addressee, (3) company name, (4) street address, (5) city and any city numbering codes or section name, (6) state or region, if applicable, and (7) destination country.

**b.**  The sequencing of the address components varies among countries. Some countries place the name of the addressee first but place the city information before the street address. Some place the house number after the street name or the zip code equivalent before the city name. Others follow the familiar street address, city, state, and zip code format used in the United States. Where possible, follow the conventions of the destination country. For mail posted from the United States, however, always place the name of the destination country in all capital letters as the last line of the mailing address.

| | |
|---|---|
| Mr. Atsushi Ishiki | Alexandria |
| 1-6-302 Wutsukusigaoka | Stanly |
| 1 Chome—1Z Midoriku | 237 Zaky Badway Mohamed St. |
| Yokohama | Mrs. Iman Gaber El-Desoky |
| JAPAN | EGYPT |

**c.**  If possible, use courtesy titles that reflect the language of the country. *Herrn*, *Frau*, and *Fraülein* (German); *Señor*, *Señora*, and *Señorita* (Spanish); and *Monsieur*, *Madame*, and *Mademoiselle* (French) are just a few examples of foreign courtesy titles that represent the English *Mr.*, *Mrs.*, and *Miss*.

In most foreign countries a comparable term for *Miss* is used for young women. Adult women are addressed with the courtesy title comparable to the English *Mrs.*, regardless of their marital status.

Use English courtesy titles in those cases where the comparable title is unknown or impractical to reproduce on English-based keyboards.

| | |
|---|---|
| Le Lien | Srta. Kristina Chagas Tavares |
| c/o M$^{r}$ Lucien Aubert | Rua 706, n° 152/178 |
| 14, rue Roger-Radisson | Balneario Camboriú, SC |
| 69322 Lyon | CEP 88330 |
| FRANCE | BRAZIL |

**d.**  When addressing foreign correspondence, use the English version of a country name (*GERMANY*, not *DEUTSCHLAND*) to ensure the correspondence is routed to the correct country from the United States. For city names, however, select the foreign spelling to hasten delivery within the country (*Köln*, not *Cologne*; *Wien*, not *Vienna*; *Ogasawara*, not *Bonin*). If possible, use all appropriate letters and diacritical marks in spelling names, streets, cities, and other parts of the address. Consult the geographical reference section of your dictionary for assistance in selecting the correct name and its spelling.[2]

Herrn Paul-Erich Rünz
Diplomat-Kaufman
Gemarkenstraße 290
5000 Köln 80–Dellbrück
GERMANY

# On-Line Address Formats

The Internet,[3] which is accessible to over 30 million users worldwide, has promoted information exchange between virtually any segment of our society. From individuals in major universities and giant corporations to the single user at a home computer, all may access the wealth of information Internet access provides and all may communicate with each other through E-mail.

## 9–9.  Internet Addresses

Internet popularity has soared with the introduction of the World Wide Web (WWW). Companies, government offices, educational institutions, organizations, and individuals have established Web sites—computer "pages" on which they provide information, sell products or services, and/or recruit employees. Each page has an address so it can be reached easily by merely typing in the address. An Internet address is known as a Universal Resource Locator—URL, pronounced "earl." A description of URL parts follows:

(1)  A typical Internet address (URL) might appear as **http://www.odci. gov/cia/publications/95fact/index.html** in a listing.

(2)  The first part, **http://**, indicates the type of protocol needed to retrieve the information at the site. In this case **http** represents *hypertext transport protocol.* World Wide Web sites are accessed with http protocols through Web browsers. Other protocols include **gopher://**, which identifies a gopher resource, and **ftp://**, which identifies a file transfer protocol resource.

(3)  The **www** following the protocol type symbolizes World Wide Web. The name of the host computer, **odci** (Office of the Director of Central Intelligence), is followed by its identifier, **gov**, which distinguishes the Web site as a government entity. Note the common URL identifier extensions in the following table:

---

[2]The spellings shown here are based on those contained in *Merriam-Webster's Collegiate Dictionary*, 10th Ed. (Springfield, Mass.: Merriam-Webster, Incorporated, 1996). Note that in this dictionary the foreign spelling is shown after the English spelling in the primary reference and also listed separately in a secondary reference.

[3]See Sections 15-11 and 15-12 for additional information on accessing and using the Internet.

| Identifier | Definition |
|---|---|
| com | commercial organization |
| edu | educational site |
| gov | government organization |
| mil | military |
| net | organization administering a network |
| org | miscellaneous organization |

(4) The link **cia** from the host computer moves to the Web site of The Central Intelligence Agency where **publications**, **95fact**, and **index. html** are accessed.

(5) Keying in **http://www.odci.gov/cia/publications/95fact/index.html**, therefore, will take you directly to the index for *The World Factbook 1995*. The **html** extension after **index** represents "HyperText Markup Language." Clicking on any item in the index will access the text in the world fact book.

## 9–10. E-Mail Addresses

**Just as everyone has an address for mail delivery by the U.S. Postal Service and private mail carriers, anyone who wishes to send and receive mail through the Internet must have an Internet E-mail (electronic mail) address.**

(1) An E-mail address is divided into two basic parts: the user name and the user domain. The user name is the combination of letters and/or numbers assigned to a specific user when the user signs up with an on-line service or other E-mail provider; formats for the user name are governed by the E-mail provider. The user domain identifies the location of the computer you are E-mailing or the location of the computer that receives your mail—the on-line service or other E-mail provider.

(2) The user name and the user domain are separated by @ (an "at" sign). Examples of E-mail addresses follow:

| Address | Explanation |
|---|---|
| ClarksHOW@aol.com[4] | The user name is *ClarksHOW*; the on-line service provider is America Online, an on-line service provider that is classified as a commercial organization. |
| 72257.1546@compuserve. com | The user name (number) is *72257.1546*; the on-line service provider is Compu-Serve, an on-line service provider that is classified as a commercial organization. |
| jdoe@swpco.com | The user name is *jdoe* (J. Doe); the E-mail provider is South-Western Publishing Company, a commercial organization. |

[4]See Section 9-9 for an explanation of extensions *com, edu, gov, mil, net*, and *org*.

| Address | Explanation |
|---------|-------------|
| Clarklr@laccd.edu | The user name is *Clarklr* (L. R. Clark); the E-mail provider is the Los Angeles Community College District, an educational site. |
| bsmith@csupomona.edu | The user name is *bsmith* (B. Smith); the E-mail provider is California State University, Pomona—an educational site. |
| lthamilton@pacificnet.net | The user name is *lthamilton* (L. T. Hamilton); the E-mail/Internet access service is an organization administering a network. |
| az876@lafn.org | The user name is *az876*; the E-mail/Internet service provider is Los Angeles Free Net, a miscellaneous organization. |
| rljones@rain.org | The user name is *rljones* (R. L. Jones); the E-mail/Internet service provider is Regional Area Information Network, a miscellaneous organization. |

# Forms of Address

## 9–11.   Personal and General Professional Titles

The following table lists the proper forms of address, salutation, and complimentary close for correspondence addressed to a general individual, two or more individuals, certain professionals, and a company.

| Addressee | Address on Letter and Envelope | Salutation and Complimentary Close |
|-----------|-------------------------------|-----------------------------------|
| Man | Mr. (full name)<br>(local address) | Dear Mr. (surname):<br>Sincerely, |
| Married Woman | Mrs. (husband's first name, last name)<br>(local address) | Dear Mrs. (surname):<br>Sincerely, |
|  | [5]Mrs. or Ms. (wife's first name, last name)<br>(local address) | Dear Mrs. or Ms. (surname):<br>Sincerely, |

---

[5]This form is also used for a woman who is separated or divorced from her husband.

Mr./Ms.

| Addressee | Address on Letter and Envelope | Salutation and Complimentary Close |
|---|---|---|
| Single Woman | Ms. or Miss (full name) (local address) | Dear Ms. or Miss (surname): Sincerely, |
| Woman, Marital Status Unknown | Ms. (full name) (local address) | Dear Ms. (surname): Sincerely, |
| Widow | Mrs. (husband's first name, last name) (local address) | Dear Mrs. (surname): Sincerely, |
|  | Mrs. or Ms. (wife's first name, last name) (local address) | Dear Mrs. or Ms. (surname): Sincerely, |
| Two or More Men | Mr. (full name) Mr. (full name) (local address) | Dear Mr. (surname) and Mr. (surname): *or* Dear Messrs. (surname) and (surname): *or* Gentlemen: Sincerely, |
| Two or More Women | Mrs. (full name) Mrs. (full name) (local address) | Dear Mrs. (surname) and Mrs. (surname): *or* Dear Mesdames (surname) and (surname): *or* Mesdames: Sincerely, |
|  | Mrs. (full name) Miss (full name) (local address) | Dear Mrs. (surname) and Miss (surname): Sincerely, |
|  | Ms. (full name) Ms. (full name) (local address) | Dear Ms. (surname) and Ms. (surname): *or* Dear Mses. (surname) and (surname): Sincerely, |
| One Woman and One Man | Ms. (full name) Mr. (full name) (local address) | Dear Ms. (surname) and Mr. (surname): Sincerely, |
| Married Couple | Mr. and Mrs. (husband's full name) (local address) | Dear Mr. and Mrs. (surname): Sincerely, |
| Married Couple With Different Surnames | (title) (full name of husband) (title) (full name of wife) (local address) | Dear (title) (husband's surname) and (title) (wife's surname): Sincerely, |
| Professional Married Couple With Same Title and Same Surname | (title in plural form) (husband's first name) and (wife's first name) (surname) (local address) | Dear (title in plural form) (surname): Sincerely, |

| Addressee | Address on Letter and Envelope | Salutation and Complimentary Close |
|---|---|---|
| Professional Married Couple With Different Titles and Same Surname | (title) (full name of husband) (title) (full name of wife) (local address) | Dear (title) and (title) (surname): Sincerely, |
| President of a College or University (Doctor) | Dr. (full name), President (name of institution) (local address) | Dear Dr. (surname): Sincerely, |
| Dean of a School or College | Dean (full name) School of (name) (name of institution) (local address) | Dear Dean (surname): Sincerely, |
| | Dr. or (Mr./Mrs./Ms.) (full name) Dean of (title) (name of institution) (local address) | Dear Dr. or (Mr./Mrs./Ms.) (surname): Sincerely, |
| Professor | Professor (full name) (name of department) (name of institution) (local address) | Dear Professor (surname): Sincerely, |
| | Dr. (full name), Professor (name of department) (name of institution) (local address) | Dear Dr. (surname): Sincerely, |
| | Dr. or (Mr./Mrs./Ms.) (full name) Assistant (or Associate) Professor (name of department) (name of institution) (local address) | Dear Dr. or (Mr./Mrs./Ms.) (surname): Sincerely, |
| Physician | (full name), M.D. (local address) *or* Dr. (full name) (local address) | Dear Dr. (surname): Sincerely, |
| Lawyer | (Mr./Mrs./Ms.) (full name) Attorney-at-Law (local address) *or* (full name), Esq. (local address) | Dear (Mr./Mrs./Ms.) (surname): Sincerely, |
| Service Personnel[6] | (full rank, full name, and abbreviation of service designation) (*Retired* is added to rank if applicable.) (unit assignment) (local address) | Dear (rank) (surname): Sincerely, |

[6]For a comprehensive listing of ranks and their abbreviations for the various military services, consult Webster's Collegiate Dictionary, 10th Ed. (Springfield, Mass.: Merriam-Webster, Incorporated, 1996), 1555–1557.

| Addressee | Address on Letter and Envelope | Salutation and Complimentary Close |
|---|---|---|
| Service Personnel (*continued*) | Example: Lieutenant Colonel, United States Air Force | |
| | Lieutenant Colonel Cory Adams, USAF | Dear Colonel Adams: |
| | Headquarters Squadron, 22nd Bomb Group | Sincerely, |
| | March Air Force Base | |
| | Riverside, California 92506 | |
| | Example: Brigadier General Retired, United States Marine Corps | |
| | Brig. Gen. Ret. Casey Rhodes, USMC | Dear General Rhodes: |
| | (local address) | Sincerely, |
| Company or Corporation, Men | (full name of organization) (local address) | Gentlemen: Sincerely, |
| Company or Corporation, Men and Women | (full name of organization) (local address) | Ladies and Gentlemen: Sincerely, |
| Company or Corporation, Women | (full name of organization) (local address) | Ladies: Sincerely, |

## 9–12.  Government Officials

**The following table shows the proper forms of address, salutation, and complimentary close for specific government officials.**

| Addressee | Address on Letter and Envelope | Salutation and Complimentary Close |
|---|---|---|
| President of the United States | The President The White House Washington, DC 20500 | Dear (Mr./Madam) President: Respectfully, |
| Former President[7] | Honorable (full name) Former President of the United States (local address) | Dear (Mr./Mrs./Ms.) (surname): Sincerely, |
| President-Elect | Honorable (full name) President-Elect of the United States (local address) | Dear (Mr./Mrs./Ms.) (surname): Sincerely, |
| Wife of the President | Mrs. (full name) The White House Washington, DC 20500 | Dear Mrs. (surname): Sincerely, |
| Assistant to the President | Honorable (full name) Assistant to the President The White House Washington, DC 20500 | Dear (Mr./Mrs./Ms.) (surname): Sincerely, |

---

[7]This form of address may be adapted to address other former high-ranking government officials.

| Addressee | Address on Letter and Envelope | Salutation and Complimentary Close |
|---|---|---|
| Vice President of the United States | The Vice President<br>United States Senate<br>Washington, DC 20510<br><br>*or*<br><br>The Honorable (full name)<br>Vice President of the United States<br>United States Senate<br>Washington, DC 20510 | Dear (Mr./Madam) Vice President:<br>Sincerely, |
| Chief Justice of the United States | The Chief Justice of the United States<br>The Supreme Court of the United States<br>Washington, DC 20543 | Dear (Mr./Madam) Chief Justice:<br>Sincerely, |
| Associate Justice | (Mr./Madam) Justice (surname)<br>The Supreme Court of the United States<br>Washington, DC 20543 | Dear (Mr./Madam) Justice:<br>Sincerely, |
| United States Senator | Honorable (full name)<br>United States Senate<br>Washington, DC 20510<br><br>*or*<br><br>Honorable (full name)<br>United States Senator<br>(local address) | Dear Senator (surname):<br>Sincerely, |
| United States Senator-Elect | (Mr./Mrs./Ms.) (full name)<br>Senator-Elect, United States Senate<br>(local address) | Dear (Mr./Mrs./Ms.) (surname):<br>Sincerely, |
| United States Representative | Honorable (full name)<br>House of Representatives<br>Washington, DC 20515<br><br>*or*<br><br>Honorable (full name), Member<br>United States House of Representatives<br>(local address) | Dear (Mr./Mrs./Ms.) (surname):<br>Sincerely, |
| Cabinet Member | Honorable (full name)<br>Secretary of (name of department)<br>Washington, DC 00000 | Dear (Mr./Madam) Secretary:<br>Sincerely, |
| | Honorable (full name)<br>Postmaster General<br>Washington, DC 20260 | Dear (Mr./Madam) Postmaster General:<br>Sincerely, |
| | Honorable (full name)<br>Attorney General<br>Washington, DC 20503 | Dear (Mr./Madam) Attorney General:<br>Sincerely, |

Mr./Ms.

| Addressee | Address on Letter and Envelope | Salutation and Complimentary Close |
|---|---|---|
| Deputy Secretary, Assistant, or Under Secretary | Honorable (full name)<br>Deputy Secretary of (name of department)<br>Washington, DC 00000 | Dear (Mr./Mrs./Ms.) (surname):<br>Sincerely, |
| | Honorable (full name)<br>Assistant Secretary of (name of department)<br>Washington, DC 00000 | |
| | Honorable (full name)<br>Under Secretary of (name of department)<br>Washington, DC 00000 | |
| Head of Independent Offices and Agencies | Honorable (full name)<br>Comptroller General of the United States<br>General Accounting Office<br>Washington, DC 20548 | Dear (Mr./Mrs./Ms.) (surname):<br>Sincerely, |
| | Honorable (full name)<br>Chairman, (name of commission)<br>Washington, DC 00000 | Dear (Mr./Madam) Chairman:<br>Sincerely, |
| | Honorable (full name)<br>Director, Bureau of the Budget<br>Washington, DC 20503 | Dear (Mr./Mrs./Ms.) (surname):<br>Sincerely, |
| American Ambassador | Honorable (full name)<br>American Ambassador<br>(address and city)<br>(country) | Sir or Madam: (formal)<br>Very truly yours,<br>*or*<br>Dear (Mr./Madam) Ambassador: (informal)<br>Sincerely, |
| American Consul General or American Consul | (Mr./Mrs./Ms.) (full name)<br>American Consul General (or American Consul)<br>(address and city)<br>(country) | Dear (Mr./Mrs./Ms.) (surname):<br>Sincerely, |
| Foreign Ambassador in the United States | His Excellency (full name)<br>Ambassador of (country)<br>(local address) | Excellency: (formal)<br>Very truly yours,<br>*or*<br>Dear (Mr./Madam) Ambassador: (informal)<br>Sincerely, |
| Governor of State | Honorable (full name)<br>Governor of (name of state)<br>(address)<br>(city), (state) 00000 | Dear Governor (surname):<br>Sincerely, |

| Addressee | Address on Letter and Envelope | Salutation and Complimentary Close |
|---|---|---|
| Lieutenant Governor | Honorable (full name) Lieutenant Governor of (name of state) (address) (city), (state) 00000 | Dear (Mr./Mrs./Ms.) (surname): Sincerely, |
| State Senator | Honorable (full name) (name of state) State Senate (address) (city), (state) 00000 | Dear Senator (surname): Sincerely, |
| State Representative, Assemblyperson, or Delegate | Honorable (full name) (name of state) House of Representatives (or State Assembly or House of Delegates) (address) (city), (state) 00000 | Dear (Mr./Mrs./Ms.) (surname): Sincerely, |
| Mayor | Honorable (full name) Mayor of (name of city) (address) (city), (state) 00000 | Dear Mayor (surname): Sincerely, |
| President of a Board of Commissioners | Honorable (full name), President Board of Commissioners of (name of city) (address) (city), (state) 00000 | Dear (Mr./Mrs./Ms.) (surname): Sincerely, |
| Judge | Honorable (full name) (name of court) (local address) | Dear Judge (surname): Sincerely, |

## 9–13.  Religious Dignitaries

The following table shows the proper forms of address, salutation, and complimentary close for specific religious dignitaries.

| Addressee | Address on Letter and Envelope | Salutation and Complimentary Close |
|---|---|---|
| Catholic Clergy Cardinal | His Eminence (given name) Cardinal (surname) Archbishop of (diocese) (local address) | Your Eminence: (formal) *or* Dear Cardinal (surname): (informal) Sincerely, |
| Archbishop | The Most Reverend (full name) Archbishop of (diocese) (local address) | Your Excellency: (formal) *or* Dear Archbishop (surname):  (informal) Sincerely, |

273

| Addressee | Address on Letter and Envelope | Salutation and Complimentary Close |
|---|---|---|
| Bishop | The Most Reverend (full name) Bishop of (city) (local address) | Your Excellency: (formal) *or* Dear Bishop (surname): (informal) Sincerely, |
| Monsignor | The Right Reverend Monsignor (full name) (local address) *or* The Very Reverend Monsignor (full name) (local address) | Right Reverend Monsignor: (formal) *or* Dear Monsignor (surname): (informal) Sincerely, Very Reverend Monsignor: (formal) *or* Dear Monsignor (surame): (informal) Sincerely, |
| Priest | The Reverend (full name), (add initials of order, if any) (local address) | Reverend Sir: (formal) Dear Father (surname): (informal) Sincerely, |
| Mother Superior | Mother (full name), (initials of order, if used) Superior, (name of convent) (local address) | Dear Mother (full name): Sincerely, |
| Nun | Sister (full name), (initials of order, if used) (name of convent) (local address) | Dear Sister (full name): Sincerely, |
| Monk | Brother (full name), (initials of order, if used) (local address) | Dear Brother (full name): Sincerely, |
| Jewish Clergy | Rabbi (full name) (local address) | Dear Rabbi (surname): Sincerely, |
| **Protestant Clergy** | | |
| Bishop | The Right Reverend (full name) Bishop of (name) (local address) *or* The Reverend (full name) Bishop of (name) (local address) | Right Reverend Sir: (formal) *or* Dear Bishop (surname): (informal) Sincerely, Reverend Sir: (formal) *or* Dear Bishop (surname): (informal) Sincerely, |

Mr./Ms.

| Addressee | Address on Letter and Envelope | Salutation and Complimentary Close |
|-----------|-------------------------------|-----------------------------------|
| Dean | The Very Reverend (full name)<br>Dean of (name of church)<br>(local address) | Very Reverend Sir:<br>(formal)<br>*or*<br>Dear Dean (surname):<br>(informal)<br>Sincerely, |
| Minister | The Reverend (full name)<br>(title, if any)<br>(name of church)<br>(local address) | Dear Reverend<br>(surname):<br>*or*<br>Dear (Dr./Mr./Mrs./Ms.)<br>(surname):<br>Sincerely, |
| Chaplain | Chaplain (full name)<br>(full rank, service designation)<br>(post office address of organization and<br>station)<br>(local address) | Dear Chaplain (surname):<br>Sincerely, |
| Lay Clergy | Deacon (full name)<br>(name of church)<br>(local address) | Dear Deacon (surname):<br>Sincerely, |
| | (Brother/Sister) (full name)<br>(name of church)<br>(local address) | Dear (Brother/Sister)<br>(surname):<br>Sincerely, |

## 9-14. Undetermined Individual or Group

Although addressing correspondence to an undefined or undetermined individual or group should generally be avoided, circumstances sometimes provide no other alternative. In these cases the letter contains no inside address. The phrase *To Whom It May Concern:* replaces the standard salutation, and the complimentary close is either *Sincerely yours,* or *Yours very truly,*.

# Chapter 10

# Business Letters
# and Memorandums

Enc.

## Business Letters and Memorandums Solution Finder

Enc.

# Letter Styles[1]

## 10–1. Full Block

**Business letters may be formatted in several styles. The full block letter style is the most streamlined letter style because all parts and all lines begin at the left margin.**

**full block letter**

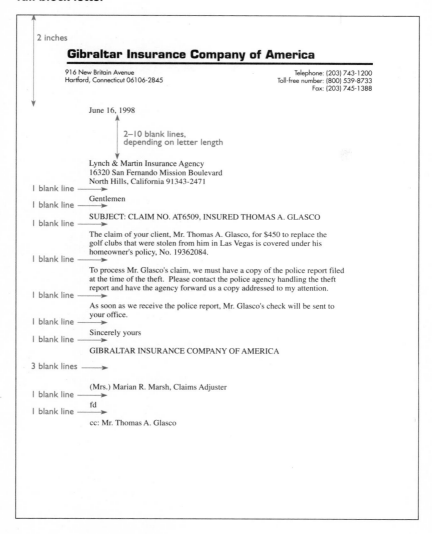

---

[1]All letters appearing in this chapter have been designed by the authors for illustrative purposes. They are not reproductions of actual letters.

## 10–2. Modified Block

**a.** The modified block letter style with blocked paragraphs is the most popular letter style used in business. All lines except the return address (if used), the date, and the closing lines begin at the left margin.

**modified block letter with blocked paragraphs**

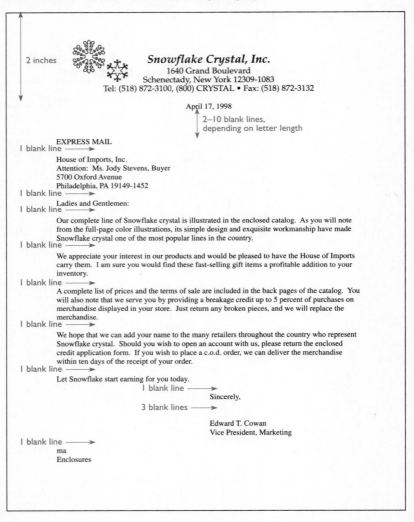

**b.** The modified block letter style with indented paragraphs is also used frequently. All lines except the first line of each paragraph, the return address (if used), the date, and the closing lines begin at the left margin.

## modified block letter with indented paragraphs

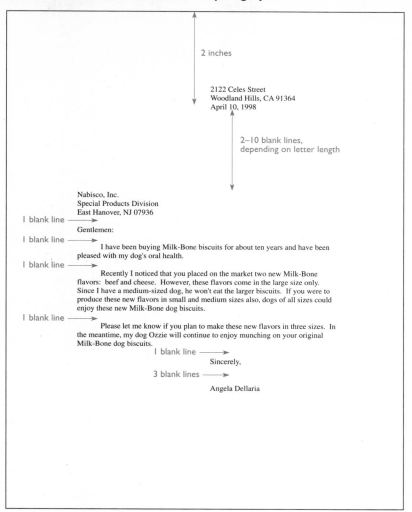

2 inches

2122 Celes Street
Woodland Hills, CA 91364
April 10, 1998

2–10 blank lines,
depending on letter length

Nabisco, Inc.
Special Products Division
East Hanover, NJ 07936

1 blank line ⟶

Gentlemen:

1 blank line ⟶

I have been buying Milk-Bone biscuits for about ten years and have been pleased with my dog's oral health.

1 blank line ⟶

Recently I noticed that you placed on the market two new Milk-Bone flavors: beef and cheese. However, these flavors come in the large size only. Since I have a medium-sized dog, he won't eat the larger biscuits. If you were to produce these new flavors in small and medium sizes also, dogs of all sizes could enjoy these new Milk-Bone dog biscuits.

1 blank line ⟶

Please let me know if you plan to make these new flavors in three sizes. In the meantime, my dog Ozzie will continue to enjoy munching on your original Milk-Bone dog biscuits.

1 blank line ⟶

Sincerely,

3 blank lines ⟶

Angela Dellaria

## 10–3.   Social Business

The social business letter style is used for social business correspondence. In this informal format the inside address is placed after the closing lines. The salutation may be followed by a comma instead of a colon, and the typed signature line is optional. Paragraphs are either indented or blocked.

No subject or attention lines are used in the social business letter style. Reference initials, enclosure notations, and copy notations are usually omitted on the original, but these parts may be included below the inside address on the file copy or on the copies for distribution. Leave a double space after the inside address, and single-space on all copies except the original the notations that are to be included.

## social business letter

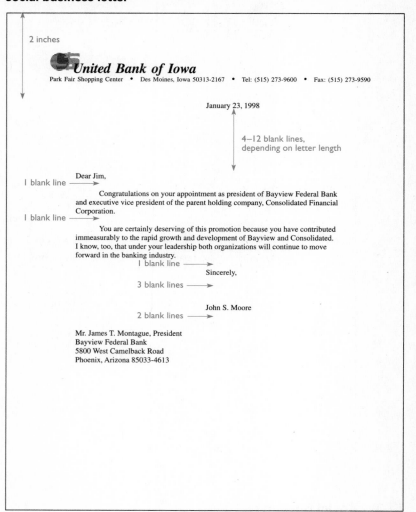

2 inches

**United Bank of Iowa**
Park Fair Shopping Center • Des Moines, Iowa 50313-2167 • Tel: (515) 273-9600 • Fax: (515) 273-9590

January 23, 1998

4—12 blank lines, depending on letter length

Dear Jim,

1 blank line ———→

Congratulations on your appointment as president of Bayview Federal Bank and executive vice president of the parent holding company, Consolidated Financial Corporation.

1 blank line ———→

You are certainly deserving of this promotion because you have contributed immeasurably to the rapid growth and development of Bayview and Consolidated. I know, too, that under your leadership both organizations will continue to move forward in the banking industry.

1 blank line ———→

Sincerely,

3 blank lines ———→

John S. Moore

2 blank lines ———→

Mr. James T. Montague, President
Bayview Federal Bank
5800 West Camelback Road
Phoenix, Arizona 85033-4613

## 10–4.  Simplified

The simplified letter style was introduced by the Administrative Management Society. All parts of the letter begin at the left margin. In this style a subject line typed in all capital letters replaces the salutation. Two blank lines are left before and after the subject line. No complimentary close is used in the simplified letter style. Instead, the signature line is typed on the fifth line (leave four blank lines) below the last line of the message. Use all capital letters and a single line for the signature line.

**simplified letter**

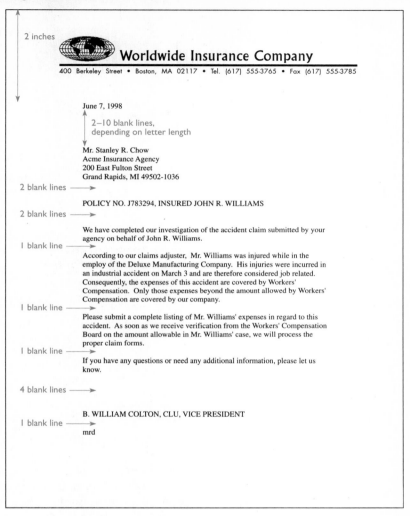

# Letter Format and Placement of Major Parts

## 10–5. Margins and Vertical Placement With Word Processing Software

**a.** Use a 2-inch top margin for the first page of a business letter printed on letterhead stationery. Any second and succeeding pages of a business letter have 1-inch top margins. Use left justification.

Select the side margins according to the number of words in the letter and the size of the font used to prepare the letter. Set the margins *after* keying the letter and using the word count feature of your word processing program.

The following tables may be used as guidelines for preparing standard and long letters. The first table applies to 12-point fonts; the second table applies to 11-point and 10-point fonts.

**12-point fonts[2]**

### *Margin Settings for Business Letters Printed in 12-Point Fonts*

| Letter Length | Number of Words | Margin Settings | | Line Length |
|---|---|---|---|---|
| | | Left | Right | |
| Standard | Up to 200 | 1.5" | 1.5" | 5.5 inches |
| Long | 200 + | 1" | 1" | 6.5 inches |

**11-point and 10-point fonts[3]**

### *Margin Settings for Business Letters Printed in 11-Point and 10-Point Fonts*

| Letter Length | Number of Words | Margin Settings | | Line Length |
|---|---|---|---|---|
| | | Left | Right | |
| Standard | Up to 200 | 1.75" | 1.75" | 5 inches |
| Long | 200 + | 1.25" | 1.25" | 6 inches |

**b.** Leave 2 or 3 blank lines between the date and inside address in letters with two or more pages. Balance single-page letters vertically by regulating the number of lines between the date and the inside address. Use the following procedures on your word processing program to achieve this balance *after* the margins have been set:

(1) Count the number of blank lines between the date and the inside address. (Example: 3 blank lines)

(2) Directly after the *last* line of the letter (usually reference initials or an enclosure notation), press the *Enter* key until the page break is reached. Count the number of blank lines from the last line of the letter until the page break. (Example: 6 blank lines)

(3) Total the two line counts. (Example: 6 + 3 = 9). Divide this total by two (Example: 9 ÷ 2 = 4.5). Disregard any fractional part. (Example: 4 blank lines)

(4) Insert or delete blank lines, if necessary, to ensure that the number of blank lines between the *date and the inside address* EQUALS the result obtained in Step (3) above. Do not, however, leave fewer than two or more than ten blank lines between the date and the inside

---

[2]This table may also be used for fonts measuring 10 characters per inch. Other names used to describe this font size are *10 cpi, 10 pitch,* and *pica.*

[3]This table may also be used for fonts measuring 12 characters per inch. Other names used to describe this font size are *12 cpi, 12 pitch,* and *elite.*

address. (Example: Insert 1 additional blank line between the date and the inside address.)

(5) Delete any extra blank lines at the bottom of the page.

### examples for balancing a letter vertically on the page

| Blank Lines Between Date and Inside Address | Blank Lines Between Letter End and Page Break | Sum of Blank Lines | Blank Lines ÷ 2 (Remainder Dropped) | Revised Number of Blank Lines Needed Between Date and Inside Address | Number of Blank Lines to Be Inserted or Deleted |
|---|---|---|---|---|---|
| 4 | 2 | 4+2=6 | 6÷2=3 | 3 | −1 |
| 3 | 7 | 3+7=10 | 10÷2=5 | 5 | +2 |
| 4 | 1 | 4+1=5 | 5÷2=2.5=2 | 2 | −2 |
| 3 | 8 | 3+8=11 | 11÷2=5.5=5 | 5 | +2 |
| 4 | −1 | 4−1=3 | 3÷2=1.5=1 | At least 2 | −2 |

## 10–6. Margins and Vertical Placement With Typewriters

a. Use a 2-inch top margin for the first page of a business letter prepared on printed letterhead stationery. Any second and succeeding pages of a business letter have 1-inch top margins.

b. For letters prepared on standard or electronic typewriters, use the following table to determine the side margins and the number of blank lines to be left between the date and the inside address.

The table takes into consideration ordinary business letters—those without delivery notations, addressee notations, attention lines, subject lines, tables, and postscripts. Letters containing supplementary parts should be readjusted (in margin settings and/or number of lines between the date and the inside address) to accommodate these parts.

### Letter Formatting Guide

| Number of Words in Letter | Left and Right Margin Settings | | Blank Lines Between Date and Inside Address |
|---|---|---|---|
| | 12 Point or 10 Pitch | 10 or 11 Point or 12 Pitch | |
| Under 200 | 1.5" | 1.75" | 4–10 |
| Over 200 | 1" | 1.25" | 2–3 |

## 10–7. Return Address

a. No return address is needed for business letters prepared on paper containing a complete company letterhead. Similarly, business letters prepared on word processing programs with a letter template do not require a return address.

**printed company letterhead**

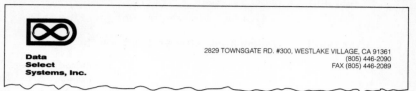

2829 TOWNSGATE RD. #300, WESTLAKE VILLAGE, CA 91361
(805) 446-2090
FAX (805) 446-2089

Data
Select
Systems, Inc.

**letterhead produced from a word processing template**

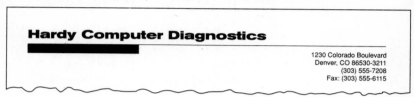

**Hardy Computer Diagnostics**

1230 Colorado Boulevard
Denver, CO 86530-3211
(303) 555-7208
Fax: (303) 555-6115

**b.** When plain bond paper or letterhead paper without a mailing address is used, a return address must be included.

On plain bond paper begin the return address so that the date is 2 inches from the top edge of the paper. Although the date appears directly below the last line of the return address, it is not considered part of the return address.

On letterhead paper without a mailing address, begin the return address a double space below the last line in the letterhead or end it so the date is 2 inches below the top edge of the paper. Select the option that places the return address in the lower position.

**c.** *Modified block or social business letter styles.* In the modified block or social business styles, each line of the return address may be centered. Lines in the return address may also (1) begin at the center of the page, (2) begin 0.5 inch to the left of the page center, or (3) align at the right margin. The return address in a modified block letter style is illustrated in Section 10-2b, page 281.

*Full block or simplified letter styles.* In the full block and simplified letter styles, all lines begin at the left margin.

**return address in modified block or social business letter style without letterhead**

2 inches

2034 Mason Street
Macon, Georgia 31204-6232
May 3, 1998

**return address in full block or simplified letter style without letterhead**

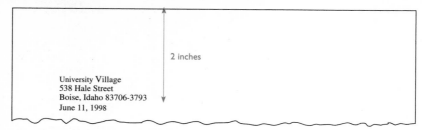

**letterhead with return address ending 2 inches from top edge of paper—modified block or social business letter**

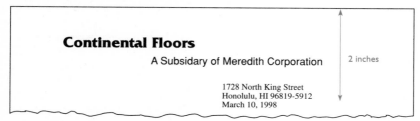

**letterhead with return address begun a double space below letterhead—full block or simplified letter**

## 10–8. Date

**a.** On letterhead paper with a mailing address, place the date a double space below the last line in the letterhead or allocate a 2-inch margin from the top edge of the paper. Select the procedure that places the date in the lower position.

*Modified block and social business letter styles.* In modified block and social business letters, the date may be (1) centered, (2) begun at the center of the page, or (3) aligned with the right margin.

*Full block and simplified letter styles.* In full block or simplified letters, place the date at the left margin.

**date 2 inches below top edge of paper—modified block or social business letter**

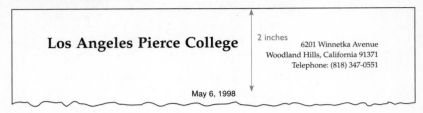

**date placed a double space below letterhead—full block letter**

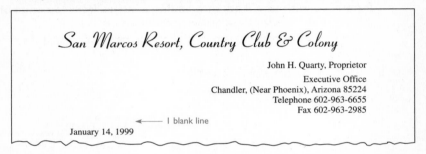

**b.** In letters requiring return addresses, place the date on the line directly below the last line of the return address. A date used with the return address in a complete letter is illustrated in Section 10-2b, p. 281.

**date with return address**

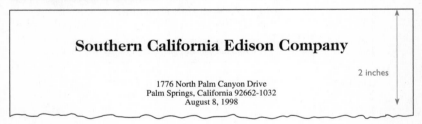

## 10–9.  Addressee and Delivery Notations

**a.** Addressee notations such as *Personal* and *Confidential* are entered in all capital letters a double space above the inside address.

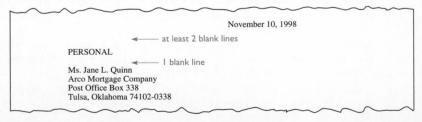

**b.** Delivery notations such as *Certified Mail, Express Mail, Federal Express, Air Mail, Registered Mail, Fax Transmittal,* and *Messenger Delivery* are entered in all capital letters either (1) a double space above the inside address or (2) a single or double space below the reference initials or enclosure notation, whichever appears last. A delivery notation is illustrated in a complete letter in Section 10-2a, p. 280.

**delivery notations a double space above inside address**

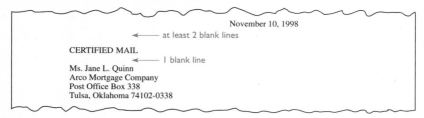

**delivery notation after reference initials or enclosure notation**

**c.** If an addressee notation and a delivery notation appear in the same letter, place the addressee notation on the third line above the inside address and the delivery notation on the line directly below. Use all capital letters for both notations. Leave *at least* two blank lines between the date and the addressee notation.

**addressee and delivery notations in same letter**

February 11, 1999

←——— at least 2 blank lines

CONFIDENTIAL
EXPRESS MAIL ←——— l blank line

Mr. Frank D. Parsons
Vice President, Sales
Western Foundry, Inc.
3210 West Polk Street
Chicago, IL 60612-6427

## 10–10. Inside Address

**a.** The inside address follows the date and any delivery or addressee notations. It contains some or all of the following: courtesy title, full name, professional title, department name, company name, street or mailing address, city, state, and zip code. Single-space and begin at the left margin those parts necessary to direct the letter to the addressee.

Place the courtesy title and full name on the first line. The professional title and department name have no specific line designations; they should be positioned to balance with the remaining parts of the inside address. The street or mailing address appears on a separate line. Arrange the city, state, and zip code together on another separate line.

**arrangement of an inside address**

Ms. Margaret A. Williamson
Manager, Accounting Department
Eastern Savings and Loan Association
6750 East Independence Boulevard
Charlotte, North Carolina 28212-7610

Mr. Jeffrey Davis, Manager
Department of Human Resources
Eastern Federal Bank
3452 West Sixth Street
Charlotte, NC 28212-4310

**b.** Abbreviate only the courtesy titles *Mr.*, *Mrs.*, and *Dr.* The courtesy title *Ms.* is not an abbreviation; its only form is *Ms.*

Spell out all street designations such as *Street*, *Avenue*, and *Boulevard*. *Boulevard* may be abbreviated, however, with exceptionally long street names. Spell out the state name or use the two-letter post office abbreviation, whichever form achieves balance with the remaining lines.

An inside address may contain from a minimum of two lines to a maximum of six lines.

**two-line inside address**

Holiday Inn
Cedar Rapids, IA 52406

**six-line inside address**

Mr. M. J. Fujimoto
Airline Training Specialist
Division of Personnel Instruction
TransAmerica-Continental Airlines
12700 East Funston Street
Wichita, Kansas 67207-3402

**c.** *Modified block, full block, and simplified letter styles.* In the modified block, full block, and simplified letter styles, the inside address usually follows the date. The number of blank lines between the date and the inside address is determined by the length of the letter.

For letters prepared with word processing software, refer to Section 10-5 for detailed instructions on setting margins and determining the number of blank lines to leave between the date and inside address. Section 10-6 provides the same information for letters prepared on electronic or regular typewriters.

**inside address in modified block letter**

<table>
<tr><td>

**Lawndale Pharmaceutical Company**

5170 Medina Road
Akron, Ohio 44321-2843
Telephone: (216) 382-4955
Fax: (216) 382-7135

March 10, 1999

Dr. Roy C. Trever
560 Yale Drive
Austin, TX 76015-4613

</td><td>2 inches</td></tr>
</table>

**d.** *The social business letter style.* In the social business letter, the inside address is placed after the closing lines. If the typed signature line is omitted, leave five or six blank lines after the complimentary close before beginning the inside address. If a typed signature line is included, leave two blank lines after the typed signature before beginning the inside address.

**social business letter without typed signature**

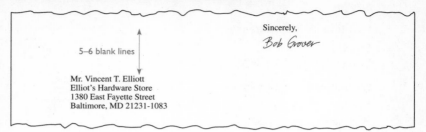

**social business letter with typed signature**

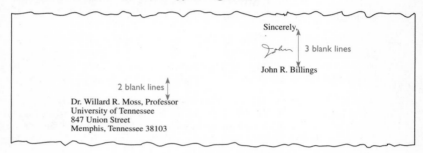

## 10–11. Attention Line

**a.** The attention line is used for directing correspondence to an individual or department within a company while still officially addressing the letter to the organization. It is especially useful in directing correspondence to a person whose name is unknown.

**b.** The modern trend is to place the attention line in the inside address on the line directly below the company name and use the same format for the envelope address.[4]

*Modified block and full block letter styles.* As an alternate to including the attention line in the inside address, it may be placed at the left margin a double space below the last line of the inside address in the modified and full block styles.

Use (1) a combination of initial capital letters and lowercase letters or (2) all capital letters. The use of a colon after the word *Attention* is optional. An attention line is illustrated in a complete letter in Section 10-2a, page 280.

*Simplified letter style.* In the simplified letter style, the attention line is included in the inside address and placed directly below the organization's name. The attention line is treated as any other line in the

---

[4]Correspondence using an attention line is addressed to the company, not an individual. Therefore, the name of the company should appear before the attention line. The U.S. Postal Service recommendation to place the attention line before the company name does not follow this protocol.

inside address. The word *Attention* may or may not be followed by a colon.

*Social business letter style.* The attention line is not used in the social business style.

**attention line included in inside address**

Valley Manufacturing Company
Attention:  General Manager
18600 Sierra Bonita Boulevard
San Bernardino, CA 91763-5201

**attention line at left margin below inside address**

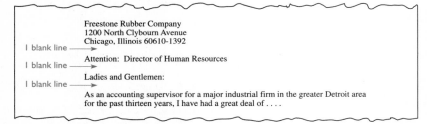

Freestone Rubber Company
1200 North Clybourn Avenue
Chicago, Illinois 60610-1392

I blank line ⟶

Attention:  Director of Human Resources

I blank line ⟶

Ladies and Gentlemen:

I blank line ⟶

As an accounting supervisor for a major industrial firm in the greater Detroit area
for the past thirteen years, I have had a great deal of . . . .

## 10–12. Salutation[5]

**a.** The content of the salutation depends upon to whom the letter is addressed in the inside address and the degree of familiarity between the addressee and the writer. See Section 10-12b–f for selecting standard salutations.

*Modified block and full block letter styles.* Begin the salutation at the left margin and place it a double space below the last line of the inside address or the attention line, if used. Conclude the salutation with a colon for the mixed punctuation format; use no ending punctuation mark for the open punctuation format.

*Simplified letter style.* Omit the salutation in the simplified letter style.

*Social business letter style.* In the social business style, position the salutation at the left margin after the date. Use the mixed punctuation format; place a colon or a comma after the salutation.

---

[5]See Sections 9-9, 9-10, 9-11, and 9-12 for additional information on the proper use of formal titles, salutations, and complimentary closes.

### salutation in a modified block or full block letter

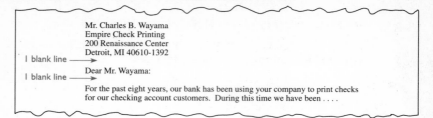

### salutation in a social business letter

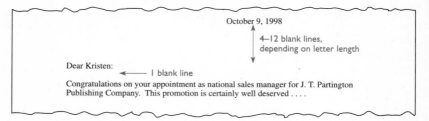

**b.** In letters addressed to individuals, use one of the following salutations, depending upon the degree of formality desired. Use a colon
after the salutation if mixed punctuation is used; use no punctuation
mark if open punctuation is used.

### informal salutation

Dear Fred:          Dear Connie:

### standard business letter salutation to a single addressee

Dear Mr. Hampton:          Dear Miss Baker:

Dear Ms. Harris:          Dear Mrs. Chin:

### standard business letter salutation to two or more men

Dear Mr. Andrews and Mr. Cranston:
*or*
Dear Mr. Andrews, Mr. Cranston, and Mr. Phillips:
*or*
Dear Messrs. Andrews, Cranston, and Phillips:
*or*
Gentlemen:

### standard business letter salutation to two or more women—courtesy title "Ms."

Dear Ms. Bailey and Ms. Johnson:
*or*
Dear Ms. Bailey, Ms. Horike, and Ms. Johnson:
*or*

Dear Mses. Bailey, Horike, and Johnson:
                    *or*
Ladies:

### standard business letter salutation to two or more women — courtesy title "Miss"

Dear Miss Frazier and Miss Goodlad:
                    *or*
Dear Miss Frazier, Miss Goodlad, and Miss Hoover:
                    *or*
Dear Misses Frazier, Goodlad, and Hoover:
                    *or*
Ladies:

### standard business letter salutation to two or more women — courtesy title "Mrs."

Dear Mrs. Koonce and Mrs. O'Donnell:
                    *or*
Dear Mrs. Bedrosian, Mrs. Koonce, and Mrs. O'Donnell:
                    *or*
Dear Mesdames Bedrosian, Koonce, and O'Donnell:
                    *or*
Mesdames:          *or*          Ladies:

### standard business letter salutation to two or more persons with different courtesy titles

Dear Ms. Knott and Mr. Wade:

Dear Ms. Gallagher, Ms. Lee, and Mrs. Moreno:

Dear Mrs. Andrino, Ms. Hopi, Mr. Lopez, and Ms. Mullens-King:

Ladies: (women only)

Ladies and Gentlemen:

Dear Colleagues: (or other appropriate general reference designation)

### standard salutations to persons with professional titles

Dear Dr. Parsons:     Dear Professor Bredow:     Dear Colonel Jones:

### formal salutations for certain government officials and religious dignitaries

Sir:                          Reverend Sir:

Excellency:                   Your Eminence:

**c.**  **If the gender of an addressee is unknown, use the full name of the person without a courtesy title. Use the courtesy title *Ms.* for a woman unless another title is specified by the addressee.**

### full name without courtesy title

Orolyn Ruenz (Dear Orolyn Ruenz:)

Chris Meister (Dear Chris Meister:)

**courtesy title for a woman**

Ms. Sharon Reember (Dear Ms. Reember:)

Ms. Laura Nguyen (Dear Ms. Nguyen:)

**d.** In correspondence addressed to companies, associations, or other groups, use one of the following salutations:

**salutations for groups composed of men and women**

Ladies and Gentlemen:      Gentlemen and Ladies:

**salutation for groups composed entirely of men**

Gentlemen:

**salutations for groups composed entirely of women**

Mesdames:     Ladies:

**e.** Letters addressed to a firm but directed to the attention of an individual within the company receive the salutation used to open a letter to a group: *Gentlemen, Ladies and Gentlemen, Gentlemen and Ladies, Mesdames,* or *Ladies.*

Arroyo Textile Manufacturing Company
Attention Accounts Receivable Manager
2850 Central Avenue, N.W.
Albuquerque, New Mexico 87105-1742
⟵ l blank line
Ladies and Gentlemen:
⟵ l blank line
On September 10 we purchased from your company twelve 50-yard bolts of Royal
Luster velvet upholstery fabric (Invoice No. GY-14953). Payment for . . . .

**f.** Letters to an undetermined individual or group of individuals should generally be avoided. When used, such letters contain no inside address and use *To Whom It May Concern:* as the salutation.

March 8, 1999
4–12 blank lines,
depending on letter length

To Whom It May Concern:
⟵ l blank line
I am pleased to recommend . . . .

## 10–13. Subject Line

**a.** The subject line briefly describes the contents of the letter.

*Modified block and full block letter styles.* For modified and full block letters, begin the subject line at the left margin a double space below the salutation. Double-space after the subject line.

Use (1) initial capital letters for the main words[6] or (2) all capital letters. The word *Subject* followed by a colon usually introduces the line. The subject line is illustrated in a full block letter in Section 10-1, p. 279.

If an attention line appears in the same letter a double space below the inside address, use the same format for both lines.

### subject line at left margin

Dear Mr. Sullivan:
           ←——— I blank line

Subject: Anticipated Cost Reductions
           ←——— I blank line

Within the next few weeks, we expect to see significant price reductions in the cost of several raw materials we use for the production of . . . .

---

Dear Mr. Sullivan:
           ←——— I blank line

ANTICIPATED COST REDUCTIONS
           ←——— I blank line

Within the next few weeks, we expect to see significant price reductions in the cost of several raw materials we use for the production of . . . .

### two-line subject with book title

Dear Ms. Kriegisch:
           ←——— I blank line

Subject: Alternate Distribution Channels for the Seventh Edition of Our Statistics Textbook, *Statistical Analysis*
           ←——— I blank line

The seventh edition of one of our best-selling textbooks, *Statistical Analysis*, has generated considerable interest among many members of the . . . .

### attention and subject lines in the same letter

ATTENTION: MANAGER, DEPARTMENT OF HUMAN RESOURCES
           ←——— I blank line

Ladies and Gentlemen:
           ←——— I blank line

SUBJECT: INSURANCE BENEFITS FOR REGULAR EMPLOYEES
           ←——— I blank line

Premium costs for group health, dental, vision care, and life insurance have been rising rapidly during the past three years. Providers of these packages . . . .

*Simplified letter style.* The subject line replaces the salutation in the simplified style. Begin the subject line at the left margin a triple space below the inside address. Type it in all capital letters without the term *Subject:*. Triple-space between the subject line and the first line of the body of the letter.

---

[6]*Main* words are (1) the first and last words and (2) all words except the articles *a, an, the*; the conjunctions *and, but, or, nor*; the word *to* used with an infinitive; and prepositions containing two or three letters (*of, for, on*, etc.).

> Ms. Susan Carson, Editor
> South-Western Publishing Company
> 5101 Madison Road
> Cincinnati, Ohio 45227
> ◄———— 2 blank lines
>
> DISK-BASED PRINTING SERVICES
> ◄———— 2 blank lines
> We appreciate receiving your inquiry about our new disk-based printing services
> and have enclosed a brochure describing the various . . . .

*Social business letter style.* A subject line is not used in the social business letter style.

**b.** Insurance and financial institutions, attorneys, and government offices often use the abbreviation *Re:* or *In re:* in place of the word *Subject:* at the beginning of the subject line.

Re:   Policy 489-6342, Insured Michael T. Block

IN RE:   TOLBERT VS. FEINBERG

**c.** When initiating or replying to correspondence that has a special policy number, order number, account number, or other such reference, include this information in a subject line or in a specific reference below and aligned with the date.

If guide words are not printed on the letterhead, supply labels such as *When replying, refer to:, File No.:, In reply to:, Re:, Your reference:, Refer to:,* etc. These notations are typed in initial capital and lowercase letters; they are placed a double space below the date.

**standard subject line**

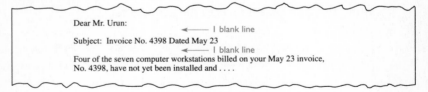

> Dear Mr. Urun:
> ◄———— 1 blank line
> Subject: Invoice No. 4398 Dated May 23
> ◄———— 1 blank line
> Four of the seven computer workstations billed on your May 23 invoice,
> No. 4398, have not yet been installed and . . . .

**notation below and aligned with date—modified block letter**

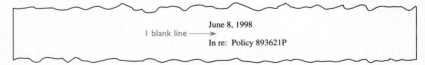

> June 8, 1998
> 1 blank line ———►
> In re:  Policy 893621P

**d.** Some companies prefer to place the subject line above the salutation. In such cases begin the subject line a double space below the inside address. If an attention line follows the inside address, then begin the subject line a double space below the attention line.

Use (1) initial capital letters with lowercase letters or (2) all capital letters. The caption *Subject, Re,* or *In re* precedes the content and is followed by a colon. If an attention line appears in the same letter, use the same format for both lines.

Double-space after the subject line to begin the salutation.

### subject line above salutation

Ms. Midori S. Washida, Manager
Great Midwestern Bank
4430 Greenbriar Street
Iowa City, IA 52247-0321  ◄——— | blank line

Subject: Account 183-573245, John R. Hagle  ◄——— | blank line

Dear Ms. Washida:

### subject and attention lines above salutation

Prudential Insurance Company
Post Office Box 2488
Salt Lake City, UT 84157-2488  ◄——— | blank line

ATTENTION:  CLAIMS DEPARTMENT  ◄——— | blank line

RE:  CLAIM NO. 845986532, INSURED JANET A. HORNE  ◄——— | blank line

Ladies and Gentlemen:

## 10–14. Body of the Letter

a.  The body of the letter contains the message. It begins a double space below the salutation or the subject line, if used. Single-space paragraphs within the body of the letter and double-space between each paragraph.

*Modified block and social business letter styles.* The first line of paragraphs in the modified block or social business letter styles may be either blocked or indented 0.5 inch.

*Full block and simplified letter styles.* Always block the first line of paragraphs in the full block and simplified letter styles.

### body of letter with blocked paragraphs

Dear Mr. Feinberg:  ◄——— | blank line

Your Zippo portable sound system arrived yesterday, along with your explanation of the needed repairs.  ◄——— | blank line

As you suggested, the station tuning mechanism has been replaced under the terms of the warranty.  In examining your system, however, our service representative noticed that the speaker had been damaged from an apparent jarring or dropping. The installation cost (parts and labor) for a new speaker would be $54.98.

### body of letter with indented paragraphs

Dear Mrs. Russell:     ←——— | blank line

    We enjoyed the presentation on color coordination that you gave to Dr. Sullivan's business management class last Saturday. Thank you for sharing your valuable ideas with us.     ←——— | blank line

    The class especially appreciated the material you gave us on the Wilson color wheel. Everyone agreed that this information will certainly be helpful in making color selections for the employee work environment and ensuring comfortable working conditions.

**b.** Quoted materials, listings, tables, and graphics are often included within the body of a letter. All these visual enhancements are placed within the left and right margins. See Section 1-25 for instructions on formatting long quotations, Section 11-9 for preparing horizontal and vertical listings, and Section 11-11 for preparing tables and charts.

### quoted material within the body of a letter

recommendations have been based on an economic forecast published in one of our leading trade magazines. This forecast appeared in an article on pages 101–103 of the September issue of *Bankers' Financial World*:     ←——— | blank line

    Although interest rates for the next quarter will remain at the same low rate, building of new homes and commercial buildings will continue to decline. The large number of bank foreclosures on real property during the last year has driven values down so low that builders are ceasing to develop new projects.

0.5"      0.5"

←——— | blank line

The article, "Foreclosures and Their Rippling Effect on the Banking Industry," was written by Joseph L. Langham, a prominent economist and professor at Stanford University. Dr. Langham is noted for his success in predicting trends . . . .

### listing within the body of a letter

To proceed with the escrow on the property you purchased at 6176 Arroyo Road in Palm Springs, please send us the following items by September 20:     ←——— | blank line

- A loan application (form enclosed) completely filled out and notarized by a bank official

0.5"      0.5"

←——— | blank line

- Verification of employment to include a letter from your employer stating your length of employment and current earnings     ←——— | blank line

- Copies of your last six months' paycheck stubs     ←——— | blank line

- Copies of your federal income tax returns for the previous two years     ←——— | blank line

As soon as we receive these items we will be able to contact prospective lenders to obtain a loan. Interest rates among lenders vary, but we will attempt to . . . .

## table within the body of a letter

We certainly appreciate your interest in purchasing a catalog that illustrates our fine Foster porcelain figurines. The following catalogs are presently available for purchase:

◄——— 1–2 blank lines

| 1998/99 Foster Catalog Set | | |
|---|---|---|
| Current Retail Pricing | | |
| Catalog or Supplement | Price for Members | Price for Nonmembers |
| Foster Core Catalog | $16.25 | $ 32.50 |
| Foster Limited Edition Catalog | 8.75 | 17.50 |
| Gres Supplement | 2.50 | 5.00 |
| Elite Catalog | 10.00 | 20.00 |
| Limited Edition Gres Catalog | 7.50 | 15.00 |
| Gres Catalog | 5.00 | 10.00 |
| Complete Catalog Set With Price List | $50.00 | $100.00 |

◄——— 1–2 blank lines

Both the *Foster Core Catalog* and the *Foster Limited Edition Catalog* contain color photographs of the figurines currently available. All other catalogs contain black-and-white photographs. As a member of the Foster Collectors' Society, you are eligible for the members' price. Shipping and handling . . . .

## 10–15. Complimentary Close

a. The complimentary close begins the closing lines of a letter. The closing selected to conclude a business letter must conform to the formality of the salutation. Sample salutations as well as suitable complimentary closes are listed here.

### formal correspondence

| Salutation | Complimentary Close |
|---|---|
| Your Excellency | Respectfully |
| | Very truly yours |

### general business correspondence

| Salutation | Complimentary Close |
|---|---|
| Dear Mr. Siebert | Sincerely yours |
| | Sincerely |

### informal business correspondence

| Salutation | Complimentary Close |
|---|---|
| Dear Karen | Sincerely yours |
| | Sincerely |
| | Cordially yours |
| | Cordially |

Enc.

**b.** The complimentary close is placed a double space below the last line of the message. Capitalize only the first word. Conclude the complimentary close with a comma for the mixed punctuation format; use no ending punctuation mark for the open punctuation format.

*Modified block and social business letter styles.* For the modified block and social business letter styles, begin the closing lines at the center of the page.

*Full block letter style.* Begin the closing lines at the left margin when using the full block letter style.

*Simplified letter style.* The complimentary close is omitted in the simplified letter style.

**complimentary close begun at page center**

**complimentary close begun at left margin**

## 10–16. Signature Block

**a.** The signature block identifies the writer of the letter by name. In most cases the writer's professional title is also included.

*Modified and full block letter styles.* Some business firms include the name of the company in the closing lines. In such cases the name of the company is placed in all capital letters a double space below and aligned with the complimentary close.

Company signature lines are used only in the modified block and full block letter styles. Use of the company name in the closing lines is illustrated in a full block letter in Section 10-1, p. 279.

## modified block letter

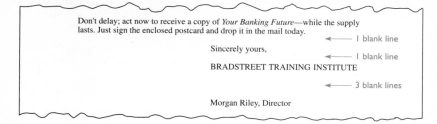

Don't delay; act now to receive a copy of *Your Banking Future*—while the supply lasts. Just sign the enclosed postcard and drop it in the mail today.

Sincerely yours, ←——— I blank line

BRADSTREET TRAINING INSTITUTE ←——— I blank line

←——— 3 blank lines

Morgan Riley, Director

## full block letter

Sincerely yours,

←——— I blank line

REDVIEW TILE COMPANY

←——— 3 blank lines

(Ms.) Gail Fleming, Director
Plant Production

**Place the writer's signature line or lines on the fourth line below the previous line, which will be either the complimentary close or the company name. Align the first letter of the individual's name with the first letter of the complimentary close and/or the company name.**

## modified block letter

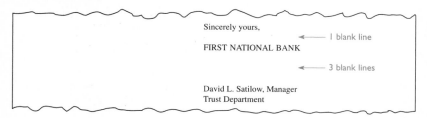

Sincerely yours,

←——— I blank line

FIRST NATIONAL BANK

←——— 3 blank lines

David L. Satilow, Manager
Trust Department

## full block letter

Sincerely,

←——— 3 blank lines

John R. Gregg
Vice President

**Place combinations of names, titles, and organizational sectors so that the contents of the signature lines appear balanced. The name and title may appear on the same line or on separate lines, depending upon the length of each item. Use commas to separate categories within the same line, but do not use commas to conclude any of the signature lines.**

### single-line signature line

Phillip Ashton, President                    Susan R. Mayfield, M.D.

### two-line signature line

Margaret T. Washington                  John S. Ross, Supervisor
Manager, Credit Department          Data Processing Department

Horace F. Tavelman
Accounts and Sales Representative

### three-line signature line

Roberta Casselman, Ed.D.
Curriculum Consultant
Division of Secondary Education

*Simplified letter style.* In the simplified letter style, the entire signature line is typed in all capital letters on a single line. It begins at the left margin on the fifth line below the last line of the message.

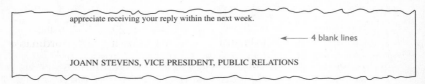

appreciate receiving your reply within the next week.

←——— 4 blank lines

JOANN STEVENS, VICE PRESIDENT, PUBLIC RELATIONS

*Social business letter style.* In the social business style, the printed signature line may be omitted. If it is included, only the individual's name, not title, is written.

### typed signature line omitted

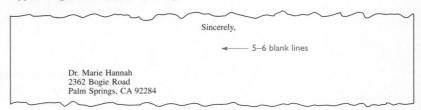

Sincerely,

←——— 5–6 blank lines

Dr. Marie Hannah
2362 Bogie Road
Palm Springs, CA 92284

### typed signature line included

Cordially yours,

←——— 3 blank lines

Phyllis Ramon

←——— 2 blank lines

Mr. Winston L. Bell
638 Ladley Avenue
Evanston, IL 60204-3246

**b.** Signature lines containing the names of men are generally not preceded by the courtesy title *Mr.* Only with initials, international names, and gender-equal names should a man use *Mr.* if the addressee does not know him. *Mr.* may be written with or without parentheses.

If a man has the title *Dr.*, either (1) place the abbreviation of the degree after the name of the individual or (2) place the title *Dr.*—with or without parentheses—before the name of the individual.

**signature lines containing name of man to be addressed as *Mr.***

George R. Bezowski
Regional Manager

(Mr.) Huy Cao Nguyen
Assistant Vice President

Mr. R. L. Rothstein
Realtor Associate

(Mr.) Leslie Neible
Customer Service Representative

**signature lines containing name of man to be addressed as *Dr.***

Cory V. Stephenson, Ph.D.
Professor of Economics

Vahi Urun, D.D.S.

(Dr.) Donald C. Cook
Occupational Coordinator

Dr. Donald C. Cook
Occupational Coordinator

**c.** Signature lines containing the names of women should be preceded by a courtesy title if the writer prefers to be addressed as *Mrs.* or *Miss* instead of the standard *Ms.* in any return correspondence. Courtesy titles (*Ms.*, *Mrs.*, or *Miss*) should also be used before female names that are not readily distinguishable as male or female, names containing only initials, and international names. The title is usually placed in parentheses, but it may appear without them.

If a woman has the title *Dr.*, either (1) place the abbreviation of the degree after the name of the individual or (2) place the title *Dr.*—with or without parentheses—before the name of the individual.

**signature lines containing name of woman**

Sally Abramowitz, Manager
Production Department

Alice H. Duffy, Coordinator
Training and Development

**signature lines distinguishing courtesy title of woman**

(Miss) Miho Tabata
Administrative Assistant

*or*

Miss Miho Tabata
Administrative Assistant

(Mrs.) Kelly Krusee
Sales Associate

*or*

Mrs. Kelly Krusee
Sales Associate

(Ms.) M. R. Stevens
General Manager

*or*

Ms. M. R. Stevens
General Manager

(Ms.) Tran Huynh
Vice President

*or*

Ms. Tran Huynh
Vice President

**signature lines containing name of woman addressed as *Dr*.**

Ermonia C. Gevorkian, D.B.A.
Associate Professor

Lynn V. Stauber, M.D.

(Dr.) Alecia Morley, Dean
Academic Affairs

Dr. Alecia Morley, Dean
Academic Affairs

**d.** **Correspondence that is signed by a person other than the one whose name appears in the signature line usually shows the initials of the person signing the letter.**

**e.** **Sometimes more than one signature is required in a business letter. Arrange the signature lines in order of rank within the organization. If ranking is unimportant, arrange the signature lines in alphabetical order.**

*Modified block letter style.* In the modified block letter, align multiple signatures vertically beginning at the horizontal center of the page. Leave three blank lines between each signature block.

*Full block letter style.* In a full block letter, arrange multiple signatures (1) side by side or (2) aligned vertically at the left margin with three blank lines separating each typed signature block.

**multiple signature lines in modified block letter**

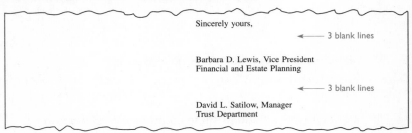

**side-by-side signature lines in full block letter**

**vertically aligned signature lines in full block letter**

~~~
Sincerely,
                        ◄─── 3 blank lines

John P. Gerberding
Vice President
                        ◄─── 3 blank lines

(Ms.) Leslie R. Leigh
Director of Marketing
                        ◄─── 3 blank lines

Mark F. Sarafian
Sales Manager, Central
~~~

## 10–17. Reference Initials

**a.** Reference initials are used to show who typed the letter. In all letter styles except the social business style, the preparer's initials are placed in lowercase letters at the left margin a double space below the last line in the signature block.

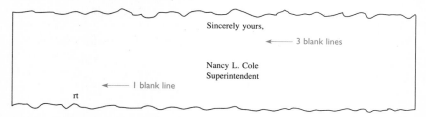

~~~
                        Sincerely yours,
                                    ◄─── 3 blank lines

                        Nancy L. Cole
                        Superintendent
                ◄─── I blank line
        rt
~~~

**b.** The initials of both the writer and the preparer *may* be included in the reference notation. When the person whose name appears in the signature lines is the one who wrote the letter, his or her initials appear in capital letters before the preparer's initials. The initials are separated by a colon or a diagonal line.

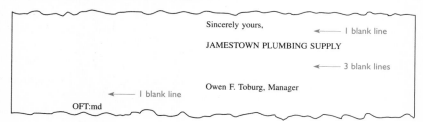

~~~
                        Sincerely yours,        ◄─── I blank line

                        JAMESTOWN PLUMBING SUPPLY

                                        ◄─── 3 blank lines

                        Owen F. Toburg, Manager
                ◄─── I blank line
        OFT:md
~~~

**c.** When correspondence is written by a person other than the one whose name appears in the signature lines, the writer's name or capitalized initials precede the initials of the preparer. Separate the name or initials of the writer from the preparer's initials by a colon or a diagonal line.

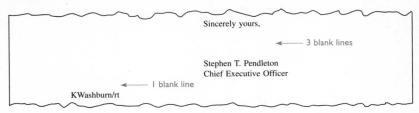

## 10–18. Enclosure or Attachment Notations

**a.** If any enclosures are included with the letter, an enclosure notation is placed on the second line (or next line to conserve space) below the reference initials. Begin the enclosure notation at the left margin. If more than one enclosure is included, be sure to list the enclosures or the number with the enclosure notation. Following are some examples of enclosure notations:

**one enclosure**

Enclosure        Enc.        Check enclosed        Enclosure: Wilson Contract

**more than one enclosure**

Enclosures:    Check for $200                 2 Enc.                    Enc. 2
                      Copy of Invoice 1362

Enclosures 2                                          Enclosures (2)      2 Enclosures

**b.** When an enclosure is attached to the letter, the word *Attachment* or its abbreviation may be used in place of the enclosure notation. If more than one item is attached, be sure to include a listing or the number with the attachment notation.

**one attachment**

Attachment          Attachment: Survey results          Att.

**more than one attachment**

Attachments:    Application for admission          Attachments 2
                      Student information form

2 Attachments                                              Att. 2

## 10–19. Copy Notations

**a.** When copies of correspondence are directed to individuals other than the addressee, note the distribution at the bottom of the letter. The copy notation is placed on the second line (or next line to conserve space) following the enclosure notation, if used. Otherwise, it appears a single or double space below the reference initials. However, if a delivery notation follows the reference initials or enclosure notation, the copy notation is placed below it.

### copy notation following reference initials

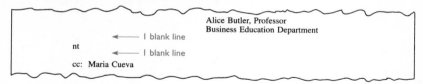

### copy notation with additional notations

**b.** Copies of correspondence are prepared with a photocopier, a printer, or—in rare cases—carbon paper. The traditional *cc* notation represents the terms *courtesy copy* or *carbon copy*, so this notation is appropriate for copies produced by any method. Some writers use only *c* for *copy*.

Copy notations may include a combination of the courtesy title, name, position, department, company, and complete address of an individual. Following are some examples of appropriate copy notations:

cc: Mr. John R. Robinson
    1865 Rinaldi Street
    Oklahoma City, OK 73103

c: Francis P. Olsen, President, Wilson Corporation

cc Alice Morley, Credit Clerk

c Vahi Urun

Some companies prefer to note copies made on a photocopier in the following ways:

copy: Ms. Janice Welch                   c: Sales Department Staff

copies: Bill Acevedo                     C: Mrs. Phuong Nguyen
        Donna Mellert

copy to Mr. Bill Hughes, Manager, Hillsdale Paper Corporation

**c.** If copies are directed to more than one individual, list the individuals according to rank. If the individuals are equal in rank or ranking is unimportant, alphabetize the list. The list may be prepared either vertically or horizontally.

**ranked list**

cc: R. F. Gillham, President
    T. L. McMillan, Vice President
    F. S. Brotherton, General Manager

**alphabetized list**

cc Marcus L. Brendero, Anne S. Langville, David M. Silverman

**d.** If sending a copy of the letter to other individuals is unnecessary or inappropriate for an addressee to know, use a blind copy notation. The blind copy notation appears only on copies of the letter, not on the original.

The blind copy notation may be placed (1) one inch from the top edge of the page at the left margin or (2) where the regular copy notation normally appears. Examples of blind copy notations follow:

bcc: David P. Dougherty       bcc  Ms. Marty Hayes

## 10–20. Postscripts

A postscript may be used to emphasize an idea or add an idea that was unintentionally omitted from the body of the letter. The postscript is placed in last position; it may appear in type or be handwritten with or without the abbreviation *P.S.* or *PS:*.

Treat the postscript as any other paragraph in the letter. If the first line is blocked, then block the first line and all succeeding lines. If the first line is indented, then indent the first line and begin the remaining lines at the left margin.

**with abbreviation *P.S.* or *PS***

rt                          ◄——— I blank line

Enclosure                   ◄——— I blank line

P.S.  Don't miss this opportunity to order your subscription of *Living World Today.*
Remember that this offer ends October 31.

at least I inch

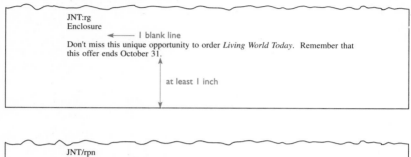

### without abbreviation *P.S.* or *PS*

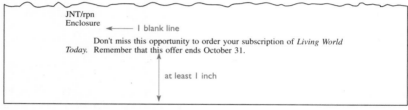

## 10–21. Second-Page Headings

**a.** Prepare headings for second and succeeding pages on plain paper. Allow a 1-inch top margin, and use the same side margins that appear on the first page. These continuation-page headings include the name of the addressee, the page number, and the date. Either a horizontal or vertical format may be used.

**b.** Before resuming the message, space down three lines from the last line of the heading. Two blank lines should separate the heading and the continuation of the message.

**horizontal format**

**vertical format**

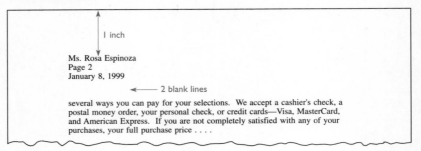

c. If a page does not end at the conclusion of a paragraph, include *at least* the first two lines of any new paragraph begun at the bottom of the page. Do not divide the last word on the page. Likewise, carry forward to the next page *at least* the last two lines from a paragraph begun on the previous page. Leave at least 1 inch, but no more than 1.5 inches, at the bottom of each page—except, of course, for the last one.

d. The closing lines of a business letter should not be isolated on a continuation page. At least two lines of the message must precede the complimentary close or signature lines (when no complimentary close is used).

# Punctuation Style

## 10–22. Mixed Punctuation

The most popular punctuation style for business letters is mixed punctuation. In this format a colon follows the salutation and a comma appears after the complimentary close. No other closing punctuation marks are used except those concluding an abbreviation or ones appearing within the body of the letter.

312

Enc.

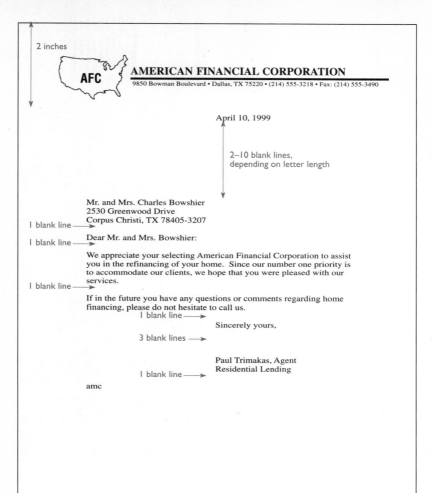

2 inches

**AMERICAN FINANCIAL CORPORATION**

AFC

9850 Bowman Boulevard • Dallas, TX 75220 • (214) 555-3218 • Fax: (214) 555-3490

April 10, 1999

2–10 blank lines,
depending on letter length

Mr. and Mrs. Charles Bowshier
2530 Greenwood Drive
Corpus Christi, TX 78405-3207

I blank line

Dear Mr. and Mrs. Bowshier:

I blank line

We appreciate your selecting American Financial Corporation to assist you in the refinancing of your home. Since our number one priority is to accommodate our clients, we hope that you were pleased with our services.

I blank line

If in the future you have any questions or comments regarding home financing, please do not hesitate to call us.

I blank line

Sincerely yours,

3 blank lines

Paul Trimakas, Agent
Residential Lending

I blank line

amc

## 10–23. Open Punctuation

Writers of business letters sometimes use open punctuation. No closing punctuation marks except those concluding an abbreviation appear after the letter parts. The only other ending punctuation marks are ones used within the body of the letter.

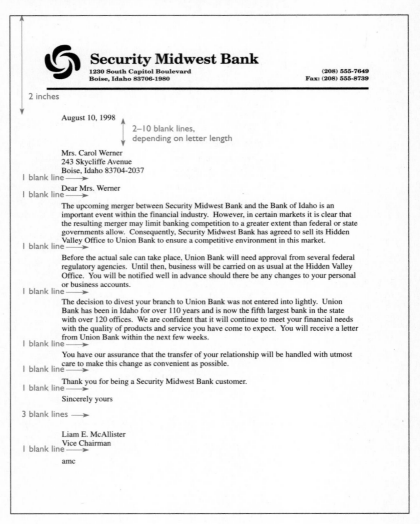

# Addressing Envelopes

## 10–24. Automated Envelope Addressing

Use the envelope feature of your word processing program to pre-pare envelopes for your correspondence and other mailings. Adapt the default settings to correspond to your needs by following these guidelines:

(1) Select the envelope size from the menu of types provided by your software. If the correct envelope size is not available, create and select it. Be sure that your printer will support the envelope size selected.

(2) Adjust the left and top margin settings of your return address placement to accommodate any lines to be added to a printed return address or to accommodate a typed return address. See Section 10-25.

(3) Adjust the left and top margin settings of your mailing address placement to accommodate the envelope size selected. See Section 10-26 for the margin settings to be used for No. 10 (legal-size), No. 6¾ (letter-size), No. 7 (monarch), and No. 5⅜ (baronial) envelopes.

(4) Use the option to insert a bar code, if desired. Before using this option, make sure your printer supports it.

**envelope printed with envelope feature of a word processing program[7]**

---

*Continental Insurance Company*
460 North Ashley Drive
Tampa, Florida 33601-1469


CONFIDENTIAL                                                    CERTIFIED MAIL


                        Mr. Thomas R. Paige, Manager
                        Allied Insurance Agency
                        6200 Beachwood Boulevard
                        Tampa, Florida 33609-2147


                        |ıllıııllıllıllıııhlııııhlıııllılıllıııhlılıl

---

[7]Prepared using the envelope feature of Corel WordPerfect 7 for Windows

## 10–25. Return Address

**a.** The return address is usually printed in the upper left corner of the envelope. In large companies the writer's or sender's initials or name and location are typed above the company name and return address. This practice facilitates routing the letter to the sender in case of non-delivery by the post office.

Jeffrey Edwards, Trust Department
**United Bank of Iowa**
1640 Medina Road
Des Moines, Iowa 50313-2167

**b.** On an envelope without a printed return address, place the return address in the upper left corner. Single-space the lines and include (1) the name of the individual; (2) the title of the individual, if applicable; (3) the company name, if applicable; (4) the mailing address; and (5) the city, state, and zip code. Begin the return address 0.3 inch from the top and 0.4 inch from the left edge of the envelope.

```
          ↕ 0.3 inch
John R. Stevens
   460 Old Dorsett Road
←→ Hazelwood, MO 63043-2367
0.4 inch
```

## 10–26. Mailing Address

**a.** Single-space the mailing address, using at least two lines. The last line of the address should contain the city, state, and zip code. If the envelope is used to mail correspondence, type the address exactly as it appears in the inside address.

**b.** On legal-size envelopes, No. 10 envelopes (9.5 by 4.13 inches), allow a 2-inch top margin. Begin the address 4.25 inches from the left edge of the envelope.

**No. 10 envelope**

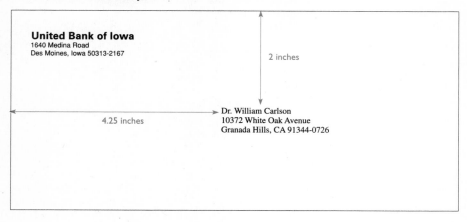

**United Bank of Iowa**
1640 Medina Road
Des Moines, Iowa 50313-2167

2 inches

4.25 inches

Dr. William Carlson
10372 White Oak Avenue
Granada Hills, CA 91344-0726

**c.** On letter-size envelopes, No. 6 3/4 envelopes (6.5 by 3.63 inches), allow a 1.75-inch top margin. Begin the mailing address 2.5 inches from the left edge of the envelope.

**No. 6 3/4 envelope**

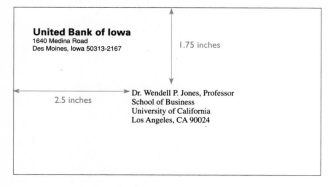

**United Bank of Iowa**
1640 Medina Road
Des Moines, Iowa 50313-2167

1.75 inches

2.5 inches

Dr. Wendell P. Jones, Professor
School of Business
University of California
Los Angeles, CA 90024

317

**d.** No. 7 (7.5 by 3.88 inches) and No. 5 3/8 (5.94 by 4.63 inches) envelopes are used less frequently than the standard No. 10 and No. 6 3/4
envelopes. On No. 7 envelopes allow a 1.75-inch top margin; on No. 5
3/8 envelopes allow a 2-inch top margin. Begin typing the mailing
address 0.5 to 1 inch left of the envelope center, depending upon the
length of the address lines.

### No. 7 envelope

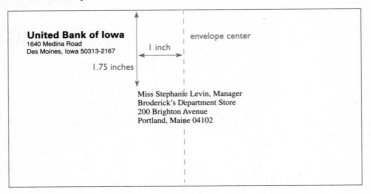

### No. 5 3/8 envelope

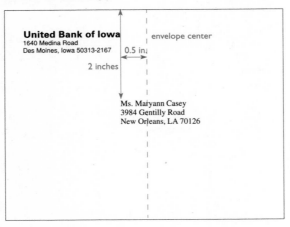

**e.** Letter-size manila envelopes (9 by 12 inches or 10 by 12 inches) may
have the address typed directly on the envelope or have a label with
the address affixed to the envelope. In either case, position the envelope so that the flap and opening are on the right side. Place the first
line of the mailing address 4.5 inches (for 9- by 12-inch envelopes) or
5 inches (for 10- by 12-inch envelopes) from the top edge and 4.5 to 5
inches from the left edge, depending upon the length of the address
lines.

## letter-size manila envelope

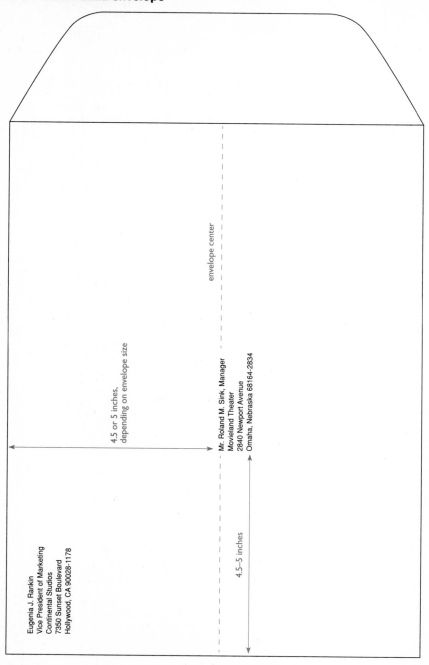

Business Letters

10

Enc.

Eugenia J. Rankin
Vice President of Marketing
Continental Studios
7350 Sunset Boulevard
Hollywood, CA 90028-1178

4.5 or 5 inches,
depending on envelope size

envelope center

Mr. Roland M. Sink, Manager
Movieland Theater
2840 Newport Avenue
Omaha, Nebraska 68164-2834

4.5–5 inches

## 10–27. Addressee Notations

If an attention line appears in the inside address of a letter, include it within the envelope address. If an attention line is placed below the inside address in the letter, treat it the same as you would any other addressee notation.

Type an attention line or an addressee notation such as *Personal*, *Confidential*, *Please Forward*, or *Hold for Arrival* a double space below the last line of the return address or 1.5 inches from the top edge of the envelope, whichever position is lower. Begin typing 0.5 inch from the left edge of the envelope, and use all capital letters.

**attention line included with address**

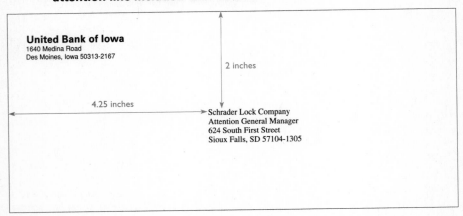

**addressee notation below return address**

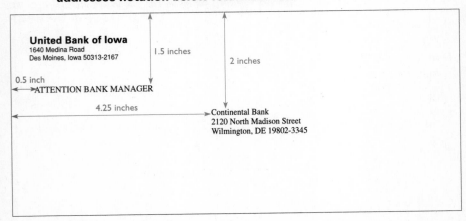

## 10–28. Delivery Notations

a.   Place delivery notations such as *Air Mail* (for foreign destinations), *Certified Mail,* or *Registered Mail* in all capital letters below the stamp, 1.5 inches from the top edge of the envelope. End the notation 0.5 inch from the right edge of the envelope.

Envelope delivery notations are of lesser significance than they were previously, except for *Air Mail*, which is used exclusively for international mailings. *Express Mail* and other fast-delivery options provided by private courier services have their own supplier-provided envelopes. *Registered Mail* must be presented at the post office for mailing, where it is marked and routed appropriately. *Certified Mail*, too, is usually taken to the post office and marked accordingly.

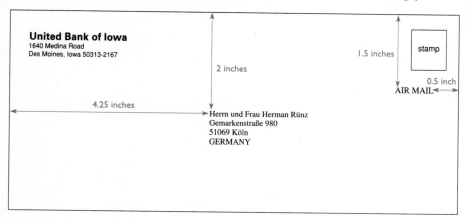

**b.** If an addressee and a delivery notation are on the same envelope, type both in all capital letters. The addressee notation appears a double space below the last line of the return address or 1.5 inches from the top edge of the envelope, whichever position is lower. Begin this notation 0.5 inch from the left envelope edge. Delivery notations are placed below the stamp, 1.5 inches from the top edge of the envelope. They end 0.5 inch from the right edge.

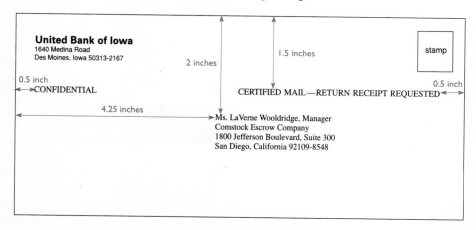

## 10–29. Addressing Envelopes for Optical Character Recognition (OCR)

In 1972 the U.S. Postal Service introduced a format for faster handling of mail addressed by plates or computerized equipment. In a 1974 publication, the U.S. Postal Service recommended that a similar addressing format be used for all other mail.

Advances in technology, however, have led to the U.S. Postal Service equipment recognizing standard address formats.[8] One publication states, "The OCR can read a combination of uppercase and lowercase letters in addresses *but prefers all uppercase letters.* Even though OCR enhancements now allow effective reading of punctuation in addresses, it is still suggested that punctuation be omitted when possible."[9]

For general business correspondence most companies prefer the formality of using the same form of address for both the inside address and the envelope. This format is described in Sections 10-24 through 10-28. If a company follows the U.S. Postal Service recommendations for bulk or regular mailings, use the following guidelines for addressing mail:[10]

a. Addresses should be placed at least 1/2 inch (0.5 inch) from the left and right edges of the envelope. The bottom of the last line must be at least 5/8 inch (0.625 inch), but no more than 2 3/4 inches (2.75 inches), from the bottom edge of the envelope. Keep the lower right half of the envelope free of extraneous printing or symbols, and be careful not to type the address at a slant. The following illustration shows the margin limitations recommended by the U.S. Postal Service.[11]

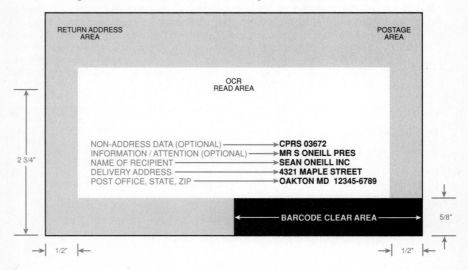

---

[8]*Postal Addressing Standards*, Publication 28 (Memphis, Tenn.: United States Postal Service, National Customer Support Center, 1995), 5–6.

[9]*Designing Letter Mail*, Publication 25 (United States Postal Service, 1995), 31.

[10]These guidelines are based on the information given in *Postal Addressing Standards*, Publication 28 (August 1995), and *Designing Letter Mail*, Publication 25 (August 1995), issued by the U.S. Postal Service.

[11]*Postal Addressing Standards*, op. cit., 49–50.

**b.** Use block-style type or print (no italic, script, or artistic fonts) and a font size between 10 and 12 points. The address area on all mail materials should be blocked, with all lines having uniform left margins. Addresses in all capital letters without punctuation are preferred.

**c.** The last line of a domestic address should include the city name spelled in its entirety, the two-character state abbreviation, and the ZIP + 4 code. Format the last line with at least one space between each segment. When addressing foreign mail, use the country name as the last line of the address block.

**last line of domestic address**

DALLAS TX  75201-2310

CITY OF INDUSTRY CA  90014-1326

**concluding lines of foreign address**

LONDON  WIP7HQ
ENGLAND

**d.** The delivery point for the mail, whether it is a street address or a box number, must be shown on the second line from the bottom, directly above the city, state, and zip code. Follow these guidelines for preparing the delivery address line:

(1) Do not use dual addresses on a piece of mail, even though a person or business may maintain both a physical and a mailing address. Normally use only the post office box address.

(2) When mail is addressed to a box number, place the box number first and then the station name, both on the same line.

(3) Use approved abbreviations for directional, street, and secondary address unit designations. A partial listing of such abbreviations follows:

### Common Address Abbreviations Used by the U.S. Postal Service

| | | | |
|---|---|---|---|
| Apartment | APT | Meadows | MDWS |
| Avenue | AVE | North | N |
| Boulevard | BLVD | Palms | PLMS |
| Building | BLDG | Park | PK |
| Department | DEPT | Parkway | PKY |
| Drive | DR | Place | PL |
| East | E | Plaza | PLZ |
| Expressway | EXPY | Post Office | PO |
| Floor | FL | Ridge | RDG |
| Heights | HTS | River | RV |
| Junction | JCT | Road | RD |
| Lake | LK | Room | RM |
| Lakes | LKS | Route | RT |
| Lane | LN | Rural | R |

*(continued)*

### Common Address Abbreviations Used by the U.S. Postal Service

| | | | |
|---|---|---|---|
| Rural Route | RR | Terrace | TER |
| Shore | SH | Turnpike | TPKE |
| South | S | Union | UN |
| Square | SQ | View | VW |
| Station | STA | Village | VLG |
| Street | ST | West | W |
| Suite | STE | | |

(4) Secondary address unit designators such as *APARTMENT* or *SUITE* should be abbreviated and placed at the end of the delivery address line. The pound sign (#) should not be used in place of *APT, DEPT,* or the like if the correct secondary unit designator is known. If the pound sign is used, space between the pound sign and the secondary number.

(5) If all delivery address line information cannot fit on a single line, place the continuation information *above* the initial line.

**street address**

8325 W HALBY ST  APT 27
DENVER CO  80202-3210

DEPT 40A
5800 SPRINGFIELD GARDENS CIR
SPRINGFIELD VA  22152-1058

**box number with station name**

PO BOX 3302 JEFFERSON STN
DETROIT MI  48214-3302

PO BOX 10846 TERMINAL ANNEX
LOS ANGELES CA  90043-0846

**e.** Place any business or firm name on the line directly above the delivery address line. Individual names, attention lines, individual titles, department names, and other such information are not required by the U.S. Postal Service for distribution and delivery and are optional for the mailer. Use the following guidelines for the placement of these lines in the address block above the second line from the bottom:

(1) Place a business or firm name on the third line from the bottom. If a business or firm name appears in the address, it is used by the U.S. Postal Service for mail delivery.

(2) Continue in reverse line order with (a) a department name (if any), (b) an individual's title (if any), and (c) the recipient's name or an attention line.

Enc.

### envelope addressed to an individual

MRS HELEN K SAUNDERS
200 SW 34TH ST UNIT 105
NEW YORK NY  10021-0905

### envelope addressed to an individual within a company

MR AARON JENKINS
VICE PRESIDENT
ABC CORPORATION
3515 INDUSTRIAL PKY STE 300
CLEVELAND OH  44135-3473

### envelope containing an attention line

ATTN MANAGER
HUMAN RESOURCES DEPARTMENT
GENERAL MANUFACTURING COMPANY
PO BOX 3302 JEFFERSON STN
DETROIT MI  48214-3302

f.  Account numbers, subscription order codes, presort codes, mailstop codes, and advertising may be located within the address block. Such items are placed immediately above the addressee's name.

973-81269346
MS ROBERTA W FRANK
8325 W HALBY ST APT 27
DENVER CO  80202-1253

### envelope prepared according to postal service recommendations

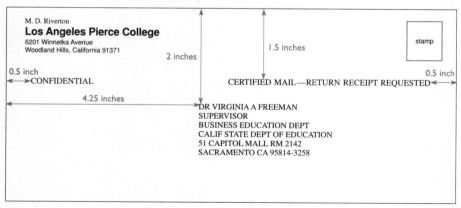

**acceptable envelope address format for OCR**

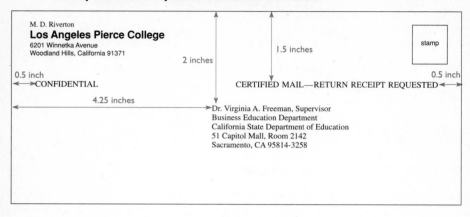

Enc.

## 10–30. Computer-Generated Address Labels

Word processing programs as well as database programs can easily generate mailing labels from a database merge file or a database file. Addresses are compiled and formatted for printing on predefined label forms prepared commercially by companies such as Avery or 3M. The following example was prepared on a word processor using an Avery 5162 address label form for a laser printer.

Mr. George R. Simms, Vice President
Great Western Bank
19300 Devonshire Street
Chatsworth, CA 93471-1046

Ms. Elizabeth Candiotti, President
Woodland Hills Chamber of Commerce
20220 Ventura Boulevard, Suite 130
Woodland Hills, CA 91365-3281

Ms. Veronica Richmond, Director
Human Resources Department
Harman International
6200 Balboa Boulevard
Northridge, CA 91324-1954

Dr. Sandra L. Washington, President
California State University, Northridge
18600 Nordhoff Street
Northridge, CA 91327

Mr. Charles E. Buchanan, Manager
Coldwell Banker Realty
8750 Arroyo Parkway
Camarillo, CA 92374-3209

Mr. Anthony Murillo, Vice President
International Operations
Amgen Corporation
30375 Victory Boulevard
Thousand Oaks, CA 94509-1001

## 10–31. Zip + 4

a. To process mail faster and more economically, the U.S. Postal Service has assigned four additional digits to the zip code of mailing addresses that do not have their own separate zip codes. This series of four digits is separated from the zip code with a hyphen.

Northridge, CA 91325-**6213**
Jackson, MS 39203-**1073**

Boise, Idaho 83702-**4819**
Reno, Nevada 89503-**2103**

**b.** The use of Zip + 4 is recommended by the U.S. Postal Service. Reduced rates for the use of Zip + 4 can be obtained by bulk mailers.

**c.** Although zip codes may be located through a directory published by the U.S. Postal Service, the additional four digits result in producing too many codes to be published in volumes free-of-charge for public distribution. Zip + 4 software, *CD-ROM ZIP + 4 Retrieval Microcomputer System*, is available for purchase from the U.S. Postal Service.[12]

## Folding and Inserting Correspondence

### 10–32. No. 10 and No. 7 Envelopes

**a.** Fold up one third of the page.

**b.** Fold down the upper third of the page so that the top edge is approximately 1/3 inch above the first fold.

 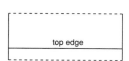

**c.** Insert the page so that the top edge is near the top edge of the envelope.

---

[12]For more information about this product and other Zip + 4 directories, telephone the National Customer Support Center, U.S. Postal Service, 1-800-238-3150.

## 10–33. No. 6 3/4 Envelopes

**a.** Fold up one half of the page so that the bottom edge is approximately 1/3 inch below the top edge.

**b.** From the right side fold over one third of the page.

**c.** Fold over the second third of the page so that the left edge is approximately 1/3 inch from the right fold.

**d.** Insert the page so that the left edge is near the top edge of the envelope.

## 10–34. Window Envelopes

**a.** Fold up one third of the letter.

**b.** Turn the folded letter face down.

**c.** Fold down the upper third of the letter so that the top edge meets the first fold.

**d.** Insert the letter so that the address appears in the window of the envelope.

# Memorandums

## 10–35. Usage

While letters generally involve the transmission of written messages sent outside an organization, memorandums comprise the major medium for internal written communication.

## 10–36. Preparation

**a.** Procedures for preparing memorandums vary widely from office to office, but there are a few general guidelines. Most organizations have printed memorandum forms. These forms contain guide words for directing the message to an addressee, specifying the name of the writer, providing the date written, and identifying the subject content. Although the arrangement and design may vary, these basic elements are found in most printed memorandum forms.

**printed memorandum forms**

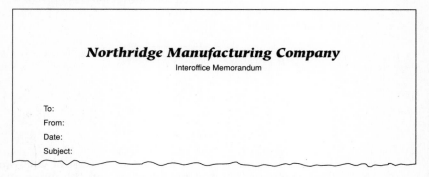

*Northridge Manufacturing Company*
Interoffice Memorandum

To:
From:
Date:
Subject:

**Mattel Toys Memo**                    MAT-3497-8

TO:                          DATE:

FROM:                        REFERENCE:
SUBJECT:

GENERAL MOTORS ACCEPTANCE CORPORATION
INTRAORGANIZATION LETTERS ONLY

TO:                   ADDRESS:
FROM:                 ADDRESS:
SUBJECT:              DATE:

**b.** Memorandums may be prepared on preprinted forms using word processing software. For standard 8 1/2- by 11-inch printed memorandum forms, create a form document or a custom template to assist you with completing the preliminary lines: *Date:, To:, From:, Subject:,* etc. Each time you are required to use this printed form, you can use the form document or template to assist you with the proper placement of information after each guide word.

(1) Use 1-inch top and bottom margins and 1.25-inch left and right margins.

(2) Use a ruler to measure the horizontal and vertical position of the first letter to be typed after each guide word contained on the memorandum form.

(3) Move your cursor to the horizontal and vertical position (as shown in the status line of your program) of the first letter to be typed after the first guide word; type an asterisk (*). Follow the same procedure for each guide word in the printed form. If any preliminary parts will be completed with standard information, key in this standard information instead of an asterisk.

(4) Triple-space after the asterisk marking the beginning of the last guide word, usually the one that introduces the subject line.

(5) Save the form document as a separate file.

When a memorandum needs to be prepared, copy the form document into a new document. Use the search feature of your program to locate the asterisks and substitute the variable information needed for the current memorandum.

c. Companies that do not have standardized forms for preparing memorandums use company letterhead, word processing templates with plain paper, or plain paper. In these cases apply the following procedures:

(1) A memorandum is usually prepared on 8 1/2- by 11-inch paper. For short memorandums, however, a half sheet (8 1/2 by 5 1/2 inches) may be used, although this size is usually avoided because of handling and filing difficulties.

(2) On 8 1/2- by 11-inch paper, begin the preliminary lines 2 inches from the top edge of the paper. For memorandums prepared on half sheets, begin the preliminary lines 1 inch from the top edge of the paper.

(3) Use 1.25-inch left and right margins for memorandums prepared on 8 1/2- by 11-inch paper and 1-inch margins for memorandums prepared on half sheets.

(4) Type in all capital letters and double-space the guide words *DATE:, TO:, FROM:,* and *SUBJECT:* at the left margin. Align the information following the guide words after the colon in the *SUBJECT:* heading. Any other guide words the company may wish to use should be placed on the same lines as the *DATE:, TO:,* or *FROM:* headings and begin after the information for those guide words.

(5) Triple-space after *SUBJECT:,* and begin typing the body of the memorandum at the left margin. Single-space the message, but double-space between paragraphs.

(6) If you regularly prepare memorandums on plain paper or letter-head stationery, create a form document or macro for the preliminary lines of the memorandum.

## memorandum prepared on company letterhead

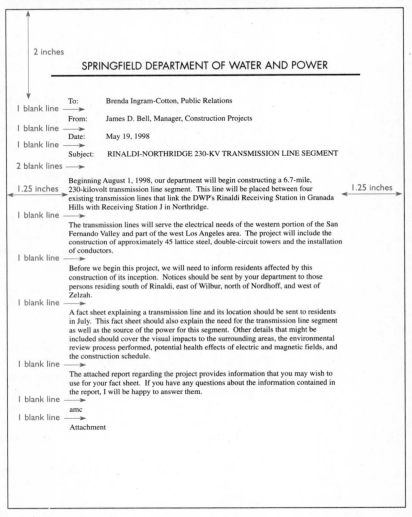

Enc.

## memorandum prepared using a word processing template

**interoffice**
MEMORANDUM

**to:**      All Employees
**from:**    Donna Anderson
**subject:** GROUP HEALTH NSURANCE
**date:**    October 21, 1998

2 blank lines ⟶

1.25 inches ⟵⟶    As you know, Stanley Hutchinson, your employee representative, proposed to the Board    ⟵ 1.25 inches
of Directors last January that we consider adopting an employee group health insurance
plan. He pointed out the many medical expenses incurred by our employees throughout
the year and the benefits a group health insurance policy would have in helping meet
some of the medical expenses resulting from sickness and injuries.

1 blank line ⟶

After careful study of several group health insurance policies, the board concluded that
the group policy proposed by the Edgewater Insurance Company would give the most
comprehensive medical coverage for its cost. As a result, the board voted unanimously
to adopt this policy at no cost to the employees, effective June 1.

1 blank line ⟶

Attached is a brochure that explains in detail the health-care services covered by the
Edgewater policy. If you have any questions, please call Don Curry at Ext. 7351. He
will be glad to assist you.

1 blank line ⟶
rm

1 blank line ⟶
Attachment

Enc.

## memorandum prepared on blank paper

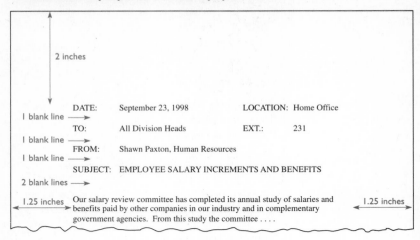

d. **When a memorandum contains more than one page, the heading for the second and succeeding pages should have a 1-inch top margin. Show the name of the person or group to whom the memorandum is addressed, the page number, and the date. This information may be arranged vertically at the left margin or be placed on a single line with the name beginning at the left margin, the page number centered, and the date aligned at the right margin. Triple-space after the heading before continuing the body of the memorandum.**

### vertical second-page heading

### horizontal second-page heading

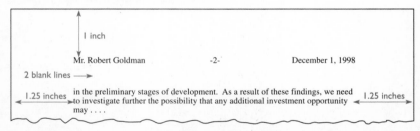

# E-Mail Messages

## 10–37. Purpose and Function

**E-mail messages are not substitutes for business letters or memorandums. They are used to convey short messages, request information, respond to inquiries, acknowledge receipt of merchandise or mail, or act as cover documents for appended files.**

(1)  The purpose of E-mail is to convey *short* messages quickly and easily without encountering the expense of long-distance telephone charges or mail carrier express charges. Not only are E-mail messages economical and easily created but also they are convenient — they may be received in a matter of hours (sometimes even minutes) and read at the recipient's discretion.

(2)  The E-mail message originator composes a message and "sends" it on its way. Interorganizational messages are directed to the recipient's computer mailbox via the organization's network. Messages directed outside an organizational network must be transmitted through the Internet.

(3)  An E-mail message sent through the Internet leaves the originator's computer and first arrives at the host computer of the originator's on-line service provider. Here the message is routed from computer to computer until it reaches the host of the recipient's on-line service provider. Once at this destination, the message is in residence until the recipient opens his or her mailbox and retrieves the message from the on-line service provider's host computer.

(4)  E-mail messages do not replace letters or memorandums that are lengthy, need paper copies, require confidentiality, or discuss significant information or issues. Messages of this nature that are for immediate delivery should be prepared on company letterhead or a memorandum form and sent by fax machine to the recipient's fax machine. Also, the U.S. Postal Service and private mail carriers offer overnight delivery to most cities in the continental United States. Keep in mind that electronic mail is not protected or private. Because network hackers can easily access anything sent through the Internet, you must assume that anyone with a computer has the potential to read your message.

## 10–38. Format

On-line service providers and Web browsers supply forms or templates from which you can create E-mail messages. These forms contain a series of boxes into which you can enter information and a series of buttons that permit you to activate E-mail options. Although these forms vary slightly from provider to provider and from browser to browser, each furnishes the following:

(1) **An E-mail address book.** In the E-mail address book, you may store the E-mail addresses of those persons to whom you write on a regular basis.[13]

(2) **The address box with the guide word *To:*.** Clicking on an address in the address book will enter the recipient's E-mail address in the address box. You may also type in the recipient's address. Do so carefully since one wrong character or space will prevent your message from being delivered—at least to its intended destination.

(3) **The courtesy copy box with the guide abbreviation *Cc:*.** If you want others to receive copies of your message, enter their E-mail addresses in the courtesy copy box—either from your address book or by typing them in. Some forms provide for sending blind courtesy copies. In this case courtesy copies are sent to the E-mail addresses listed, but the recipient specified in the address box is not shown that the message was also sent to these addresses.

(4) **The subject line box with the guide word *Subject:*.** Type in the subject line box a brief and descriptive phrase that summarizes the topic of your E-mail message. Use initial capital letters for each principal or main word[14] in the subject line; or, if space permits, use all capital letters.

(5) **The message composition window.** Type your message in the message composition window. If possible, limit your message to a screenful of data.

(6) **The attachments window or button.** Use the attachments window or button to select the path and file name of any file you wish to send with your E-mail message or to designate a Web page you wish to attach to your message.

(7) **The send button.** The send button sends the message and any attachments.

(8) **The outbox and the inbox.** E-mail messages should be composed off-line by accessing the Mail feature of your Internet browser or Internet service provider's software. Messages are saved in the outbox until you connect to your Internet access provider and send them. Once connected to your Internet access provider, you may also "get mail" and retrieve it from your inbox.

(9) **The print feature.** Through the **File-Print** menu in your E-mail program, you may print incoming and outgoing messages.

(10) **Other features.** Depending upon the software you are using for E-mail, you may create signature files, forward mail, reply directly to incoming messages, mark messages as "unread" (to be read later), automatically file messages, or delete messages.

---

[13]See Section 9-10 for an explanation of E-mail addresses.
[14]See Section 3-6 for an explanation of principal or main words.

**on-screen E-mail message**

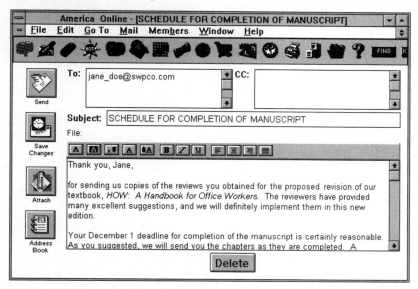

## 10–39. Message Preparation

**a.** Just as business letters and memorandums are forms of one-way communication, so are E-mail messages. Since an E-mail message will not be accompanied by facial expressions or voice inflections, it will be taken at face value. No opportunities exist for the receiver to ask questions, clarify statements, or obtain feedback. Therefore, writers of E-mail messages must plan and write their messages as carefully as they would any other form of written communication.

**b.** Begin your E-mail message with a friendly greeting. Examples of such greetings follow:

| | |
|---|---|
| Hi, Bob, | Thank you, Paula, |
| Hello, Anna | Dear John Morrow, |
| Greetings, Don, | Dear Sandra, |

**c.** Use the following guidelines to construct your messages. Review them to ensure that they are

(1) **Courteous.** Make your message "smile" by using words such as *please, thank you, appreciate,* and *gladly.* Select positive words to convey your ideas; avoid negative words, innuendos, and accusations. Above all, keep your tone friendly.

(2) **Complete.** Has all the necessary information been included to achieve the purpose of your E-mail message? Make sure you have not left out any important data.

(3) **Coherent.** Have all the ideas been placed in logical order so that one idea flows naturally from the previous one? Make sure that the reader can easily follow your train of thought and that you finish discussing one idea before moving on to the next.

(4) **Clear.** Construct your sentences so that they are worded clearly. Make sure that "who does what" and "what is what" leaves no question in the reader's mind. Avoid long, complicated sentences. Place modifiers as closely as possible to the words they modify, and do not use ambiguous pronouns.

(5) **Concrete.** Write in terms of specifics, and use concrete nouns instead of generalities. Dates and times should be expressed explicitly. Likewise, assignments and expectations need to be described in precise terms that are understood similarly by both the writer and the reader.

(6) **Concise.** Use as few words as possible to construct your message, but make sure you have included all the necessary information. Avoid including extra words and extraneous ideas. Remember to keep your E-mail messages as short as possible.

(7) **Correct.** E-mail software does not have a spelling checker, so keep handy a dictionary as you compose your messages. Proofread your messages carefully for typographical errors, repeated words, omitted words, words used incorrectly, spelling errors, and grammar errors. E-mail messages represent you as much as any other kind of written communication.

d. Conclude your E-mail message with a "signature," even if it is only your first name. Some people prefer also to sign off with a cordial farewell remark such as *Best wishes,* especially in informal messages to people whom they know.

Signature lines vary in content. Some people may use only their name. Others will include their name, title, organization, and telephone number. Whatever you choose to use, place the information in no more than four lines.

## 10–40. E-Mail Netiquette

Netiquette (net etiquette) is a set of behaviors that should be adhered to when using the Internet. Excluding conduct prohibited by federal laws, the Internet community itself has devised etiquette standards for Internet use. Those applying to E-mail follow:

(1) Construct your E-mail messages off-line so you do not unnecessarily tie up the network.

(2) Use E-mail to accomplish a specific purpose. Do not tie up the network with E-mail messages that are needless or unnecessary. At the same time, send courtesy copies only to people who will benefit from or who need the information contained in your E-mail message.

(3) When replying to E-mail messages on-line, make your reply as succinct as possible. If courtesy copies were routed to others, evaluate

whether these individuals need your response before sending your reply. Avoid cluttering the network with unnecessary replies.

(4) Be courteous in your E-mail messages. Sending rude messages is known as *flaming* and is frowned upon by the Internet community.

(5) Avoid using a series of all capital letters in the body of your letter. Besides hindering readability, all capital letters are considered the E-mail equivalent of shouting and may be construed as rude.

(6) Because E-mail software does not generally support font attributes (boldface, italics, underlining), use the following substitutions. Enclosing a word or phrase in asterisks indicates a mild emphasis and may be equated with using italics. Placing an underline before and after a published work may be construed as a continuous underline, thus distinguishing it as a title.

**asterisks for italics**

Please mark the package *Fragile*.

Megatone Utilities checks for boot sector viruses, often called *system sector viruses*, as well as for file viruses.

**single underlines for a continuous underline**

On page 23 of the July 28 issue of _Business Week_, you will find an analysis of profits in the telecommunications industry for the last three years.

Please send me three copies of _Business Communication: Process and Product_.

(7) Confine your E-mail messages to short ones, generally no more than a screenful of data. If you send a long message, tell the recipient at the beginning so he or she has the option to download it for later reading.

(8) Do not send chain letters over the Internet. Many Internet service providers prohibit chain letters and sending them may result in a revocation of Internet privileges.

# Chapter 11

# Reports and Other Business Documents

# Ibid.

## Reports and Other Business Documents Solution Finder

# General Formats for Reports and Manuscripts

## 11–1. Purpose, Content, and General Style

Reports are used in business mainly to convey information, analyze data, or support proposals. Those reports written for public distribution, such as reports to stockholders, are printed and usually appear in booklet form. Other reports, those for internal use or limited distribution, are generated internally using computer-based software. Regardless of its final form—printed, desktop published, keyed and printed from computer-based software, or typewritten—the formats recommended here should be used for the preparation and editing process. Except for printed and desktop published reports, these formats also represent the final product.

All reports and manuscripts contain a title page and the body of the report. Other parts may be added, depending upon the length, complexity, and formality of the document. The parts of a report or manuscript may include the following:

Title page
Letter of transmittal
Summary (or Executive summary)
Table of contents
List of tables (and/or List of illustrations)
Contents of the report
Endnotes (if applicable)
Bibliography
Appendix (or Appendixes)

a. Reports and manuscripts may be prepared with *either* 1.25-inch left and right margins *or* 1-inch left and right margins, depending upon the preference of the originator. If the report or manuscript is to be left bound, allow an additional 0.25 inch for the left margin.

b. The first page of major parts (title page, table of contents, bibliography, etc.) and the opening page of sections or chapters require a 2-inch top margin, 2.25 inches for top-bound documents.

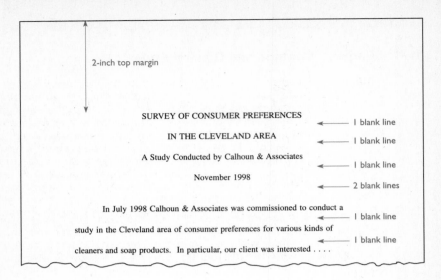

The opening pages of major sections are included in the page count, but the page number is usually not printed on the page.

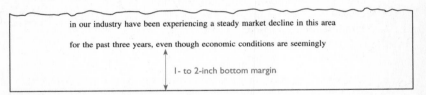

If a page number is to be included on the section opener, select one of the following formats:

(1) **Page number 1 inch from bottom edge of page.** Center the page number on a line 1 inch from the bottom edge of the paper. Leave at least one blank line separating the page number from the last line of text.

(2) **Page number 0.5 inch from bottom edge of page.** Center the page number on a line 0.5 inch from the bottom edge of the paper. Leave at least two blank lines separating the page number from the last line of text.

in our industry have been experiencing a steady market decline in this area

for the past three years, even though economic conditions are seemingly

←——— at least 2 blank lines

1

↕ 0.5-inch bottom margin

**c.** Number preliminary pages (those preceding the contents of the report) consecutively in lowercase Roman numerals (*i, ii, iii, iv, v,* etc.). Count the title page as page *i* even though no number is shown on that page; number the letter of transmittal *ii,* if used.

Create a footer or use the page numbering feature of your word processing program to number any preliminary pages. Suppress the footer or page numbering on the title page. Use one of the following two formats:

**(1)** **Page number 1 inch from bottom edge of page.** Center the page number on a line 1 inch from the bottom edge of the paper. Leave at least one blank line separating the page number from the last line of text.

XI.   Ethics in Law Enforcement . . . . . . . . . . . . . . . . . . . . . . . . . . . . . . . . . . . . 142

XII.   Regional Recruiting Efforts . . . . . . . . . . . . . . . . . . . . . . . . . . . . . . . . . . . . 164

←——— at least 1 blank line

iii

↑

I-inch bottom margin

**(2)** **Page number .05 inch from bottom edge of page.** Center the page number on a line 0.5 inch from the bottom edge of the paper. Leave at least two blank lines separating the page number from the last line of text.

VI.   Income Projections from United States Regions . . . . . . . . . . . . . . . . . . . . . . . 92

Eastern Region Projections . . . . . . . . . . . . . . . . . . . . . . . . . . . . . . . . . . . . 94

Western Region Projections . . . . . . . . . . . . . . . . . . . . . . . . . . . . . . . . . . . . 103

←——— at least 2 blank lines

iii

↕ 0.5-inch bottom margin

Discontinue the footer or this mode of pagination at the conclusion of the preliminary parts.

**d.** Use a 1-inch top margin (1.25 inches for top-bound documents) for all pages except those with main headings. The page number may begin the page.

Reports

11

Ibid.

Create a header or use the page numbering feature of your program to number pages. Select one of the following page-numbering formats; use consistent formats for numbering the preliminary pages and the remaining pages of the report or manuscript.

(1) **Page number 1 inch from top edge of page.** Place the page number in Arabic numbers 1 inch below the top edge of the paper. Align the page number with the right margin, and leave one or two blank lines before beginning the text.

(2) **Page number 0.5 inch from top edge of page.** Place the page number in Arabic numbers 0.5 inch below the top edge of the paper and 0.5 inch from the right edge of the paper. Leave two blank lines before beginning the text.

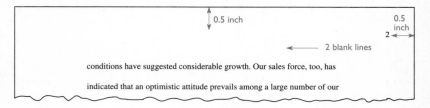

e. In the body of the report, indent the first line of paragraphs 0.5 inch. Indent long quotations and vertical listings 0.5 inch from both the left and right margins.

Use a tab to indent each paragraph and the "left-right indent" feature of your word processing program to indent long quotations and vertical listings.

0.5 inch
Besides providing local advertising, screening prospective tenants, and

collecting rents for your rental property, we provide you with an annual statement

for your income tax records. In addition, we have available at cost to each of our

clients the following services:

0.5 inch 0.5 inch

- Appliance, electrical, or plumbing repairs by a reputable, licensed
  service center

- Daily, weekly, or monthly cleaning service to include linen
  change, kitchen and bathroom maintenance, dusting and
  vacuuming, and window cleaning

- Painting and general maintenance or repairs

0.5 inch
As you can see, we are a full-service rental agency. We have been serving

the Coachella Valley for over . . . .

**f.** **A single line that belongs to a paragraph may not be isolated at the top or bottom of a different page. In addition, an isolated text heading may not be the last line on a page. Conclude the report or manuscript text 1 to 2 inches from the bottom edge of the page, ensuring that *at least* two lines of a paragraph appear at the bottom of a page. A minimum of two lines (one full line and at least one word on a second line) must appear at the top of a page for any paragraph carried over from a previous page.**

**Use the widow/orphan protection feature of your word processing program to prevent single lines of a paragraph from appearing on a separate page. For any text headings appearing as the last line on the page, use the block protect feature to force the heading to the next page.**

### concluding lines of page

We have been advertising this product line for the past six months in the

Dallas area. Television, radio, and newspaper campaigns have focused on the

Reports

11

Ibid.

**continuation of paragraph on next page**

> 6
>
> on all the hair-care products in our Lustre Plus line. Billboard advertising has been
>
> confined to featuring only our shampoo and conditioner.
>
> Preliminary results from this advertising campaign show between a 25 and
>
> 30 percent increase in sales for . . . .

g. In your word processing program, create macros, create styles, or use system shortcuts to change line spacing instantly (single spacing, double spacing, triple spacing). Use these macros, styles, and/or shortcuts to produce the following results in formatting the report or manuscript:[1]

(1) Double-space and center main headings (all capital letters) and any secondary headings (uppercase and lowercase letters); triple space before beginning the first line of text. Always triple-space after a main heading if no secondary heading is used.

(2) Double-space the textual material in the body of the report; indent the first line of each paragraph 0.5 inch.

(3) Triple-space before and double-space after first- and second-degree text headings. Third-degree headings are considered part of the paragraph they introduce and are spaced like regular text.

(4) Single-space and indent 0.5 inch from the left and right margins any long quotations; omit the quotation marks. Long quotations are those consisting of more than three lines *or* more than two sentences. Double-space before and after the long quotation.[2]

(5) Vertical listings consisting of single-line items may be single or double spaced. For listings with items containing more than one line, single-space the items and leave one blank line between items. Double-space before and after the vertical listing.

(6) Tables and illustrations should be centered between the left and right margins. Either double- or triple-space before and after any tables and illustrations interrupting the text narrative. Be consistent in your choice of spacing before and after all visual displays within the text material.

See the example report page on page 349.

h. Use the spell check feature of your word processing program to correct any spelling or typographical errors.

---

[1]See following sections in this chapter for specific instructions and examples for the preparation of report and manuscript parts, main headings, secondary headings, text headings, vertical listings, report or manuscript text (body), tables, and illustrations.

[2]See Chapter 1, Punctuation, Section 1-48, for further information on using and formatting long quotations in manuscripts and reports.

i. **If you must frequently prepare manuscripts or reports, use the styles feature of your word processing program to format your reports.**

### example of report page with table

34

for inventories valued at LIFO, inventories at December 31 would have been $66.5 million and $66.4 million higher than reported for 1998 and 1999, respectively. The FIFO cost of inventories at these dates approximated replacement cost or net realizable value.

Inventories at December 31 consisted of the following:

| Table 4 **INVENTORIES 1998-1999** | | |
|---|---|---|
| Type | 1998 (in millions) | 1999 (in millions) |
| Finished goods | $ 187.5 | $ 175.0 |
| Work-in-process | 96.4 | 115.1 |
| Raw materials | 70.0 | 69.5 |
| Inventories | $ 353.9 | $ 359.6 |

**Dispositions and Restructuring**

In 1997 the company's Board of Directors approved plans to offer for sale the businesses that comprised the Industrial Products and Technetics Divisions of the company's Technical segment except for Technetics' golf shaft operation, which was transferred to the Marsh-Barnhardt Division on January 1, 1997. The disposition of these businesses was completed in 1997. A pretax gain on the dispositions of $84.2 million ($46.7 million after taxes) was recorded in 1998. Net proceeds from the sale of assets of

Ibid.

# Parts of a Report or Manuscript

### 11–2.  Title Page

**a.** The title page generally contains the following information, but its contents are not restricted to these items:

(1)  The name or title of the report or manuscript

(2)  The name and title of the person and/or the name of the group or organization for whom it was written

(3)  The name and title of the person and/or the name of the group who wrote it

(4)  The date it was submitted

**b.** Use the following guidelines to prepare a title page. To prepare the title page easily, access the center page feature of your word processing program.

(1)  Allow 2-inch top and bottom margins.

(2)  Center all lines horizontally.

(3)  Type the title of the report or manuscript in all capital letters. Single-space any titles containing more than one line.

(4)  Space equally between the top and bottom margins all other parts following the title.

(5)  Count the title page in the pagination, but do not number the page.

An illustration of a title page appears on page 351.

### 11–3.  Letter of Transmittal

**a.** The letter of transmittal, if used, introduces the reader to the report or manuscript. Although the content of the transmittal letter will depend upon the complexity and scope of the report or manuscript, it should basically tell the reader the following:

(1)  What the topic is

(2)  Why the report was written

(3)  How the report was compiled (method of research)

(4)  Who worked on it or helped with its development

(5)  What major findings or conclusions resulted (if a synopsis or summary page is not included)

**b.** The letter of transmittal should be friendly and concise, usually concluding with the writer showing appreciation for the opportunity to do the report or manuscript. Use the following guidelines to prepare the transmittal letter:

(1)  Use any acceptable business letter style.

(2)  Place the letter of transmittal after the title page.

(3) Number the page with a lowercase Roman numeral centered at the bottom of the page. Place the page number 1 inch or 0.5 inch from the bottom edge of the page, depending upon the page-numbering format selected for the document. See Section 11-1c for further information on the page-numbering formats.

**c.** **An illustration of a letter of transmittal appears on page 352.**

**title page**

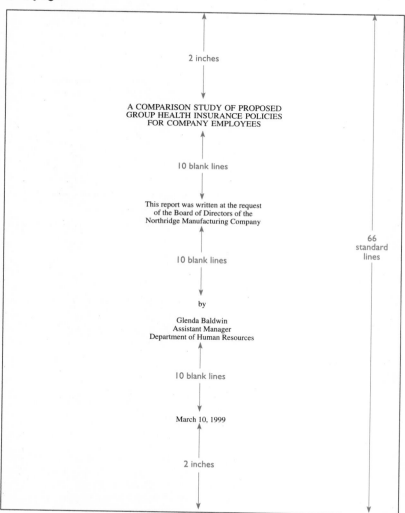

**letter of transmittal**

---

## Northridge Manufacturing Company

170 East Parkland Avenue
Dallas, Texas 75214

(214) 383-5757
Fax: (214) 383-5783

March 10, 1998

Mr. Don Washington, President
Northridge Manufacturing Company
170 East Parkland Avenue
Dallas, Texas 75214

Dear Mr. Washington:

As requested by our Board of Directors, here is the report comparing the employee group health insurance policies that were submitted by eight companies.

The policies were compared in the following ways:

1. Company cost per employee
2. Cost to employees
3. Kinds of illnesses and/or injuries covered
4. Hospital, out-patient, and home-visit coverage
5. Total annual health benefits allowed
6. Miscellaneous coverages such as medicines, X rays, physical therapy, private nursing, etc.
7. Family members covered

As shown by the summary table on page 19, the Edgewater policy is superior in all categories except one—company cost per employee. I recommend we select the Edgewater proposal. The additional $3.16 annual cost per employee is relatively small considering the substantial benefits over any one of the other less expensive policies.

Thank you for the opportunity to conduct this study. I appreciate the help and cooperation I received from the employees' representative and from the representatives of the insurance companies.

If you have any questions or if I can be of further help, please let me know.

Sincerely,

*Glenda Baldwin*

Glenda Baldwin, Assistant Manager
Department of Human Resources

ba

ii

0.5 inch

---

*Ibid.*

## 11–4. Summary of the Report

Long reports—especially those not including a letter of transmittal or those including a letter of transmittal without a synopsis—usually require a summary, sometimes referred to as an *executive summary*. Use the following guidelines to prepare the summary:

(1) Allow a 2-inch top margin. Center the main heading *SUMMARY* or *EXECUTIVE SUMMARY* in all capital letters on the line directly following the top margin. Triple-space after the main heading.

(2) Double-space the text of the summary; indent each paragraph 0.5 inch. Begin with stating the purpose of the report. Briefly

describe the procedures used in preparing the report, and conclude with a concise presentation of the conclusions and recommendations.

(3) Number the summary page or pages with lowercase Roman numerals centered at the bottom of the page. Place the page number 1 inch or 0.5 inch from the bottom edge of the page, depending upon the page-numbering format selected for the document. See Section 11-1c for further information on the page-numbering formats.

## 11–5. Table of Contents

**The content and format of a table of contents vary with the length and complexity of the report or manuscript, but the following guidelines may be used for its preparation:**

(1) Allow a 2-inch top margin. Center the main heading *TABLE OF CONTENTS* or *CONTENTS* in all capital letters on the line directly following the top margin.

(2) Place the word *Page* a triple space below the *TABLE OF CONTENTS* heading; align it with the right margin.

(3) Use all capital letters and double-space the listing for the preliminary sections of the report (e.g., letter of transmittal, summary, list of tables, or list of illustrations). Begin a double space below *Page* and at the left margin. Although it is counted and paginated with a lowercase Roman numeral, the table of contents is not included in this listing.

(4) Begin the major division heading of the report (e.g., *Chapter, Section, Unit,* or *Topic*) at the left margin. The major division heading may either appear on the same line as *Page* or be placed a double space below the preliminary parts.

(5) Number major sections of the report, if desired, by using uppercase Roman numerals. Align the longest numeral with the left margin, and indent the shorter numerals so the periods following the numerals are aligned. Use a decimal tab in your word processing program to achieve this alignment.

(6) Use all capital letters for listing major sections of the report. Those sections of lesser degree should be indented, placed in capital and lowercase letters, and arranged in the same sequence they appear in the report.

(7) Use leaders (a line of alternating periods and spaces) to assist the reader in locating the page number of a particular section, and align vertically the leaders for each section or subsection of the report. Although all major headings must have corresponding page numbers, the assignment of page numbers to subheadings appearing in the table of contents is optional. To obtain leaders in your word processing program, set a right decimal with dot leaders adjacent to the right margin.

(8) Number the table of contents with lowercase Roman numerals centered at the bottom of the page. Place the page number 1 inch or 0.5 inch from the bottom edge of the page, depending upon the page-numbering format selected for the document. See Section 11-1c for further information on the page-numbering formats.

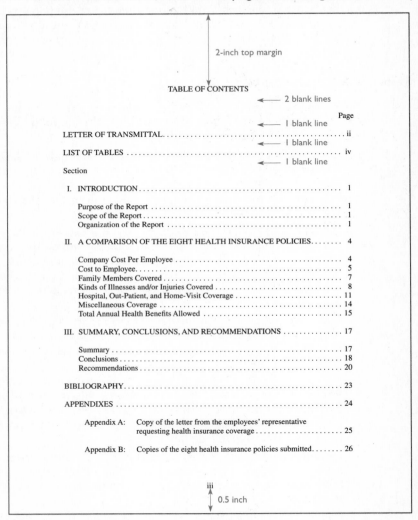

2-inch top margin

TABLE OF CONTENTS

← 2 blank lines

Page

← 1 blank line

LETTER OF TRANSMITTAL.................................................. ii

← 1 blank line

LIST OF TABLES ......................................................... iv

← 1 blank line

Section

iii

0.5 inch

## 11–6.  List of Tables or List of Illustrations

a. When a report or manuscript contains several tables, include as a helpful reference to the reader a list of tables after the table of contents. Guidelines for formatting the list of tables follow:

(1) Center the heading *LIST OF TABLES* in all capital letters 2 inches from the top edge of the page.

(2) Triple-space after the *LIST OF TABLES* heading. Place the word *Table* at the left margin, and align the last letter of the word *Page* with the right margin.

(3) Indent 0.25 inch from the left margin. Key the number of each table followed by spacing of 0.25 inch and the table title in all capital letters. Single-space each title; double-space between titles.

(4) Use leaders (a line of alternating periods and spaces) to assist the reader in locating the page number of a particular table. To obtain leaders in your word processing program, set a right decimal with dot leaders adjacent to the right margin.

(5) Number the list of tables with lowercase Roman numerals centered at the bottom of the page. Place the page number 1 inch or 0.5 inch from the bottom edge of the page, depending upon the page-numbering format selected for the document. See Section 11-1c for further information on the page-numbering formats.

LIST OF TABLES

◄──── 2 blank lines

Table                                              Page

◄──── l blank line

1    A COMPARISON OF THE ANNUAL COST PER EMPLOYEE OF HEALTH INSURANCE POLICIES SUBMITTED BY EIGHT COMPANIES . . . . . . . . . . . . . . . . . . . . . . . . . . . . . . . . . . . . . . . . 8

2    EMPLOYEE CLAIMS SUBMITTED OVER A TEN-YEAR PERIOD BY THREE COMPANIES OF EQUAL SIZE . . . . . . . . . . . . . . . . . . . . . . . . . 14

3    ESTIMATED COST (WITHOUT HEALTH INSURANCE) OF HEALTH CARE PER EMPLOYEE OVER A TEN-YEAR PERIOD . . . . . . . . 17

4    A COST COMPARISON OF GROUP INSURANCE VS. INDIVIDUAL HEALTH POLICIES . . . . . . . . . . . . . . . . . . . . . . . . . . . . . . 25

**b.** A list of illustrations may be used for a report or manuscript that contains figures or a combination of tables and figures. For one that contains only figures, use the same format described in the previous section for a list of tables. Change the title to *LIST OF ILLUSTRATIONS* and the word *Table* to *Figure*. Use the following guidelines to format a list of illustrations that contains both tables and figures:

(1) Center the heading *LIST OF ILLUSTRATIONS* in all capital letters 2 inches from the top edge of the page.

(2) Triple-space after the *LIST OF ILLUSTRATIONS* heading, and center the subheading *A. Tables* in capital and lowercase letters. Double-space after the subheading. Place *Table* at the left margin, and align the last letter of *Page* with the right margin. Double-space before beginning the listing.

(3) Indent 0.25 inch from the left margin. Key the number of each table followed by spacing of 0.25 inch and the table title in all capital letters. Single-space each title; double-space between titles. Use leaders (a line of alternating periods and spaces) to assist the reader in

355

locating the page number. To obtain leaders in your word processing program, set a right decimal with dot leaders adjacent to the right margin. Triple-space after the last title.

(4) Center the subheading *B. Figures* in capital and lowercase letters. Double-space after the subheading; place *Figure* at the left margin and align the last letter of *Page* with the right margin. Double-space before beginning the listing.

(5) Indent 0.25 inch from the left margin. Key the number of each figure followed by spacing of 0.25 inch and the figure title in all capital letters. Use leaders to assist the reader in locating the page number. Single-space each title; double-space between titles.

(6) Number the list of illustrations with lowercase Roman numerals centered at the bottom of the page. Place the page number 1 inch or 0.5 inch from the bottom edge of the page, depending upon the page-numbering format selected for the document. See Section 11-1c for further information on the page-numbering formats.

LIST OF ILLUSTRATIONS
←— 2 blank lines

A. Tables
←— 1 blank line

Table                    Page
←— 1 blank line

1   A COMPARISON OF THE ANNUAL COST PER EMPLOYEE OF HEALTH INSURANCE POLICIES SUBMITTED BY EIGHT COMPANIES . . . . . . . . . . . . . . . . . . . . . . . . . . . . . . . . . . . . . . . . . 8
←— 1 blank line

2   EMPLOYEE CLAIMS SUBMITTED OVER A TEN-YEAR PERIOD BY THREE COMPANIES OF EQUAL SIZE . . . . . . . . . . . . . . . . . . . . . . . . . 14

3   ESTIMATED COST (WITHOUT HEALTH INSURANCE) OF HEALTH CARE PER EMPLOYEE OVER A TEN-YEAR PERIOD. . . . . . . . . 17

4   A COST COMPARISON OF GROUP INSURANCE VS. INDIVIDUAL HEALTH POLICIES . . . . . . . . . . . . . . . . . . . . . . . . . . . . . . . . 25
←— 2 blank lines

B. Figures
←— 1 blank line

Figure                 Page
←— 1 blank line

1   PER CAPITA DOLLAR INCREASE IN MEDICAL CARE FOR WORKING-AGE POPULATION, 1989–1998 . . . . . . . . . . . . . . . . . . . . . . . . . . . 5
←— 1 blank line

2   PER CAPITA DOLLAR INCREASE OF GROUP MEDICAL INSURANCE COVERAGE FOR WORKING-AGE POPULATION, 1989–1998 . . . . . . . . . . . . . . . . . . . . . . . . . . . . . . . . . . . . . . . . . . . . . . . . 6

3   COMPARISON OF ASSETS OF EIGHT MAJOR HEALTH INSURANCE CARRIERS (IN MILLIONS OF DOLLARS) . . . . . . . . . . . . . . 28

## 11–7.   Preparing the Body of the Report or Manuscript

**a.**   Allow a 2-inch top margin on pages that begin the body of the report or manuscript or major sections of the body. Center the heading in all capital letters; double-space multiple-line main headings. Triple-space after the main heading if it is not followed by a secondary heading.

**b.** Secondary headings are often used to explain or elaborate on a main heading. These headings begin a double space below the main heading and appear in capital and lowercase letters. All lines are centered, and multiple lines are double spaced. Triple-space after the secondary heading.

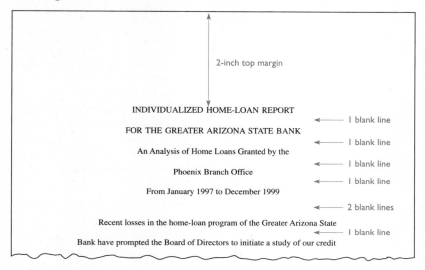

**c.** Double-space the body of the report or manuscript. Each paragraph should be indented 0.5 inch to offset it clearly from the previous one.

Use the widow/orphan feature of your word processing program to adjust page endings so that single lines from a paragraph are not at the top or bottom of a page. (These single lines are often called *widow and orphan lines*.) If page and paragraph endings do not coincide, be sure to place at least two lines of a new paragraph at the end of a page and carry over at least two lines from the previous paragraph to a new page (one complete line and a minimum of one word on a second line). Example pages from the body of a report appear on pages 358 and 359.

**d.** Use the following guidelines to number the pages of the report or manuscript:

(1) For pages with main headings, either omit the page number or center it at the bottom of the page. Place the page number either 1 inch or 0.5 inch from the bottom edge of the page, depending upon the page-numbering system selected. See Section 11-1b for further explanation and illustrations.

(2) For pages without main headings, place the page number either 1 inch or 0.5 inch from the top edge of the page, depending upon the page-numbering system selected. See Section 11-1d for further explanation and illustrations.

## body of report

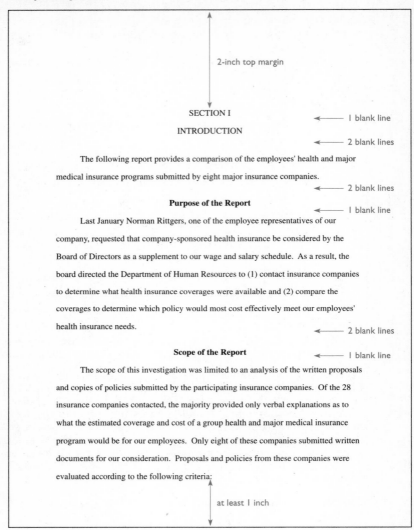

2-inch top margin

SECTION I                                    ◄——— 1 blank line

INTRODUCTION                                 ◄——— 2 blank lines

     The following report provides a comparison of the employees' health and major

medical insurance programs submitted by eight major insurance companies.

                                                  ◄——— 2 blank lines

**Purpose of the Report**

                             ◄——— 1 blank line

     Last January Norman Rittgers, one of the employee representatives of our

company, requested that company-sponsored health insurance be considered by the

Board of Directors as a supplement to our wage and salary schedule.  As a result, the

board directed the Department of Human Resources to (1) contact insurance companies

to determine what health insurance coverages were available and (2) compare the

coverages to determine which policy would most cost effectively meet our employees'

health insurance needs.

                             ◄——— 2 blank lines

**Scope of the Report**                      ◄——— 1 blank line

     The scope of this investigation was limited to an analysis of the written proposals

and copies of policies submitted by the participating insurance companies.  Of the 28

insurance companies contacted, the majority provided only verbal explanations as to

what the estimated coverage and cost of a group health and major medical insurance

program would be for our employees.  Only eight of these companies submitted written

documents for our consideration.  Proposals and policies from these companies were

evaluated according to the following criteria:

at least 1 inch

**body of report (*continued*)**

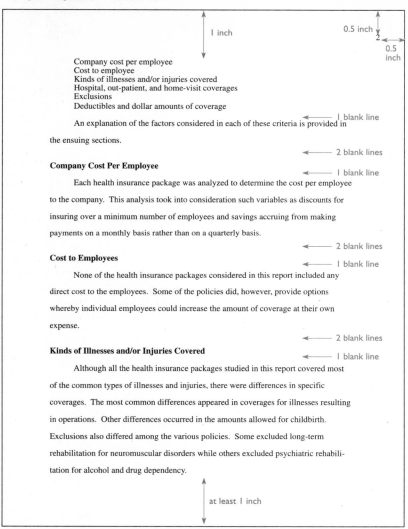

Company cost per employee
Cost to employee
Kinds of illnesses and/or injuries covered
Hospital, out-patient, and home-visit coverages
Exclusions
Deductibles and dollar amounts of coverage

An explanation of the factors considered in each of these criteria is provided in

the ensuing sections.

**Company Cost Per Employee**

Each health insurance package was analyzed to determine the cost per employee

to the company.  This analysis took into consideration such variables as discounts for

insuring over a minimum number of employees and savings accruing from making

payments on a monthly basis rather than on a quarterly basis.

**Cost to Employees**

None of the health insurance packages considered in this report included any

direct cost to the employees.  Some of the policies did, however, provide options

whereby individual employees could increase the amount of coverage at their own

expense.

**Kinds of Illnesses and/or Injuries Covered**

Although all the health insurance packages studied in this report covered most

of the common types of illnesses and injuries, there were differences in specific

coverages.  The most common differences appeared in coverages for illnesses resulting

in operations.  Other differences occurred in the amounts allowed for childbirth.

Exclusions also differed among the various policies.  Some excluded long-term

rehabilitation for neuromuscular disorders while others excluded psychiatric rehabili-

tation for alcohol and drug dependency.

*Annotations in the illustration:* 1 inch · 0.5 inch · 2 · 0.5 inch · 1 blank line · 2 blank lines · 1 blank line · 2 blank lines · 1 blank line · 2 blank lines · 1 blank line · at least 1 inch · Reports · 11 · Ibid.

## 11–8.　Text Headings

a.　**Text headings of different degrees signal content in a report or manuscript and contribute to its readability. A common classification of text headings includes first-, second-, and third-degree headings. Text headings are usually boldfaced, but they may have a larger font size with or without bolding. Guidelines for formatting each text heading follow and are repeated in the context of its corresponding illustration.**

(1) **First-degree text headings**. Center a first-degree heading, and capitalize the first letter of each main word. The heading may be boldfaced and/or typed in a larger font size than the report or manuscript text. Triple-space before a first-degree heading, and double-space after it.

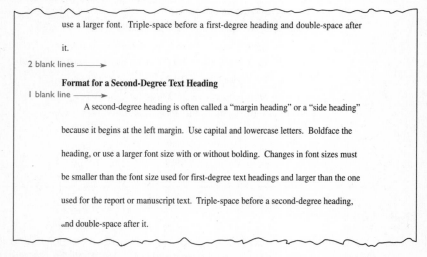

that main headings and secondary headings introduce the report or a main section of the

report.

2 blank lines ———➤

**Format for a First-Degree Text Heading**

I blank line ———➤

   A first-degree text heading, also referred to as a "centered heading," is centered

and typed in capital and lowercase letters.  The heading may be boldfaced and/or typed

in a larger font size.  Triple-space before a first-degree heading and double-space after it.

(2) **Second-degree text headings**. Begin the second-degree heading at the left margin. Capitalize the first letter of each main word. Boldface the heading, or use a larger font size with or without bolding. Changes in font sizes must be smaller than the one used for first-degree headings and larger than the one used for the report or manuscript text. Triple-space before a second-degree heading, and double-space after it.

use a larger font.  Triple-space before a first-degree heading and double-space after

it.

2 blank lines ———➤

**Format for a Second-Degree Text Heading**

I blank line ———➤

   A second-degree heading is often called a "margin heading" or a "side heading"

because it begins at the left margin.  Use capital and lowercase letters.  Boldface the

heading, or use a larger font size with or without bolding.  Changes in font sizes must

be smaller than the font size used for first-degree text headings and larger than the one

used for the report or manuscript text.  Triple-space before a second-degree heading,

and double-space after it.

(3) **Third-degree text headings**. The third-degree heading begins a paragraph, so it is indented from the left margin the same amount of space as any other paragraph—usually 0.5 inch. Capitalize only the first word and any proper nouns. Boldface the heading and conclude it with a period. Use the same font size as the report or manuscript text. Double-space before a third-degree heading, and begin

Ibid.

typing the paragraph text two spaces after the period concluding the heading.

> used for the report or manuscript text.  Triple-space before a second-degree text heading
>
> and double-space after it.
>
> I blank line ⟶
>
>     **Format for a third-degree text heading.**  Because the third-degree heading is
>
> part of the paragraph that follows, it is also referred to as a "paragraph heading."  Only
>
> the first word and proper nouns in the heading are capitalized.
>
>     The third-degree heading is boldfaced (in the same typeface and size as the
>
> report or manuscript text) and followed by a period.  Double-space before a third-
>
> degree heading, and begin typing the paragraph on the same line directly after the
>
> heading.

**b.** Text headings indicate divisions of a topic or subtopic; therefore, if a first-, second-, or third-degree heading is used, it must be followed by at least one or more matching headings. For example, if you use one first-degree heading in the report or manuscript, you must use at least one other first-degree heading in the same document.

**c.** All text headings should be separated by at least two lines of text, regardless of their place in the heading hierarchy. In other words, a lesser-degree text heading may not follow another heading without any intervening text.

**d.** Text headings must be used in ascending order of degree from first degree to third degree, *but* the first-degree heading may be omitted if only one or two levels of headings are required in a report. The following table illustrates what heading levels may be used based upon the number of levels or divisions required:

| Number of Text Headings Required | Levels of Text Headings to Be Used |
|---|---|
| 3 | First-degree heading, Second-degree heading, and Third-degree heading |
| 2 | First-degree heading and Second-degree heading *or* Second-degree heading and Third-degree heading |
| 1 | First-degree heading *or* Second-degree heading |

## 11–9.  Listings

**a.**  Both vertical and horizontal listings are often used in letters, memorandums, reports, and manuscripts. Whether to use a horizontal listing or a vertical listing depends upon (1) the number of items in the listing, (2) the number of words contained in each item, and (3) the degree of emphasis the writer wishes to assign to the listing.

Vertical listings are more emphatic than horizontal listings. They may be numbered, unnumbered, or bulleted. Lengthy and complex listings are more readily understood in the vertical format.

Horizontal listings are less emphatic. They are generally used with short listings that are few in number. Each item in a horizontal listing is preceded by an Arabic number or a lowercase letter enclosed in parentheses.

**b.**  *Numbered vertical listings* are numbered in consecutive order with Arabic numerals. In all business letters, memorandums, reports, and manuscripts, use the following guidelines for listing numbered items vertically:

(1)  Introduce a vertical listing with a complete sentence.

(2)  Indent the listing 0.5 inch from both the left and right margins. In business letters and memorandums, vertical listings *may* assume the left and right margins of the main text.

(3)  Number each item; use the left indent feature of your word processing program to align the text after the period in the number. (Any second and succeeding lines should begin directly under the first word, not the number, of the item.) Single-space items that are more than one line.

(4)  Use parallel construction; that is, use all complete sentences, all the same kind of phrases, or all single words that begin with the same part of speech and have the same form. Place a period after each item *only* in listings containing complete sentences.

(5)  Capitalize the first word in each listed item.

(6)  Double-space before the first item, between items, and after the last item in the listing.

### numbered vertical listing—complete sentences

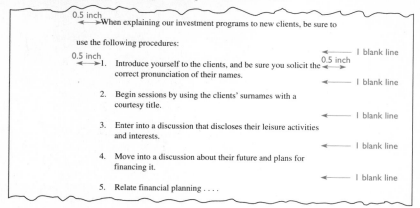

c. *Unnumbered vertical listings* are similar in most respects to numbered vertical listings. Use the following guidelines for listing unnumbered items vertically:

(1) Introduce a vertical listing with a complete sentence.

(2) Indent the listing 0.5 inch from both the left and right margins.

(3) Use parallel construction; that is, use all complete sentences, all the same kind of phrases, or all single words that begin with the same part of speech and have the same form. Place a period after each item *only* in listings containing complete sentences.

(4) Capitalize the first word in each listed item.

(5) Double-space before the first item, between items, and after the last item in the listing. Single-space items that are more than one line.

Unnumbered vertical listings consisting of words or phrases that are typed on single lines *may be* single-spaced, although a double space still appears before and after the listing. Such a listing is shown on page 364 and in the report page illustrated on page 359.

### unnumbered vertical listing—words or phrases

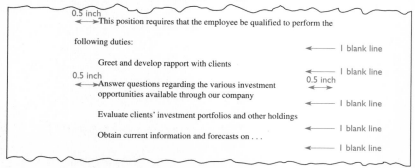

### unnumbered vertical listing—words or phrases single-spaced

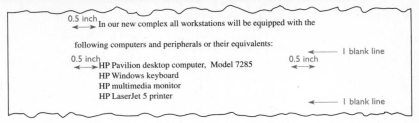

d. *Bulleted listings* are similar to numbered listings. Typographic symbols (small circles, hollowed circles, squares, hollowed squares, check marks, etc.) replace the number. These symbols may be accessed through the extended character set feature of a word processing program. In all business letters, memorandums, reports, and manuscripts, use the following guidelines for listing bulleted items vertically:

(1) Introduce a vertical listing with a complete sentence.

(2) Indent the listing 0.5 inch from both the left and right margins. In business letters and memorandums, vertical listings *may* assume the left and right margins of the main text.

(3) Insert the typographical symbol; use the left indent feature of your word processing program to align the text after the typographical symbol. (Any second and succeeding lines should begin directly under the first word, not the symbol, of the item.) Single-space items that are more than one line.

(4) Use parallel construction; that is, use all complete sentences, all the same kind of phrases, or all single words that begin with the same part of speech and have the same form. Place a period after each item *only* in listings containing complete sentences.

(5) Capitalize the first word in each listed item.

(6) Double-space before the first item, between items, and after the last item in the listing.

### bulleted vertical listing—complete sentences

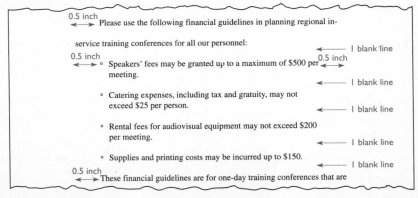

**e.** Horizontal listings may be part of a sentence, or they may be introduced by a complete thought followed by a colon. Whenever a horizontal listing contains three or more items, the items are separated by commas or semicolons. Use commas to separate words or phrases; use semicolons to separate complete thoughts or items that contain internal commas. The following guidelines are used for listing items horizontally:

(1) Use a colon to introduce the list *only when it is preceded by a complete thought.*

(2) Capitalize the first word of each item only if it is a proper noun.

(3) Identify the listed items by enclosing either lowercase letters or numbers in parentheses before each item. Do not conclude a line with only a letter or number enclosed in parentheses; at least one word of the item must appear after the letter or numeral.

**horizontal listing—items separated by commas**

as requested. Each team will consist of (a) an administrator, (b) a scientist, (c) two engineers, (d) an administrative assistant, and (e) a secretary. The team will function under the supervision of our project coordinator, who will

**horizontal listing—items separated by semicolons**

on Tuesday, June 10. While I am in New York, would you please take care of the following items: (1) complete the negotiations with AAA Computer System Services for an additional one-year contract; (2) respond to and follow through on the inquiry from Medco Financial Services regarding our medical software line; and (3) contact reviewers to test and evaluate our newly developed line of software for dental offices. If you are unable to

## 11–10. Methods of Citing Sources

When either direct quotations or other information needs to be cited in a report or manuscript, any one of a number of methods may be used. The most common ones include footnotes, bibliographical notes, endnotes, the MLA (Modern Language Association) style of notation, and the APA (American Psychological Association) style of notation.

The MLA style of notation is generally used in literary writings while the APA style of notation is predominantly used by writers in the social sciences. Business writers, on the other hand, usually employ a conventional footnote or endnote style because it is easier to associate the cited information with its source and authenticate its contents. Therefore, the following styles shown for footnotes and endnotes are recommended for use in business reports.[3]

a.  Use the *footnote* feature of your word processing program to ensure that notations and corresponding documentation appear consistently on the same page. Guidelines for preparing footnotes are listed below:

(1)  Indicate the presence of a footnote by typing a superior (slightly raised) figure after the material to be documented. Place the footnote itself at the bottom of the page on which the reference notation appears. By accessing the footnote feature of a word processing program, these procedures will be performed automatically.

(2)  Set off the footnotes from the rest of the page with a 1.5-inch or 2-inch line at the left margin, at least a single space after the last line of text on the page. Double-space after this line. By accessing the footnote feature of a word processing program, these procedures will be performed automatically.

(3)  Indent 0.5 inch, and number each footnote consecutively with a superior (slightly raised) figure at the beginning of the footnote. By accessing the footnote feature of a word processing program, these procedures will be performed automatically.

(4)  Single-space each footnote, but double-space between footnotes.

(5)  Type the name of the author, if any, in a first-name, last-name sequence.

(6)  Provide the complete title of the cited reference. Place the titles of magazine articles, sections of books, newspaper columns, and other such section or segment titles in quotation marks. Italicize (or underline) the titles of books, pamphlets, magazines, newspapers, and other complete works with subdivisions.

(7)  Include next where applicable the publishing information. Enclose in parentheses the geographical location of the publisher followed by a colon, the name of the publisher, and the date of publication. Eliminate the state name from the geographical location when the city is commonly known; otherwise, use the standard state abbreviation with the city name.

(8)  Follow the complete title of magazines and newspapers with the date of publication.

---

[3]The formats suggested here for footnotes and endnotes for published and unpublished works (except for noted deviations) are based on the traditional format alternatives contained in the following sources:

*The Chicago Manual of Style*, 14th ed. (Chicago and London: The University of Chicago Press, 1993), 487–635.

Kate L. Turabian, *A Manual for Writers of Term Papers, Theses, and Dissertations*, 5th ed., revised and expanded by Bonnie Birtwistle Honigsblum (Chicago and London: The University of Chicago Press, 1987), 120–164.

*The AMA Style Guide for Business Writing* (New York: American Management Association, 1996), 44, 81–84.

(9) Conclude footnotes with the page location of the cited material.

(10) Separate the parts of a footnote with commas.

**Formats for citing online Internet sources (FTP [File Transfer Protocol] sites, World Wide Web [WWW] sites, Telnet sites, GOPHER sites, synchronous communications, listserv messages, newsgroup [USENET] messages, E-mail messages, and linkage data) are emerging.[4] Use the following guidelines for citing World Wide Web sites:**

(1) Use the footnote feature of your word processing program to achieve the formats used for other types of sources.

(2) Begin with the author's full name, if known. Continue with the full title of the document in quotation marks, the title of the complete work (if applicable) in italics, and the date of publication or last revision (if available; otherwise, use *n.d*). Separate each item with a comma.

(3) Enclose within angle brackets (< >) the full http address (URL).

(4) Enclose in parentheses the date (day, month, year) the site was visited.

(5) Conclude the citation with a period.

### book, one author

[1]Susan A. McAllister, *An Introduction to Microcomputers: Basic Concepts*, 3rd ed. (Cincinnati: South-Western Publishing Company, 1998), 87–91.

### book, two authors

[2]E. Bryant Phillips and Andrea Kessler, *Principles of Management*, 2nd ed. (New York: John Wiley & Sons, Inc., 1997), 108.

### book, more than two authors

[3]Patricia Whitman, David Kane, James E. Wellington, and Ida Mason, *Fundamentals of Finance and Banking* (New York: McGraw-Hill, Inc., 1997), 208–214.

### book, editor(s) only

[4]John M. Sakasian and Carol L. Jones, eds., *Readings in Management Theory* (Belmont, Calif.: Wadsworth Publishing Company, 1997), 307–309.

### CD-ROM

[5]"Securities and Exchange Commission," *Microsoft Bookshelf '96*, CD-ROM (Microsoft Corporation, 1996).

---

[4]For a simple, comprehensive guide to citing on-line Internet sources, consult "Citing the Sites: MLA-Style Guidelines and Models for Documenting Internet Sources," Version 1.3, 23 October 1996 <http://falcon.eku.edu/honors/beyond-mla/#citing_sites> (3 November 1996). Guidelines presented here are based on Andrew Harnack and Eugene Kleppinger, *Online! A Reference Guide to Using Internet Sources* (New York: St. Martin's Press, 1997).

## company memorandum

[6]Meredith Garcia, "Medical Insurance Programs Available to Employees" (Boston:  Interstop Corporation memorandum, 8 June 1997).

## company report—published

[7]Shel Holtz, "A Partnership in Japan," *Insights* (Irvine, Calif.:  Allergan, Inc., published report, May 1998), 2.

## company report—unpublished (internal)

[8]Terry Thomsen, *An Analysis of Current Manufacturing Facilities* (Detroit: General Motors, Chevrolet Division, unpublished report, March 1998),  32–37.

## correspondence

[9]George Bush (as vice president of the United States), response letter to author, 17 October 1986.

## encyclopedia article—signed

[10]Robert D. Patton, "Management," *The World Book Encyclopedia* (Chicago:  Field Enterprises Educational Corporation, 1994), 13:97.

## encyclopedia article—unsigned

[11]"Adams, John," *The Encyclopaedia Britannica*, 17th ed. (Chicago: Encyclopaedia Britannica, Inc., 1997), 1:83–84.

## film, videocassette, or audiocassette

[12]*Barriers to Effective Global Communication*, videocassette (Chicago:  Visual Education Corporation, 1997).

## government publication

[13]*Statistical Abstract of the United States*, U.S. Bureau of the Census (Washington, D.C.:  U.S. Government Printing Office, 1990), 256.

## Internet, World Wide Web  (WWW)

[14]Janice R. Walker, "Style Sheet," *MLA-Style Citations of Electronic Sources*, Version 1.0, April 1995, <http://www.cas.usf.edu/english/walker/mla.html> (12 November 1996).

## interview

[15]James Montgomery (CEO, Great Western Federal Bank), interview by author, Woodland Hills, Calif., 24 July 1997.

### magazine article with author

[16]A. T. Stadthaus, "The Common Market With a Reunified Germany," *Business Week*, 20 August 1992, 32–33, 57.

### magazine article without author

[17]"The Declining Dollar in Our International Economy," *Changing Times*, December 1997, 40–42.

### newspaper article with author

[18]Richard A. Donnelly, "Commodities Corner," *Los Angeles Times*, 10 November 1997, San Fernando Valley edition, sec. D, p. 6, cols. 3–4.

### paperback book

[19]Mark T. Mathews, *Managerial Psychology in a Global Economy* (Chicago: The University of Chicago Press, 1997), 105.

### professional journal article (with volume number)

[20]Mary Vielhaber Hermon, "Building a Shared Understanding and Commitment to Managing Diversity," *The Journal of Business Communication* 33 (October 1996): 427–442.

### radio or television broadcast

[21]"Work Camps in China," *60 Minutes* (Los Angeles: Repeat KCBS telecast, 26 July 1996).

### secondary source citation

[22]Stuart Williams and Peter Conway, *Internationally Known* (New York: Penguin Books USA Inc., 1990), 79, as cited in Michael Doran, *Succeeding in the Global Marketplace* (New York: Random House, Inc., 1992), 109.

### table, source in

[23]Lennie Copeland and Lewis Griggs, table "U.S. Merchandise Trade by Area," *Going International* (New York: Plume of Penguin Books USA Inc., 1988), xviii.

### unpublished book or booklet

[24]John Wooden, *John Wooden Basketball Fundamentals Camp, Player's Notebook* (Unpublished and undated booklet), 9.

### unpublished book or booklet without author, section

[25]"History of Bruin Basketball," *The UCLA Alumni Association, Occasional Paper #9* (Unpublished booklet, 1975), 2.

Once a reference has been cited, a shortened form *may be* used when the same reference is shown again. These shortened forms—*Ibid.*, *loc. cit.*, and *op. cit.*—are explained and illustrated in the following discussion.

*Ibid.* is used when the reference cited is identical to the one in the preceding footnote. If the reference source is the same but the page numbers differ, use *Ibid.* with appended page numbers.

### Ibid.—identical reference

³Patricia Whitman, David Kane, James E. Wellington, and Ida Mason, *Fundamentals of Finance and Banking* (New York: McGraw-Hill, Inc., 1997), 208–214.

⁴Ibid.

### Ibid.—same reference but different page number(s)

⁵Mark T. Mathews, *Managerial Psychology in a Global Economy* (Chicago: The University of Chicago Press, 1997), 105.

⁶Ibid., 134.

The notation *loc. cit.* means "in the place cited." It is used when the reference and the same page numbers have been previously cited but intervening citations have occurred. Begin the citation with the last name of the author. For two authors separate the last names with *and*; for more than two authors, just add *et al.* after the last name of the first author. Conclude the citation with *loc. cit.*[5]

³Patricia Whitman, David Kane, James E. Wellington, and Ida Mason, *Fundamentals of Finance and Banking* (New York: McGraw-Hill, Inc., 1997), 208–214.

⁴Ibid.

⁵Mark T. Mathews, *Managerial Psychology in a Global Economy* (Chicago: The University of Chicago Press, 1997), 105.

⁶Ibid., 134.

⁷Whitman et al., loc. cit.

The notation *op. cit.* (meaning "in the work cited") also refers to a previously cited reference, but different page numbers are being

---

[5] *The Chicago Manual of Style* recommends the use of the short-title form in place of the term *loc. cit.* (pp. 582–583).

referenced and intervening references have occurred.[6] Begin the citation with the last name of the author. For two authors separate the last names with *and*; for more than two authors, merely add *et al.* after the last name of the first author. Conclude the citation with *op. cit.* and the new page number(s).

[5]Mark T. Mathews, *Managerial Psychology in a Global Economy* (Chicago: The University of Chicago Press, 1997), 105.

[6]Ibid., 134.

[7]E. Bryant Phillips and Andrea Kessler, *Principles of Management*, 2nd ed. (New York: John Wiley & Sons, Inc., 1997), 108.

[8]Mathews, op. cit., 147.

**b.** *Bibliographical notes,* references to the bibliography, may be used as alternatives to formal footnotes. The reference to the bibliography is shown in parentheses at the end of the cited material by referring first to the number of the reference in the bibliography followed by a colon and the page number(s) of the source. The complete source appears in the bibliography following the body of the paper (see Section 11-12).

**bibliographical note**

. . . Income has risen 16 percent during the last fiscal period. To offset this

increased income, however, expenses have risen 21 percent over the same

period. (6:10–11)

**c.** Another alternative to footnotes or bibliographical notes is *endnotes.* Indicate the presence of an endnote by typing a superior (slightly raised) figure after the reference material to be documented. Endnotes are placed on a separate page at the end of the body of the report or at the end of each chapter in a long report. Use the endnotes feature of your word processing program and the following guidelines to prepare endnotes:

(1) Allow a 2-inch top margin. Center the heading *NOTES* or *END-NOTES* in all capital letters.

(2) Triple-space after the heading. Single-space each note, but double-space between notes.

(3) Number the notes consecutively using Arabic numerals followed by a 0.3-inch left indent.

[6]*The Chicago Manual of Style* recommends the use of the short-title form in place of the term *op. cit.* (pp. 582–583).

(4) Use the same content and sequence for endnotes as shown for footnotes in Section 11-10a. Use a footer to number the page at the bottom, or omit (but count) the page number—select whichever style was used for the beginning pages of other major sections in the body of the report.

(5) Use a 0.5- or 1-inch top margin for any second and succeeding pages, depending upon the page numbering format selected. Be sure to follow the same format used for the body of the report.

**endnotes page**

2 inches

NOTES

2 blank lines

1. Michael J. Hendrix, R. Louise Preston, and Ornorio Torti, *Effective Management Principles* (Eden Prairie, Minn.: Paradigm Publishing International, 1998), 118–122.

2. Maria L. Cueva and Richard C. Follett, *Employee Motivation in the International Workplace*, 2nd ed. (New York: McGraw-Hill, Inc., 1998), 206.

3. Ibid., 212.

4. Barbara S. Kawakami, *Union and Employee Relations*, 4th ed. (Englewood Cliffs, N.J.: Prentice Hall, Inc., 1997), 49–51.

5. E. Bryant Phillips and Andrea Kessler, *Principles of Management*, 2nd ed. (New York: John Wiley & Sons, Inc., 1997), 108.

6. Hendrix et al., op. cit., 139–141.

7. Mark T. Mathews, *Managerial Psychology in a Global Economy* (Chicago: The University of Chicago Press, 1997), 105.

8. Phillips and Kessler, loc. cit.

**d.** The *MLA (Modern Language Association) referencing style*,[7] used predominantly in literary works, is another method for citing sources. In this style a short description of the source and the pertinent page number(s) appear in parentheses after the information to be cited. The main purpose of the parenthetical reference is to point the reader to a specific work in the Works Cited, the MLA version of a bibliography.

Use the following guidelines to cite sources according to the MLA referencing style:

---

[7]For a complete discussion of the preparation of reports and manuscripts according to the MLA style, consult Joseph Gibaldi, *MLA Handbook for Writers of Research Papers*, 4th ed. (New York: The Modern Language Association of America, 1995).

(1) Begin with the last name of the author or authors. If the work has more than three authors, use only the first author's last name followed by *et al.* with no intervening punctuation, e.g., Greenburg et al.

(2) Begin the citation with the title of the work or a shortened version of the title, e.g., *Employment Trends in Manufacturing* or *Employment Trends,* if a work has no author listed.

(3) Follow the author or title reference with the relevant page number(s).

(4) Place the citation in parentheses directly after the referenced material. Examples of such references would be (Greenburg et al. 113) and (*Employment Trends in Manufacturing* 65–67).

(5) Include only the page number(s) in the citation if the author(s) or source is named in the context of the text.

(6) Provide a full description of all cited sources in the Works Cited.[8]

## MLA referencing style

> According to recent surveys, investment in personal computers continues to be a major investment item for United States corporations. Advances in technology have forced corporations to update continually with hopes of obtaining a competitive edge. (McAllister and Doyle 32). Between now and the year 2000, corporations will spend between $20 billion and $25 billion on personal computers and their peripherals (*U.S. News and International Report* 114).

## MLA page reference only

> According to McAllister and Doyle (32), investment in personal computers continues to be a major investment item for United States corporations. Advances in technology have forced corporations to update continually with hopes of obtaining a competitive edge. Between now and the year 2000, as reported in *U.S. News and International Report*, corporations will spend between $20 billion and $25 billion on personal computers and their peripherals (114).

---

[8]Refer to Section 11-12c of this manual for information on preparing the Works Cited, the MLA version of a bibliography.

**e.** Another method for citing sources is the *APA (American Psychological Association) style*,[9] which is used predominantly by writers in the social sciences.

To cite a specific part of a source or a direct quotation in this style, place in parentheses a short description of the source, the year of publication, and the pertinent page number(s) after the information to be cited. To cite a complete source, place in parentheses a short description and the year of publication. Each item is separated by a comma.

The main purpose of the parenthetical reference is to point the reader to a specific work in the reference list—the bibliography. Use the following guidelines to cite sources according to the APA referencing style:[10]

(1) Begin the citation with the last name of the author. If a source has two authors, cite both authors' last names each time the source is referenced. For sources with three to six authors, cite each author's last name in the first reference; additional references require only the first author's last name followed by *et al.*

(2) Join the names in a multiple-author citation with an ampersand (&) instead of the word *and* when they appear in parentheses or in the reference list, e.g., (Hendrix, Preston & Torti, 1997).

(3) Begin the citation with the first two or three words of the entry in the reference list—usually the title of the work—if a work has no author listed. Use quotation marks around titles of articles or chapters; underline the names of books or magazines. Capitalize the main words, e.g., (Employment Trends, 1997).

(4) Follow the author or title reference with the date of publication. For direct quotations or specific material, include any relevant page number(s) preceded by *p.* or *pp.* Additional examples of such references are (Hendrix et al., 1997) and ("Marketing Aspects," 1998, pp. 87–88).

(5) Include only the date of publication (and any applicable page numbers for direct quotations or specific material) in the citation if the author(s) or source is named in the context of the text. Omit the parenthetical reference for an entire work if both the source and date appear in the text.

(6) Provide a full description of cited sources in the reference list, the APA version of a bibliography.[11] However, personal letters, telephone calls, and other material that cannot be retrieved are not listed in *References*; they are cited only in the text, e.g., "Brenda Baity (E-mail message, November 5, 1997) confirmed that . . . ."

---

[9]For a complete discussion of the preparation of reports and manuscripts according to the APA style, consult *Publication Manual of the American Psychological Association,* 4th ed. (Washington, D.C.: American Psychological Association, 1994).

[10]For an on-line abstract of the APA referencing style, consult *A Guide for Writing Research Papers Based on American Psychological Association (APA) Documentation* (<http://155.43.225.30/apa.htm>, 3 November 1996).

[11]Refer to Section 11-12d of this manual for information on how to prepare a reference list, the APA version of a bibliography.

## APA referencing style

> According to recent surveys, investment in personal computers continues to be a major investment item for United States corporations. Advances in technology have forced most corporations to update continually with hopes of obtaining a competitive edge. (McAllister & Doyle, 1998). "Between now and the year 2000, corporations will spend between $20 billion and $25 billion on personal computers and their peripherals" (U.S. News, 1998, p. 114).

## APA year and page reference only

> According to McAllister and Doyle (1998), investment in personal computers continues to be a major investment item for United States corporations. Advances in technology have forced most corporations to update continually with hopes of obtaining a competitive edge. "Between now and the year 2000, as reported in *U.S. News and International Report*, corporations will spend between $20 billion and $25 billion on personal computers and their peripherals" (1998, p. 114).

**f.** Business writers may use a reference style that suits their purpose. In citing sources, though, use a style that meets the following criteria:

(1) The citation can be easily located from its point of reference within the report.

(2) The citation contains sufficient information so that the reader can readily locate the source and authenticate the information cited.

(3) All citations, regardless of media, are complete and expressed in a similar and consistent format.

## 11–11. Illustrations

Visuals in the form of tables, pie charts, bar charts (column charts), or line charts may be used to illustrate data in a report or manuscript. Where possible, a table or chart should appear on the same page as the narrative describing it. If there is insufficient space on the same page for the table or chart and its explanation, then the illustration should be placed on the following page. A statement such as "As shown in Table 3 on page 9, . . . ." must be used in the narrative to direct the reader to the illustration. The type of illustration used will vary according to the kind of data presented; guidelines for preparing each type of illustration follow.

a. *Tables* arrange data in an orderly fashion by employing a system of headings and columns to present information. Either open tables or ruled tables may be used in business documents.

Although the length, style, and number of columns will vary according to the type of data presented, use the following general procedures to set up tables:

(1) Use the Tables feature of your word processing program to create tables. For open tables eliminate the lines and condense the row height. For ruled tables select the line enhancements or one of the preformatted table formats provided by your word processing program.

(2) Leave two blank lines before and after a table if it does not appear on a separate page. (Some authorities prefer three blank lines before and after the table; be consistent in the use of whichever of the two formats you choose.)

(3) Number each table consecutively with Arabic numerals if more than one table appears in the report. Center *Table* and its corresponding number over the proposed position of the table. (If only one table appears in a report, begin the table with its title.)

(4) Double-space, and then center under the table number the title of the table; use all capital letters. If a subtitle is needed, center and use capital and lowercase letters. Place the subtitle a double-space below the main title. Triple-space after the final line of either the main title or the subtitle.

(5) Center the entire table between the left and right margins of the report or manuscript. Allow a sufficient amount of space for each column, keeping in mind that the column heading is part of the column.

(6) Use capital and lowercase letters for column headings. Bold and center each column heading.

(7) Center both horizontally and vertically a table appearing on a separate page.

## an open table

Table 1

I blank line ⟶

**A COMPARISON OF THE MONTHLY COST PER EMPLOYEE
OF HEALTH INSURANCE POLICIES
SUBMITTED BY EIGHT COMPANIES**

I blank line ⟶

March 3, 1999

2 blank lines ⟶

| Company | Plan A[1] | Plan B[2] | Plan C[3] |
|---------|---------|---------|---------|
| Chicago General | $375.00 | $492.50 | $545.00 |
| Concord | 325.00 | 450.00 | 520.00 |
| D & D Life | 385.50 | 485.50 | 585.50 |
| Edgewater | 312.50 | 443.50 | 513.50 |
| Lincoln | 415.00 | 500.00 | 635.00 |
| Morgan | 309.34 | 440.25 | 524.15 |
| New Jersey | 350.00 | 475.00 | 530.00 |
| Western | 405.60 | 585.00 | 620.30 |

I blank line ⟶ (Company row)

[1]$500,000 maximum coverage
[2]$1,000,000 maximum coverage
[3]$1,500,000 maximum coverage

## ruled table

Table 1

I blank line ⟶

**A COMPARISON OF THE MONTHLY COST PER EMPLOYEE
OF HEALTH INSURANCE POLICIES
SUBMITTED BY EIGHT COMPANIES**

I blank line ⟶

March 3, 1999

2 blank lines ⟶

| Company | Plan A[1] | Plan B[2] | Plan C[3] |
|---------|---------|---------|---------|
| Chicago General | $375.00 | $492.50 | $545.00 |
| Concord | 325.00 | 450.00 | 520.00 |
| D & D Life | 385.50 | 485.50 | 585.50 |
| Edgewater | 312.50 | 443.50 | 513.50 |
| Lincoln | 415.00 | 500.00 | 635.00 |
| Morgan | 309.34 | 440.25 | 524.15 |
| New Jersey | 350.00 | 475.00 | 530.00 |
| Western | 405.60 | 585.00 | 620.30 |

[1]$500,000 maximum coverage
[2]$1,000,000 maximum coverage
[3]$1,500,000 maximum coverage

Reports

11

Ibid.

**b.** *Pie charts* are used to illustrate the parts of a whole when that whole represents 100 percent of something. To achieve maximum clarity in this type of visual, do not exceed seven or eight segments in the illustration.

### simple pie chart

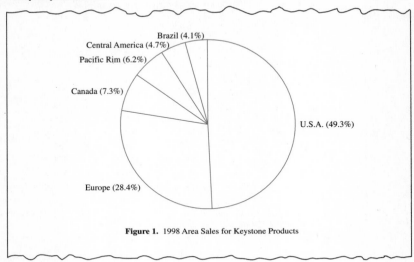

**Figure 1.** 1998 Area Sales for Keystone Products

### enhanced pie chart

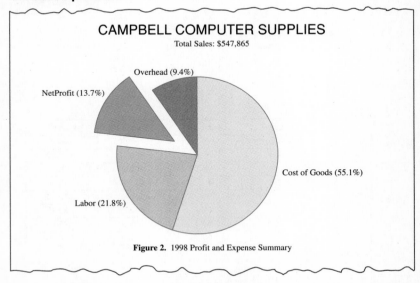

**Figure 2.** 1998 Profit and Expense Summary

If possible, use the graphics feature of your spreadsheet program to create and import charts into your word processing program. Follow these guidelines to create pie charts:

(1) Begin the illustration approximately three blank spaces below the last line of text.

(2) Slice the pie in appropriate wedges, showing the largest wedge first. Start at the 12 o'clock position of the circle and move clockwise. The remaining wedges may or may not be in descending order of size, but the size of each wedge should be proportional to the percentage of the whole it represents.

(3) Identify what each wedge represents and its corresponding percentage. If the wedges are too small, use a legend to identify what each wedge represents.

(4) Center numbers and titles of pie charts in capital and lowercase letters a triple space below the bottom of the chart. Some software, however, may not permit this format. In those cases where the program requires a different format, use the format dictated by the program. Leave three blank lines before resuming the narrative.

c. *Bar charts* are used to compare quantities within a class or over a time period. They may be oriented either horizontally or vertically. Bar charts require both a vertical axis and a horizontal axis. One axis represents the quantity and the other represents the varying items in the class or the time period over which the quantities are measured.

**horizontal 3-D bar chart comparing a single variable**

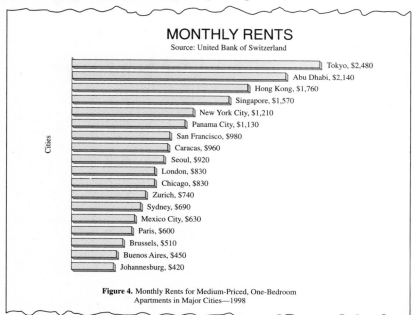

**MONTHLY RENTS**
Source: United Bank of Switzerland

Tokyo, $2,480
Abu Dhabi, $2,140
Hong Kong, $1,760
Singapore, $1,570
New York City, $1,210
Panama City, $1,130
San Francisco, $980
Caracas, $960
Seoul, $920
London, $830
Chicago, $830
Zurich, $740
Sydney, $690
Mexico City, $630
Paris, $600
Brussels, $510
Buenos Aires, $450
Johannesburg, $420

Cities

**Figure 4.** Monthly Rents for Medium-Priced, One-Bedroom Apartments in Major Cities—1998

**vertical bar chart comparing a single variable**

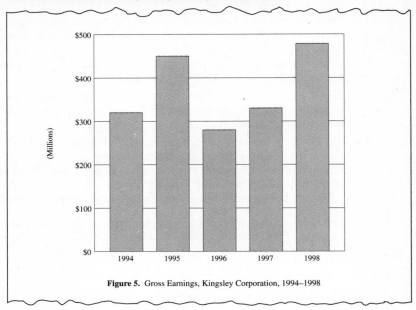

**Figure 5.** Gross Earnings, Kingsley Corporation, 1994–1998

**vertical bar chart comparing multiple variables**

**Figure 6.** May 1999 Product Sales Summary

Use your spreadsheet program and the following guidelines for constructing bar charts:

(1) Leave three blank lines before and after a bar chart when it interrupts the narrative.

(2) Use the horizontal axis in horizontal bar charts to represent the different quantities for each variable or time period; use the vertical axis to represent the variable or time period.

(3) Use the vertical axis in vertical bar charts (column charts) to represent the different quantities for each variable or time period; use the horizontal axis to represent the variables or time periods.

(4) Label clearly both the horizontal and vertical axes.

(5) Ensure that all bars are of uniform width. If the bars are not touching, they should be placed equidistantly in the chart.

(6) Center the figure numbers and titles of bar charts in capital and lowercase letters a triple space below the bottom of the chart. Some software, however, may not permit this format. In those cases where the program requires a different format, use the format dictated by the program.

d. *Line charts* are used to illustrate movement or trends over a time period. They may also be used to compare two or more sets of data over a time period.

**line chart plotting a single variable**

**Figure 9.** Average Hourly Pay, Factory Workers, 1993–1998

**line chart plotting multiple variables**

Use your spreadsheet program and the following guidelines to construct line charts that plot both single and multiple variables:

(1) Leave three blank lines before and after a line chart that interrupts text.

(2) Place a straight vertical line at the left of the line chart to portray the quantity scale. The bottom of the scale represents the lowest quantity, and the top of the scale represents the largest quantity.

(3) Place at a right angle to the bottom of the vertical line a horizontal line that extends to the right side of the line chart. This horizontal line represents the time periods encompassed by the chart.

(4) Mark each quantity and time period equidistantly on its respective scale.

(5) Plot quantities above their respective time periods. Connect the cross points with a line, mark the cross points with a symbol, or use both symbols and connecting lines. When two or more factors are plotted on the same graph, a different color, symbol, or line style must be used for each set of data.

(6) Center the figure numbers and titles of line charts a triple space below the last line contained in the chart. Capitalize all main words in the title. Some software, however, may not permit this format. In those cases where the program requires a different format, use the format dictated by the program.

## 11–12. Bibliography[12]

**a.** The bibliography follows immediately after the body of the report or manuscript and contains all sources cited in the text. Any source material that is not cited but that has contributed directly to the development of a report or manuscript should also be included.

**b.** List the items in the bibliography alphabetically by authors' last names or the first entry of the reference. Consecutively number each item in the bibliography if the bibliographical form of footnoting is used (Section 11-10b). Use the following guidelines to prepare a bibliography:

(1) Center the heading *BIBLIOGRAPHY* in all capital letters 2 inches from the top edge of the page.

(2) Triple-space between the heading and the first reference.

(3) Single-space each reference and double-space between references. If a reference requires more than one line, use the hanging indent feature of your word processing program to indent the second and succeeding lines 0.5 inch.

(4) Type a 0.5-inch underline in place of an author's name if he or she has more than one reference listed. Begin this procedure with the second reference for that author.

(5) Alphabetize the reference by title when the author is unknown.

(6) End the citations for magazines, journals, or other such source articles with page references.

(7) Enclose within angle brackets (< >) the full Universal Resource Locator (URL) for Internet sites.

**unsigned encyclopedia article**

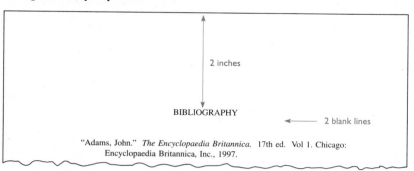

2 inches

BIBLIOGRAPHY ◄────── 2 blank lines

"Adams, John." *The Encyclopaedia Britannica.* 17th ed. Vol 1. Chicago: Encyclopaedia Britannica, Inc., 1997.

---

[12]The formats suggested here for bibliographical references (except for noted deviations) are based on the traditional format alternatives contained in the following sources:

*The Chicago Manual of Style*, 14th ed. (Chicago and London: The University of Chicago Press, 1993), 487–635.

Kate L. Turabian, *A Manual for Writers of Term Papers, Theses, and Dissertations*, 5th ed., revised and expanded by Bonnie Birtwistle Honigsblum (Chicago and London: The University of Chicago Press, 1987), 165–228.

*The AMA Style Guide for Business Writing* (New York: American Management Association, 1996), 41–44, 221.

### film, videocassette, or audiocassette

*Barriers to Effective Global Communication.* Videocassette. Chicago: Visual
    Education Corporation, 1997.

### business correspondence

Bush, George (as vice president of the United States). Response letter to author,
    17 October 1986.

### source in table

Copeland, Lennie, and Lewis Griggs. Table "U.S. Merchandise Trade by Area."
    *Going International.* New York: Plume of Penguin Books USA Inc., 1988,
    xviii.

### newspaper column with author

Doran, Lawrence J. "Computer File." *Los Angeles Times,* 19 November 1998.

### magazine article with author

Drew, Richard. "Multinational Corporations in the International Marketplace."
    *Business Week,* 17 August 1998, 19–20.

### magazine article without author

"Electronic Games Still the No. 1 Toy." *Consumer Reports,* March 1998, 47–51.

### company memorandum

Garcia, Meredith. "Medical Insurance Programs Available to Employees." Boston:
    Interstop Corporation memorandum, 8 June 1997.

### article in a professional journal with volume number

Hermon, Mary Vielhaber. "Building a Shared Understanding and Commitment to
    Managing Diversity." *The Journal of Business Communication* 33 (October
    1996): 427–442.

### section in unpublished book or booklet without author

"A History of Bruin Basketball." *The UCLA Alumni Association, Occasional Paper
    #9.* Unpublished booklet, 1975, 1–4.

### published company report

Holtz, Shel. "A Partnership in Japan." *Insights.* Irvine, Calif.: Allergan, Inc.,
    published report May 1998, 2–3.

### signed encyclopedia article

Karlen, Delmar. "Criminal Justice: 1. Criminal Justice in England and the U.S."
    *The Encyclopedia Americana.* International Edition. Vol. 8. Danbury, Conn.:
    Grolier Incorporated, 1997.

### paperback book

Larson, Harold G., and Charlene L. Morimoto. *Principles of Small Business
    Management.* 5th ed. Chicago: The University of Chicago Press, 1998.

### interview

Montgomery, James (CEO, Great Western Federal Bank). Interview by author,
    Woodland Hills, Calif., 24 July 1997.

### book, one author

Morrison, Alice T. *Microcomputers: Introductory Concepts and Applications.* 2nd ed. Cincinnati: South-Western Publishing Company, 1999.

### book, same author

_____. *Microcomputers: Business and Accounting Spreadsheet Applications.* Cincinnati: South-Western Publishing Company, 1998.

### book, two authors

Patterson, L. David, and Kathy Lim. *Principles of Real Estate.* 3rd ed. New York: John Wiley & Sons, Inc., 1998.

### book, three or more authors

Rodriguez, Rose P., Charles T. Bove, and Saad Najjar. *Fundamentals of Accounting.* 2nd ed. Pittsfield, Mass.: The Financial Press, 1997.

### book, editor(s) only

Sakasian, John M., and Carol L. Jones, eds. *Readings in Management Theory.* Belmont, Calif.: Wadsworth Publishing Company, 1997.

### CD-ROM

"Securities and Exchange Commission." *Microsoft Bookshelf '96.* CD-ROM. Microsoft Corporation, 1996.

### government publication

*Statistical Abstract of the United States.* U.S. Bureau of the Census. Washington, D.C.: U.S. Government Printing Office, 1990.

### internal unpublished company report

Thomsen, Terry. "An Analysis of Current Manufacturing Facilities." Detroit: General Motors, Chevrolet Division, unpublished report, March 1998.

### Internet, World Wide Web (WWW)

Walker, Janice R. "Style Sheet." *MLA-Style Citations of Electronic Sources.* Version 1.0. April 1995. <http://www.cas.usf.edu/english/walker/mla.html> (12 November 1996).

### secondary source citation

Williams, Stuart, and Peter Conway. *Internationally Known.* New York: Penguin Books USA Inc., 1990. As cited in Michael Doran, *Succeeding in the Global Marketplace.* New York: Random House, Inc., 1992.

### unpublished book or booklet

Wooden, John. *John Wooden Basketball Fundamentals Camp, Player's Notebook.* Unpublished and undated booklet.

### radio or television broadcast

"Work Camps in China." *60 Minutes.* Los Angeles: Repeat KCBS telecast, 26 July 1996.

**c.** Reports prepared according to the MLA (Modern Language Association) style title the bibliography *Works Cited.*[13] References are listed alphabetically as in any other bibliography. Guidelines for formatting the Works Cited follow:

(1) Place the title *Works Cited* 1 inch from the top edge of the page; number the page in the upper right corner, 0.5 inch from the top edge and aligned with the right margin.

(2) Double-space after the heading, and double-space within and between the entries. Begin each entry at the left margin, but use the hanging indent feature of your word processor to indent any subsequent lines 0.5 inch from the left margin.

**Works Cited—MLA bibliographical style**

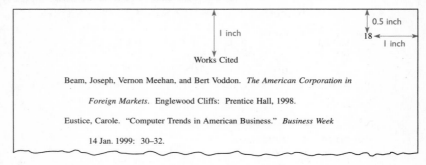

I inch

0.5 inch

18

I inch

Works Cited

Beam, Joseph, Vernon Meehan, and Bert Voddon. *The American Corporation in*

*Foreign Markets.* Englewood Cliffs: Prentice Hall, 1998.

Eustice, Carole. "Computer Trends in American Business." *Business Week*

14 Jan. 1999: 30–32.

**d.** Reports prepared according to the APA (American Psychological Association) style refer to the bibliography as a *reference list.*[14] References are listed alphabetically as in any other bibliography. Guidelines for formatting the reference list follow:

(1) Begin the reference list on a new page, and place the title *References* 1 inch from the top edge of the page (use 1-inch bottom, left, and right margins).

(2) Number all pages of the reference list in the upper right corner. Align numbers with the right margin between the top edge of the page and the first line of text. Place a shortened version of the report or manuscript title on the same line, separating the title and page number by approximately 0.5 inch.

(3) Double-space after the heading, and double-space within and between the entries.

---

[13]For a complete discussion of arrangements and formats for the Works Cited according to the MLA style, consult Joseph Gibaldi, *MLA Handbook for Writers of Research Papers,* 4th ed. (New York: The Modern Language Association of America, 1995).

For a simple, comprehensive guide to citing on-line Internet sources, consult "Citing the Sites: MLA-Style Guidelines and Models for Documenting Internet Sources," Version 1.3, 23 October 1996 <http://falcon.eku.edu/honors/beyond-mla/#citing_sites> (3 November 1996).

[14]For a complete discussion of arrangements and formats for the reference list according to the APA style, consult *Publication Manual of the American Psychological Association,* 4th ed. (Washington, D.C.: American Psychological Association, 1994).

(4) Indent the first line of each entry the same amount of space used for paragraphs within the body of the report or manuscript (usually 0.5 inch).

(5) Provide authors' last names and first initials in inverted order for book entries. Use an ampersand (&) instead of the word *and* to link multiple names. Follow the authors' names with the date of publication enclosed in parentheses.

(6) Capitalize only the first word and any proper nouns in the title or subtitle of a work. Underline the name of the work.

(7) Provide next the facts of publication, listing the city first. Give the two-letter U.S. Postal Service designation for little-known cities. The name of the location is followed by a colon and the name of the publisher.

(8) List the names of magazine article authors in the same format used for authors of books. Follow with the publication date enclosed in parentheses. Do not place quotation marks around magazine article titles, and capitalize only the first word or proper nouns. Capitalize all main words and underline the titles of periodicals; include the volume or issue number (if any). Conclude the reference with page numbers.

**reference list—APA bibliographical style**

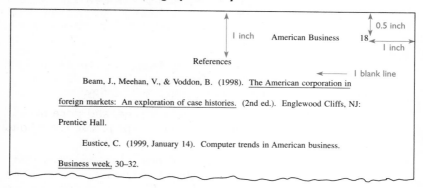

## 11–13. Appendix

**a.** The appendix follows the bibliography and contains supportive material. This material may include such items as letters, copies of questionnaires, maps, contracts, lists, tables, and other documents not shown elsewhere.

**b.** The appendix may be preceded by a page entitled *APPENDIX* or *APPENDIXES* (typed in all capital letters and centered both horizontally and vertically). The introductory page may also include a list of the items contained in the appendix. In this case (1) both the title and the listing are centered vertically or (2) the title is placed 2 inches from the top edge of the page with the listing beginning a triple space thereafter. The material should be numbered with alphabetic letters if more than one item appears in the appendix.

**introductory appendix page**

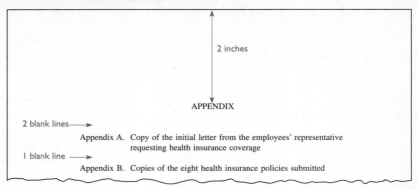

## 11–14. Word Processing Templates

Recent versions of word processing programs—WordPerfect and Microsoft Word, specifically—provide templates to simplify the process of preparing and formatting reports. These programs provide a variety of styles and formats.

WordPerfect has templates for creating a simple report and reports following the Chicago style manual, The Modern Language Association (MLA), and the American Psychological Association (APA) styles. Microsoft Word has three report templates—Contemporary, Elegant, and Professional.

**Contemporary report template—Microsoft Word**

# SECTION I
# INTRODUCTION

The following report provides a comparison of the employees' health and major medical insurance programs submitted by eight major insurance companies.

### Purpose of the Report

Last January Norman Rittgers, one of the employee representatives of our company, requested that company-sponsored health insurance be considered by the Board of Directors as a supplement to our wage and salary schedule. As a result, the board directed the Department of Human Resources to (1) contact insurance companies to determine what health insurance coverages were available and (2) compare the coverages to determine which policy would most cost effectively meet our employees' health insurance needs.

### Scope of the Report

The scope of this investigation was limited to an analysis of the written proposals and copies of policies submitted by the participating insurance companies. Of the 28 insurance companies contacted, the majority provided only verbal explanations as to what the estimated coverage and cost of a group health and major medical insurance program would be for our employees. Only eight of these companies submitted written documents for our consideration. Proposals and policies from these companies were evaluated according to the following criteria:

# Meeting Minutes

## 11–15. Purpose and Contents

Minutes are compiled to provide a written record of announcements, reports, significant discussions, and decisions that have taken place during a meeting. Although the degree of formality and extent of coverage may vary, the specific information contained in meeting minutes usually includes the following:

(1) Name of group and meeting

(2) Date, place, time meeting called to order, and time of adjournment

(3) Names of persons present (if applicable, names of persons absent)

(4) Disposition of any previous minutes

(5) Announcements

(6) Summaries of reports

(7) Motions presented and actions taken on motions

(8) Summaries of significant discussions

(9) Name and signature of person compiling minutes

## 11–16. Organization and Format of Formal Minutes

**a.** Use 8 1/2- by 11-inch white bond paper, and set 1.25-inch left and right margins. Count the first page in the pagination, but do not number it. Begin page numbering on the second page, and place the number 0.5 inch from the top and right edge of the page.

Center the name of the group and/or meeting in all capital letters 2 inches from the top edge of the page. Double-space down; then center in capital and lowercase letters the date and scheduled time of the meeting. The place where the meeting was held appears another double space below the time and date. This information, too, is centered in capital and lowercase letters. See page 392 for an illustration of the heading format for meeting minutes.

**b.** A listing of those persons attending the meeting follows the preliminary information. This listing is placed a triple space below the meeting place. Begin the listing with a phrase such as *Members Present:*, *Managers Present:*, or *Persons Present:*. Then list horizontally or vertically the names of the individuals present at the meeting in the order of their importance or in alphabetical order.

In addition to showing the members or persons in attendance, those regular members absent from a meeting may be noted. In this case a separate listing appears a double space below the listing of members present. It is usually preceded by *Members Absent:*, *Persons Absent:*, or another such designation. An example of a vertical attendance listing appears on page 392.

**c.** The initial paragraph of the meeting minutes appears a triple space below the attendance listing or listings. It generally begins with a

Ibid.

statement giving the exact time the meeting was called to order and by whom. This statement is usually followed by one giving the dispensation of any previous minutes.

d.  If there were any announcements, these are listed after the opening paragraph. Use a side heading to introduce the announcements, allowing two blank lines above the heading and one blank line below it. Then number and list each announcement made. If only one announcement occurred, show it in paragraph form without a number.

e.  Many meeting agendas are organized according to old business and new business. These two categories may be used for topic headings (use side headings) in presenting the motions and discussions that have taken place during short meetings. For lengthy meetings, however, readers can more easily locate information in the minutes if the topic headings describe concretely the subject matter discussed, reported, or voted upon.

f.  Reports presented at a meeting should be noted and in some cases summarized. The amount of information provided in the minutes will depend upon their purpose, formality, and use. Include with the reference to the report contents the name of the person giving the report as well as its disposition.

g.  The exact wording of motions must be given in the meeting minutes. Persons making and seconding the motions may be named in the motion statement. Include a brief summary of the discussion for each motion. Finally, indicate whether the motion was passed, defeated, or tabled. The number of yeses, noes, and abstentions for each motion should be recorded.

h.  If the meeting is not concluded with a motion for adjournment, the person preparing the minutes should indicate the time the meeting was adjourned and by whom. This information is placed in the concluding paragraph of the meeting minutes.

i.  The printed or typed signature of the person preparing the minutes usually appears on the fourth line below the concluding paragraph. It may be placed at the left margin or begun at the page center. The preparer's signature is placed directly above the printed signature line.

The complimentary closing *Respectfully submitted* may precede the signature line. In this case the entire signature block simulates the signature block of a business letter. Place *Respectfully submitted* a double space below the concluding paragraph, and leave three blank lines for the written signature before displaying the preparer's name. This style of signature block may also begin at the left margin or page center.

The major components of formal meeting minutes are illustrated in the following example on pages 392–393.

## formal meeting minutes

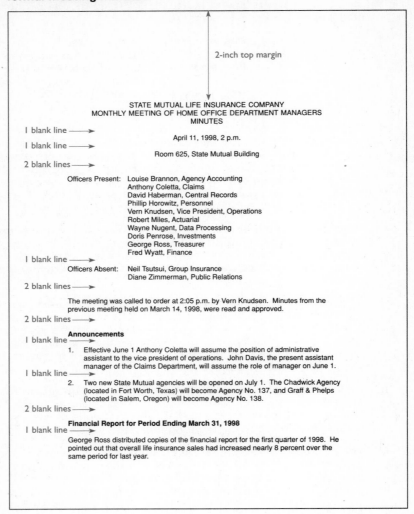

2-inch top margin

STATE MUTUAL LIFE INSURANCE COMPANY
MONTHLY MEETING OF HOME OFFICE DEPARTMENT MANAGERS
MINUTES

I blank line ⟶

April 11, 1998, 2 p.m.

I blank line ⟶

Room 625, State Mutual Building

2 blank lines ⟶

Officers Present:   Louise Brannon, Agency Accounting
Anthony Coletta, Claims
David Haberman, Central Records
Phillip Horowitz, Personnel
Vern Knudsen, Vice President, Operations
Robert Miles, Actuarial
Wayne Nugent, Data Processing
Doris Penrose, Investments
George Ross, Treasurer
Fred Wyatt, Finance

I blank line ⟶

Officers Absent:   Neil Tsutsui, Group Insurance
Diane Zimmerman, Public Relations

2 blank lines ⟶

The meeting was called to order at 2:05 p.m. by Vern Knudsen.  Minutes from the previous meeting held on March 14, 1998, were read and approved.

2 blank lines ⟶

**Announcements**

I blank line ⟶

1.   Effective June 1 Anthony Coletta will assume the position of administrative assistant to the vice president of operations.  John Davis, the present assistant manager of the Claims Department, will assume the role of manager on June 1.

I blank line ⟶

2.   Two new State Mutual agencies will be opened on July 1.  The Chadwick Agency (located in Fort Worth, Texas) will become Agency No. 137, and Graff & Phelps (located in Salem, Oregon) will become Agency No. 138.

2 blank lines ⟶

**Financial Report for Period Ending March 31, 1998**

I blank line ⟶

George Ross distributed copies of the financial report for the first quarter of 1998.  He pointed out that overall life insurance sales had increased nearly 8 percent over the same period for last year.

## formal meeting minutes (*continued*)

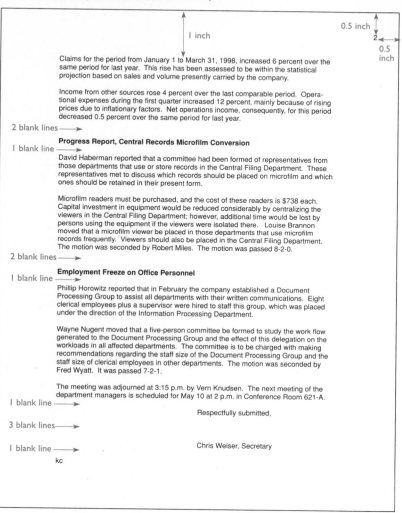

0.5 inch

1 inch

0.5 inch

Claims for the period from January 1 to March 31, 1998, increased 6 percent over the same period for last year. This rise has been assessed to be within the statistical projection based on sales and volume presently carried by the company.

Income from other sources rose 4 percent over the last comparable period. Operational expenses during the first quarter increased 12 percent, mainly because of rising prices due to inflationary factors. Net operations income, consequently, for this period decreased 0.5 percent over the same period for last year.

2 blank lines ──►

1 blank line ──►

**Progress Report, Central Records Microfilm Conversion**

David Haberman reported that a committee had been formed of representatives from those departments that use or store records in the Central Filing Department. These representatives met to discuss which records should be placed on microfilm and which ones should be retained in their present form.

Microfilm readers must be purchased, and the cost of these readers is $738 each. Capital investment in equipment would be reduced considerably by centralizing the viewers in the Central Filing Department; however, additional time would be lost by persons using the equipment if the viewers were isolated there. Louise Brannon moved that a microfilm viewer be placed in those departments that use microfilm records frequently. Viewers should also be placed in the Central Filing Department. The motion was seconded by Robert Miles. The motion was passed 8-2-0.

2 blank lines ──►

1 blank line ──►

**Employment Freeze on Office Personnel**

Phillip Horowitz reported that in February the company established a Document Processing Group to assist all departments with their written communications. Eight clerical employees plus a supervisor were hired to staff this group, which was placed under the direction of the Information Processing Department.

Wayne Nugent moved that a five-person committee be formed to study the work flow generated to the Document Processing Group and the effect of this delegation on the workloads in all affected departments. The committee is to be charged with making recommendations regarding the staff size of the Document Processing Group and the staff size of clerical employees in other departments. The motion was seconded by Fred Wyatt. It was passed 7-2-1.

The meeting was adjourned at 3:15 p.m. by Vern Knudsen. The next meeting of the department managers is scheduled for May 10 at 2 p.m. in Conference Room 621-A.

1 blank line ──►

Respectfully submitted,

3 blank lines ──►

1 blank line ──►

Chris Weiser, Secretary

kc

## 11–17. Organization and Format of Informal Minutes

**The organization and format of informal minutes may vary. The only requisite is that the minutes provide an adequate record of the information needed by the group or organization and that this information be presented in an easy-to-understand fashion. Use the tables feature of your word processing program to format easily informal minutes.**

## informal meeting minutes

COMPUTER APPLICATIONS ADVISORY COMMITTEE
PIERCE COMMUNITY COLLEGE
TUESDAY, APRIL 4, 1998, 2–4 P.M.
BUSINESS 3216

### MINUTES

| Activity/Discussion | Issues/Relative Information | Resolution |
|---|---|---|
| Survey of Classrooms and Laboratories | The faculty familiarized the committee with the equipment presently used for classroom instruction. | Information only. |
| Language Skills | The faculty described the five departmental courses that meet the requirements for its certificate programs. Two additional courses are required for students completing a degree program in business.<br><br>The committee emphasized the importance of language skills and how these skills relate to the productive use of a computer. | Information only. |
| Equipment Training: Hardware Issues | The committee discussed the pros and cons of purchasing IBM computers, IBM clones, Macintoshes, or a combination of vendors' models and equipment. | **MSP** to purchase IBM clones with 2 GB hard disks. |
| | | **MSP** to seek additional funding to acquire Macintosh computers. |
| | A discussion about printer usage in business indicated that laser printers and color printers are used predominantly. Although dot-matrix printers are appropriate for rough-draft copies, all final work is produced on laser printers. In addition, laser printers are required to produce output formatted with desktop publishing software. | **MSP** to acquire two laser printers and one color printer so that more sophisticated kinds of software can be taught; e.g., desktop publishing. |
| | The committee felt that students should understand the use of modems, facsimiles, and other telecommunicating equipment. | **MSP** that modems and a facsimile machine be purchased and incorporated into our instructional program. |
| Equipment Training: Software Issues | Telecommunications and the Internet have a paramount role in business and industry today. Students should be well trained in these areas. | **MSP** that a course in telecommunications and the Internet be implemented. |
| | A discussion was held concerning the philosophy of upgrading software versions in the business community. | Recommendation: Upgrade software as soon as possible. |
| | skills at all levels. | |
| Recommendations for Future Meetings | Survey technology, software, and business trends by circulating a questionnaire to all advisory committee members prior to the meeting date. | Information only. |

Submitted by: Barbara Jacobson, Professor
Computer Applications and Administrative Support Department

Format developed by and used with permission of K. Basil and Associates.

Ibid.

## 11–18. Meeting Agendas

**a.** Meeting agendas forecast the items to be considered at a scheduled meeting. Basic information that appears on an agenda includes the following:

(1) Name of committee, name of group, or purpose of meeting

(2) Date, time, and location of meeting

(3) Kind of document—*Meeting Agenda* or *Agenda*

(4) List of items to be considered, along with the names of any persons designated to present the item.

**agenda**

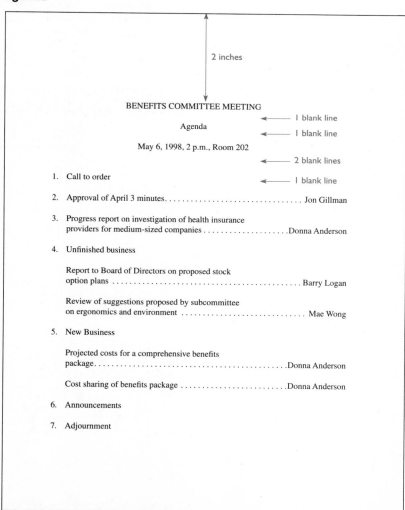

2 inches

BENEFITS COMMITTEE MEETING      ← I blank line

Agenda      ← I blank line

May 6, 1998, 2 p.m., Room 202

← 2 blank lines

1. Call to order      ← I blank line

2. Approval of April 3 minutes. . . . . . . . . . . . . . . . . . . . . . . . . . . . . Jon Gillman

3. Progress report on investigation of health insurance providers for medium-sized companies . . . . . . . . . . . . . . . . . .Donna Anderson

4. Unfinished business

   Report to Board of Directors on proposed stock option plans . . . . . . . . . . . . . . . . . . . . . . . . . . . . . . . . . . . . . . . . . Barry Logan

   Review of suggestions proposed by subcommittee on ergonomics and environment . . . . . . . . . . . . . . . . . . . . . . . . . . . Mae Wong

5. New Business

   Projected costs for a comprehensive benefits package. . . . . . . . . . . . . . . . . . . . . . . . . . . . . . . . . . . . . .Donna Anderson

   Cost sharing of benefits package . . . . . . . . . . . . . . . . . . . . . . .Donna Anderson

6. Announcements

7. Adjournment

**b.** **Use the agenda template of your word processing program or the following guidelines to create an agenda:**

(1) Use a 2-inch top margin and the default left and right margins of your word processing program.

(2) Center and place in all capital letters the name of the committee, the name of the group, or the purpose of the meeting. Double-space.

(3) Center and place in capital and lowercase letters *Meeting Agenda* or *Agenda*. Double-space.

(4) Center and place in capital and lowercase letters the date, time, and location of the meeting. Triple-space.

(5) Number with Arabic numerals the items to be considered at the meeting. Follow the topic with the name of the presenter, if any. Single-space the items and double-space between them.

**agenda prepared with a Microsoft Word template**

## Agenda — Weekly Sales Meeting

7/21/98
2:00 PM to 3:35 PM
Conference Room 2

| | |
|---|---|
| **Meeting called by:** | Bill Armstrong |
| **Type of meeting:** | Weekly Sales Meeting |
| Facilitator: | Bill Armstrong |
| **Note taker:** | Janice Morris |
| Timekeeper: | Jerry Phillips |
| **Attendees:** | Bill Armstrong |
| | Barbara Berkowitz |
| | Anita Gonzalez |
| | Daniel Ho |
| | Janice Morris |
| | Jerry Phillips |
| | Laura Sullivan |
| | Mark Turbian |
| **Please read:** | The attached article |
| **Please bring:** | Copy of national sales report |

### Agenda topics

| | | |
|---|---|---|
| 2:00-2:10 PM | Minutes from July 21 meeting | Janice Morris |
| 2:10-2:20 PM | Weekly sales summary and report | Bill Armstrong |
| 2:20-2:35 PM | New sales promotions | Anita Gonzalez |
| 2:35-2:45 PM | Discontinued products | Daniel Ho |
| 2:45-3:05 PM | Introduction of new products | Daniel Ho |
| 3:05-3:25 PM | Discussion of problem areas | Bill Armstrong |
| 3:25-3:35 PM | Adjournment | |

| | |
|---|---|
| **Observers:** | Andrea Schwartz, Intern, Cromwell University |
| **Resource persons:** | Robert Goldman, National Sales Manager |
| **Special notes:** | Note that our usual meeting place has been changed. |

Ibid.

## 11–19. Itineraries

**Itineraries plot out specifically events in a travel plan. Use the tables feature of your word processing program and the following guidelines to prepare an itinerary:**

(1) Begin the itinerary with a heading that describes the purpose of travel, the name of the person traveling, and the dates of travel.

(2) Use a table or column format with three columns. Set up *Date*, *Time*, and *Activity* as columnar headings.

(3) Specify all airline flights, hotel reservations, car rental reservations, business appointments, and meal reservations. Include addresses, telephone numbers, and confirmation numbers.

**itinerary**

| | MEETING WITH NationsBank REPRESENTATIVES<br>Itinerary for Kym Freeman<br>March 23–26, 1999 | |
|---|---|---|
| **Date** | **Time** | **Activity** |
| **Monday, March 23** | 7:13 a.m. | Depart Burbank airport, American Airlines Flight 1502, light breakfast, Seat 23D, check-in at gate required |
| | 12:13 p.m. | Arrive Dallas-Fort Worth airport |
| | 2:25 p.m. | Depart Dallas-Fort Worth airport, American Airlines Flight 1564, beverage service only, Seat 19D, check-in at gate required |
| | 5:46 p.m. | Arrive Tampa airport |
| | | Reservations at the Marriott Airport Hotel; hotel located on airport premises; Tel: (813) 879-5151; Confirmation No. 987T385R |
| **Tuesday, March 24** | 8:00 a.m. | Obtain rental car at Hertz airport booth, Confirmation No. ZBT4314 |
| | 10:00 a.m. | Meet with Robin Fielding and Chris Perez, NationsBank downtown offices, 400 North Ashley Drive, Room 450, (813) 555-2236 |
| | 12 noon | Lunch with Robin Fielding, Chris Perez, and Michael Morris at the Tampa Club, Barnett Bank Building, 22nd Floor, 437 North Commonwealth Street, (813) 555-8732 |
| | 2:30 p.m.–<br>4:30 p.m. | Conduct orientation session of DLDS computerized loan tracking system for all members of the Loan Department at NationsBank downtown office |
| | 7:30 p.m. | Dinner with Jeff and Janet Spiegel at the Outrigger Steak House, 814 Bayview Drive, (813) 555-7892 |
| **Wednesday, March 25** | 8:30 a.m.–<br>11:30 a.m. | Conduct training sessions on DLDS computerized loan tracking system for all members of the Loan Department |
| | 1:00 p.m.–<br>4:00 p.m. | Conduct training sessions on DLDS computerized loan tracking system for all members of the Loan Department |
| | 6:00 p.m. | Dinner with Robin Fielding and Chris Perez at the University Club, 1120 University Avenue, (813) 555-0930 |
| **Thursday, March 26** | 6:57 a.m. | Depart Tampa airport, American Airlines Flight 1573, light breakfast, Seat 20B, check-in at gate required |
| | 8:42 a.m. | Arrive Dallas-Fort Worth airport |
| | 9:22 a.m. | Depart Dallas-Fort Worth airport, American Airlines Flight 1465, beverage service only, Seat 20B, check-in at gate required |
| | 10:43 a.m. | Arrive Burbank airport |

## 11–20. Press Releases

Press releases contribute to an organization's visibility and goodwill within the community. Important events and occurrences within an organization should be described on a press release and sent to the news media in the area.

Use the press release template of your word processing program and/or the following guidelines to prepare a press release on your word processor:

(1) Label the document in large bold letters *Press Release* or *News Release*.

(2) Specify the date for release or the words *For immediate release*.

(3) Include the name, address, telephone number, and fax number of the contact person.

(4) Provide a headline (centered and in all capital letters) that summarizes the content of the press release.

(5) Begin the opening paragraph with the city, state, and date. State immediately the essence of your news—who, what, when, where, and why. Follow with the details in subsequent paragraphs.

(6) Prepare the news release on letterhead or 8½- by 11-inch white bond paper. Use a 2-inch top margin and the default left and right margins of your word processor. Triple-space before and after the headline and double-space the text.

(7) Number multiple-page press releases with Arabic numbers in the upper right corner beginning with page 2. Center the word *-more-* at the bottom of the first page and all other pages except the last.

(8) Conclude the press release by centering a double space below the last line one of the following: *-30-*, *-# # #-*, or *-end-*.

**press release prepared on company letterhead**

2 inches

## Northridge Manufacturing Company

170 East Parkland Avenue
Dallas, Texas 75214

(214) 383-5757
Fax: (214) 383-5783

## Press Release

*For Immediate Release*

From Donna Anderson
Phone: (214) 363-5757
Fax: (214) 363-5788

BYRON R. TEAGUE NEW PRESIDENT OF NORTHRIDGE MANUFACTURING

Dallas, Texas, March 10. The Board of Directors of Northridge Manufacturing Company announced yesterday the appointment of Byron R. Teague as its new president effective June 30.

Mr. Teague, 47, has been with Northridge Manufacturing for nine years. He is presently serving as vice president of operations, a position he has held for the past three years. During this time the company has increased its sales 32 percent and expanded operations into New Mexico, Oklahoma, and Louisiana. Mr. Teague resides with his wife and two children in Dallas.

Mr. Teague will replace William R. Byrd, who will retire on May 30. Mr. Byrd has served as president of Northridge Manufacturing for the past sixteen years.

-30-

Reports

11

Ibid.

**press release prepared on word processing template—WordPerfect**

# PRESS RELEASE

**Northridge Manufacturing Company**
170 East Parkland Avenue
Dallas, Texas 75214

FOR MORE INFORMATION, CONTACT:

Donna Anderson
Northridge Manufacturing Company
(214) 363-5757   Fax: (214) 363-5783

**FOR IMMEDIATE RELEASE**

**BYRON R. TEAGUE NEW PRESIDENT OF NORTHRIDGE MANUFACTURING**

Dallas, Texas, March 10, 1999– The Board of Directors of Northridge Manufacturing Company announced yesterday

the appointment of Byron R. Teague as its new president effective June 30.

Mr. Teague, 47, has been with Northridge Manufacturing for nine years.  He is presently serving as vice president

of operations, a position he has held for the past three years.  During this time the company has increased its sales

32 percent and expanded operations into New Mexico. Oklahoma, and Louisiana.  Mr. Teague resides with his wife

and two children in Dallas.

Mr. Teague will replace William R. Byrd, who will retire on May 30.  Mr. Byrd has served as president of Northridge

Manufacturing for the past sixteen years.

-30-

# Chapter 12

# Employment Application Documents

$

## Solution Finder for Employment Application Documents

During the employment process candidates seeking positions are usually faced with preparing several kinds of documents: a résumé, a letter of application, an application form, reference request letters, and follow-up letters. Candidates may be required to prepare each of these documents or just one or two before obtaining the position they wish. Guidelines for formulating these kinds of job-seeking instruments are presented here.

# Résumés

A résumé provides the prospective employer with a capsulized visual of an applicant's qualifications. Its chart-like features summarize for the busy executive the attributes a candidate will bring to the position. See pages 407, 415, 416, 418, and 420 for examples of résumés.

## 12–1. Preparation for Computerized Résumé Searches

a. Large companies are increasingly relying on automated applicant tracking systems to screen candidates. These computers are not programmed to assess personal skills, initiative, motivation, drive, attitude, disposition, or other such attributes. Instead, they look for the marketable skills possessed by a candidate. Automated applicant tracking systems generally operate in the following way:

(1) On-line résumés are loaded directly into the tracking system. A paper résumé is scanned, and its scanned image is sent to a computer equipped with optical character recognition (OCR) software. Here the computer "reads," classifies, and stores each résumé quickly.

(2) When a job opening occurs, the employer tells the tracking system the keywords for the position. The computer looks for keywords (nouns that match the candidates' education, experience, skills, abilities, and knowledge with the job requirements).

(3) Applicants' résumés are selected and ranked according to the number of keywords appearing in the résumé. Only applicants whose résumés contain the keywords are candidates for the interview. These résumés are then subjected to human scrutiny for a decision as to whether the applicant will be invited for an interview.

(4) Automated applicant tracking systems generate response letters to prospective job candidates—interview offers, acknowledgments, and rejections. Most résumés are stored for a stipulated time period before they are purged from the system.

b. Keywords are the core of automated applicant tracking systems. Computers assess what a person can *do*. They look for substantiated facts, definitive quantities, and concrete nouns that describe specific, identifiable skills and accomplishments.

Keywords *differ* for each job title and each industry. Some companies will use keywords for the specific job opening and other keywords to

Employment

12

**assess familiarity with terms in the industry. Consider the following examples:**

(1) If a company were looking for a tax accountant with at least two years' experience with a Big 6 accounting firm, keywords for this position might be as follows:

| | |
|---|---|
| B.A. in Accounting | public accounting experience |
| B.S. in Accounting | Excel |
| Masters of Accounting | computer skills |
| Masters of Tax Law | communication skills |
| CPA | Arthur Andersen |
| auditing | Coopers & Lybrand |
| tax accounting | Deloitte & Touche |
| tax law | Ernst & Young |
| corporate tax | KPMG Peat Marwick |
| tax return preparation | Price Waterhouse |

(2) A major pharmaceutical company posted the following job opening for an "Admin Coordinator II" at its Web site, informing applicants that their résumés would be processed using an "electronic résumé database system."

Duties: provide administrative support for two associate directors including traveling and meeting coordination; agenda and minutes preparation; development and preparation of spreadsheets and databases; administrative support for extramural studies; preparation of routine and nonroutine correspondence; assist in preparing monitoring of research agreements through computer tracking; other duties as required.

Education: high school or equivalent.

Experience: typically, three years of general secretarial experience is expected for this position.

Skills required: Excel, MS Word, E-mail; good organizational skills; familiarity with financial and administrative process requirements of a large firm; ability to exercise judgment and support a team-oriented environment.

Based on the job description provided, an applicant might assume that the employer would suggest the following keywords for the automated applicant tracking system:

| | |
|---|---|
| Excel | travel coordination |
| MS Word | meeting coordination |
| E-mail | correspondence preparation |
| organizational skills | spreadsheet |
| team-oriented | database |
| high school diploma | administrative support |
| general secretarial experience | meeting agendas |
| computer tracking | meeting minutes |

Additional industry-specific keywords this employer may look for include these:

| | |
|---|---|
| biology | health industry |
| medical terminology | research |
| chemistry | pharmaceutical |
| life science | anatomy |

**c.** Check with prospective employers to see if your résumé will be evaluated by an automated applicant tracking system. If so, devise a list of keywords from your qualifications that you think may be used by the employer to select people for the position in which you are interested.

After the personal information (name, address, and telephone number) in your resumé, begin your listing of qualifications with a keyword summary. Use the following guidelines to prepare this section of your resumé:

(1) Label the section *Keyword Summary*, *Keywords*, or *Keyword Profile*. Use no font attributes such as boldface, italics, or underlining.

(2) Use nouns to show what you can do or what you have accomplished. Follow each keyword with a period, and list the keywords horizontally across the page.

(3) Begin the listing with the most important qualifications, and follow these keywords with those of lesser significance.

(4) Use variants of the keywords in the main text of your résumé to increase your chances of matching the keyword images of the optical character reading (OCR) software; for example, substitute *Associate in Arts* for *A.A.*, *spreadsheet* for *Excel*, or *administrative assistant* for *secretary*.

> Keyword Profile
>
> Microsoft Word. WordPerfect. Excel. Lotus 1-2-3. Access. PowerPoint. E-mail. 3 years' general secretarial experience. Office Administration. Administrative support. A.A. Help Desk. Typing. Filing. Agendas. Meeting minutes. Itineraries. Phones. Scheduling. Mail. Correspondence. Well organized. Good written and oral communication skills. Team-oriented.

**d.** Paper résumés submitted to automated applicant tracking systems are scanned and forwarded to optical scanning equipment (OCR) for reading. To ensure that your résumé is read correctly, you need to make certain it meets the following criteria:

(1) Use black print equal to the quality of a laser or an inkjet printer on 24-pound, smooth-surfaced white bond paper.

(2) Avoid fancy font styles and attributes such as boldfacing, underscores, or italics that are hard for optical scanning equipment to read. Keep your résumé free from graphics, boxed text, and shading; you may use solid bullets or asterisks for a listing. Confine your

**Employment**

**12**

résumé to a single-column format; multiple columns often run together in translations by OCR software.

(3) Place your name on the first line of the résumé. Following lines should include your complete address and telephone number. Include also your fax number and E-mail address, if applicable.

(4) Begin your description of qualifications with a keyword summary (nouns used by the computer to match candidates' traits with job requirements).

(5) Continue to employ keywords to describe specifically what you can do in relation to the job for which you are applying. Examples are (1) perform bookkeeping and accounting functions such as payroll, accounts receivable, and accounts payable; (2) use computer programs such as Microsoft Word, WordPerfect, Lotus, Excel, and Access; (3) work in retail sales and customer relations; and (4) prepare, edit, and proofread reports.

(6) Avoid using abbreviations; use them only if they are common to your profession or after you have spelled them out in full.

(7) Send the résumé in a large envelope; do not fold or crease it. Be sure to include a cover letter.

**An example of a résumé prepared for an automated applicant tracking system is shown on page 407.**

## résumé prepared for an automated applicant tracking system

Corey T. Roberts
2380 Vista Avenue
Thousand Oaks, California 95609
(805) 553-2196

### Keyword Profile

Microsoft Word. WordPerfect. Excel. Lotus 1-2-3. Access. PowerPoint. E-mail. 4 years' general secretarial experience. A.A. Office Administration. Administrative assistant. Help Desk. Typing. Filing. Agendas. Meeting minutes. Itineraries. Phones. Scheduling. Mail. Correspondence. Well organized. Good written and oral communication skills.

### Objective

Administrative support position in a large pharmaceutical corporation

### Experience

1994 to Present, ABCO Resource and Consulting Services, Administrative Assistant to the General Manager, Woodland Hills Office
- Handle phones and incoming calls on Help Desk
- Schedule meetings, prepare agendas, take minutes, and prepare meeting minutes for distribution
- Make travel arrangements and prepare itineraries
- Use word processing equipment to prepare all written documents and answer routine incoming correspondence
- Use spreadsheet software for budget and expense reports
- Use presentations software to assist staff in developing sales presentations
- Maintain a database of current and potential contract employees
- Maintain a filing system
- Process incoming mail

1993 to 1994, Salvation Corps, Administrative Clerk
- Handled all incoming phone calls and greeted visitors
- Scheduled pickup of nonmonetary donations
- Used spreadsheet software to track monetary donations, prepare budgets, and record expenses
- Used a Macintosh to prepare fliers
- Processed all incoming mail and handled the filing system

1991 to 1993, Secretary to Professor Linda Atkinson (part-time)
- Used a personal computer to prepare manuscript for publication
- Proofread page proof

### Education

Associate in Arts, Office Administration, Office Automation option, Brookview Community College, 1993. Additional courses taken include biology, anatomy, and medical terminology.

High school diploma, Wilson High School, 1990.

---

## 12–2. Posting Résumés on the Internet

The Internet furnishes access to a large variety of career services. These career services usually provide information about employers, post employment opportunities, assist candidates in placing their résumés on-line, and grant employers access to candidates' résumés. Many of these career services are free of charge to the prospective employee and employer, but others charge the employer or both the employer and employee. Follow these guidelines to locate an appropriate career service for posting your résumé on the Internet:

(1) Use a search engine (WebCrawler, Excite, etc.) to locate a listing of career services for your area of interest and expertise—business, health services,[1] law, entertainment, computing, etc.[2]

(2) Explore a number of the career services listed to determine the one or ones suitable for you. Consider job classifications, location of opportunities, kinds of applicants targeted, kinds of employers, scope of coverage, and cost (if any). You may wish to visit the Online Career Center,[3] Intellimatch,[4] or JobTrak,[5] which posts job openings listed with college and university career centers.

(3) Select one or more career services on which to post your résumé. Use the chronological style résumé described in Section 12-3 and follow the formats required by the career service.

# The Chronological Résumé

### 12–3. Information to Include in the Chronological Résumé

The résumé is often the only document an employer will use to screen individuals for an interview; therefore, it must succinctly describe your abilities and present you in a favorable light. The résumé style favored by most employers is the *chronological résumé* because it is easy to follow and assess. Guidelines for preparing this résumé style follow:

(1) Select carefully the information you include in your résumé so that the information can be presented on a single page. Only in those situations where an applicant has considerable experience or other qualifications related specifically to a position should the résumé exceed one page.

(2) Incorporate facts about your education, employment background, abilities, achievements, and awards. Besides the usual name, address, and telephone number, information in a résumé should also designate an employment or career objective. Optional categories include college extracurricular activities, professional memberships, willingness to relocate, and references. Personal

---

[1]MedSearch America <http://www.medsearch.com> posts résumés and lists job opportunities in a wide range of health-related occupations throughout the United States.

[2]The authors' search yielded a number of listings for business employment opportunities. The following site provided an extensive listing of career services: "Yahoo! - Business and Economy:Employment:Jobs," 1994–1996 <http://www.yahoo.com/business/employment/jobs> (20 November 1996).

[3]The Online Career Center <http://www.occ.com> is among the most frequently accessed on-line career centers. Résumés may be posted without charge.

[4]Intellimatch <http://www.intellimatch.com/yahoo/> offers on-line résumé posting and on-line application to posted jobs for registered applicants. Registration is free of charge. Nonregistrants may peruse posted jobs.

[5]JobTrak <http://www.jobtrak.com/> provides on-line listings of jobs posted with college and university career centers. Students and alumni from 400+ colleges may view job listings posted with their institution by obtaining a password from that college or university.

statistics (age, height, weight, gender), marital status, race, religion, ethnicity, birthplace, high school grades and activities, church responsibilities, hobbies, and interests should not be included in the résumé—unless they relate specifically to the job for which you are applying.

(3) Begin your résumé with a main heading (name, address, telephone number, fax number [if applicable], and E-mail address [if applicable]) followed by your career objective. Whether you begin the presentation of your credentials with a profile of your educational history and performance, special skills and aptitudes, or work experience depends upon where your greatest strengths lie. Launch the display of your abilities with the category that is most likely to get you the job. Follow up with other categories in the order of their importance to the career objective stated initially. Use text headings such as the following for the categories in your résumé:

*Objective* or *Career Objective*

*Education, Educational Background, Academic Preparation,* or *Professional Training*

*Employment, Experience,* or *Employment Experience*

*Skills and Abilities*

*Activities; Honors and Awards;* or *Honors, Awards, and Activities*

*References*

## 12-4. Main Heading

**The main heading opens the résumé and displays your name, address, and telephone number. If you have a fax number and/or an E-mail address, include these also. Follow these guidelines for the main heading:**

(1) Set up the main heading so that a prospective employer can easily spot your name and where to reach you for an interview.

(2) Include the addresses and telephone numbers for your *temporary* and *permanent* residences if you have both a college and home residence. If you know an ending date for your temporary residence, indicate it in the heading also.

**main heading showing single residence**

**Jeffrey D. Schultz**
2430 Brockton Drive
Upper Marlboro, Maryland 20772
(301) 555-4374

**main heading showing temporary and permanent residences**

**Brian R. Garvey**

Temporary Residence:                              Permanent Residence:
830 Willow Street, Apt. 6                     5460 Roundtree Circle
Columbia, South Carolina 29207            Atlanta, Georgia 30315
(803) 555-7863                                 (404) 555-9066

## 12–5.   Career or Employment Objective

**a.**   Include in your résumé a career or employment objective so that prospective employers know the kind of position you are seeking. Prepare an objective related to a specific job or one that would make you employable in a number of job categories, depending upon your qualifications and interests.

**specific employment objective**

> Objective:    To obtain a position as a legal office trainee in a medium-size legal office

**general employment objective**

> *Career Objective*
>
> To begin a career in marketing with exposure to retail sales, customer relations, market research, and advertising. Long-range goal is to become a department manager in a large metropolitan area department store.

**b.**   Prepare separate résumés if you have more than one employment area in which you wish to apply. Write the career objective to pertain to each of the positions in which you are interested, and tailor the other sections to emphasize the position stated in your objective.

## 12–6.   Educational History and Performance

Résumés furnish the opportunity to provide prospective employers with information substantiating an applicant's academic preparation to perform the job for which he or she is applying. Use these guidelines to present your academic qualifications in the chronological résumé:

(1)   Begin this section with the college, university, or other postsecondary institution you attended most recently. Include the name and location of the institution, school or department within the institution, major and minor fields of study, degrees or diplomas received, and dates of attendance. If the awarding of a degree is anticipated, list the degree supported by the anticipated date or a statement such as *to be granted June 2000.*

(2) Provide your grade-point average within this section, but only if it reflects favorably upon you. You may wish to provide your overall grade-point average and/or a grade-point average in your major courses of study. Include the scale on which the grade-point average is based—e.g., 3.65/4.00.

(3) Avoid listings of courses completed. Furnish only those course names and other educational experiences that are directly related to performing successfully in the desired position.

(4) List all collegiate or other postsecondary institutions attended. Include your high school education only if your postsecondary education has not resulted in a degree, anticipated degree, diploma, or certificate.

**example of educational background entry in a résumé**

> **Education**
>
> • University of Southern California, Los Angeles, Graduate School of Business Administration, Master of Science Degree in Management of Human Resources to be awarded May 2000, 3.9/4.0 grade-point average
>
> Courses in management of human resources, management-union relations, contract negotiations, and international resource development
>
> • University of Montana, Missoula, Montana, College of Engineering, Bachelor of Science in Mechanical Engineering, June 1996, 3.2/4.0 grade-point average

## 12–7. Work Experience

Reportings of successful work experiences tell prospective employers that applicants have been productive in the work environment. This section gives you an opportunity to show that you respond positively to supervision, have good work habits, and work well with others.

**a.** If your work experience is limited, include all the positions you have held—even though they do not relate to the position for which you are applying. They indicate to the employer that you are familiar with the work world and have performed successfully in its environment.

**b.** If your work experience is vast and varied, select only for inclusion those positions that are most recent and/or are related to the job for which you are applying.

**c.** In the chronological résumé list your work experience in reverse chronological order, that is, your most recent employment first. Include the following information for each position listed:

(1) **Employer's or company name and address.** Include only the city and state for the address.

(2) **Dates of employment.** State the month and year you began work and the month and year you terminated. You need not state a reason for leaving the position or provide salary information.

411

(3) **Job title.** Supply only the title of the most important or the last position held before leaving the employer.

(4) **Significant duties, activities, accomplishments, and promotions.** Use parallel construction and action verbs to describe succinctly and concretely the activities involved in your employment. Use action verbs such as *composed, conducted, created, designed, initiated, maintained, organized, prepared*, and *upgraded*. For previous employment activities, use the past tense; for ongoing employment activities, use the present tense. As much as possible select those responsibilities and accomplishments that feature your attributes for the position you are seeking.

d. In cases of part-time employment, indicate the part-time status in parentheses after the dates of employment. No notation is necessary for positions held as a full-time employee.

**example of work experience entry in a résumé**

**Work Experience**

Freestone Industries, Inc., Portland, Oregon, *Payroll Accountant*, July 1997–present
    Enter and maintain payroll records using a computerized payroll system
    Issue weekly and monthly payroll checks
    Complete payroll and tax reports for local, state, and federal agencies
    Submit withholding and other payroll taxes

Ritter's Clothing Emporium, Eugene, Oregon, *Bookkeeper-Accountant*,
    September 1995–March 1997 (part-time)
    Entered daily sales receipts and expense disbursements
    Prepared checks for signature
    Maintained payroll records

Barton-Hagan Ice Cream Parlor, Eugene, Oregon, *Service Representative*,
    September 1994–August 1995 (part-time)
    Served and packed ice cream
    Cashiered customer purchases

## 12–8. Skills and Abilities

a. Your educational background and work experience may not show all the traits and abilities that relate to the job you are seeking. Qualities that fall into the skills and abilities category include knowledge of specific computer programs or the ability to speak a foreign language. In some cases extensive travel in another country or knowledge pertaining to another culture might prove of value. Include in this category only those skills and abilities that pertain to your job objective. Omit this section in your résumé if the information can be incorporated into another part.

b. Follow these guidelines to list your skills and abilities:

(1) Begin, if possible, each item in the listing with an action verb stated in the present tense.

(2) Use parallel construction to list your special abilities.

**example of skills and abilities entry in a résumé**

> **Skills and Abilities**
>
> Use proficiently the following computer application programs: Excel,
> Lotus 1-2-3, Access, dBase, WordPerfect, and Microsoft Word
>
> Speak and write Spanish fluently

## 12–9. Awards, Honors, and Activities

**a.** If you have a number of awards and honors (at least three) and also a number of collegiate extracurricular activities (at least three), you may wish to show these items in two categories (*Honors and Awards* and *Activities*) instead of just one.

**b.** If your career experiences are more important than your education in obtaining the desired position, this category may well be replaced by a listing of your activities in professional and community organizations.

**c.** Use these guidelines to present any activities, honors, or awards in the chronological résumé:

(1) Begin with the most recent occurrence.

(2) List the names of the honors and awards and the dates they were earned or received.

(3) List the name of the organization, any offices held, and the dates of participation for each activity.

**example of honors, awards, and activities entry in a résumé**

> **Honors, Awards, and Activities**
>
> Awarded *The Wall Street Journal* scholarship for academic excellence,
> February 1998
>
> Dean's Honor Roll, September 1997–Present
>
> Fenton College Student Council, Associated Student Body Representative, Business
> Department, Spring 1997 and Fall 1997 semesters
>
> Alpha Gamma Sigma, honor society, February 1996–Present
>
> Phi Beta Lambda, business fraternity, September 1996–Present
> • Treasurer, Spring 1997 semester
> • Vice President, Fall 1997 semester
> • President, Spring 1998 semester

## 12–10. References

**a.** The inclusion of references in the chronological résumé is optional. The statement *References furnished upon request* is not necessary if you decide not to furnish names, addresses, and telephone numbers on the résumé itself. Prospective employers assume that at the point of interview you will be able to furnish them from three to five former professors and/or employers who will be able to provide firsthand information about you.

**b.** Select your references carefully. A bad reference is worse than no reference at all. Before giving the name of a reference, check with that person to ensure that he or she is agreeable to giving you a recommendation. Give each reference a copy of your résumé.

**c.** Use the following guidelines for including references in your résumé:

    (1) Limit the number of references to two or three. Space is better allocated to a presentation of your qualifications for the job you are seeking.

    (2) Provide the name and title of the individual; the company or institution name; the street address; the city, state, and zip code; and the telephone number for each reference cited.

Examples of references are shown in the résumé on page 415. Examples of chronological résumés are shown on pages 415 and 416.

# chronological résumé

**LORRAINE V. HOOVER**

Temporary Address:
3460 S.W. 16th Street, #12
Gainesville, FL 32608
(904) 555-3250

Permanent Address:
7520 Beachway Drive
Tampa, FL 33609
(813) 555-2840

| | | |
|---|---|---|
| *Objective* | To begin a career in accounting with immediate objective to gain experience for certification as a Certified Public Accountant | |
| *Education* | **Master of Accounting (3/2 program)** | **May 1997** |
| | **Bachelor of Science in Accounting** | **May 1996** |
| | Fisher School of Accounting | |
| | University of Florida, Gainesville, Florida | |
| | GPA 3.53/4.0 (accounting), 3.68/4.0 (overall) | |
| *Honors* | Beta Alpha Psi | Spring 1995 |
| | Becker CPA Review Scholarship | Spring 1995 |
| | Golden Key Honor Society | Spring 1995 |
| | Dean's List | Summer 1994–present |
| | President's Honor Roll | Spring 1994 |
| *Activities* | **Beta Alpha Psi** | |
| | Reporting Secretary | Spring 1995–present |
| | **Fisher School of Accounting Council** | |
| | Vice President | Spring 1995–Spring 1996 |
| | Audit Team | Spring 1995 |
| | Student Representative to Programs Board | Spring 1995 |
| | Class Representative | Fall 1994–Spring 1995 |
| | **Becker CPA Review** | |
| | Student Representative | May 1995–present |
| | **Florida Accounting Association** | Fall 1995–present |
| | **American Marketing Association** | |
| | Promotion Co-chairman | Fall 1994 |
| *Work Experience* | **Alpert, Josey and Grilli, P.A.**, Tampa, Florida | Summer 1993 |
| | Assistant Bookkeeper | |
| | • Reconciled monthly bank statements and daily deposits | |
| | • Recorded and updated billable time for legal fees | |
| | • Prepared clients' monthly bills | |
| | • Revised clients' financial files | |
| | **Zudar's Cafe**, Tampa, Florida | Summer 1992 |
| | Server | |
| | **Tampa Eye Clinic**, Tampa, Florida | August 1991–May 1992 |
| | Doctor's Assistant | |
| | • Updated patients' files | |
| | • Prepared patients for examination | |
| *Computer Knowledge* | Lotus 1-2-3, Excel, dBaseIV, WordPerfect | |
| *References* | Peter Grilli | Dr. Lewis Lauring |
| | Alpert, Josey and Grilli, P.A. | Tampa Eye Clinic |
| | 100 Ashley Drive South | 3000 Dr. Martin Luther King Jr. West |
| | Tampa, Florida 33601 | Tampa, Florida 33601 |
| | (813) 555-4131 | (813) 555-2020 |

Employment

12

## chronological résumé

---

### DANIEL HO

---

*6201 Rathburn Avenue • Northridge, California 91325 • (818) 555-9770*

---

**Objective**

To obtain a responsible and challenging position as an administrative assistant
where my education and work experience will be of value

**Education**

| | |
|---|---|
| Los Angeles Pierce College | |
| Woodland Hills, California | |
| Certificate in Office Administration, General Administrative | May 1998 |
| Associate in Arts degree, Quality Control Engineering | June 1995 |
| Associate in Arts degree, Landscape Maintenance | June 1993 |

**Work Experience**

Los Angeles Pierce College     August 1996–
Woodland Hills, California     Present
Computer Laboratory Assistant     (part-time)
     Assist students with computer assignments
     Provide instructional support during evening classes
     Maintain equipment in working order

Nordskog Industries, Inc.     July 1991–
Van Nuys, California     September 1995
CNC Operator
     Assembled and operated CNC (Computerized Numerical
     Control) machine
     Checked and modified CNC program
     Assembled and bonded parts for commercial airplane
     galleys

**Computer Skills**

Training in the following computer programs emphasizing the production of
documents typically found in business and office applications:
- WordPerfect
- Microsoft Word for Windows
- Excel
- Lotus 1-2-3
- dBASE IV

Ability to type 50 wpm

# The Functional Résumé

## 12–11. Preparation of the Functional Résumé

The functional résumé, shown on page 418, focuses on an applicant's accomplishments, abilities, and skills. Rather than beginning with an education or employment history, the functional résumé presents competencies and accomplishments in special categories.

**a.** You may wish to use a functional résumé if you have changed jobs frequently or if there are gaps in your employment history. Applicants with little employment experience also find this form of résumé appealing.

**b.** Although the functional résumé emphasizes abilities, it should also include information regarding a candidate's education; previous employment; and any pertinent honors, activities, and affiliations. Use the following guidelines to prepare a functional résumé:

(1) Begin with a main heading that displays your name, address, and telephone number. If you have a fax number and/or an E-mail address, include these also. Follow the main heading with your employment objective.

(2) Continue the functional résumé with a listing of your significant abilities, skills, activities, and accomplishments. As much as possible select items that feature your attributes for the position you are seeking. Group the items into meaningful categories, and use a descriptive heading for each category.

(3) Use parallel construction and action verbs to describe succinctly and concretely the items in your listing. Use action verbs such as *assisted, compiled, coordinated, developed, edited, established, managed, planned*, and *translated*. For previous accomplishments, use the past tense; for present skills and abilities, use the present tense.

(4) Include in the functional résumé a history of your academic preparation (see Section 12-6) and a brief account of your previous employment (see Section 12-7).

(5) Conclude the functional résumé with a listing of any awards, extracurricular activities, or professional affiliations (see Section 12-9).

Employment

12

**functional résumé**

---

### Claudia Martinez
3221 Nordhoff Street · Northridge, California 91326 · (818) 555-6497

---

OBJECTIVE
Obtain a secretarial or word processing position with opportunity for advancement

SKILLS AND ABILITIES
- Operate proficiently the following software programs: Microsoft Word for Windows, WordPerfect for Windows and DOS, Excel, Lotus 1-2-3, Access, DOS 6.22, Windows 3.1, and Windows 95
- Transcribe and proofread business documents accurately
- Compose and prepare routine correspondence
- Perform computerized accounting functions using BusinessWorks
- Speak and write English and Spanish fluently
- Type 55 words a minute

ACCOMPLISHMENTS
- Trained and supervised student workers
- Performed database entries using FileMaker Pro on a Macintosh computer and Microsoft Access on a personal computer
- Reorganized instructional media for easier access and availability to faculty
- Maintained audio and video equipment
- Filed invoices and catalogs
- Answered telephone inquiries and took reservations for equipment loans
- Duplicated audiocassettes for students

EDUCATION
Los Angeles Pierce College, Woodland Hills, California. Associate in Arts degree, May 1997, Office Administration–General Administrative. Overall GPA 3.9/4.0.

EXPERIENCE
Instructional Media Center, Los Angeles Pierce College, Woodland Hills, California. August 1995 to present (part-time).

HONORS AND AWARDS
- Certificate of Recognition from Alpha Gamma Sigma, the scholastic honor society, for 'Outstanding Scholarship and Placement' on the Dean's List each semester
- Frances M. Heinze Memorial Scholarship for outstanding scholastic achievement, May 1996
- Teresa A. Caruana Memorial Award for overall outstanding achievement, May 1997
- Office Administration Department, Highest GPA Award, May 1997

---

# The Combination Résumé

## 12–12. Preparation of the Combination Résumé

The combination résumé, shown on page 420, blends the strongest qualities of the chronological and functional résumés.

a.  For candidates who are recent graduates but have some full-time experience, the combination résumé offers the opportunity to highlight both their competencies and their experience.

**b.** The combination résumé continues to focus on an applicant's abilities, skills, and accomplishments. It differs from the functional résumé in that the combination résumé provides a complete employment history. Use the following guidelines to prepare a combination résumé:

(1) Begin with a main heading that displays your name, address, and telephone number. If you have a fax number and/or an E-mail address, include these also. Follow the main heading with your employment objective.

(2) Continue the combination résumé with a listing of your significant abilities, skills, activities, and accomplishments. As much as possible select items that feature your attributes for the position you are seeking. Group the items into meaningful categories, and use a descriptive heading for each category.

(3) Use parallel construction and action verbs to describe succinctly and concretely the items in your listing. Use action verbs such as *assisted, compiled, coordinated, developed, edited, established, managed, planned*, and *translated*. For previous accomplishments, use the past tense; for present skills and abilities, use the present tense.

(4) Include in the combination résumé a history of your academic preparation (See Section 12-6) and your previous employment (See Section 12-7). Place first the category that is more likely to qualify you for the job for which you are applying.

(5) Conclude the combination résumé with a listing of any awards, extracurricular activities, or professional affiliations (See Section 12-9).

# Résumé Formats

## 12–13. Formats for the Résumé

The appearance of your résumé creates a first impression, the first impression a prospective employer forms of you. If the résumé is well designed and well written, it is more likely to be read and to lead to an interview. Use the following guidelines to prepare your résumé:

(1) Use 20- or 24-pound high-quality white bond paper to prepare your résumé. Ensure that the print quality is high density, equal to that of a laser printer.

(2) Strive for optimal top, bottom, left, and right margins—1 inch. Use no less than 0.75 inch for each of these margins.

(3) Select a font or typeface that is easy to read. Use no smaller than an 11-point font, and do not condense the line spacing so that the copy becomes difficult to read.

(4) Use headings for each of your major categories. Differentiate through size and/or attribute (bold or italic) these text headings

## combination résumé

**MARLENE CAPPETTO**

6240 Winnetka Avenue ♦ Encino, CA 91371 ♦ (818) 555-4210 ♦ mcappetto213@aol.com

| | |
|---|---|
| **EMPLOYMENT OBJECTIVE** | To obtain a paralegal position offering challenge, responsibility, and personal growth |
| **CAPABILITIES AND SKILLS** | ♦ Draft complaints/answers<br>♦ Compose interrogatories/answers<br>♦ Prepare motions<br>♦ Conduct legal research<br>♦ Access and use WESTLAW<br>♦ Compose and prepare business correspondence<br>♦ Operate proficiently WordPerfect, Microsoft Word for Windows, Lotus 1-2-3, Quicken, and dBASE IV<br>♦ Type 70 words per minute<br>♦ Operate the numeric 10-key pad proficiently<br>♦ Speak and write English and Spanish fluently |
| **EDUCATION** | **University of California, Los Angeles, Extension, Attorney Assistant Training Program**, Certificate in Litigation, November 1995<br>This program is offered in cooperation with the UCLA School of Law and is approved by the American Bar Association.<br><br>**Los Angeles Pierce College**, Woodland Hills, Associate in Arts degree, Office Administration—Word Processing, May 1995 |
| **EXPERIENCE**<br>July 1995–Present | **Litigation Assistant, O'Melveny & Myers, Los Angeles**<br>Perform automated document management on multiple projects<br>Review documents and prepare information for discovery<br>Investigate facts and case law |
| February 1995–<br>July 1995<br>(part-time) | **Legal Secretary, Law Offices of Duane Lübbe, Encino**<br>Composed and prepared business correspondence using WordPerfect<br>Managed documents for personal injury cases<br>Transcribed dictation<br>Maintained business calendars |
| **HONORS** | Dean's Honor List, 1991–1994<br>The National Dean's List Award, 1994–95<br>Teresa A. Caruana Memorial Award, May 1995<br>2,000 Notable American Women Award |
| **AFFILIATIONS** | Phi Theta Kappa International Honor Society<br>UCLA Extension Attorney Assistant Alumni Association<br>Los Angeles Paralegal Association<br>National Association for Female Executives<br>National Association of Legal Assistants |

from the regular text. Use regular second-degree text headings as shown in Section 11-8a and page 416 or parallel headings as shown in the example résumés on pages 415 and 420.

(5) Use font attributes (bold, italic, all capital letters) to make your résumé more attractive and easily comprehensible. Be careful, though, not to overuse these attributes and to apply them consistently for the same features.

(6) Single-space the items listed within each section, but double-space between the items. Use parallel construction for all entries within a section, and place a period only at the end of complete sentences. Use no punctuation mark to conclude incomplete word groups unless they are followed by complete sentences or another word group.

# The Application Letter

Although the letter of application functions as a cover letter in the transmittal of your résumé, its importance must not be minimized. This document is your initial introduction to the employer, so care must be taken to make a good first impression. This letter represents you. If it is prepared poorly, there is a good chance that your résumé will not be read.

## 12–14. Contents of the Application Letter

**a.** Begin the letter of application with a statement that attracts the interest of the reader and is related to the purpose of the letter. If an opening has been announced and applications are being solicited, use a direct approach. If, on the other hand, you are investigating whether an opening may exist, use a different strategy by approaching your purpose indirectly.

### direct opening for solicited application

> The opening for an administrative assistant in your Publications Department that you filed with the Loma Vista College Career Center appears to be interesting and challenging. As you can see by the enclosed résumé, my specialty in the office administration area has been desktop publishing.

### indirect opening for unsolicited application

> My high regard for Allerman Corporation and its products has prompted me to inquire whether you could use the services of a knowledgeable administrative assistant who has specialized in desktop publishing.

**b.** Continue the letter of application with information that explains the purpose of your letter and convinces the reader to consider your qualifications further. Do not summarize your résumé; instead, amplify and briefly explain one or two of your strongest qualifications and relate them to the job for which you are applying. Refer the reader to the enclosed résumé.

**body of application letter**

> My formal study of computer application programs—word processing, desktop publishing, spreadsheet, and database—at Loma Vista College culminated with an internship program at Data Select. Here I was able to use my word processing and desktop publishing skills to produce an instructional manual for one of the company's new software programs.
>
> In addition to my course work and experience in applications software, courses in business English, transcription, and business communication have enabled me to develop the proofreading, editing, and writing skills needed to produce error-free business documents. Information regarding my other qualifications is included in the enclosed resumé.

**c.** A request for action closes the letter of application. Usually the action requested is an invitation for an interview. It may, however, merely be that the reader mail an employment application or refer your letter and résumé to a local office or representative. Whatever the request may be, preface it with *please* or another such appreciative expression.

In requesting an interview, make it easy for the reader to reply by furnishing your telephone number and the times you may be reached at that number. Serious job seekers, however, invest in answering machines, beepers, and even portable cellular phones so they are readily reachable when opportunities arise.

**closing for application letter**

> May I have an opportunity to discuss my qualifications with you further? To arrange an interview, please call me at (212) 555-5865. I can be reached personally before 10 a.m. and after 3 p.m., and my answering machine picks up messages between 10 a.m. and 3 p.m. I can arrange to meet with you at any time convenient for your schedule.

## 12–15. Preparation of the Application Letter

Like the résumé, the application letter represents you and forms a first impression. To form a favorable first impression, follow these guidelines:

(1) Use 20- or 24-pound high-quality white bond paper to prepare your application letter. Ensure that the print quality is high density, equal to that of a laser printer. Select a typeface and font size that complement the ones used in your résumé.

(2) Use one of the three following business letter formats: full block, modified block with blocked paragraphs, or modified block with indented paragraphs. Detailed instructions for preparing letters in these formats are contained in Sections 10-1 and 10-2. An example application letter is shown on page 423.

(3) Limit your application letter to one page. Keep in mind that it is a transmittal letter for your résumé and, in most cases, a request for

an interview. Highlight and expand only one or two of your major qualifications. Letters that are too long are less likely to be read. Similarly, letters prepared in fonts smaller than 11 points will receive less attention.

(4) Be sure to begin the application letter with a return address. Although your address and telephone number are prominently displayed in the résumé, your address must also appear on the application letter.

(5) Other parts of a business letter to be used include an inside address, a salutation, the letter body, a complimentary close, a signature line, and an enclosure notation. Specific instructions for the placement and format of these letter parts are contained in Sections 10-7 through 10-18.

Employment

12

**letter of application**

1116 East 59th Street, Apt. 301
Chicago, IL 60615-3022
March 1, 1998

Ms. Denise R. Cueva, Vice President
Human Resources and Development
First National Bank of Arizona
10370 Camelback Road
Phoenix, Arizona 85030-1900

Dear Ms. Cueva:

As a growing bank in the Phoenix area, does First National have a need for a qualified representative in its trust and estate planning area?

In June I will earn a bachelor of science degree in business finance from Chicago State University. Besides fulfilling all the requirements for the regular curriculum in finance, I have completed additional course work in estate planning, trust initiation and management, tax law for trusts, and ethics in trust management.

As you can see by the enclosed résumé, for the past year the knowledge gained in my course work has been applied in a part-time position at Illinois Federal Bank. Here I met with new customers and assisted in setting up trusts to meet their individual needs. I also worked closely with trust officers in establishing and maintaining present clients' trusts.

May I have an opportunity to discuss with you how my education and experience can be put to work for First Federal? I plan to be in Phoenix from April 12 to 16 and would appreciate your scheduling an interview during that time. You may reach me by mail at the above address, by E-mail at 104450.1502@compuserve.com, or by telephone at (312) 555-8732. I look forward to hearing from you.

Sincerely,

Robert Ferreira

Enclosure

# The Application Form

Many organizations require candidates to complete formal application forms even though they have submitted résumés. Application forms permit employers to obtain and organize standardized information about applicants—and those whom they hire as employees.

## 12–16. Procedures for Completing Application Forms

Use the following guidelines to assist you in completing application forms efficiently and completely:

(1) Carry with you a copy of your résumé when visiting prospective employers' offices. Much of the information contained in your résumé will be needed to complete the application form.

(2) Write on the reverse side of your résumé copy any information that may be needed for the application form but is not included on your résumé. Such information may include the following:

Social security number

Driver's license number

Beginning and ending dates of *all* employment

Salary history

Name, title, complete address, and telephone number of all former supervisors

Name, title, complete address, and telephone number of all references

(3) Read over all the questions before you begin to answer them. Write neatly and legibly. If you have poor handwriting, print your responses.

(4) Answer all questions on the application form. If a question is not applicable to your situation, respond with a statement such as *Not applicable*.

(5) Write *Negotiable* or *Open* on application forms that contain questions regarding the salary you expect to earn. This strategy is best used when you are uncertain what others in comparable positions are earning.

# Reference Request Letters

## 12–17. Reference Request Letters

a. Prospective employers will undoubtedly request you to furnish two or three references, persons who can verify your abilities and/or former employment. Provide the names of former professors or employers who will present you in a favorable light. Do not provide "character" references from family friends, personal friends, or relatives.

b. Request permission from potential references to use their names; select people who you feel will enthusiastically endorse you. Remember that a poor recommendation is worse than no recommendation at all.

c. Solicit the recommendation endorsement in person or by telephone, and follow-up a "yes" response with an acknowledgment letter. Use the following guidelines for writing this letter:

(1) Express appreciation for the person's willingness to provide you with a recommendation should a prospective employer contact him or her.

(2) Provide a description of the job for which you are applying. If appropriate, relate one of your accomplishments or skills (that the person has observed personally) to the qualifications for the job.

(3) Include and refer to a copy of your résumé.

(4) Invite the reference to contact you if he or she has any questions.

**reference request letter**

Dear Professor Simons:

I appreciate your willingness to provide me with a reference for a position as a legal assistant should you be contacted by a prospective employer.

My immediate objective is to obtain a position in a large legal firm where I will have an opportunity for advancement. The courses I took from you—word processing, legal office procedures, and legal transcription—have certainly prepared me well to begin my career in a legal office.

After graduating from Pierce College, I continued my education in the area of legal assisting. As you can see by the enclosed résumé, I enrolled in the Attorney Assistant Training Program at the University of California, Los Angeles, Extension. Here I earned a Certificate in Litigation.

Thank you for your support. If you have any questions or wish any additional information, please let me know.

# Follow-up Letters

Follow-up letters may be written when no response is received to an application letter or form. They are also written after an interview. The follow-up letter reminds the prospective employer that you are interested in a position with that employer or company.

## 12–18. Application Follow-Up Letter

If you have not received a response to an application letter or an application form within a reasonable period of time, you may wish to send an application follow-up letter. Such a letter shows serious interest and reminds the personnel officer of your qualifications.

(1) Begin the application follow-up letter with a statement reaffirming your interest in the job for which you formerly applied. Remind the addressee of your letter or application and mention one of your qualifications—or provide any new information that may enhance your likelihood of obtaining the position. Close with a statement anticipating that your application will be kept active.

(2) Use one of the following three business letter formats: full block, modified block with blocked paragraphs, or modified block with indented paragraphs. Detailed instructions for preparing letters in these formats are contained in Sections 10-1 and 10-2. An example application follow-up letter is shown on page 427.

(3) Be sure to begin the application follow-up letter with a return address. Other parts of a business letter to be used include an inside address, a salutation, the letter body, a complimentary close, and a signature line. Specific instructions for the placement and format of these letter parts are contained in Sections 10-7 through 10-18.

**application follow-up letter**

Dear Ms. Cueva:

I am still very interested in becoming a representative in the Estate Planning and Trust Department of First National Bank of Arizona.

As I mentioned in my March 1 letter, I will be in Phoenix from April 12 through April 15 and would be available for an interview anytime that week. If these dates are not convenient for you, please write me at the above address, E-mail me at 104450.1502@compuserve.com, or call me at (312) 555-8732 to set up an appointment to meet with you another time.

If you do not have an opening at the present time, please let me know. I would appreciate, however, your keeping my application in your active file and notifying me when an opportunity with First National arises.

## 12–19. Interview Follow-Up Letter

**After you have been interviewed, send a brief letter of appreciation to the interviewer. Not only will this courtesy thank the interviewer for his or her time but also it will remind that person of your meeting. Sending a follow-up letter will reaffirm your interest in the position and at the same time distinguish you from the other candidates. More than likely, others will not take this extra step.**

(1) Write and send the interview follow-up letter immediately after the interview. Delays will impair its effectiveness. In addition to expressing appreciation and thanks, remind the interviewer of a topic discussed during your conversation and conclude with a positive statement indicating your interest in the position.

(2) Use one of the following three business letter formats: full block, modified block with blocked paragraphs, or modified block with indented paragraphs. Detailed instructions for preparing letters in these formats are contained in Sections 10-1 and 10-2. An example interview follow-up letter is shown on page 428.

(3) Be sure to begin the interview follow-up letter with a return address. Other parts of a business letter to be used include an inside address, a salutation, the letter body, a complimentary close, and a signature line. Specific instructions for the placement and format of these letter parts are contained in Sections 10-7 through 10-18.

## interview follow-up letter

Dear Ms. Cueva:

Thank you for meeting with me in Phoenix last week. My interview with you and Mr. Sabian has convinced me even more that I would like to become part of the First National Bank of Arizona staff.

Since there are no openings in your Estate Planning and Trust Department at the present time, I appreciate your suggesting the management training program in the interim. Please consider me for an opening in this program.

Because of my experience at Illinois Federal Bank, I could be a productive member of your staff. I look forward to hearing your decision about my entering the management training program at First National.

# Mail and Electronic Messaging

E-mail

# Mail and Electronic Messaging Solution Finder

E-mail

In today's rapidly paced business world, the mode of transmission and transmission time are in many cases as important as the contents of a written message or a package. If information or materials are needed for a scheduled event, they must be received in time or they are of no value. Mail delays in the exchange of information, contracts, and payments can impede the progress of a project and affect potential profits.

Electronic messaging systems, contemporary transportation systems, and modern dispatch methods have enabled businesses to hasten the delivery of messages, packages, and freight to all parts of the United States and to almost all countries in the world. Computer networks, facsimile (fax) transmissions, and electronic mail (E-mail) ensure the receipt of written messages worldwide within minutes. Private delivery services and the U.S. Postal Service ensure same-day and overnight delivery of messages, packages, and—in some cases—freight.

# Electronic Messaging Services

## 13–1. Networks

Computer communication is a key factor in information exchange. Computers that are linked together can communicate with each other and are part of a network.

**a.** Local area networks use telephone wires, radio waves, coaxial cable, or fiber optics to link computers that are geographically close; that is, computers within a building, several adjacent buildings, or the same geographical area. Data can be transmitted within seconds from one location to another. The receiving station may store or print the information for further use.

**b.** Local networks can be linked to larger networks that enable individuals and companies to send and receive information throughout the United States and worldwide. These wide area networks or global networks use combinations of telephone lines, satellites, and microwave radio links to transmit information within minutes.

## 13–2. Facsimile Transmissions (Fax)—Fax Machine-to-Fax Machine Messaging

Facsimile transmission of computer-generated, typewritten, and handwritten documents; charts, graphs, and diagrams; photographs; and other kinds of hard copy has become an everyday occurrence. It is the most popular method of electronic document transmission used by modern businesses today.

**a.** Businesses, individuals, or other kinds of stations using facsimiles (faxes) require a telephone line to which they connect their fax machine. The fax machine scans any hard copy, and a built-in modem converts the scanned images to analog signals that are transmitted over telephone lines to a receiving fax machine. Here the signals are reconverted to images and a replica of the hard copy is produced at

E-mail

Mail and E-mail

13

the receiving station, often thousands of miles from the sending source. Fax machines are capable of both sending and receiving documents to and from locations locally or around the world.

b. Costs include the purchase of a facsimile, paper to reproduce the transmitted replicas, installation and monthly service charges for a telephone line, and regular local and long-distance telephone rates for on-line transmission. Simple documents are sent and received in just a matter of minutes.

c. Fax machine transmissions require a cover sheet that contains the following information or provisions:

(1) Name of the addressee

(2) Company name, if any

(3) Destination fax number

(4) Destination city (include state or country also if lesser-known city)

(5) Name, complete address, fax number, and telephone number of originator

(6) Space for any message

(7) Number of pages transmitted

(8) Request to telephone if transmission unsuccessful

An example of a fax cover sheet is shown on page 434.

d. Use of fax transmission is not restricted to those individuals and businesses that have stations on-site. This high-speed, low-cost method of document transmission is also available to the general public through the U.S. Postal Service, private mail receiving and forwarding services, stationery stores, and various other businesses in major cities throughout the United States.

## 13–3. Facsimile Transmissions — Computer Fax-to-Computer Fax, Computer Fax-to-Fax Machine, and Fax Machine-to-Computer Fax Messaging

Most computers purchased in today's market are equipped with built-in fax software, a modem, and a fax management system. These features enable fax transmissions to occur between computers and between computers and fax machines.

a. Businesses, individuals, or other kinds of stations using computer faxes require a telephone line to which they connect their modem. On-screen documents or computer files are transmitted by the fax software and modem to their destination. The modem converts the data to analog signals that are transmitted over telephone lines to a receiving computer or fax machine. Here the signals are reconverted to their former images and a replica of the original file is produced at the receiving station—in file form at a computer station and in hard copy form at a fax machine station.

b. Computers are capable of sending and receiving documents to and from locations locally or around the world. To receive fax messages, the computer must be turned on and the "fax manager" must be resident. Messages received in computer files may be printed if a printer is attached to the computer.

**c.** Costs include the purchase of a computer (with fax software and a modem), installation and monthly service charges for a telephone line, and regular local and long-distance telephone rates for on-line transmission. Simple documents are sent and received in just a matter of minutes.

**d.** The fax management system of a computer generally provides a fax cover sheet that may be sent with each transmission. These cover sheets make provisions for entering some or all of the following information:

(1) Name of the addressee

(2) Company name, if any

(3) Destination fax number

(4) Destination telephone number

(5) Destination address or city name

(6) Standardized and personalized sender information—name, company (if any), complete address, fax number, and telephone number of originator

(7) Space for any message

**fax machine cover sheet**

James
and Lyn
Clark

17225 Superior Street, Northridge, CA 91325
(818) 701-9770
**Fax: (818) 772-8108**

### Fax Transmittal and Cover Letter

Date:     July 13, 1997

Please deliver the following pages to

Name:     Susan Carson

Firm:     South-Western Publishing Company

City:     Cincinnati

Fax No.:  (513) 555-6134

From:     Jim and Lyn Clark

Message:

Following are manuscript pages for Chapter 12, "Employment Application Documents," for *Handbook for Office Workers*, Eighth Edition.

We are transmitting    23    page(s) (including this cover letter).  If you do not receive all the pages, please call us as soon as possible.

## 13–4.  E-Mail

**a.**   E-mail (electronic mail) is a system by which people communicate with one another through computers and networks. Individuals each have an electronic "mailbox" in their computers and an "address" to which communiqués are directed. Messages sent to the mailbox by other E-mail participants are stored until the recipients open their "mailboxes." After reading the messages, recipients may print them, store them on the computer, or delete them.

**b.**   E-mail messages within organizations are commonly sent through a computer network established to serve the organization. Stations are connected by either coaxial cable (within a building) or by phone lines (between buildings or sites). Messages are transmitted from station to station by cable or phone lines.

**c.** E-mail messages sent outside an organizational network or messages sent by individuals are transmitted through the Internet, a worldwide global network. The rate of information exchange through E-mail messages conveyed on the Internet is rising faster than any other method of message transmission. Advances in accessing the Internet have brought E-mail messaging to the "fingertips" of anyone who has a computer.

**d.** Individual users of Internet electronic mail must have the following:

(1) A computer, monitor, and keyboard

(2) A modem and connection to a telephone line

(3) A subscription to an Internet service provider (ISP), which supplies the connection to the Internet. Commonly known Internet service providers are America Online, CompuServe, and Prodigy. Thousands of others are scattered in cities throughout the United States and may be easily located through a city's *Yellow Pages*. Internet service providers usually furnish the communications software needed for E-mail and other Internet access. See Section 15-11 for additional information.

**e.** Internet service providers supply each subscriber with a screen name (a user I.D.) that is unique for that subscriber. The screen name followed by the *at* sign (@) and the Internet name of the Internet service provider comprise the subscriber's E-mail address. Examples of E-mail addresses are *ClarksHOW@aol.com*, *104450.1502@ compuserve.com*, and *jlclark214@pacificnet.net*. An explanation of commonly used extensions following the Internet name of the E-mail provider follows:

| Extension | Definition |
|-----------|------------|
| com | commercial organization |
| edu | educational site |
| gov | government organization |
| mil | military |
| net | organization administering a network |
| org | miscellaneous organization |

**f.** Messages are sent from one E-mail address to another through the Internet service providers. An originator's message is sent to the computer of his or her provider, where it is directed along the Internet to the computer of the recipient's Internet service provider. Here it is stored until the recipient logs on to his or her provider's computer and retrieves the message.

**g.** On-line service providers furnish an on-screen form to compose and send messages. The E-mail message illustrated on page 436 was written on the template provided by CompuServe.

E-mail

Mail and E-mail

13

E-mail

## Private Delivery Services

### 13–5. Private Delivery Services

**a.** A number of private delivery services specialize in expediting the delivery of letters, packages, and freight worldwide. Companies such as Airborne Express, DHL Worldwide Express, Federal Express, Sky Courier International, and United Parcel Service (UPS) are among the nationally based companies that offer worldwide service.

**b.** Other private delivery or courier companies offer statewide or nationwide services. These companies offer a variety of services, but the majority specialize in overnight delivery of letters and small packages to major cities within their state or throughout the United States. Consult your local *Yellow Pages* to determine which private delivery companies have offices in your area.

**c.** Private delivery companies vary somewhat in their offerings of services. A sampling of services obtainable through private delivery companies follows:

Domestic Delivery

(1) Overnight delivery of letters and packages

(2) Two-day delivery of letters and packages

(3) Regular delivery (3 to 5 days) of packages (UPS)

(4) Overnight freight service

(5) Two-day freight service

(6) Air cargo services

(7) Air charter services

International Delivery

(1) Overnight delivery of letters and packages from New York to several designated European cities

(2) One- to three-day express delivery of nondutiable letters, packages, and freight

(3) One- to three-day airport-to-airport service

(4) Delivery of dutiable packages and freight—schedule dependent upon travel time and customs considerations

(5) Three- to six-day mail service for letters and printed matter

(6) Air and sea cargo services

(7) Air charter services

Services Provided

(1) Complimentary assortment of mailers and packaging

(2) Pickup service

(3) Convenient offices or drop locations

(4) Transportation-cost refunds for delayed deliveries

(5) COD services

(6) Package tracking

(7) Confirmation of delivery

(8) Volume discounts

(9) Hold-for-pickup service

(10) Saturday service

**d.** For the same cost, private delivery services are often able to provide faster delivery than the United States Postal Service, especially to smaller United States cities. Obtain literature from the major providers (Airborne, DHL, Federal Express, United Parcel Service) and local services to determine if any will meet your mailing needs.

**e.** Verify with the delivery company the delivery time of any mail piece that must reach its destination by a certain time and date. Do not assume from reading the literature that a letter or package will reach its destination as generally described.

E-mail

Mail and E-mail

13

# U.S. Postal Service Domestic Mail Classes and Services[1]

There are a number of domestic mail classes. Each varies in (1) the type, weight, and size of the matter that may be sent; (2) the cost of mailing; and (3) the priority in which the mail will be delivered.

The U.S. Postal Service limits single-piece mailings to 70 pounds and 108 inches, combined length and girth. To determine the combined length and girth of a parcel, use the following procedures:

(1)   Measure the length of the longest side.

(2)   Measure the distance around the parcel at its thickest part.

(3)   Add the two measurements. The result may not exceed 108 inches.

A brief description of the domestic mail classes and services offered by the U.S. Postal Service follows.

## 13–6.   Express Mail Service

Express Mail service receives the highest priority handling in terms of destination arrival time. It is a high-speed intercity delivery system geared to the special needs of business and industry for the fast transfer of letters, documents, or merchandise.

a.    Express Mail is the only overnight service offering delivery 365 days a year, including weekends and holidays. To use Express Mail Next-Day Service, (1) take the article to a designated Express Mail post office (generally by 5 p.m.), (2) deposit it in an Express Mail collection box (with appropriate postage affixed), (3) call for a pickup (extra charges apply), or (4) hand it to your letter carrier (with appropriate postage affixed). Depending upon the destination, your mailing will be delivered by 12 noon or 3 p.m. the next day. Some destinations may not be reached overnight, but second-day delivery is guaranteed.[2]

---

[1]Visit the U.S. Postal Service's Web site at <www.usps.gov> for current information on domestic and international services and rates.

[2]Telephone (800) 222-1811 for Express Mail pickup, rates, tracking, and general information.

b. All merchandise shipments sent by Express Mail are insured for $500 against loss or damage at no extra charge; negotiable instruments are limited to $15. Document reconstruction insurance is available at an additional cost.

Postage varies by weight and type of service selected. However, the 2-pound flat-rate envelope (supplied by the U.S. Postal Service) is convenient to use. Any amount of material that fits into the envelope, regardless of the weight, may be sent at the rate charged for a 2-pound piece of Express Mail—currently $15. A full postage refund is made for all domestic shipments delivered later than the guaranteed commitment.

c. The maximum weight for domestic Express Mail is 70 pounds; the combined length and girth permitted is 108 inches. Types of Express Mail service include, but are not limited to, the following:

*Express Mail Next-Day or Second-Day Service* is available to all five-digit zip codes. Express Mail Next-Day Service is provided in major cities throughout the United States, and each city has its list of other cities to which it guarantees this service. Express Mail Second-Day Service is available for shipments to service areas not eligible for same-day service.

If next-day delivery is a priority, be sure to check whether your destination zip code has guaranteed next-day delivery from the originating post office. If not, you may wish to use the services of a private delivery service that can guarantee delivery. (See Section 13-5.)

*Express Mail Same-Day Airport Service* provides service between major airports within the United States. Items are brought to the airport mail facility by the customer and sent on the first available flight to the destination airport. They are to be picked up upon arrival at the destination airport mail facility by the addressee.

*Express Mail Custom-Designed Service* is offered 24 hours a day, 365 days a year, under an agreement for customers with regularly scheduled shipments. Each agreement is custom tailored to meet the customer's individual needs.

## 13–7. Priority Mail

Priority Mail offers expedited delivery when the speed of Express Mail is not needed. Between major business centers, this class of mail is generally delivered within two days.

a. All First-Class Mail over 11 ounces is delivered as Priority Mail. Mail weighing less than 11 ounces may be sent as Priority Mail. All Priority Mail should be clearly marked as such; the U.S. Postal Service supplies customers with special containers and labels.

b. Priority Mail flat-rate envelopes are convenient to use. Any amount of material that fits into the envelope, regardless of the weight, may be sent at the rate charged for a 2-pound piece of Priority Mail—currently $3.

E-mail

Mail and E-mail

13

c.  The maximum weight for Priority Mail is 70 pounds, and its dimensions are limited to 108 inches in combined length and girth, the maximum standard set for mailings handled by the U.S. Postal Service.

d.  Priority Mail may be insured, registered, certified, or sent COD for an additional charge.

## 13–8.  First-Class Mail

The following examples are always considered First-Class mail if the weight is 11 ounces or less:

(1)  Handwritten and keyboarded (typewritten) messages, including identical copies

(2)  Bills and statements of account

(3)  Notebooks or account books containing handwritten or keyboarded (typewritten) entries

(4)  Postcards and postal cards

(5)  Greeting cards

(6)  Canceled and uncanceled checks

(7)  Money orders

(8)  Printed forms filled out in writing

(9)  Printed price lists with written or typed changes

(10)  Business-reply mail

(11)  Matter having the characteristics of actual or personal correspondence

(12)  Matter closed against postal inspection

(13)  Any other type of mailable matter weighing 11 ounces or less sent as first class at the option of the mailer

Any First-Class Mail items weighing more than 11 ounces must be sent as Priority Mail.

a.  All First-Class Mail pieces must be at least 0.007 inch thick. First-Class Mail pieces that are 0.25 inch or less in thickness are nonmailable unless they are (1) rectangularly shaped, (2) at least 3.5 inches high, (3) and at least 5 inches long.

A surcharge is assessed on each piece of First-Class Mail weighing 1 ounce or less if it exceeds any one of the following criteria: (1) a height of 6.125 inches, (2) a length of 11.5 inches, (3) a thickness of 0.25 inch. In addition, the surcharge is assessed if the length divided by the height is less than 1.3 or more than 2.5.

Be sure to assess the dimensions of nonstandard-sized mailings before affixing the postage. Original or creative invitations and announcements often exceed the criteria for standard First-Class Mail. If there is any doubt, consult a postal supervisor before mailing the pieces.

b.  For oversized materials (larger than legal-sized envelopes), use the white envelopes with a green diamond border available for purchase

E-mail

at the post office. This border automatically indicates that these materials are to be sent first class.

c. Services such as certificates of mailing, certified, registered, COD, and restricted delivery may be purchased for First-Class Mail. Insurance is also available for purchase; however, only merchandise and material not required to be sent as First-Class Mail may be insured.

d. *Business-Reply Mail* is a First-Class Mail service supplied to mailers who want to encourage responses by paying the postage. Mailers guarantee they will pay the postage plus a fee for all replies returned to them. Anyone wishing to use this service must obtain a permit from the U.S. Postal Service and prepare the replies to conform to a specified format.

## 13–9.  Periodicals

*Periodicals*, formerly known as *Second-Class Mail*, is used by newspaper and magazine publishers to mail publications at a special bulk rate. Only publishers and registered news agents may mail at the Periodicals rates of postage. The general public must pay First-Class Mail or single-piece Standard Mail (A) rates for magazines and newspapers.

## 13–10.  Standard Mail (A)

*Standard Mail* is mail matter not required to be mailed as First-Class Mail nor does it require expedited or first-class service. Although *Standard Mail (A)*, formerly known as *Third-Class Mail*, may be sent by anyone, it is most commonly used by businesses and community organizations who take advantage of significant discounts when mailing at least 200 addressed pieces or 50 pounds of addressed pieces at a time.

a. *Standard Mail (A)* consists of circulars, booklets, catalogs, and other printed materials such as form letters (printed or computer generated), newsletters, or proofs. It also includes merchandise, farm and factory products, photographs, keys, identification devices, and printed drawings. Each piece of Standard Mail (A) is limited in weight to fewer than 16 ounces. The same material weighing 16 ounces or more is classified as *Standard Mail (B)*.

Standard Mail (A) may be sent at a single-piece rate or at a bulk rate. Additionally, certain nonprofit organizations qualify for a special Standard Mail (A) postage rate. Before affixing the postage for a single piece, compare the Standard Mail (A) rate with the First-Class Mail or Priority Mail rate. Often there are just pennies' difference in postage. You may wish to send the mailing first class in view of its priority handling.

## 13–11.  Standard Mail (B) (Parcels)

*Standard Mail (B)*, formerly called *Fourth-Class Mail* or *Parcel Post*, includes such items as merchandise, bound printed matter, books, films, manuscripts, and library materials. The minimum weight for

E-mail

Mail and E-mail

13

Standard Mail (B) is 16 ounces per item; mail weighing less than 16 ounces is usually sent at Standard Mail (A) rates. Maximum weight and size restrictions are 70 pounds and 108 inches combined length and girth. Postage rates for this class are determined by the weight of the parcel and the distance from its point of origin to its destination.

a. *Bulk-Rate Standard Mail (B)* is available for (1) mailings of 300 or more pieces or (2) mailings of at least a 2,000-pound total weight with individual pieces having identical weights.

b. A *Special Standard Mail (B) Rate* may be used for mailing books, certain kinds of films, printed music, printed test materials, sound recordings, manuscripts, educational reference charts, and medical information. Items mailed at this Special Standard Mail (B) Rate may weigh less than 16 ounces. Books containing advertising for merchandise, telephone directories, corporation reports, house organs, and periodicals do not qualify for this special rate.

All items mailed with the Special Standard Mail (B) Rate should be marked as such. In addition, a description of the item should be included, such as "Books," "Sound Recordings," "Films," etc.

c. *Library Rate* is used for certain kinds of materials that are loaned to, exchanged between, mailed to, or mailed by schools, colleges, libraries, museums, and other similar kinds of nonprofit organizations. Materials include books, printed music, academic theses, sound recordings, etc. All items must be marked "Library Rate."

d. Securely bound advertising, promotional, directory, or educational material may be sent at a special *Bound Printed Matter Rate*. Material may not have the nature of personal correspondence and cannot be a book.

## 13–12. Mixed Classes

A first-class letter may be attached to or enclosed in a parcel sent by Standard Mail. If the letter is attached to the parcel, each item should have separate postage. If the letter is enclosed in the package, "First-Class Mail Enclosed" should be marked on the outside of the parcel, along with the correct postage affixed for both items.

## 13–13. Special Delivery

This special service provides for delivery, even on Sundays and holidays, during prescribed hours that extend beyond the hours for delivery of ordinary mail. It is available to all customers served by city carriers and to other customers within a 1-mile radius of the delivery post office.

a. The purchase of special delivery does not always mean the article will be delivered by messenger; it may be delivered by a regular carrier if it is available before the carrier departs for morning deliveries. Although sending an item special delivery virtually ensures delivery on the day received at that post office, it does not necessarily speed up the transportation time to that point from its origin.

**b.** All classes of mail except Express Mail and bulk Standard Mail (A) may be sent special delivery for an additional fee.

## 13–14. Special Handling

A special handling service is provided for preferential handling in the dispatch and transportation of Standard Mail only. A special handling fee must be paid on parcels that take special care, such as baby chicks, baby alligators, packaged bees, etc. This service is not necessary for sending ordinary parcels, even when they contain fragile items. Just mark the package "FRAGILE," and use sufficient cushioning to pack the item.

## 13–15. Insured Mail

**a.** *Registered Mail* is the safest way to send valuables through the mail. This service may be used only for First-Class mail, Priority Mail, or COD parcels with prepaid postage at the First-Class Mail rate. Except for COD parcels, each mailing may be insured for its full value up to $25,000; COD service is limited, however, to items valued at a maximum of $600. Registered mail may not be deposited in collection boxes since a receipt must be issued at the point of mailing.

This service is offered for the protection of negotiable instruments, jewelry, and other items of value. The registry fees, in addition to First-Class Mail or Priority Mail postage, are scaled according to the declared value of the mail. For an additional fee a mailer can obtain a return receipt and/or restrict to whom the mail is delivered.

**b.** *Insured Mail* consists of Standard Mail items insured for protection against loss or damage. This service is also available for any Standard Mail items that are mailed at First-Class mail or Priority Mail rates.

Insured mail has a maximum indemnity of $600. A receipt is given to the mailer at the time of mailing, and a signature is required upon delivery for articles insured for more than $50. You may also purchase the following additional services for articles insured for more than $50: return receipt, restricted delivery, special delivery, and special handling.

**c.** *COD (Collect on Delivery)* may be used for merchandise sent by Express Mail, Priority Mail, First-Class Mail, and Standard Mail. When the mail is delivered, the addressee pays the amount due for the contents. The addressee may also be required to pay the postage and the COD fee, depending upon the prior agreement between the sender and the receiver.

The COD fee includes insurance against loss, damage, or failure to receive the amount collected from the addressee. The maximum amount that can be collected for one item is $600. The goods shipped must have been ordered by the addressee, and the sender agrees to pay any return postage unless specified differently on the mail.

**d.** *Postal Money Orders* provide for sending money through the mail safely. If they are lost or stolen, they can be replaced by presenting your customer receipt. Domestic money orders up to $700 may be purchased and redeemed at any post office. Copies of paid money orders are available for a small fee up to two years after the payment date.

### 13–16. Proof of Mailing and Delivery

The U.S. Postal Service provides ways in which proof may be obtained that an item has been mailed or received. These optional services are available to any mailer.

a. *Certified Mail* is used for First-Class Mail and Priority Mail items that have no monetary value since there is no insurance feature with this service. Certified Mail provides for a record of delivery to be maintained by the post office from which the item was delivered. The carrier delivering Certified Mail obtains a signature from the addressee on a receipt form that is kept for two years. In this way the sender can prove that items were received by the addressee. Proof of delivery may be obtained at a later time during the two-year period following delivery.

b. *Return Receipts* showing to whom, when, and where items were delivered may be obtained for an additional charge for mail that is Registered, Insured, Certified, or sent COD. During the two-year period after delivery, proof of delivery may be obtained from the post office from which the items were delivered.

c. A *Certificate of Mailing* for any item may be obtained from the sender's post office, but only at the time of mailing. Unlike certified mail, however, the post office does not keep any record of the certificate issued or of the delivery of the item. It only provides proof that the item was mailed.

## U.S. Postal Service International Classes and Services

Because the regulations regarding international mailings vary according to country, the information presented here provides only general guidelines for international mailings through the United States Postal Service. For details regarding a specific country, consult the main post office serving your area or the *International Mail Manual* (*IMM*).[3]

### 13–17. Classes of International Mail

Classes of international mail may be separated into three categories. *LC mail*, derived from the French words *Lettres et Cartes* (letters and cards), consists of letters, letter packages, aerogrammes, and postcards. *AO mail*, derived from the French expression *Autres Objets* (other articles), includes regular printed matter, books, sheet music, matter for the blind, small packets, and publishers' periodicals. The

---

[3]Copies of the *International Mail Manual* are available through your local post office or the Superintendent of Documents, U.S. Government Printing Office, Washington, D.C. 20402-9371 [Tel: (202) 783-3238].

third category, *CP mail*, is an abbreviation for *Colis Postaux*, the French version of *parcel post*.

**a.** Letters and Letter Packages. Mail items containing current correspondence, handwritten or typewritten, must be sent as *Letters* or *Letter Packages*. Merchandise or other articles may also be mailed at Letter postage rates as long as they are allowed by the destination country. Letters and Letter Packages may be sent at either air rates or surface rates, and the weight limit to all countries for this class is 4 pounds.

**b.** Postcards. Postcards and postal cards consist of single cards sent without an envelope or wrapper. They may be sent at either air or surface rates. Folded (double) cards must be mailed in envelopes at the Letter postage rate.

**c.** Aerogrammes. Aerogrammes are air letter sheets that are folded into the form of an envelope and sealed with tape or stickers. Enclosures are not permitted in this class of mail.

**d.** Printed matter. Printed matter refers to paper on which words, letters, characters, figures, and/or images not resembling a bill or statement of account or correspondence have been reproduced by a process other than handwriting or typewriting. Included in this classification are publishers' periodicals, books, sheet music, and other regular printed matter. Items not permitted under this classification include articles of stationery, postage stamps, framed photographs or certificates, photographic negatives or slides, films, microfilm or microfiche, and playing cards. Weight limits to various countries vary, depending upon the contents and country of destination. Printed matter may be sent at either air or surface rates.

**e.** M-Bag Mail. Printed matter in quantities of 15 pounds or more may, under certain circumstances, be enclosed in mail sacks addressed directly to a single addressee. The combined weight of the sack and its contents may not exceed 66 pounds. M-Bag Mail may be sent by airmail, ISAL (International Surface Air Lift), or surface mail.

**f.** Matter for the Blind. Weight limit for this class is 15 pounds, and the surface rate is free. Consult your local post office for matter eligible for this class and for air rates.

**g.** Small Packets. Items of merchandise, commercial samples, or documents that do not resemble current or personal correspondence may be sent by this class. The postage rates are lower than those for Letter Packages or Parcel Post, and the weight limit for most countries is 4 pounds. Small Packets may be sent at either air or surface rates.

**h.** Parcel Post. Packages of merchandise or any other articles that are not required to be mailed as Letters or Letter Packages may be sent as Parcel Post. Any written communication resembling current or personal correspondence is not permitted. Parcel Post offers insurance protection against loss. The maximum weight limit per package depends upon the destination country, but this limit is usually either 22 or 44 pounds. International Parcel Post resembles domestic zone-rated Standard Mail (B).

E-mail

Mail and E-mail

13

**i.** Express Mail International Service (EMS). Express Mail International Service offers reliable, high-speed mail service to nearly 200 countries and territories around the world. In addition to the regular service, there are options tailored for specific business needs. EMS includes merchandise and document reconstruction insurance at no extra charge. The weight limit is generally 33 or 44 pounds, depending upon the country of destination. Unlike domestic Express Mail, there is no service guarantee for Express Mail International Service.

**j.** Global Priority Mail. Urgent items weighing up to 4 pounds, including merchandise, may be sent to designated countries around the world by Global Priority Mail.

**k.** International Surface Air Lift (ISAL). International Surface Air Lift (ISAL) provides expedited dispatch and transportation for all types of printed matter. Mailing costs are lower than airmail while the service is faster than that provided by surface mail. ISAL shipments are brought by the customer to a designated airport mail facility from which they are sent by air to their foreign destination. Upon arrival the shipments are placed into the surface mail system for delivery to the addressee.

**l.** INTELPOST. International Electronic Post, INTELPOST, offers same- or next-day delivery of facsimile documents from post offices in major cities to addresses in about 50 foreign countries. Any item that can be photocopied can be sent in minutes. It can be picked up by the addressee within an hour, delivered by special delivery the same day (depending on time differences around the world), or delivered by regular mail the next day.

## 13–18. Special Services for International Mail

**a.** Registered Mail. Registered Mail arranges for the secure handling of mail and provides an indemnity of $42.30 (up to $1,000 in Canada). This service is available only for Letter mail, Small Packets, and all Printed Matter.

**b.** Insurance. Insurance offers indemnity for loss of or damage to items sent as Parcel Post. Insurance is not available for Letter mail, Small Packets, or Printed Matter. The maximum indemnity is $600, but only certain countries are eligible for this service and the maximum limits vary according to country.

**c.** Return Receipt. Return Receipts provide mailers evidence of delivery of Registered or Insured mail. Return receipts must be purchased at the time of mailing.

**d.** Restricted Delivery. Restricted Delivery limits who may receive an item. This service is available to many countries for Registered Mail. Details of the service, however, are governed by the internal legislation of the destination country.

**e.** Special Delivery. Special delivery provides for faster delivery of Letter mail, Small Packets, and Printed Matter at the post office serving the addressee, according to the special delivery regulations of the destination country. This service is not available for items sent as Parcel Post. Special Delivery is available to most countries.

**f.** Special Handling. Special Handling provides for preferential handling to the extent practical in dispatch and transportation from the office of mailing to the U.S. office of dispatch. This service does not offer preferential dispatch from the U.S. or special treatment in the destination country. Special Handling is available only for Parcel Post, Printed Matter, Matter for the Blind, and Small Packets sent at surface rates.

**g.** Collect on Delivery (COD). Collect on Delivery is not available for international items.

**h.** Certified Mail. Certified Mail is not available for international mail items.

E-mail

Mail and E-mail

13

# Chapter 14

# Indexing for Filing

ABC

## Indexing for Filing Solution Finder

### Filing Process, The

### Indexing and Alphabetizing

ABC

# The Filing Process

## 14–1. Purpose of Indexing

You may find that you need to set up communication indexers, (telephone, fax, E-mail, address), customer/client files, patient files, vendor files, or some other kind of database involving individual and/or organizational names. To organize names so they can be located easily, you will first need to place the separate words in each name in a sequence to be alphabetized. This process is known as *indexing*. Once placed in the proper order, the units may be alphabetized.

So that filed names may be located easily (retrieved), all names must be indexed and alphabetized in the same manner; that is, you need to follow the same set of guidelines in preparing each name for filing. The most commonly used set of guidelines is called the *Simplified Filing Standard Rules*.

## 14–2. Simplified Filing Standard Rules

The rules presented here for indexing and alphabetizing individual and organizational names are the Simplified Filing Standard Rules endorsed by the Association of Records Managers and Administrators, Inc. (ARMA International).[1]

The ARMA publication for alphabetic filing explains and illustrates accepted deviations from the Simplified Filing Standard Rules but cautions that these deviations must be documented for all users. Otherwise, inconsistencies in indexing records for alphabetizing will lead to difficulties in locating and retrieving records.

The following rules and examples are based solely on the Simplified Filing Standard Rules.

# Indexing and Alphabetizing

## 14–3. Indexing and Alphabetizing the Names of Individuals

a. To index the names of individuals, arrange the units (words and initials) in each name in the following order:

(1) Complete last name as written (includes hyphenated last names and *all* prefixes such as *D', Da, De, Del, De La, Della, Den, Des, Di, Du, El, Fitz, L', La, Las, Le, Les, Lo, Los, M', Mac, Mc, O', Saint, San, St., Ste., Te, Ten, Ter, Van, Van de, van Der, Von,* and *Von der*.

(2) Complete first name or initial (includes two-word first names such as *Jo Ann, Mary Ellen, John Paul,* and *Billy Bob*)

(3) Complete middle name(s) or initial(s)

[1]*Alphabetic Filing Rules*, 2nd Ed. (Prairie Village, Kans.: ARMA International, 1995), 3–4, 7–9, 17–22. [Copies of this publication may be purchased from ARMA International by telephoning (913) 341-3808.]

Do not use suffixes and titles as filing units unless they are needed to distinguish between or among identical names. Titles and suffixes include the following:

(1) Seniority suffix (rank designated by a Roman numeral or the abbreviation *Jr.* or *Sr.*)

(2) Professional suffix (position designated by a certification such as *CPA, Ph.D.,* or *R.N.*)

(3) Title (such as *Mr., Mrs., Ms., Dr., Professor, Sergeant, Dean,* or *Governor*)

Titles followed only by a first name or a last name are indexed in the order they are written. Examples of such names are *Queen Elizabeth, Brother John,* and *Mr. Damico.*

## complete names of individuals placed in indexing order

| Last (Unit 1) | First (Unit 2) | Middle (Unit 3) | Suffixes and Titles (Unit 4) |
|---|---|---|---|
| Clark | James | L. | Jr. |
| Clark | James | L. | Sr. |
| Hoover | Han Nang | Kim | Mrs. |
| Hoover | Herb | Michael | Mr. |
| Clark | William | James | Mr. |
| Clark | William | James | Dr. |
| Costellano | Maria Elena | Murillo Lopez | |
| Hoover | Hannah | Kim | Ms. |
| Clark | Wm. | Bradley | |
| Clark-Hoover | Karen | Lynelle | Ms. |
| Clemson | B. | Thomas | II |
| Ho | Hung | | Mr. |
| Clemson-Clark | Alice | Marie | |
| Harper | Mary | | Sister |
| Hoover | BettyBruce | Howard | |
| Hoover | Betty Lou | H. | Ms. |
| Hertig | Thomas | J. | Major |
| De Hertog | Thos. | I. | R.N. |
| De Hertog | Thomas | James | |
| Hertig | Thomas | J. | Mr. |
| Clemson | B. | Thomas | III |
| Hoover | Herbert | Charles Marsh | Mr. |
| Hoover | Herb | Michael | M.D. |
| Debrosian | John | T. | |
| Delano | Marisa | Torti | Mrs. |
| Hoover | Billy Bob | Scot | |

## title with first or last name only

| Title (Unit 1) | First or Last (Unit 2) |
|---|---|
| Sister | Mary |
| Mr. | Hoover |
| General | Clark |

**b.** Indexed names are alphabetized in indexing order. In alphabetizing names, place (1) nothing before something, (2) numerals before alphabetic letters, and (3) initials before names containing that letter.

Compound names (those containing more than one word) in an indexing unit are treated as a single word, whether they are hyphenated or separated by a space. All punctuation marks—such as periods, apostrophes, hyphens, and commas—are disregarded.

Abbreviated and shortened names such as *Wm.* and *Sandy* are alphabetized as they are written.

| Unit 1 | Unit 2 | Unit 3 | Unit 4 |
| --- | --- | --- | --- |
| Clark | James | L. | Jr. |
| Clark | James | L. | Sr. |
| Clark | William | James | Dr. |
| Clark | William | James | Mr. |
| Clark | Wm. | Bradley | |
| Clark-Hoover | Karen | Lynelle | Ms. |
| Clemson | B. | Thomas | II |
| Clemson | B. | Thomas | III |
| Clemson-Clark | Alice | Marie | |
| Costellano | Maria Elena | Murillo Lopez | |
| Debrosian | John | T. | |
| De Hertog | Thomas | James | |
| De Hertog | Thos. | I. | R.N. |
| Delano | Marisa | Torti | Mrs. |
| General | Clark | | |
| Harper | Mary | | Sister |
| Hertig | Thomas | J. | Major |
| Hertig | Thomas | J. | Mr. |
| Ho | Hung | | Mr. |
| Hoover | BettyBruce | Howard | |
| Hoover | Betty Lou | H. | Ms. |
| Hoover | Billy Bob | Scot | |
| Hoover | Hannah | Kim | Ms. |
| Hoover | Han Nang | Kim | Mrs. |
| Hoover | Herb | Michael | M.D. |
| Hoover | Herb | Michael | Mr. |
| Hoover | Herbert | Charles Marsh | Mr. |
| Mr. | Hoover | | |
| Sister | Mary | | |

## 14–4. Indexing and Alphabetizing the Names of Organizations

**a.** Words in business and organizational names are arranged in the order they are written, even the full names of individuals. Each word—including articles, prepositions, conjunctions, and symbols—is a separate unit. Except for the word *The* appearing as the first word, index the words in the order they are written. When the word *The* begins a business or organizational name, consider it the last filing unit.

Spell out any symbols such as & (*and*), $ (*dollar*), or # (*number*). Disregard all punctuation marks such as hyphens, apostrophes, periods, commas, or quotation marks. Close up any letters or words and index them as a single unit.

### business names containing articles, lowercase words, and symbols

| Business/ Organizational Name | Unit 1 | Unit 2 | Unit 3 | Unit 4 | Unit 5 |
|---|---|---|---|---|---|
| Fortune $ Saver | Fortune | Dollar | Saver | | |
| Jane Ryan & Associates | Jane | Ryan | and | Associates | |
| Jane Ryan and Sons | Jane | Ryan | and | Sons | |
| The Jane Ryan Realty Company | Jane | Ryan | Realty | Company | The |
| Rings and Things | Rings | and | Things | | |

### business names containing punctuation

| Business/ Organizational Name | Unit 1 | Unit 2 | Unit 3 | Unit 4 | Unit 5 |
|---|---|---|---|---|---|
| Dr. Ryan's Hospital and Clinic | Dr. | Ryan's | Hospital | and | Clinic |
| Foreman-Ryan Furniture | Foreman-Ryan | Furniture | | | |
| In-and-Out Burger King | In-and-Out | Burger | King | | |
| Mark C. Bloom Tires | Mark | C. | Bloom | Tires | |
| Ryan, Irwin, Kirk, and Janns | Ryan | Irwin | Kirk | and | Janns |
| Ryan's Automotive Repair | Ryan's | Automotive | Repair | | |

**b.** Single letters separated by spaces in business and organizational names are considered separate indexing units. Single letters hyphenated or written without spaces, letters representing the full organizational name (such as *IBM*, *GM*, and *YMCA*), acronyms (names made from initial letters such as *MADD* and *D.A.R.E.*), and call letters for radio and television stations are indexed as single units.

### letters indexed as separate units

| Business/ Organizational Name | Unit 1 | Unit 2 | Unit 3 | Unit 4 | Unit 5 |
|---|---|---|---|---|---|
| A B C Linen Service | A | B | C | Linen | Service |
| A to Z Rentals | A | to | Z | Rentals | |
| H L T Express | H | L | T | Express | |

## letters indexed as a single unit

| Business/ Organizational Name | Unit 1 | Unit 2 | Unit 3 | Unit 4 | Unit 5 |
|---|---|---|---|---|---|
| ABC Learning Systems | ABC | Learning | Systems | | |
| ARMA | ARMA | | | | |
| A-to-Z Data Systems | A-to-Z | Data | Systems | | |
| ITT | ITT | | | | |
| KABC Radio | KABC | Radio | | | |
| KNXT Television | KNXT | Television | | | |
| TWA | TWA | | | | |
| ZZZ Freight Express | ZZZ | Freight | Express | | |

c. In business and organizational names, all abbreviated words such as *Inc.*, *Co.*, and *Mfg.* are indexed as written. Names of cities appearing in business and organizational names are also indexed as written; however, prefixes (see Section 14-3a) and names appearing together are indexed as one unit.

## abbreviations indexed as written

| Business/ Organizational Name | Unit 1 | Unit 2 | Unit 3 | Unit 4 | Unit 5 |
|---|---|---|---|---|---|
| A & A Paper Co. | A | and | A | Paper | Co. |
| The Clothing Factory, Ltd. | Clothing | Factory | Ltd. | The | |
| Mrs. Ryan's Cookies, Inc. | Mrs. | Ryan's | Cookies | Inc. | |

## cities indexed as written or combined with prefixes

| Business/ Organizational Name | Unit 1 | Unit 2 | Unit 3 | Unit 4 | Unit 5 |
|---|---|---|---|---|---|
| El Centro Produce Market | El Centro | Produce | Market | | |
| Ft. Lauderdale Resorts, Inc. | Ft. | Lauderdale | Resorts | Inc. | |
| The Kansas City Inn | Kansas | City | Inn | The | |
| Las Vegas Credit Bureau | Las Vegas | Credit | Bureau | | |
| Los Angeles Flower Exchange | Los Angeles | Flower | Exchange | | |
| New York Stock Exchange | New | York | Stock | Exchange | |
| Newark Yellow Cab Co. | Newark | Yellow | Cab | Co. | |
| San Diego Gas and Electric Co. | San Diego | Gas | and | Electric | Co. |
| San Francisco Travel Agency | San Francisco | Travel | Agency | | |
| South Pasadena Cleaners | South | Pasadena | Cleaners | | |
| St. Louis Flowers and Gifts | St. Louis | Flowers | and | Gifts | |
| Terre Haute Pharmacy | Terre | Haute | Pharmacy | | |
| West Covina Pet Hospital | West | Covina | Pet | Hospital | |
| The West Haven Motor Lodge | West | Haven | Motor | Lodge | The |
| The Westfield Motor Lodge | Westfield | Motor | Lodge | The | |

**d.** Spelled-out numbers in business and organizational names are treated as any other word in alphabetizing names. Arabic numerals, however, precede all alphabetic letters in arranging indexing units; Roman numerals follow directly after any Arabic numerals—before any alphabetic letters. Arrange the numerals in ascending order, and disregard any ordinal endings such as *st*, *nd*, or *rd*.

### spelled out numbers

| Business/<br>Organizational Name | Unit 1 | Unit 2 | Unit 3 | Unit 4 | Unit 5 |
|---|---|---|---|---|---|
| Twelfth Street Cafe | Twelfth | Street | Cafe | | |
| Twentieth Century Insurance | Twentieth | Century | Insurance | | |
| Two-for-One Sundries | Two-for-One | Sundries | | | |

### Arabic or Roman numerals

| Business/<br>Organizational Name | Unit 1 | Unit 2 | Unit 3 | Unit 4 | Unit 5 |
|---|---|---|---|---|---|
| $1 Outlet | 1 | Dollar | Outlet | | |
| 2-for-1 Photos | 2-for-1 | Photos | | | |
| 5 Star Realty | 5 | Star | Realty | | |
| 20th Century Realtors, Inc. | 20 | Century | Realtors | Inc. | |
| 99¢ Store | 99 | Cent | Store | | |
| A1 Photos | A1 | Photos | | | |
| Aaron Bros. Art Studios | Aaron | Bros. | Art | Studios | |
| Pier 1 Imports | Pier | 1 | Imports | | |
| Pier I Food Imports | Pier | I | Food | Imports | |
| Sixth Avenue Pharmacy | Sixth | Avenue | Pharmacy | | |
| Star 4 Studios | Star | 4 | Studios | | |
| Star III Studios | Star | III | Studios | | |

**e.** Names of domestic government entities are indexed first under the level of government: United States Government, (state name) State of, (county name) County of, (city name) City of, or (village name) Village of. These levels are a single indexing unit.[2]

Departments and agencies of the federal government are first indexed under *United States Government*. The second indexing unit is the main word that identifies the department, bureau, or office. Terms such as *Bureau of* or *Department of* follow the second indexing unit.

Subdivisions of departments and agencies are subsequently indexed according to their order of authority. Again, use main words for the primary indexing units.

---

[2]Ibid., 31.

### federal government entities

| Unit 1 | Unit 2 | Unit 3 | Unit 4 | Unit 5 |
|---|---|---|---|---|
| United States Government | Agriculture | (Department of) | | |
| United States Government | Commerce | (Department of) Economic International | Development Trade | Administration Administration |
| United States Government | State | (Department of) Passport | Agency | |
| United States Government | Transportation | (Department of) Coast Federal | Guard Aviation | Administration |
| United States Government | Treasury | (Department of) Alcohol | Tobacco (and) | Firearms (Bureau of) |
| | | Customs Internal | Service Revenue | Service |

### state and local government entities

| Unit 1 | Unit 2 | Unit 3 | Unit 4 | Unit 5 |
|---|---|---|---|---|
| California State of | Consumer | Affairs | Department of | |
| California State of | Employment | Development | Department | |
| Glendale City of | Building | Permits | | |
| Glendale City of | Community | Development | and | Housing |
| Los Angeles County of | Animal | Care | and | Control |
| Los Angeles County of | Disabilities | Commission on | | |

    **f.** Index government agencies in foreign countries first by their country. To prevent confusion, use English names. If appropriate, index any additional units in the country name, e.g., *China, Republic of*. States, colonies, provinces, cities, and other such government entities follow, with their names spelled in English.

| Unit 1 | Unit 2 | Unit 3 | Unit 4 | Unit 5 |
|---|---|---|---|---|
| Belgium | Kingdom of | Taxation | Department of | |
| China | Republic of | Internal | Affairs | Bureau of |
| South Korea | Seoul | City of | | |
| Uruguay | Republic of | Public | Education | Secretary of |

## 14–5.  Handling Identical and Alternate Names

    **a.** Use the address to determine the correct filing order of identical individual or organizational names. Compare addresses in the following order: (1) city names, (2) state names, (3) street names (with street numbers appearing before street names), and (4) house or building numbers. Use these address components in the order listed only until the names are distinguished.

| Identical Name | City | State | Street | House No. |
|---|---|---|---|---|
| John R. Smith | Springfield | Connecticut | | |
| John R. Smith | Springfield | Illinois | 23rd Street | |
| John R. Smith | Springfield | Illinois | Dover Avenue | 910 |
| John R. Smith | Springfield | Illinois | Dover Avenue | 3640 |

**b.** Individuals or organizations that are known by more than one name should be cross-referenced. These second (and even third) names are an additional filing entry indexed in the order of the alternate name. When persons look for the entry under the alternate name, the cross-reference entry refers them to the original record.

Cross-referencing is often used for (1) unusual names, (2) persons or businesses having more than one name, (3) abbreviated names, and (4) foreign business names.

**cross-reference entry**

PSI

See: Professional Secretaries International

**examples of cross-referenced names**

| | |
|---|---|
| Thomas Howard | See: Howard, Thomas |
| Hung Ho | See: Ho, Hung |
| Duncan, Thelma R. | See: Nicklin, Thelma R. Duncan |
| Yama Motors | See: Matsuyama Motor Imports, Inc. |
| ABC | See: Association for Business Communication |
| Bonn Chemische Fabrik AG | See: Bonn Chemical Works Inc. |

# Information Sources

http:/

# Information Sources Solution Finder

## Electronic Media

Basic resource materials
    Almanacs   15-9
    Atlases   15-9
    Biographies   15-9
    Dictionaries   15-9
    Encyclopedias   15-9
    Quotations   15-9
    Thesauri   15-9
Directories and other locators
    800 numbers directory   15-10
    Census information   15-10
    Fax numbers directory   15-10
    Internet directories   15-9, 15-10
    Street directories, U.S.A.   15-10
    Telephone directories,
       national   15-10
    Web site directories   15-10
    Yellow pages, national   15-10
    Zip code directories   15-9, 15-10

## On-Line Resources

Connecting to the Internet   15-11
    Equipment needed 15-11b
    Kinds of information on the
       Internet   15-11a
    On-line service providers   15-11b
    Software needed   15-11b
Internet Web sites   15-13
    Airline reservations   15-13e
    Almanacs   15-13a
    Atlases   15-13a
    Biographies   15-13g
    Conversion tables   15-13g
    Delivery services   15-13c, d
    Dictionaries   15-13a
    Directories and other locators
       15-13e, g

Encyclopedias   15-13a
Government information   15-13c
Hotel reservations   15-13g
News sources   15-13b
Quotations   15-13g
Stock market information   15-13g
Style manuals   15-13f
Thesauri   15-13a
Weather information   15-13g
World Wide Web on the Internet
    15-12
    Browsers   15-12b
    Hypertext   15-12a
    Locating information   15-12c
    Search engines   15-12c

## Published Materials

Almanacs   15-3
Atlases   15-4
Business information   15-8
    Career information   15-8
    Corporate information   15-8
    Directories   15-8
    Internet Yellow Pages   15-8
    Office equipment   15-8
    Robert's Rules of Order   15-8
    World Wide Web sites   15-8
    Writing style   15-8
Dictionaries   15-1
    Specialized   15-1c
    Standard   15-1a, b
Encyclopedias   15-3
Etiquette standards   15-7
Quotations   15-6
Style manuals   15-5, 15-8
Thesauri   15-2

http:/

Business people often need to consult reference material to gather information for general operations, decision making, and document preparation. Major sources were previously confined to printed reference materials. With advances in technology, however, other forms of information exchange—electronic media and on-line resources—provide access to the information needed by today's fast-paced business environment.

Reference materials are abundant. Numerous kinds and extensive listings are available in libraries, in bookstores, from software vendors, and on the Internet. Some are valuable tools for the business person; others are not. The intent of this chapter is to provide a selective listing of printed materials, electronic media, and on-line resources that will be most valuable for a business person. The sources listed may be (1) purchased at reasonable prices from bookstores or software vendors, (2) located at local public or university libraries, or (3) accessed on the Internet.

# Published Materials

## 15–1. Dictionaries

a. Although word processing programs provide a spell checker, this feature has its limitations. It does not differentiate between words that sound alike but are spelled differently, flag words that are used incorrectly, or assess whether a term should be spelled as one or two words (e.g. *mark down* or *markdown*). Dictionaries provide spellings, syllabication, pronunciation guides, definitions, irregular verb and adjective forms, and synonyms in their entries—all useful information in preparing business documents.

b. Dictionaries are generally published in paperback-pocket format, collegiate editions, or complete unabridged versions. Collegiate editions—because of their compact, comprehensive nature and annual update printings—are considered the best source for office use. Update your office dictionary every three years, and select an authoritative one such as those listed below:

*The American Heritage Dictionary of the English Language.* 3rd ed. Boston: Houghton Mifflin Company, 1996. (Published annually)
*Merriam-Webster's Collegiate Dictionary.* 10th ed. Springfield, Mass.: Merriam-Webster, Incorporated, 1996. (Published annually)
*Random House Webster's College Dictionary.* New York: Random House, Inc., 1995.
*Webster's New World College Dictionary.* 3rd ed. New York: Macmillan, Inc., 1996. (Published annually)
*Webster's Third New International Dictionary of the English Language, Unabridged.* Springfield, Mass.: Merriam-Webster, Incorporated, 1993.

c. Consider whether specialized dictionaries are needed in your office. Besides the regular array of foreign language-English dictionaries, investigate the usefulness of dictionaries that define business terms, computer terms, legal terms, medical terms, and foreign expressions.

Information

15

461

> *The American Heritage Stedman's Medical Dictionary*. Boston: Houghton Mifflin Company, 1995.
>
> *Black's Law Dictionary*. St. Paul, Minn.: West Publishing Company, 1992.
>
> *Computer Dictionary*. 2nd ed. Redmond, Wash.: Microsoft Press, 1994.
>
> Cross, Wilbur. *Encyclopedic Dictionary of Business Terms*. Englewood Cliffs, N.J.: Prentice Hall, 1995.
>
> Gifis, Steven H. *Law Dictionary*. Hauppauge, N.Y.: Barron's Educational Series, Inc., 1996
>
> Guinagh, Kevin, translator and compiler. *Dictionary of Foreign Phrases and Abbreviations*. 3rd ed. New York: The H. W. Wilson Company, 1983.
>
> *Merriam-Webster's Medical Desk Dictionary*. Springfield, Mass.: Merriam-Webster, Incorporated, 1993.

## 15–2. Thesauri

Use a thesaurus to add variety to your writing style. Locate words with the same meaning for those words you tend to overuse. A partial listing of thesauri follows:

> *Bartlett's Roget's Thesaurus*. Boston: Little, Brown and Company, 1996.
>
> Chapman, Robert L., ed. *Roget's International Thesaurus*. 5th ed. New York: HarperCollins Publishers, 1992.
>
> *Roget's II, The New Thesaurus*. 3rd ed. Boston: Houghton Mifflin Company, 1995.

## 15–3. Encyclopedias and Almanacs

Encyclopedias and almanacs provide answers for questions that might arise concerning events and trends.

Almanacs, published annually, describe significant events of the past year; provide information about government officials, states, the United States, and other nations; and supply facts on weather and other topics.

For people involved in international communication, encyclopedias furnish background information about countries' political systems, history, customs, and other relevant information. In addition, encyclopedias provide a concise synopsis on virtually thousands of topics.

The following sources may prove valuable in collecting facts and information:

> *Collier's Encyclopedia* (24 volumes). New York: P. F. Collier, Inc.
>
> *The Encyclopaedia Britannica* (30 volumes). Chicago: Encyclopaedia Britannica, Inc.
>
> *The Encyclopedia Americana* (30 volumes). New York: Grolier Incorporated.
>
> Godin, Seth, ed. *The 1996 Information Please Business Almanac and Sourcebook*. Boston: Houghton Mifflin Company. (Published annually)
>
> *Information Please Almanac, Atlas & Yearbook*. Boston: Houghton Mifflin Company. (Published annually)
>
> *The Old Farmer's Almanac*. Dublin, N.H.: Old Farmer's Almanac. (Published annually)
>
> *The World Almanac and Book of Facts*. Mahwah, N.J.: World Almanac Books. (Published annually)

## 15–4. Atlases

Atlases provide maps of cities, states, countries, continents, and the world. Accompanying a wide variety of maps is often information on areas such as population, weather, terrain, agricultural production, and economic orientation. Consult atlases such as the following:

*Hammond Atlas of the World, Concise Edition.* Maplewood, N.J.: Hammond Incorporated, 1996.
*Oxford Concise Atlas of the World.* New York: Oxford University Press, Inc., 1995.
*The World, Afghanistan to Zimbabwe.* U.S.A.: Rand McNally.
*World Facts & Maps, 1996 Edition.* U.S.A.: Rand McNally, 1996. (Published annually)

## 15–5. Style Manuals

Style manuals govern the presentation style of reports and manuscripts. Three styles dominate the preparation of reports and manuscripts: (1) the Modern Language Association (MLA) style is endorsed by those writing in the fields of language and arts; (2) the American Psychological Association (APA) style is endorsed by those writing in the social sciences; and (3) *The Chicago Manual of Style* prescribes a traditional style usable for business, researchers, and students.

The following listing gives the latest authoritative published sources for preparing manuscripts or reports according to the MLA, APA, or Chicago Style Manual style. Two other sources—popular among students and business people—have also been included.

*The AMA Style Guide for Business Writing.* New York: American Management Association, 1996.
*The Chicago Manual of Style.* 14th ed. Chicago: The University of Chicago Press, 1993.
Gibaldi, Joseph. *MLA Handbook for Writers of Research Papers.* 4th Ed. New York: The Modern Language Association of America, 1995.
*Publication Manual of the American Psychological Association.* 4th Ed. Washington, D.C.: American Psychological Association, 1994.
Turabian, Kate L. *A Manual for Writers of Term Papers, Theses, and Dissertations.* 6th Ed. Chicago: The University of Chicago Press, 1996.

## 15–6. Quotations

Books of famous quotations are often useful in preparing speeches, written presentations, or marketing brochures. Collections of famous quotations are organized according to topic so suitable selections can be made easily. Several books of quotations are listed below:

Bartlett, John. Justin Kaplan, ed. *Bartlett's Familiar Quotations.* 16th ed. Boston: Little, Brown and Company, 1992.
Donadio, Stephen, Joan Smith, Susan Mesner, and Rebecca Davison, eds. *The New York Public Library of 20th-Century American Quotations.* New York: The Stonesong Press, Inc., and The New York Public Library, 1992.
Peter, Laurence J. *Peter's Quotations, Ideas for Our Time.* New York: William Morrow and Company, Inc., 1977.

Information

15

## 15–7. Etiquette Standards

Business etiquette and general etiquette standards are important in establishing and maintaining business relationships. Etiquette standards and customs differ throughout the world so the international business person should be well acquainted with not only American standards but also standards of other cultures. The following books address a variety of domestic situations and international customs:

*The Amy Vanderbilt Complete Book of Etiquette.* Revised and expanded by Leticia Baldrige. Garden City, N.Y.: Doubleday & Company, Inc., 1978.

Axtell, Roger E. *The Do's and Taboos of International Trade.* New York: John Wiley & Sons, Inc., 1991.

Baldrige, Leticia. *Leticia Baldrige's New Complete Guide to Executive Manners.* New York: Rawson Associates, 1993.

Morrison, Terri, Wayne A. Conaway, and George A. Borden. *Kiss, Bow, or Shake Hands: How to Do Business in Sixty Countries.* Holbrook, Mass.: Bob Adams, Inc., 1994.

Post, Emily. *Emily Post's Etiquette.* 15th ed. New York: HarperCollins, 1992.

## 15–8. Business Information Sources

The following publications contain information that may be used for job seeking, meetings, research, mailings, writing style, or general information:

Derrick, John. *The Office Equipment Adviser.* 3rd ed. Santa Barbara, Calif.: What to Buy for Business, Inc., 1995.

English, Katharine, ed. *Most Popular Web Sites.* Emeryville, Calif.: Lycos Press, 1996.

Glossbrenner, Alfred and Emily. *Finding a Job on the Internet.* New York: McGraw-Hill, Inc., 1995.

*Guide to the FORTUNE 500 U.S. Corporations.* By the editors of *Fortune* and *Hoover's Handbooks.* Austin, Tex.: The Reference Press, Inc., and Time Inc., 1996.

Holmberg, Erin E., ed. *Directories in Print.* 13th ed. Vol 1, Descriptive Listings. New York: Gale Research Inc., 1996. (Published annually)

Holmberg, Erin E., ed. *Directories in Print.* 13th ed. Vol 2, Indexes. New York: Gale Research Inc., 1996. (Published annually)

Kennedy, Joyce Lain, and Thomas J. Morrow. *Electronic Résumé Revolution.* New York: John Wiley & Sons, Inc., 1994.

Newby, Gregory B., ed. *Mecklermedia's Official World Internet Yellow Pages.* Foster City, Calif.: IDG Books Worldwide, Inc., 1996. (Published annually)

Rositano, Dean J., Robert A. Rositano, and Jay Lee. *Que's Mega Web Directory.* 2nd ed. Indianapolis: Que Corporation, 1996.

Rozakis, Laurie. *New Robert's Rules of Order.* New York: Smithmark Publishers, 1996.

Strunk, William, and E. B. White. *The Elements of Style.* 3rd ed. New York: Macmillan Publishing Co., Inc., 1979.

http://

# Electronic Media

## 15–9. Basic Resource Materials

CD-ROM drives on recent-generation computers permit access to volumes of data previously believed accessible only through printed material. CD-ROMs contain volumes of information that can be read and/or captured while working on a Windows program.

The following listing focuses on dictionaries, thesauri, encyclopedias, atlases, and other such general reference material. Some are single-source references; other packages contain multiple volumes. CD-ROM publishers generally maintain Web sites on the Internet for users to obtain product information and updates. Internet addresses are shown in angle brackets (< >).

*American Heritage Dictionary With Roget's II Thesaurus*. CD-ROM. Palo Alto, Calif.: DUX Software, 1995.
*Compton's Interactive World Atlas*. CD-ROM. Cambridge, Mass.: Compton's New Media, Inc., 1997.
*Grolier Multimedia Encyclopedia*. CD-ROM. Danbury, Conn.: Grolier Interactive Inc., 1997. <http://www.grolier. com>.
*The Merriam-Webster Dictionary*. CD-ROM. Dallas: Zane Publishing, Inc., 1996.
*Merriam-Webster's Biographical Dictionary*. CD-ROM. Hiawatha, Iowa: Parsons Technology.
*Merriam-Webster's Collegiate Dictionary* (with thesaurus). 10th ed. CD-ROM and Book. Dallas: Zane Publishing, Inc., 1996.
*Merriam-Webster's Collegiate Dictionary, Deluxe Electronic Edition*. CD-ROM. Springfield, Mass.: Merriam-Webster Electronic Publishing, 1995.
*Microsoft Bookshelf*. 1996-97 ed. CD-ROM. Microsoft Corporation, 1996. (Published annually) <http://www.microsoft.com/bookshelf>.
  *Internet Directory 96*
  *Concise Encarta 96 World Atlas*
  *The American Heritage Dictionary, 3rd ed.*
  *The Original Roget's Thesaurus*
  *The World Almanac and Book of Facts 1996*
  *The Concise Columbia Encyclopedia, 3rd ed.*
  *The Columbia Dictionary of Quotations*
  *The People's Chronology*
  *National Five-Digit Zip Code and Post Office Directory*
*Microsoft Encarta '97 Encyclopedia*. CD-ROM. Microsoft Corporation, 1997. (Published annually) <http://www.encarta.com>.
*Microsoft Encarta '97 World Atlas*. CD-ROM. Microsoft Corporation, 1997. (Published annually) <http://www.encarta.com>.
*The Plain-Language Law Dictionary*. Disk. Hiawatha, Iowa: Parsons Technology. <http://www.parsonstech.com>.
*The Random House Health and Medicine Dictionary*. Disk. Hiawatha, Iowa: Parsons Technology. <http://www.parsonstech.com>.
*Time Magazine Multimedia Almanac*. CD-ROM. Cambridge, Mass.: SoftKey, 1995.
*Webster's Concise Encyclopedia*. CD-ROM. Chatsworth, Calif.: Cambrix Publishing, 1995.
*Webster's New World College Dictionary*. 3rd ed. CD-ROM. Dallas: Zane Publishing, Inc., 1996.

Information
15

## 15–10. Directories and Other Locators

Businesses often wish to locate names of individuals and other businesses, addresses, phone numbers, fax numbers, zip codes, Web sites, and other such kinds of information on a nationwide basis. Printed volumes are costly and cumbersome. Inexpensive and easy access to these nationwide lists is now possible through CD-ROMs. Following are several kinds of directories and locators presently available:

*1-800 Directory.* CD-ROM. Hiawatha, Iowa: Parsons Technology. <http://www.parsonstech.com>.

*2 Million Fax Numbers Directory.* CD-ROM. Omaha, Neb.: CDUSA, 1997. <http://www.LookupUSA.com>.

*9-Digit Zip Code Directory.* CD-ROM. Omaha, Neb.: CDUSA, 1997. <http://www.LookupUSA.com>.

*88 Million Households Phone Book Deluxe.* CD-ROM. Omaha, Neb.: CDUSA, 1997. <http://www.LookupUSA.com>.

*103 Million Listings.* CD-ROM. Omaha, Neb.: CDUSA, 1997. <http://www.LookupUSA.com>.
*American Yellow Pages*
*Streets USA*
*9-Digit Zip Code Directory*
*2 Million Fax Numbers Directory*
*88 Million Households Phone Book Deluxe*

*American Yellow Pages.* CD-ROM. Omaha, Neb.: CDUSA, 1997. <http://www.LookupUSA.com>.

*Census USA.* CD-ROM. Omaha, Neb.: CDUSA, 1997. <http://www.LookupUSA.com>.

*Directory USA 2.0.* CD-ROM. Hiawatha, Iowa: Parsons Technology, 1996. <http://www.parsonstech.com>.

English, Katharine, ed. CD-ROM and Book. *Most Popular Web Sites.* Emeryville, Calif.: Lycos Press, 1996.

*Health and Medical Yellow Pages.* CD-ROM. Omaha, Neb.: CDUSA, 1997. <http://www.LookupUSA.com>.

*Microsoft Automap Streets Plus.* CD-ROM. Microsoft Corporation, 1997. <http://www.microsoft.com/automap>.

*Phone Search USA.* CD-ROM. Freeport, Maine: DeLorme. <http://www.phonesearchusa.com>.

*Rand McNally Street Finder.* CD-ROM. Rand McNally, 1997.

Rositano, Dean J., Robert A. Rositano, and Jay Lee. *Que's Mega Web Directory.* 2nd ed. CD-ROM and Book. Indianapolis: Que Corporation, 1996.

*Street Atlas USA.* v. 4.0. CD-ROM. Freeport, Maine: DeLorme. <http://www.streetatlasusa.com>.

*Streets USA.* CD-ROM. Omaha, Neb.: CDUSA, 1997. <http://www.LookupUSA.com>.

*The Thomas Guide on CD-ROM for (Local Area).* CD-ROM. Thomas Bros. Maps.

# On-Line Resources

The Internet, an extensive system of connected computers, comprises over 25,000 networks that are made up of more than 2 million host computers. This on-line global network, which is accessible to over 30 million users worldwide, has promoted information exchange between virtually any segment of our society. From major universities and giant corporations to the single user at a home computer, all may access the wealth of information Internet access provides.

## 15–11. Connecting to the Internet

a. Although business people may wish to use the Internet to visit famous museums, plan a vacation, or join a newsgroup, these personal applications are separate from accessing information that relates directly to business operations. Major interest today lies in accessing the Internet's World Wide Web and its exploding abundance of resources.

The Internet and other on-line resources provide the following kinds of information often needed for research, planning, and implementation:

(1) General references such as directories of reference materials, dictionaries, encyclopedias, thesauri, and atlases

(2) Stock and bond market quotations and other business and financial resources

(3) Airline schedules and reservations

(4) Current news and weather in various parts of the world

(5) Articles in major newspapers and magazines

(6) Services and rates of mail service providers

(7) Products and services provided by companies throughout the world

(8) Career services and company profiles

(9) Government information and services

b. Access to on-line media requires a computer, a modem, a telephone line connection, communications software, and an on-line service provider.

Most modern computers provide as standard features a built-in modem with preloaded communications software. Users need only to plug in to a regular telephone jack, and they are ready to be connected to an on-line service.

Computer connections to on-line services may be achieved in one of the following ways:

(1) **Through an Internet service provider with a local telephone number.** Internet service providers (ISPs) supply E-mail capabilities and access to the Internet. Some providers furnish software for accessing (browsing) the Internet's World Wide Web (WWW); others require members to

Information

15

467

purchase their own software. Two popular Web browsers are NetScape Navigator and Microsoft Internet Explorer. To locate an Internet Service Provider in your local area, consult your *Yellow Pages* under Telecommunications. Internet service providers may also be located through an Internet connection at <http:// www.thelist.com>.

(2) **Through a commercial on-line service such as America Online, CompuServe, Prodigy, Delphi, or Genie.** In addition to providing E-mail capabilities, Internet access, and a World Wide Web browser, commercial on-line services provide features such as these:

News and weather
Stock reports and other financial news
Sports scores, headlines, and news
Key magazine and newspaper articles
Reference (dictionaries and encyclopedias) and education sources
Computing support
Professional forums
Travel information
Entertainment options
Shopping opportunities
Home and leisure activities

(3) **Through a local corporation, university, college, or government agency that provides an Internet connection.** Large corporations, universities, colleges, and government agencies furnish free of charge Internet access to their employees and students. On-site computers are available for easy access. Remote sites (home computers) may dial into the host computer at the university, college, or agency site and gain Internet access from there.

## 15–12. Using the World Wide Web on Your Internet Connection

a. The World Wide Web, the Internet's most popular source, provides an interactive, graphical presentation of information that connects similar data at different locations. On-line documents known as Web pages contain hypertext, highlighted words that link you to other areas containing related information. With just a mouse click, hypertext will enable you to do the following:

(1) Migrate easily to documents, graphics, or other Web pages

(2) Connect to other kinds of Internet resources such as newsgroups and ftp (file transfer protocol) files

(3) Download graphics, photos, sounds, music, and movies to your computer

b. Using the World Wide Web requires a Web browser in addition to the standard communications software that usually comes preloaded on today's computers. Commercial on-line service providers supply their subscribers with a browser; many local Internet service providers make available Web browsers to their members at no cost or for a nominal fee. In any case, two popular commercial browsers, NetScape Navigator and Microsoft Internet Explorer, are available at a low cost.

c. **Locating information through your Web browser is accomplished in several ways:**

(1) **Through an Internet address.** Any Internet site may be reached through its address. Web sites each have specific addresses, and by typing the correct address in the appropriate box shown on your Web browser screen, you will be transported to that site.

All World Wide Web addresses begin with *http://* (HyperText Transfer Protocol); the following letters, spaces, and symbols must be entered exactly as shown in order to access the site. In this reference manual, all Internet addresses are shown in angle brackets (< >) to avoid confusion with any sentence punctuation marks. Enter only the information within the angle brackets. For example, the U.S. Postal Service's Web site may be reached by entering the following address: <http://www.usps.gov>.

(2) **Through a search engine.** All Web browsers have at least one search engine readily available, or search engines can be accessed through their Web site. Search engines such as WebCrawler, Excite, Alta Vista, Yahoo, HotBot, Infoseek, Magellan, and Search.com permit you to locate information by entering key words.

If you were trying to find job listings on the Internet, you might enter *employment resources jobs resumes career.* This search will give you the information you need; it relies on a series of synonyms to capture the various employment-related information that is available. From the listing produced by this search, you can connect directly to any of the sites listed.

(3) **Through a link in a Web site.** Hypertext permits Web sites to link to other Web sites. By clicking on an icon, underlined text, or highlighted text, you can be transported from one information source to another. Related information is frequently linked through hypertext, so oftentimes you can locate needed information through a link.

## 15–13. Sampling of Internet Web Sites

The wealth of information available on the Internet is overwhelming. Not all of it is valid or reliable — and not all of it is obtainable free of charge. The Internet user must use good judgment and discretion in selecting sources. Also, the Internet user must decide if subscription membership fees to access certain kinds of information are worth their costs.

a. Reference sources such as dictionaries, thesauri, encyclopedias, almanacs, and atlases are available for access on the Internet. Several such sites follow. The dates in parentheses show when these sites were visited and evaluated for inclusion in this listing.

*Britannica Online.* Encyclopaedia Britannica, 1996. <http://www.eb.com/> (17 January 1997).

*Dictionary.com* (listing of dictionaries on the Internet). n.d. <http://www2.dictionary.com/dictionary/> (2 January 1997).

Howe, Denis. *FOLDOC: The Free On-line Dictionary of Computing.* n.d. <http://wombat.doc.ic.ac.uk/> or <http://www.instantweb.com/foldoc/> (2 January 1997).

*Hypertext Webster Interface*. San Diego, Calif.: University of California, San Diego, Infopath, <http://www.ucsd.edu/>, n.d. <http://c.gp.cs.cmu.edu:5103/prog/webster/> (2 January 1997).

*The Internet Public Library Reference Center*. Ann Arbor, Mich.: University of Michigan, School of Information, 1996. <http://www.ipl.org/ref/> (3 January 1997).

*Merriam-Webster Online*. Springfield, Mass.: Merriam-Webster, Incorporated, 1996. <http://www.m-w.com/> (2 January 1997).

*Roget's Thesaurus of English Words and Phrases*. Nothing Limited, 1996. <http://home.thesaurus.com/thesaurus/search.html> (3 January 1997).

*The World Factbook 1995*. Washington, D.C.: Central Intelligence Agency, 1995. <http://www.odci.gov/cia/publications/95fact/index.html> (2 January 1997).

*The WorldWideWeb Acronym and Abbreviation Server*. n.d. <http://www.ucc.ie/info/net/acronyms/index.html> (3 January 1997).

**b.** **News sources—news channels, newspapers, and magazines—are available on-line. Several sites are listed here:**

*CNN Interactive*. <http://www.cnn.com/> (5 January 1997).

*New York Times*. <http://www.nytimes.com/> (5 January 1997).

*Top Ten News Media Resources List*. Internet Training & Consulting Services, 1996. <http://www.itcs.com/topten/newsres.html> (5 January 1997).

*United States: Newspaper Services on the Internet*. The Internet Company, 1996. <http://www.mediainfo.com/ephome/npaper/nphtm/e-papers/e-papers.us.html> (5 January 1997).

*USA Today*. <http://www.usatoday.com/> (5 January 1997).

*U.S. News and World Report Online*. <http://www.usnews.com/> (6 January 1997).

*The Wall Street Journal Interactive Edition*. <http://www.wsj.com/> (6 January 1997).

**c.** **Government offices provide information through the Internet. Mailing, tax, and census information may be obtained at the following sites:**

*1995 Statistical Abstract of the United States*. Washington, D.C.: U.S. Census Bureau, 1996. <http://www.census.gov/ftp/pub/prod/1/gen/95statab/95statab.html> (7 January 1997).

*1996 Statistical Abstract of the United States*. Washington, D.C.: U.S. Census Bureau, 1996. <http://www.census.gov/statabstract/> (7 January 1997).

*FedWorld Information Network*. Springfield, Va.: United States Department of Commerce, National Technical Information Service, 1996. <http://www.fedworld.gov/> (7 January 1997).

*Forms and Publications—IRS*. Washington, D.C.: United States Treasury Department, Internal Revenue Service, 1996. <http://www.irs.ustreas.gov/prod/forms_pubs/index.html > (7 January 1997).

*THOMAS: Legislative Information on the Internet*. Washington, D.C.: United States Library of Congress, 1997. <http://thomas.loc.gov/> (12 January 1997).

United States Postal Service Home Page. Washington, D.C.: U.S. Postal Service, n.d. <http://www.usps.gov/> (7 January 1997).

Census Bureau Home Page. Washington, D.C.: U.S. Census Bureau, n.d. <http://www.census.gov/> (8 January 1997).

USPS ZIP+4 Code Lookup. Washington, D.C.: U.S. Postal Service, n.d. <http://www.usps.gov/ncsc/lookups/lookup_zip+4.html> (7 January 1997).

**d.** Private delivery services maintain Web sites that allow package tracking and provide information about their services. Web site addresses for several such providers are listed below:

Airborne Express Home Page. Airborne Freight Corporation, 1996. <http://www.airborne-express.com/> (8 January 1997).

DHL Worldwide Express Home Page. DHL Systems, Inc., 1996. <http://www.dhl.com/> (8 January 1997).

FedEx Home Page. FedEx, 1996. <http://www.fedex.com/> (8 January 1997).

UPS Home Page. United Parcel Service of America, Inc., 1996. <http://www.ups.com/> (8 January 1997).

**e.** On-line directories provide addresses, telephone numbers, fax numbers, E-mail addresses, Web site addresses (URLs—Universal Resource Locators), and other similar types of information for individuals, businesses, organizations, and government agencies. A select list of on-line locators follows:

*Airline Toll-Free Numbers and Web Sites.* n.d. <http://www.princeton.edu/Main/air800.html> (9 January 1997).

*AT&T Toll-Free Internet Directory.* AT&T, 1996. <http://www.tollfree.att.net/> (9 January 1997).

*The Electronic Embassy* (embassies in Washington, D.C.). TeleDiplomacy, Inc., 1996. <http://www.embassy.org/> (10 January 1997).

*The Embassy Page* (embassies around the world). GlobeScope Internet Services, 1996. <http://www.embpage.org/> (10 January 1997).

*InfoSpace* (phone, E-mail, and fax listings). Redmond, Wash.: InfoSpace, Inc., 1996. <http://www.infospace.com/> (9 January 1997).

*Map It USA!* Worldview Systems, n.d. <http://ps.worldview.travelocity.com/PS/html/ps_driving.html> (11 January 1997).

*WhoWhere?* (yellow and white pages and E-mail addresses). WhoWhere? Inc., 1997. <http://www.whowhere.com/> (9 January 1997).

*WorldPages* (address, telephone, E-mail, web site connections, and mapping). WorldPages Inc. 1995. <http://www.worldpages.com/> (9 January 1997).

*Yellow Pages Online* (business directory). Yellow Pages Online, Inc., 1996. <http://www.ypo.com/> (12 January 1997).

**f.** Adaptations of writing style manuals are available on the Internet:

*A Guide for Writing Research Papers Based on American Psychological Association (APA) Documentation.* Hartford, Conn.: Humanities Department and the Arthur C. Banks, Jr., Library, Capital Community-Technical College, 1997. <http://155.43.225.30/apa.htm> (14 January 1997).

*A Guide for Writing Research Papers Based on Modern Language Association (MLA) Documentation*. Hartford, Conn.: Humanities Department and the Arthur C. Banks, Jr., Library, Capital Community-Technical College, 1997. <http://155.43.225.30/mla.htm> (14 January 1997).

*Chicago Manual of Style: Documentation Style I, Footnotes and Bibliographies*. Bethlehem, Penn.: Lehigh University Libraries, n.d. <http://www.lib. lehigh.edu/footnote/chicago.html> (30 January 1997).

*Chicago Manual of Style: Footnoting Electronic Sources*. Bethlehem, Penn.: Lehigh University Libraries, n.d. <http://www.lib.lehigh.edu/footnote/chicelec.html> (30 January 1997).

Dewey, Russ. *APA Publication Manual Crib Sheet*. 1996. <http://www.gasou.edu/psychweb/tipsheet/apacrib.htm#top> (4 January 1997).

Harnack, Andrew, and Gene Kleppenger. *Beyond the MLA Handbook: Documenting Electronic Sources on the Internet*. Richmond, Ky. Eastern Kentucky University, 1996. <http://falcon.eku.edu/honors/beyond-mla/> (30 January 1997).

List of Writers' Sources on the Internet. Green Bay, Wisc.: University of Wisconsin, David A. Cofrin Library, 1996. <http://gbms01.uwgb.edu/~library/refdesk/writers/> (2 January 1997).

Strunk, William, Jr. *Elements of Style*. New York: Columbia University, Bartleby Library, n.d. <http://www.columbia.edu/acis/bartleby/strunk/> (5 January 1997).

Walker, Janice R. *MLA-Style Citations of Electronic Resources*. Tampa, Fla.: University of South Florida, Department of English, 1995. <http://www.cas.usf.edu/english/walker/mla.html> (30 January 1997).

**g.** **Several other kinds of information sources on the Internet that may be of value to persons involved in business, industry, or government are listed below:**

*All the Hotels on the Web*. Internet Marketing Services, Ltd., 1996. <http://www.all-hotels.com/> (16 January 1997).

Bartlett, John. *Familiar Quotations*. New York: Columbia University, Bartleby Library, n.d. <http://www.cc.columbia.edu/acis/bartleby/bartlett/> (17 January 1997).

*Biography*. n.d. A&E Television Networks, 1996. <http://www.biography.com/> (16 January 1997).

*Hotels and Travel on the Net*. Stelcom, Inc., and WebScope, 1996. <http://www.hotelstravel.com/> (16 January 1997).

*Measurement Conversion Calculator (The Internet Version)*. Entisoft Units, Entisoft Tools 1.01, 1996. <http://entisoft.earthlink.net/scripts/unitscgi.exe> (17 January 1997).

Reference Listings. Yahoo!, n.d. <http://www.yahoo.com/> (14 January 1997).

Rudolph, Dana. *Really Useful Web Sites*. n.d. <http://www.tac.nyc.ny.us/%7Erudolph/useful/> (19 January 1997).

*StockMaster*. Marketplace.net Inc., 1996. <http://www.stockmaster.com/> (19 January 1997).

*TravelNow Hotel Reservations*. TravelNow Network Inc., n.d. <http://www.travelnow.com/> (16 January 1997).

Wallin, Peter. *Conversion Factor Table*. Oshkosh, Wisc.: University of Wisconsin, 1996. <http://www.uwosh.edu/students/wallip27/convert.html> (17 January 1997).

*Weather by Intellicast.* WSI Corp., 1996. <http://www.intellicast.com/>
   (18 January 1997).
*WeatherOnline.* Weatherboy and Weather Network, 1995. <http://www.
   weatheronline.com/> (18 January 1997).

**h.**  Remember that the Internet is still in its infancy. As this information
      source continues to grow, new Web sites will emerge as others dis-
      appear. Some Web sites will be updated almost daily, some periodi-
      cally, and others not at all. Not every source contains valid
      information, so evaluate its contents and origin judiciously.

      Learn to use search engines to gather the information you need.
      Bookmark those sites that you use frequently or that you feel will
      be useful to you sometime in the near future. Continually search out
      Web sites that will assist you in carrying out your responsibilities.

# Glossary

## Grammatical Terms Used in
## *A Handbook for Office Workers*

**Abbreviation**

A shortened form of a word or word group. Examples: *in.* for *inches* and *AMA* for *American Medical Association.*

**Absolute adjective**

An adjective that cannot be compared because it represents a definite and exact state. Examples: *dead, perfect*, and *full.*

**Action verb**

A verb that shows or represents movement. Examples: *run, talk*, and *breathe.*

**Active voice**

A method of constructing sentences that identifies who does what. The person or thing performing the action is the subject of the sentence. Example: The *stockholders* rejected the proposal.

**Adj.**

Abbreviation of *adjective.*

**Adjective**

A word or word group that describes a noun or pronoun. It tells what kind, which one, or how many. Examples: *good* investment, *this* bank, and *three* employees.

**Adverb**

A word that describes a verb, an adjective, or another adverb. It tells when, where, how, or to what degree. Many adverbs end in *ly.* Examples: arrive *early*, come *here*, drive *carefully*, and *too* small.

**Adverbial clause**

A word group containing a subject and a verb that begins with a subordinating conjunction such as *if, when, since, because,* or *as.* An adverbial clause modifies the verb in the main clause. Example: *If you wish an appointment*, please *call* me.

**Ampersand**

A symbol (&) meaning *and* used mainly in organizational names. Example: We have signed a contract with Robert White *&* Associates.

**Animate object**

Any person, any living thing, or any group composed of persons or living things. Compare with *inanimate object.* Examples: *manager, tree, company*, and *flock of sheep.*

## Antecedent

A noun (or an indefinite pronoun) to which a pronoun or any number of pronouns refer. Examples: Our last newsletter asked all *clients* in this area *who* are interested in bond investment to indicate *their* willingness to attend a free seminar by phoning this office. *Anyone* in the office *who* is interested in carpooling should submit *his* or *her* name to our director of human resources.

## Apostrophe

A symbol (') used to show noun possession, the omission of letters in contractions, and the beginning and ending of quotations within quotations. Examples: (1) *Carol's* salary; (2) we *haven't*; and (3) He asked, "Have you read my latest article, 'Western Travels'?"

## Apposition, Appositive, Appositive expression

A word or word group that renames or explains the noun or pronoun it follows. These descriptive words usually add extra information. Example: Ms. Johnson, *our new manager*, has been with the company for three years.

## Article

The words *a, an*, and *the*. These words are used as adjectives. Examples: *a* method, *an* interesting tour, *the* stock market.

## "Being" verb

A form of the verb *to be* when it is used as a main verb, that is, when it appears alone or as the last verb in a verb phrase. These forms are *am, is, are, was, were, be*, and *been*. Examples: (1) Jill *was* here yesterday. (2) He has *been* our client for three years.

## "Being" verb helper

A form of the verb *to be* when it is used in a verb phrase as a helping verb. These forms are *am, is, are, was, were, be*, and *been*. Example: Whitmore appliances *have* not *been sold* in our store for the past three years.

## Cardinal number

A number such as 3 (three), 10 (ten), 32 (thirty-two), 541, or 1,856 that is used in simple counting.

## Case form

A category used to classify nouns or pronouns in a sentence as subjective, objective, or possessive.

## Celestial body

A planet, star, or other heavenly form. Examples: *Mars, North Star*, and *sun*.

## Clause

A word group that contains a subject and a verb.

## Collective noun

A noun composed of individual persons or things. Examples: *committee, team, jury, herd*, and *class*.

476

## Colon

A punctuation mark (:) used to indicate that the following words explain further the word or word group appearing before the punctuation mark. Example: Our company specializes in the manufacture of the following women's clothing accessories: shoes, boots, handbags, and belts.

## Command

A sentence in which the subject *you* is not stated but instead is implied. The sentence directs the understood subject *you* to perform (or refrain from) an action. Examples: (1) (You) Mail this information to me as soon as possible. (2) (You) Do not slam the door as you leave.

## Common noun

A noun that does not name a specific person, place, or thing. Examples: *supervisor, building, city council, university,* and *company.*

## Common noun element

That part of a proper noun that is not a specific name. Examples: *university* in Rutgers University, *building* in Tishman Building, and *city council* in Miami City Council.

## Comparative form

The spelling or form of an adjective or an adverb when it compares two nouns or pronouns or two conditions. Compare with *superlative form.* Examples: (1) This year's sales are *greater* than last year's. (2) We have progressed *more slowly* in this area than we had hoped.

## Complement pronoun

A pronoun that completes a being verb. It follows a form of the verb *to be—am, is, are, was, were, be,* and *been.* Example: The contest winners were *they*, Karen and Bill.

## Complete thought

A word group that contains a subject and a verb. The word group must make sense and be able to stand alone as a complete sentence. A complete thought is also known as an *independent clause.* Example: *Mr. Reed agreed to the terms of the contract,* but *his attorney advised him not to sign it.*

## Complex sentence

A sentence that contains a dependent clause and an independent clause. Example: As soon as we receive your reply, we will send you a replacement or issue a credit to your account.

## Complimentary close

The first closing line of a business letter. Example: *Sincerely yours.*

## Compound adjective

Two or more words acting together as a single thought to describe or modify a noun or pronoun. Same as *compound modifier.* Example: *part-time* job.

## Compound modifier

Same as *compound adjective.*

## Compound noun

Two or more words used as a single unit to name a person, place, or thing. Examples: *sister-in-law, notary public, high school, word processing,* and *income tax.*

## Compound number

A number requiring more than one word when written in word form. Examples: *twenty-seven, ninety-eight, one hundred, two hundred fifty.*

## Compound sentence

A sentence containing two independent clauses (complete thoughts) joined by (1) a semicolon; (2) a transitional expression (such as *therefore, consequently,* or *nevertheless*); or (3) the conjunction *and, but, or,* or *nor.* Examples: (1) Please call me when the shipment arrives; I will pick it up immediately. (2) The Model 432 cart you ordered has been discontinued; *however,* our Model 434 cart has all the features of the cart you ordered. (3) The manufacturer has promised to send us another shipment of these disks by next week, *and* we will fill your order immediately upon its arrival.

## Compound subject

A subject that contains two or more nouns or pronouns joined by *and, or,* or *nor.* Example: *Ellen and Jack* have already reached their quotas for this month's sales.

## Compound verb

Two or more words combined to produce a single thought unit that functions as a verb. Compound verbs appear as one word, as two words, or hyphenated. Examples: *upgrade, mark up, double-space.*

## Compound-complex sentence

A sentence containing two independent clauses (complete thoughts) and a dependent clause. Example: This suite of offices is currently available for occupancy, and we will release the keys to you as soon as you return the signed lease agreement with a certified check for $3,000.

## Conjugation

The various forms of a verb that show person. Examples: I *see,* he or she *sees,* we *see,* you *see,* they *see;* I *am,* he or she *is,* we *are,* you *are,* they *are.*

## Conjunction

A part of speech that serves as a connector of words or word groups within a sentence. Examples: *and, but, or, nor, either . . . or,* and *not only . . . but also.*

## Conjunctive adverb

An adverb—such as *consequently, however,* or *therefore*—that connects the main clauses of a compound sentence. Example: Most of our advertising budget has already been allocated; *therefore,* we are unable to take advantage of your offer.

## Conjunctive pair

A class of connecting words—conjunctions—that link contrasting or dependent ideas. These connectors consist of two parts. Examples: *either . . . or, neither . . . nor, if . . . then,* and *not only . . . but also.*

### Consonant
Any letter of the alphabet other than *a, e, i, o,* and *u.*

### Contingent expression
An expression that is based upon a similar expression for completion. Example: *The sooner* you take advantage of this offer, *the more often* you will be able to enjoy your personal home movie selections.

### Contraction
Shortened forms that use an apostrophe to show the omission of letters or numbers. These shortened forms may be applied to certain words, verb phrases, and dates. Examples: *internat'l* for *international, doesn't* for *does not,* and *'98* for *1998.*

### Coordinating conjunction
A part of speech (conjunction) that joins equal words or word groups. Examples: *and, but, or,* and *nor.*

### Courtesy title
A title used to address individuals. Examples: *Mr., Ms., Mrs., Miss,* and *Dr.*

### Dash
A mark of punctuation (— or --) used to precede summary statements or for emphasis in setting off words or word groups. The em dash (—) is used in computer-based and printed copy. In typewritten copy the dash is formed by keying two hyphens consecutively (--); no space appears before, between, or after the hyphens. Examples: (1) Sofas, chairs, bedroom suites, dining room sets—we have a large variety of styles and brands from which you may choose. (2) Three employees--Clyde Jones, Janice Lee, and Dennis Martinez--have agreed to work overtime next week.

### Decimal
A small dot (.) used in numbers to separate a whole number from a portion of the next number in the sequence. Examples: *12.5, 0.07, 147.38, 6.75 percent,* and *$1.4 million.*

### Declarative sentence
A complete sentence that makes a statement. Example: Our company president announced our merger with Cory Industries yesterday.

### Dependent adverbial clause
A word group that (1) contains a subject and a verb and (2) begins with a subordinating conjunction such as *if, when, since, because,* or *as.* An adverbial clause modifies the verb in the main clause. Example: *When the shipment arrives,* we will *call* you immediately.

### Dependent clause
A word group that contains a subject and a verb but cannot stand alone as a complete sentence. Same as a *subordinate clause.* Example: John told me last week *that he expects to win this month's sales contest.*

### Direct address
The act of calling a person by name, title, or classification in written or oral communication *with that person.* Examples: (1) Thank you, *Ms. Burwell,* for responding so promptly. (2) Yes, *Professor,* we will have this textbook available for use during the spring semester. (3) Only you, *fellow citizens,* can prevent a further decline of our schools.

### Direct object

A noun or pronoun acted upon by the subject and verb of a sentence. Example: Our accountant mailed the *check* yesterday.

### Direct quotation

The exact words spoken or written by a person or group. Example: According to the committee's report, "The property was sold in 1993 for $10,950,000."

### Ellipsis

A series of three periods ( . . . )—with spaces before, between, and after the periods—used to show omissions in quoted material or hesitations in other printed material. Example: According to his latest journal article, Professor Haley concludes, "Social conditions will continue to improve in this area . . . unless the government withdraws its funding commitment."

### Essential subordinate clause

A word group that contains a subject and a verb but cannot stand alone as a complete sentence. The word group is needed to complete the main idea of the sentence by furnishing *who, what, which one, when, why, how, whether,* or *to what degree.* An *essential subordinate clause* is the same as a *restrictive clause,* a *restrictive dependent clause,* or a *restrictive subordinate clause.* Example: John told me last week *that he expects to win this month's sales contest.*

### Exclamation mark

A mark of punctuation (!) used to show strong feeling or emotion. Example: Take advantage of our free offer today—while this letter is in front of you!

### First person

*I* or *we* used as subjects in writing or speaking. Example: After analyzing the specimen, *we* contacted several contagious disease specialists.

### Fraction

A part of a whole number expressed in proportion to the whole. Example: The legislature is proposing a *1/2* percent increase in our state's sales tax.

### Future perfect tense

A verb phrase used to express an action that will occur before a certain time in the future. This tense is formed by using the verb helpers *will have* and the past participle of a verb. Example: If donations continue to be made at this same rate, we *will have paid* for this new hospital wing before its completion.

### Future progressive tense

A verb phrase used to express an action that will be ongoing in the future. This tense is formed by using the verb helpers *will be* and the present participle of a verb. Example: Our volunteers *will be calling* other alumni during the next month to solicit donations for the newly formed college foundation.

### Future tense

A verb phrase used to express an action that will happen in the future. This tense is formed by using the verb helper *will* and the present part of a verb. Example: I *will call* you next week.

## Gender

A term used to refer to the sexual classification of nouns, pronouns, and their modifiers. Classifications include feminine, masculine, and neuter.  Examples: (1) *Maria* lost *her* purse. (2) *He* sold all *his* stock. (3) The *company* has just purchased dental insurance for all *its* employees.

## Gerund

A verb form ending in *ing* that functions as a noun in a sentence.  Example: His *refusing* our offer came as a surprise to all of us.

## Helping verb

A verb that appears with the present part, present participle, or past participle of another verb to form tenses.  Examples: *will* go, *are* planning, *have been* employed.

## Horizontal listing

A listing of items that continues across the page like ordinary text. Compare with *vertical listing*.  Example: Check the following sources for current employment opportunities: *classified ads appearing in your local newspaper, postings in your college or university employment office, and listings provided by career centers on the Internet.*

## Hyphen

A mark of punctuation (-) used in some word groups to join two or more words that function as a single idea. In typewritten copy this mark is also used to represent *through* when placed between two numbers.  Examples: *mother-in-law, up-to-date*, and pages 34-35.

## Hyphenated compound

A word group joined by hyphens that functions as a single thought unit.  Examples: *trade-in, self-employment, well-to-do.*

## Imperative sentence, Imperative statement

A complete sentence in which the subject *you* is not stated; it is understood.  Example: (You) Please mail your check in the enclosed envelope today.

## Implied verb

A word group in which an intended verb is not stated. Compare with *stated verb*.  Examples: (1) If possible (If it *is* possible), we would appreciate your shipping this order by July 10. (2) John has more seniority with the firm than I (I *have*).

## Inanimate object

A nonliving thing. Compare with *animate object*.  Examples: *computer, lease*, and *insurance.*

## Indefinite pronoun

A pronoun that does not represent a specific person, place, or thing.  Examples: *each, every, either, someone, anyone*, and *something.*

## Independent adjective

An adjective that describes a noun without relying on other adjectives to enhance its meaning. Two or more independent adjectives modifying a noun are separated by commas.  Examples: an *intelligent, conscientious* student vs. printed in *large bold* print.

481

### Independent clause

A word group that (1) contains a subject and a verb and (2) can stand alone as a complete sentence. An *independent clause* is the same as a *main clause.* Example: Although he was at first reluctant, *Senator Richards has agreed to seek reelection for a third term.*

### Independent phrase

A word group that represents a complete sentence although it is not. Example: *Now to the point.*

### Independent question

A word group stated in question format that stands alone as a complete sentence. Example: Who is responsible for closing the office on Friday evenings?

### Indirect object

A noun or pronoun acted upon by a subject, a verb, and a direct object. Example: Chris gave *him* the check yesterday.

### Indirect question

A statement that describes the content of a question or questions. Example: Several customers have asked whether we will extend our shopping hours for the holiday season.

### Indirect quotation

A statement that describes the written or spoken word of another person or source but does not employ the exact words used by that person or source. Example: Sharon said that if she was not promoted within the next three months, she would begin to look for another position.

### Infinitive

The present part of a verb preceded by the word *to.* Example: You will probably need *to work* overtime *to finish* this project by its deadline date.

### Infinitive phrase

A word group beginning with an infinitive and ending with a noun or pronoun. Example: *To obtain more information,* just mail the enclosed card.

### Inside address

The part of a business letter that lists the addressee's name, professional title (if any), company name (if any), street address, city, state, and zip code.

### Intransitive verb

A verb that does not have a direct or an indirect object. Compare with *transitive verb.* Examples: (1) The governor will *campaign* heavily in the southern part of the state next week. (2) Responsibility for the success of this project *lies* with the project manager. (3) Prices *rise* when manufacturers encounter increased costs.

### Introductory clause, Introductory dependent clause

A word group that (1) contains a subject and a verb and (2) starts with a subordinating conjunction such as *if, when, since, because,* or *as.* The word group begins the sentence, ends with a comma, and is followed by the main clause. Example: *Because we are unable to obtain this merchandise,* we are returning your check.

482

### Introductory phrase

A word group without a subject and corresponding verb that starts with a preposition, an infinitive, or a participle. Such word groups that begin a sentence and appear directly before the main clause are introductory. Examples: (1) *By this time next year*, we will have moved our home office to Louisville. (2) *To receive your free copy*, simply sign and mail the enclosed card. (3) *Lured by the promise of large profits*, investors poured millions of dollars into this fraudulent development project.

### Introductory prepositional phrase

A word group that starts with a preposition but does not contain a subject or a verb. The word group begins the sentence and is followed directly by the main clause. Example: *During this time* we will need to gather more information about the economic conditions of this area.

### Irregular verb

A verb that does not form its parts in the usual way, that is, by adding *ed* to the present part to form the past part and the past participle. Examples: *eat, ate, eaten; go, went, gone;* and *sing, sang, sung.*

### Limiting adverb

A word or word group that restrains, confines, or negates the meaning of a verb. Examples: *not, barely, scarcely,* and *hardly.*

### Limiting expression

A word group that restrains or confines another word group. Example: You may petition for a grade change, *but only for a valid reason.*

### Linking verb

A form of the verb *to be* used as a main verb or a form of another nonaction verb. Examples: (1) She *is* a conscientious employee. (2) I *feel* bad that our manager is being transferred.

### Lowercase

Refers to the format of alphabetic characters; letters that are not capitalized. Examples: *a, d, m,* and *u.*

### Main clause

A word group that (1) contains a subject and a verb and (2) can stand alone as a complete sentence. A *main clause* is the same as an *independent clause*. Example: When we receive your signed contract, *we will order the equipment needed for your installation.*

### Main verb

A single verb or the last verb in a verb phrase. Examples: (1) Please *call* me tomorrow. (2) The display *was* too large to fit into a suitcase. (3) Only three candidates have been *called*. (4) Our manager was *disappointed* with the results of the advertising campaign.

### Main word

The most descriptive or definitive word in a compound noun. Examples: *mother*-in-law, personnel *manager*, *notary* public, and vice *president*.

### Main words in a heading or title to be capitalized

All words except the articles *a*, *an*, and *the*; the conjunctions *and*, *but*, *or*, or *nor*; and prepositions with three or fewer letters such as *of*, *for*, *to*, *in*, or *out* UNLESS any of these words appear as the first or last word. Examples: (1) Normal Climate Conditions in the Northeastern Part of the United States, (2) Corporate Goals and Strategies for 1999, (3) An Analysis of Marketing Strategies Used by an Independent Mail Order House.

### Modifier

An *adjective* that describes a noun or pronoun. An *adverb* that describes or limits a verb, an adjective, or another adverb.

### N.

An abbreviation for *noun*.

### Nominative case, Nominative case form

A noun or pronoun used as the subject of a sentence, the complement of a *being* verb, or the object of the infinitive *to be* when this infinitive has no subject. Nouns always maintain the same form; pronouns require a specific form: *I, he, she, you, we, they, who, whoever.* Same as *subjective case, subjective case form.* Examples: (1) *We* called you yesterday. (2) The winner was *she*, Joyce Moore. (3) I would not want to be *he* when the mistake is discovered.

### Nonaction verb

A verb that does not demonstrate action. Examples: *am, is, was,* and *were*.

### Nonessential subordinate clause

A word group that (1) contains a subject and a verb and (2) starts with a subordinating conjunction such as *if, when, as, after,* or *although* or a relative pronoun such as *who* or *which*. This word group is an additional thought unit that does not change or modify the main clause of the sentence. It is the same as a *nonrestrictive clause* or a *nonrestrictive subordinate clause*. Examples: (1) Our major advertising campaign is scheduled to begin on November 1, *after all our dealers nationwide have the new product line in their stores*. (2) Jan Davidson, *who has been with our company for three years*, has been placed in charge of the project.

### Nonrestrictive

A word or word group that is not essential to the meaning of the main idea.

### Nonrestrictive clause

A word group that (1) contains a subject and a verb and (2) appears with a main clause. This word group is subordinate to the main idea and does not alter its meaning. It complements the main idea by adding additional information. A *nonrestrictive clause* is the same as a *nonessential subordinate clause* or a *nonrestrictive subordinate clause*. Examples: (1) This proposal, *as I explained to you earlier*, has not yet been approved by the Board of Directors. (2) The profit and loss statement for this project was shown in our last annual report, *which was distributed to the stockholders on March 1*.

### Nonrestrictive phrase

A word group beginning with a preposition, an infinitive, or a participle and ending with a noun or pronoun. This word group does not affect the meaning of the main clause; it adds an additional idea that does not modify the main idea. Examples: (1) You cannot, *in my estimation*, expect a greater return on your investment at this time. (2) Susan and Randy, *to name at least two people*, were among those staff members in our department who were affected by the abolishment of our child care center. (3) Our president, *concerned about the steady sales decline*, has decided to invest more heavily in research and development.

### Nonrestrictive subordinate clause

Same as *nonessential subordinate clause*.

### Noun

A person, place, thing, animal, quality, concept, feeling, action, measure, or state. Examples: *employee, city, chair, cat, sincerity, democracy, love, swimming, inch*, and *happiness*.

### Object

A noun or pronoun acted upon by another part of speech, e.g., a verb or a preposition. Examples: (1) Scott sent *me* the *check* yesterday. (2) For the next three *months*, you will receive a free trial *subscription*.

### Object of a preposition

The noun or pronoun that follows a preposition. Examples: of our *clients*, for the last few *months*, from *her*, and through your *efforts*.

### Objective case, Objective case form

A noun or pronoun used as the object of a verb, the object of a preposition, the subject or object of an infinitive other than *to be*, or the object of the infinitive *to be* when this infinitive has a subject. Nouns always maintain the same form; pronouns require a specific form: *me, him, her, you, us, them*. Examples: (1) You may *contact me* at this number after 3 p.m. (2) Please send this information *to me* directly. (3) I do not want *to give her* too much information about our new product. (4) I would not want our new *supervisor to be him*.

### Open compound

Two or more words used to represent a single idea. The words appear as separate words and are not hyphenated. Examples: *information processing, golf club*, and *vice president*.

### Ordinal number

A number form that indicates order in a series. Cardinal numbers like *3, 10*, and *246* are numbers used in counting; ordinal numbers like *first (1st), second (2nd)*, and *twenty-fourth (24th)* indicate order or position in a series. Example: Our sales report for the *fourth* quarter must be ready by January 15 for inclusion in the annual report.

### Parallel structure

Words or word groups used in a similar fashion that are expressed in the same format. Parallel structure applies to words joined by a conjunction, joined by a conjunctive pair, appearing in a series, and appearing in a listing. Examples: (1) Our receptionist's main duties are to *answer the telephone* and *greet office visitors*. (2) You may order supplies from not only *our standard supply catalog* but also *Kalleen's Computer Supply Catalog*. (3) The whole day was spent *returning phone calls, reading the mail*, and *dictating correspondence*.

**Parenthesis**
A mark of punctuation signifying the beginning [(] of a side thought and the ending [)] of a side thought. Example: Please request copies of any ancillary materials (at least an instructor's manual and key) that may accompany the text.

**Parenthetical element, Parenthetical expression, Parenthetical remark**
A word or word group that does not contribute to the meaning of the main clause but merely acts as a transitional thought or provides an additional idea. Examples: (1) *Therefore,* we are returning this order for credit. (2) The meeting scheduled for October 24, *as you probably already know,* has been canceled.

**Participial phrase**
A word group beginning with a past or present participle and followed by a noun or pronoun. Examples: (1) *Encouraged by last month's increased sales,* our Advertising Department has decided to extend the present campaign another month. (2) *Hoping to sell the property immediately,* Mr. Rice agreed to drop the price $10,000.

**Parts of a verb**
The forms of a verb that are used to construct tenses, that is, those spellings of a verb used in expressing time periods. The parts of a verb include the *infinitive, present, past, present participle*, and *past participle*. Examples: *to send, send, sent, sending, sent.*

**Passive voice**
A form of sentence construction in which the doer of the action is not the subject of the sentence. This form is used primarily to deemphasize the person performing the action by focusing instead on the results. The passive voice is constructed by using a form of the verb *to be* as a helper and the past participle of the main verb. Example: These reports *were mailed* last week.

**Past part**
One of the five verb parts used in constructing tenses. For most verbs this part is formed by adding *ed* to the present part, the form listed in the dictionary. The past part for verbs not following this pattern is shown in the dictionary directly after the main entry. Examples: (1) *called* (call), *discussed* (discuss), and *answered* (answer). (2) *saw* (see), *wrote* (write), and *went* (go).

**Past participle**
One of the five verb parts used in constructing tenses. For most verbs this part is formed by adding *ed* to the present part, the form listed in the dictionary. The past participle for verbs not following this pattern is shown in the dictionary directly after the main entry. Examples: *called* (call), *discussed* (discuss), and *answered* (answer). (2) *seen* (see), *written* (write), and *gone* (go).

**Past perfect tense**
Used to describe a past action that has taken place before another past action. This tense is formed by using the helping verb *had* and the past participle of the main verb. Example: The applicant *had accepted* another position before he *received* our offer.

## Past progressive tense

Used to describe an ongoing action that took place in the past. This tense is formed by using the helping verb *was* or *were* with the present participle of the main verb. Example: Last year our company *was hiring* additional personnel; this year the company is reducing its staff in all departments.

## Past tense

Used to report a single past action or occurrence. This tense is formed by using the past part of a verb. Example: We *finished* the report last Friday.

## Perfect tense

Describes the present, past, or future by using a form of *have* as a helping verb and the past participle of the main verb. Examples: *have completed, had completed,* and *will have completed.*

## Permanent compound

Dictionary entries consisting of more than one word to represent a single idea. Examples: *air-conditioning, high school, community college, up-to-date,* and *full-time.*

## Personal pronoun

A word that substitutes for the name of a person or thing. Examples: *I, he, she, it, we, they, you, me, him, her, us,* and *them.*

## Phrase

A group of two or more grammatically related words that act upon one another in a modifying, coordinating, or composite relationship. The word group does not have a subject and a verb. Examples: (1) Our sales have increased *during the past few months.* (2) Mr. Lee requested the custodial crew *to wash the windows, vacuum the carpeting,* and *set up the chairs.* (3) Our supply *of printer ribbons* is diminishing rapidly.

## Plural

More than one. Nouns, pronouns, and verbs have plural forms.

## Plural noun

More than one person, place, or thing. These nouns usually require a special form and appear with a plural verb. Examples: *files* (file), *bosses* (boss), *companies* (company), *curricula* (curriculum), and *potatoes* (potato).

## Polite request

A command worded like a question that requests the reader or listener to perform a specific action. Example: Will you please send us your remaining application materials by November 16.

## Possessive

A noun or pronoun that shows ownership. Examples: (1) The *company's* liability in this case has not yet been determined. (2) The company awarded all *its* employees a bonus.

## Possessive case, Possessive case form

The spelling of a noun or pronoun that shows ownership. Examples: *Sally's* desk, an *accountants'* convention, *his* books, *your* paycheck, and *their* tickets.

### Predicate
That part of the sentence that includes the verb or verb phrase and all its modifiers—all parts of the sentence except the complete subject. Example: All parts in this assembly *will need to be replaced within the next few months*.

### Prefix
A syllable attached to the beginning of a word that forms a derivative word or an inflectional form. Compare with *suffix*. Examples: *un*able, *dis*cover, *mis*pronounce, and *ful*fill.

### Preposition
A part of speech that links a noun or pronoun to another word in the sentence. Examples: *of, for, behind, in, through, during, around, above, between,* and *except*.

### Prepositional phrase
A word group that begins with a preposition and ends with a noun or pronoun. The phrase modifies another noun or pronoun or a verb in the sentence. Examples: (1) Our new line *of office equipment* will be on display at the convention. (2) Do not park your car *between these posts*.

### Present part
One of the five verb parts used in constructing tenses. This part is the form shown as the main dictionary entry of the verb. Examples: *call, discuss, answer, see, write,* and *go*.

### Present participle
One of the five verb parts used in constructing tenses. For most verbs this part is formed by adding *ing* to the present part, the form listed in the dictionary. The present participle for verbs not following this pattern is shown in the dictionary directly after the main entry. Examples: (1) *calling* (call), *discussing* (discuss), and *answering* (answer). (2) *omitting* (omit), *writing* (write), and *starring* (star).

### Present perfect tense
Used to describe an action that began in the past but has continued during the time leading to the present. This tense is formed by using the helping verb *has* or *have* and the past participle of the main verb. Example: We *have sent* this client at least three reminders about his past-due account.

### Present progressive tense
Used to describe an action in progress during the present time. This tense is formed by using the helping verb *am, is,* or *are* and the present participle of the main verb. Example: We *are* now *taking* applications for this position.

### Present tense
Used to describe an ongoing action or an existing condition. This tense is formed by using the present part of the verb. Examples: (1) Lisa *drives* 20 miles each day to work. (2) Your company *has* too many employees.

### Principal parts of a verb
Same as *parts of a verb*.

## Principal word

The word in a compound noun that describes or defines the noun most explicitly, if any. Examples: *brother*-in-law, *sergeant* at arms, lieutenant *colonel*, and high *school*.

## Principal words in a heading or title to be capitalized

See *Main words in a heading or title to be capitalized.*

## Professional title

A title related to a person's employment. Examples: *Professor* Scot Ober, *Governor* Joyce Arntson, *Dean* Dolores Denova, *Vice President* Norlund, *General* Rodriguez, and *Mayor* Bradley.

## Progressive tenses

Used to describe actions in progress during various time periods. Describes the present, past, or future by using a form of *to be* as a helping verb and the present participle of the main verb. Examples: *are processing, were processing*, and *will be processing*.

## Pronoun

A word that functions as the substitute for a noun. Examples: *I, her*, and *they; that* and *who*; and *this, each*, and *everyone*.

## Proper noun

The name of a specific person, place, or thing. Examples: *Jane Thompson, San Francisco Bay Bridge*, and the *Empire State Building*.

## Question mark

A mark of punctuation (?) used to end a word group or complete sentence that is a direct question. Example: Have you received any further information about the proposed project?

## Quotation mark

A mark of punctuation (") used primarily to set off the exact words spoken or written by another person. Example: As the author stated in his article, "As interest rates decline, investments in the municipal bond market become less attractive."

## Reflexive pronoun

A pronoun that refers back to and is acted upon by another noun or pronoun in the sentence. Example: *We* can certainly give *ourselves* a pat on the back for this accomplishment.

## Regular verb

A verb that forms its parts by adding standard endings to the present form; that is, by adding *ed* for the past part, *ed* for the past participle; and *ing* for the present participle. Example: *check, checked, checked, checking.*

## Relative clause

A word group (containing a subject and a verb) introduced by a pronoun that refers back and relates to a noun or pronoun in the main clause. Relative clauses are most commonly introduced by *who, whom, that*, and *which*. Example: Dr. Williams is the physician *who will handle your case.*

### Relative pronoun

The noun substitutes *who, whoever, whom, whomever, that,* and *which* used to introduce a clause that refers back and relates to a noun or pronoun in the main clause. Example: The *subsidiary* of our company *that* handles this product is Belegrath Tool & Die.

### Relative pronoun clause

A word group containing a subject and a verb that appears with a main clause; it begins with *who, whom, whoever, whomever, that,* or *which.* Example: Heritage Inc. is the real estate agency *that is handling the sale of our Springfield warehouse.*

### Restrictive

A word or word group that contributes substantially to the main idea of the sentence and is needed for it to convey the same meaning. Without the word or word group, the meaning of the sentence would be changed or incomplete.

### Restrictive appositive

A word or word group used to rename or describe a previous noun or pronoun. The word or word group is needed to identify *which one.* Example: The *book The Pentagon Heroes* has been on the best-seller list for the past eight weeks.

### Restrictive clause

A word group that (1) contains a subject and a verb and (2) appears with a main clause. Although this word group is subordinate to the main idea, it does clarify, limit, or otherwise affect its meaning. A *restrictive clause* is the same as an *essential subordinate clause,* a *restrictive dependent clause,* or a *restrictive subordinate clause.* Examples: (1) This order will be shipped *as soon as I receive approval from our Credit Department.* (2) The only person *who can approve this request* is the vice president of financial services.

### Restrictive dependent clause

Same as an *essential subordinate clause,* a *restrictive clause,* or a *restrictive subordinate clause.*

### Restrictive phrase

A word group beginning with a preposition, an infinitive, or a participle and ending with a noun or pronoun. This word group affects the meaning of the main clause by answering such questions as *who, what, which one, when, why, how, whether,* or *to what degree.* Examples: (1) The auction will be held *on Saturday, December 4.* (2) Please mail the enclosed postcard *to obtain further information.* (3) The books lying *in this corner* are yours.

### Restrictive subordinate clause

Same as an *essential subordinate clause,* a *restrictive clause,* or a *restrictive dependent clause.*

### Return address

The complete address of the person writing a business letter that is not prepared on letterhead stationery. On envelopes prepared for mailing, the complete address of the person mailing the envelope and its contents.

## Roman numeral

One of a sequence of numbering based on the ancient Roman system. In business this system is used primarily for numbering the major divisions in an outline, the chapters in a report, and the preliminary pages of a report. Examples: *I, II, III, IV, V* and *i, ii, iii, iv, v.*

## Salutation

The opening greeting in a business letter. Examples: *Gentlemen, Ladies and Gentlemen, Dear Dr. Gates, Dear Ms. Howell,* and *Dear Bob.*

## Semicolon

A mark of punctuation (;) used primarily to join two complete thoughts in a sentence. Example: We have not received any responses to our advertisement for an administrative assistant; therefore, please do not renew our ad in the *Valley Star.*

## Sentence fragment

A word group ending with a period, question mark, or exclamation mark that is not a complete sentence or does not represent a complete thought. Example: We are interested in sponsoring a number of spot announcements. *That describe how our services and employees benefit the community.*

## Series

Three or more words or word groups that have the same structure within a sentence. Items in a series consist of words, phrases, or clauses. The last item is joined to the others with a coordinating conjunction: *and, or,* or *nor.* Example: You may *telephone, fax, or mail* your orders.

## Signature block

The closing lines of a business letter that contain the signature of the writer, the typewritten name of the writer, and the title of the writer, if any.

## Simple fraction

Any portion of a whole number that is less than *one.* Examples: *1/4* or *one fourth, 2/3* or *two thirds,* and *3/5* or *three fifths.*

## Simple noun

The name of a person, place, or thing that consists of one word. Examples: *Mary, computer, state,* and *manager.*

## Simple sentence

A word group that contains only one subject and one verb and makes sense. Example: I received the package of materials yesterday.

## Simple subject

The single word in the main clause of a sentence that answers *who* or *what* in relation to the verb. Example: All *employees* in our division *have received* copies of the employee newsletter.

## Simple tenses

The present, past, and future tenses. Examples: (1) He *writes* well. (2) He *wrote* this letter yesterday. (3) He *will write* the letter tomorrow.

### Singular
A mode or form of nouns, pronouns, and verbs signifying *one*.  Examples: *truck* (vs. *trucks*), *she* (vs. *they*), and *drives* (vs. *drive*).

### Singular noun
The form used to name a person, place, or thing that signifies *one*.  Examples: *supervisor, country,* and *bank*.

### Slash
A symbol (/) used primarily for expressing fractions and certain expressions. Same as a *solidus* and a *virgule*.  Examples: *3 3/4, c/o* (in care of), and *and/or*.

### Solidus
Same as a *slash* and a *virgule*.

### Stated verb
A verb expressed orally or in written format. Compare with *implied verb*.  Examples: (1) If this *is* so, please *call* me.  (2) He *is* older than I *am*.

### Statement
A word group that presents facts or ideas. It is concluded with a period.  Example: Our company was established in 1953.

### Subject
The word or word group in the main or subordinate clause of a sentence that answers *who* or *what* in relation to the verb.  Examples: (1) The *stockholders* of the corporation *approved* the merger last month.  (2) Both *answers and explanations* for this test *are contained* in the instructor's manual.  (3) *We will notify* you when your order arrives.

### Subject of a clause
The word or word group in the subordinate clause of a sentence that answers *who* or *what* in relation to the verb.  Example: If *you are interested* in this position, please send us your résumé.

### Subject complement
The noun, pronoun, or adjective following a being verb (*am, is, are, was, were, be, been*) that either renames or describes the subject.  Examples: (1) The former *supervisor* of our department *is* the new *vice president*.  (2) The *paintings* in this exhibition *are* exceptionally *valuable*.

### Subject of a sentence
The word or word group in the main clause of a sentence that answers *who* or *what* in relation to the verb.  Example: As I mentioned in my previous memorandum, any further *delays* in the completion of this contract *will cost* the company thousands of dollars.

### Subject of an infinitive
A noun or pronoun that appears directly before an infinitive.  Example: I did not expect *him to have* the authority to release this kind of information.

**Subjective case, Subjective case form**

A noun or pronoun used as the subject of a sentence, the complement of a *being* verb, or the object of the infinitive *to be* when this infinitive has no subject. Nouns always maintain the same form; pronouns require a specific form: *I, he, she, you, we, they, who, whoever.* Same as *nominative case, nominative case form.* Examples: (1) *They* signed the papers this morning. (2) The only person who responded was *he*. (3) I would not want to be *she* when our manager discovers her mistake.

**Subjunctive mood**

Used to describe events that cannot or probably will not happen and conditions that are not true or highly unlikely. The plural form *were* is used with *if, as if, as though*, or *wish* for singular subjects when the situation described is not true or unlikely. Examples: (1) *If* I *were* you, I would refer this letter to my attorney. (2) During the meeting Tina acted *as if* she, not Ms. Elliott, *were* the department manager.

**Subordinate clause**

A word group that contains a subject and a verb but cannot stand alone as a complete sentence. Same as a *dependent clause.* Example: Please notify our office *if you need any additional sales literature.*

**Subordinating conjunction**

A specific kind of conjunction used to introduce a dependent or subordinate word group that contains a subject and a verb. Examples: *if, as, when, because*, and *since.*

**Suffix**

A syllable attached to the ending of a word or word root that forms a derivative word or an inflectional form. Compare with *prefix.* Examples: invest*ment*, account*ing*, and fruit-*ful.*

**Superlative form**

The spelling or form of an adjective or an adverb when it compares more than two nouns or pronouns or more than two conditions. Compare with *comparative form.* Examples: (1) Sales figure for this year are the *highest* in our company's history. (2) Your firm is the *most* highly *respected* one in the industry.

**Suspending hyphen**

A hyphen following the first word of a compound adjective in which the second word of the compound appears later with a compatible compound adjective. Examples: (1) Most of our automobile loans extend over a *four-* or five-year period. (2) This carpeting may be purchased in *10-, 12-*, and 15-foot widths.

**Syllable**

A unit of spoken language used to make up words. Syllables are marked off in main dictionary entries; a small dot separates each syllable. Written words may be divided at the end of a line only between syllables. Examples: *syl·la·ble, di·vi·sion*, and *ir·re·vo·ca·ble.*

**Temporary compound**

A compound adjective not appearing in the dictionary. This compound is hyphenated only when it precedes the noun it modifies. Examples: (1) These *easy-to-follow instructions* were written by one of our staff members. (2) These *instructions* are *easy to follow.*

**Tense**
The form of a verb that places an action or a condition in a time frame.

**Transitional expression, Transitional words**
A word or phrase that does not contribute to the meaning of a sentence but takes the listener or reader smoothly from one concept to another by bridging two ideas or signaling a turn in thought. Examples: (1) Our supplier is unable to obtain any additional pieces of Harwood china by Lexington; *therefore*, we are returning your deposit. (2) You may, *however*, wish to upgrade the memory of your computer to 32 megabytes.

**Transitive verb**
A verb that has an object. Compare with *intransitive verb*. Examples: (1) Mr. Morris *called me* yesterday. (2) Please *place the book* on the table. (3) Our supervisor *gave her* an excellent *rating*.

**Uppercase**
Capital letters. Examples: *A, M*, and *IBM*.

**Verb**
A part of speech that shows action or movement or describes a situation or condition. Examples: *write, listen, send, be, appear*, and *look*.

**Verb phrase**
A verb part combined with helpers such as *was, have, did*, and *will* to form tenses. Examples: *were divided, had reached, does work, will have finished*, and *may be reached*.

**Vertical listing**
A listing of items in which each item begins a new line on the page. Compare with *horizontal listing*. The following entries are an example of a vertical listing:
> *First entry in the listing*
> *Second entry in the listing*
> *Third entry in the listing*
> *Fourth entry in the listing*
> *Last entry in the listing*

**Virgule**
Same as a *slash* and a *solidus*.

**Vowel**
Letters of the alphabet *a, e, i, o*, and *u*.

# Index

# Abbreviations of States and Territories

| State or Territory | Two-Letter Postal Designation | Standard Abbreviation |
|---|---|---|
| Alabama | AL | Ala. |
| Alaska | AK | — |
| Arizona | AZ | Ariz. |
| Arkansas | AR | Ark. |
| California | CA | Calif., Cal. |
| Canal Zone | CZ | C.Z. |
| Colorado | CO | Colo., Col. |
| Connecticut | CT | Conn. |
| Delaware | DE | Del. |
| District of Columbia | DC | D.C. |
| Florida | FL | Fla. |
| Georgia | GA | Ga. |
| Guam | GU | — |
| Hawaii | HI | — |
| Idaho | ID | — |
| Illinois | IL | Ill. |
| Indiana | IN | Ind. |
| Iowa | IA | — |
| Kansas | KS | Kans., Kan. |
| Kentucky | KY | Ky. |
| Louisiana | LA | La. |
| Maine | ME | — |
| Maryland | MD | Md. |
| Massachusetts | MA | Mass. |
| Michigan | MI | Mich. |
| Minnesota | MN | Minn. |
| Mississippi | MS | Miss. |
| Missouri | MO | Mo. |
| Montana | MT | Mont. |
| Nebraska | NE | Nebr., Neb. |
| Nevada | NV | Nev. |
| New Hampshire | NH | N.H. |
| New Jersey | NJ | N.J. |
| New Mexico | NM | N. Mex. |
| New York | NY | N.Y. |
| North Carolina | NC | N.C. |
| North Dakota | ND | N. Dak. |
| Ohio | OH | — |
| Oklahoma | OK | Okla. |
| Oregon | OR | Oreg., Ore. |
| Pennsylvania | PA | Pa., Penn., Penna. |
| Puerto Rico | PR | P.R. |
| Rhode Island | RI | R.I. |
| South Carolina | SC | S.C. |
| South Dakota | SD | S. Dak. |
| Tennessee | TN | Tenn. |
| Texas | TX | Tex. |
| Utah | UT | — |
| Vermont | VT | Vt. |
| Virgin Islands | VI | V.I. |
| Virginia | VA | Va. |
| Washington | WA | Wash. |
| West Virginia | WV | W. Va. |
| Wisconsin | WI | Wis., Wisc. |
| Wyoming | WY | Wyo. |